A Brit's Guide
to
rlando
and
Walt Disney World

2003

Simon Veness

foulsham

The Publishing House, Bennetts Close, Cippenham, Berkshire, SL1 5AP, England

ISBN 0-572-02822-9

Other books in this series:
A Brit's Guide to Las Vegas and the West 2002–3, Karen Marchbank, 0-572-02746-X
Choosing A Cruise, Simon Veness, 0-572-02738-9
A Brit's Guide to New York 2003, Karen Marchbank, 0-572-02823-7

DEDICATION

To my wife and children – my support and inspiration.

SPECIAL THANKS

Special thanks for this edition go to: Travel City Direct, The Walt Disney Company, Alamo Rent A Car, Universal Orlando, Orlando Convention and Visitors Bureau, Kissimmee Convention and Visitors Bureau, St Petersburg/Clearwater Area Convention & Visitors Bureau, Daytona Beach Area Convention & Visitors Bureau, the Best Western Lake Buena Vista Resort, the Gaylord Palms Resort and Airwave Communications.

My sincere thanks also go to all the hard-working people at Foulsham who help to bring my work to life every year.

Printed in Malaysia

Contents

8. Off The Beaten Track

(or, When You're All Theme-Parked Out). A taste of the real Florida: Winter Park, Aquatic Wonders Boat Tours, Boggy Creek Airboats and Parasail, Cypress Glades Adventure Tours, Orange Blossom Balloons, Everglades and the Bahamas, Flying Tigers Warbird Restoration Museum and Warbird Adventures, Green Meadows Petting Farm, Disney and Cruising, Seminole County, Mount Dora Railway, Forever Florida, Disney's Wilderness Preserve; The Beaches: St Pete's/Clearwater, Cocoa Beach and Daytona; Sports, including golf, fishing, water sports, horse riding, spectator sports and Disney's Wide World of Sports™, Motorsport.

9. Orlando by Night

(or, Burning the Candle at Both Ends). Downtown Disney, Pointe*Orlando, Universal's CityWalk, Downtown Orlando, Disney Shows, Arabian Nights, Pirate's Dinner Adventure, Medieval Times, Sleuth's, SoulFire Theatre, Dixie Stampede, nightclubs, live music, discos, bars.

10. Eating Out

(or, Man, These Portions Are *Huge!*). Full guide to local-style eating and drinking, rundown of the fast-food outlets, best family restaurants, American diners and speciality restaurants.

11. Shopping

(or, How to Send Your Credit Card into Meltdown). Your duty-free allowances, full guide to the main tourist shopping complexes, discount outlets, flea markets, malls, supermarkets and speciality shops.

12. Going Home

(or, Where Did the Last Two Weeks Go?). Avoiding last-minute snags, returning the car, full guide to Orlando International and Orlando Sanford Airports and their facilities for the journey home.

13. Your Holiday Planner

Examples of how to plan for a 2-week holiday, with a Disney 5-Day Hopper PLUS Ticket and blank forms for your holiday! Plus, the Theme Parks', Busy Day Guide.

Foreword

*In business terms, 2002 was a testing and challenging year for Orlando's tourism business in the post-September 11 climate. In tourist terms, it was a brilliant year to visit the world's most exciting holiday destination, with lower crowds than average, some genuine travel bargains and the thrills of **Disney's 100 Years of Magic celebration**. Plus, for a destination that prides itself on service, value for money and friendliness, Orlando went to new lengths in a bid to woo visitors back. That spirit of co-operation, coupled with even more attractions, promises to make the experience better than ever in 2003 – and you are in pole position to prepare for and look forward to all the fun that lies in store with this book. Whether you are a first timer to the Sunshine State of Florida or one of the many repeat visitors (and one of our regular readers – hello again!), I would like to extend a hearty* Brit's Guide *welcome to the next best thing to actually being in Orlando.*

As you will probably be aware (you've already flicked through the pages and looked at the Contents list, right?!), this is a massively complex and extensive destination, and you need the best possible advice to get the maximum enjoyment from your holiday. Well, rest assured you are in possession of the best aid for all that – and more. This latest edition (the eighth) of Britain's best-selling guidebook continues to represent, I firmly believe, the most user-friendly and authoritative companion to all that lies in store for you in this holiday wonderland, especially if used in conjunction with our friends at the website www.wdwinfo.com, by far the best Internet resource on all things Disney out there. I like to think this book is researched and written with a real tourist's eye for detail and value, including all the information you really need to know, not just what the brochures want you to believe. It aims to give you a good idea of what to expect and (most importantly) how to plan and budget for it. The three principal areas that comprise this vast 'resort' (the counties of Orange, Osceola and Seminole) also remain vigorously engaged in making things newer, bigger and better almost by the day. It is quite a challenge keeping up with it all, even on an annual basis, but I can't pretend it isn't also great fun! I even had to try parascending!

Over the course of the last 10 years (and almost 50 visits), Orlando has become a home away from home for me and so, knowing all the fun and excitement that lies in store, it is with an enduring enthusiasm that I ask you to read on and allow me to escort you through my second 'home'. More significantly, you will get the inside track on how to have the best holiday you can, at the best price and with the least fuss. Prepare to be amazed (and exhausted!) by what's in store, but don't say I didn't tell you so. Now, excuse me while I put my feet up for a while… have a nice day now.

Simon Veness

(email me at simon.veness@spitfireuk.net or join me on the Discussion Forums at www.wdwinfo.com)

1 Introduction

(or, Welcome to the Holiday of a Lifetime)

Welcome to the most exciting holiday experience in the world, bar none, guaranteed. This area of central Florida we call Orlando is a vast conglomeration of adventure rides, thrills, fun and fantasy the like of which exists nowhere else, and we are not talking just about the *Walt Disney World Resort in Florida* here.

First off, you need to be aware of the bewilderingly extensive and complex nature of most of what lies in wait in this tourist wonderland. Disney remains the leading attraction in town, but there is a strong supporting cast, of which Universal Orlando and SeaWorld are outstanding examples.

There is something to suit all tastes and ages – young or old, families, couples or singles – but it exacts a high physical toll. You'll walk a lot, queue a lot and probably eat a lot. You will have a fabulous time, but you'll end up exhausted as well. It is not so much a holiday as an exercise in military planning.

Eight theme parks

In simple terms, there are now eight major theme parks that are generally reckoned to be essential holiday fare, and at least one of those will require 2 days to make you feel it has been well and truly done. Add on a day at one of the water parks, a trip to see some of the wildlife or other more 'natural' attractions, and the lure of the nearby Kennedy Space Center, and you're talking at least 12 days of pure adventure-mania. Then mix in the night-time attractions of *Downtown Disney*, Universal's CityWalk and a host of dinner shows, and you get an idea of the awesome scale of the entertainment on offer. Even given 2 weeks, something has to give – just make sure it isn't your patience/pocket/sanity!

So, how do we innocents abroad, many of us making our first visit to the good ol' USA, get full value from what is still, without doubt, a truly magical holiday?

There is no set answer of course, but there are some pretty solid guidelines to steer you in the right direction and help avoid some of the more obvious pitfalls. Central to most of them is **planning**. At the back of this guide there is a useful 'calendar' to fill in and use as a ready reference guide. Don't be inflexible, but be aware of the time demands of the main parks, and give yourself a few quiet days by the pool or at one of the smaller attractions to recover your strength. With so much on offer, it simply isn't possible to do it all, so try to ensure you get full value for what you do decide to do.

Also, be aware of the vast scale and complexity of this wonderland, and try to take in as much of the clever detail and breadth of imagination on offer, especially in the Disney parks.

Orlando

Orlando itself is a relatively small but bright young city which has been taken over to the immediate south-west by *Walt Disney World Resort in Florida*, to give it its full title, which opened with the *Magic Kingdom Park* in 1971 and has encouraged a massive tourist expansion ever since. New attractions are being added all the time and it is easy to get carried away by the artificial (and highly commercial) fantasy of it all. However, there is still a genuine concern for the environment, and there are only a few areas where the development looks as if it has got out of hand.

The tourist area generally known as Orlando actually consists of three counties. Orange County is the home of the city of Orlando, but much of Disney's fun and frolics are to be found in Osceola County, with Kissimmee its main town. Seminole County, home of Orlando Sanford Airport, is immediately to the north of Orange County.

The local population numbers slightly above 1.7 million, of which some 200,000 are actively employed in the tourist business, but in 2000 some 43.3 million people made Orlando their holiday destination, spending $20.9 billion in the area!

Britain accounts for more than a third of all foreign visitors to Orlando, and in 2000 that was 1,312,000 of us. Those figures represent a near 100% increase in the last 10 years, with the international airport seeing its traffic boom from 8 million passengers in 1983 to a massive 30 million plus just 17 years later. In addition, the full Orlando area boasts more than 105,000 hotel rooms and more than 4,500 places to eat. And for shopaholics there are 250 shopping centres with 29 malls.

Walt Disney World Resort in Florida

This actually consists of four distinct, separate theme parks, 21 speciality hotel resorts, a camping ground, two water parks, a state-of-the-art spectator sports complex, five 18-hole golf courses, four mini-golf courses and a huge shopping and entertainment complex *(Downtown Disney)*. It covers 47 square miles (almost 31,000 acres). Alton Towers and Thorpe Park would comfortably fit into its car park. Indeed, Alton Towers, Britain's biggest theme park, is 60 times smaller. Disney's most-frequented park, the *Magic Kingdom*, has a single-day record attendance in the region of 92,000 – most British parks peak at around 20,000. The Disney organisation does things with the most style, but the others have caught on fast and they are all creating new amenities almost as fast as they can think of them.

Intriguingly, less than half of Disney's massive site has been developed so far, leaving plenty of room for new accommodation and attractions, while even the existing parks have potential for an extra ride or two, and there are several major projects on the drawing board. Disney maintains an extremely high customer service ethic and is always looking at ways to refresh the existing attractions. From October 2001 to December 2002, *100 Years of Magic* celebration added still more novelty and freshness to the overall experience, while Mission: SPACE, due to open in summer 2003, should provide a new benchmark in theme park thrills.

Here's a quick rundown of what's on offer:

Magic Kingdom Park: this is the essential Disney, including the fantasy of their wonderful animated films, the adventures of the Wild

FLORIDA

How far from Orlando to . . .

Bradenton	130 miles	Miami	220 miles
Clearwater	110 miles	Naples	230 miles
Cocoa Beach	40 miles	Sarasota	140 miles
Daytona	60 miles	Silver Springs	80 miles
Fort Lauderdale	205 miles	St Augustine	120 miles
Fort Myers	190 miles	St Petersburg	105 miles
Jacksonville	155 miles	Tampa	75 miles
Key West	375 miles	Venice	160 miles

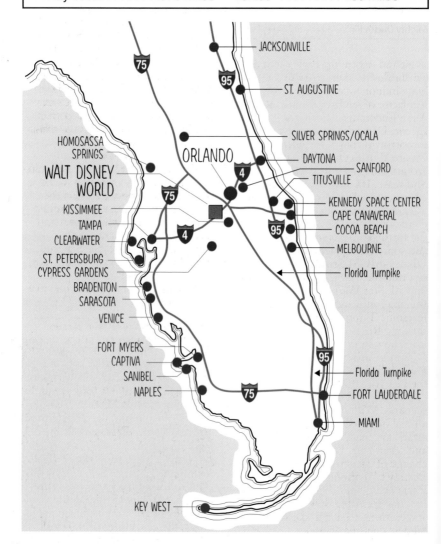

Mighty Duck's Pinball Show at DisneyQuest

West and Africa, the excitement of thrill rides like Space Mountain, a huge indoor roller-coaster, and the fear factor of the ExtraTERRORestrial Alien Encounter.

Epcot: Disney's look at the world of tomorrow through the gates of Future World, plus a potted journey around our planet in World Showcase. It's more educational than adventurous, but still possesses some memorable rides, including Test Track and Universe of Energy – plus the forthcoming Mission: SPACE – and some great places to eat.

Disney-MGM Studios: here you can ride the movies in style, meeting up with Star Wars, the Muppets, Indiana Jones and drop into the fearsome Tower of Terror or the thrilling Rock 'n Roller Coaster and learn how films are really made.

Disney's Animal Kingdom Theme Park: billed as 'a new species of theme park', this delivers another contrasting and hugely entertaining scenario. With cleverly realistic animal habitats, including a 100-acre safari savannah, captivating shows and several terrific rides, it offers a change of pace from the other parks.

Disney's Typhoon Lagoon Water Park: bring your cossie and spend a lazy day splashing down water slides and learning to surf in the world's biggest man-made lagoon.

Disney's Blizzard Beach Water Park: this is the big brother of all the water parks, with a massive spread of rides and slides in a 'snowy' environment.

Disney's Wide World of Sports Complex™: offers the chance to watch world-class events like baseball, basketball, athletics, volleyball and many others.

Downtown Disney area: incorporates Pleasure Island, Marketplace and the West Side with themed restaurants, a cinema complex, the *DisneyQuest* arcade of interactive games, Virgin Megastore and the world-famous Cirque du Soleil® company. New Year's Eve is the Pleasure Island theme, with eight night-clubs on offer. This is where Disney's superb range of hotels can be found, while the picture-perfect **Wedding Pavilion** features in many brochures offering marriage ceremonies in fairytale style.

Most people buy one of the multi-day passes which allow you to move between the various parks on the same day, while all grant unlimited access to the monorails, buses and ferries (always get your hand stamped if you leave one park but intend to return). Make no mistake, you can't walk between the parks, and trying to do more than one in a day is a recipe for disaster. The

Share a Dream Come True parade

choice of tickets for Disney in particular is bewildering, so make sure you buy only what you need.

The main options at the ticket booths are: **1-day tickets,** giving access to one of the four main parks; **4-Day Park Hopper,** providing 4 days at the main parks, with multiple parks on the same day; **5-Day Park Hopper,** 5 main park days, with multiple same-day visits; **5-Day Park Hopper Plus,** 5 days at the four parks, with multiple same-day visits, plus two visits to any of *Disney's Blizzard Beach* and *Typhoon Lagoon* water parks, *Pleasure Island* and *Disney's Wide World of Sports Complex*™ (excluding special events at WWoS); **6-Day Park Hopper Plus,** 6 days at the main parks, plus three of the options above; and the **7-Day Park Hopper Plus,** a week at the main parks, plus four of the options. All multi-day passes give savings on 1-day tickets, and unused days never expire, so can be saved for any time in the future. In the UK, you can buy the 5- and 7-Day Park Hopper Plus through tour operators, ticket brokers and *Disney Stores,* while the special **World Ticket** is available ONLY in the UK, giving 10 days' entry to the four main parks, water parks, Pleasure Island, *DisneyQuest Indoor Interactive Theme Park* and *Wide World of Sports Complex*™ (excluding special events), plus a FREE character breakfast. However, the World Pass (priced at £259 for adults and £208 for children aged 3–9 at the time of writing) expires 20 days after its first use (unlike the Hopper passes).

Guests at Disney's hotels can also buy **Ultimate Park Hopper** tickets, giving entry to all the parks, *Pleasure Island, Disney's Wide World of Sports Complex*™ AND *DisneyQuest Indoor Interactive Theme Park* or the length of their stay, plus a choice of one extra item. The price varies according to how long you stay. For stays in excess

of 2 weeks, it is worth considering the **Annual Pass** or **Premium Annual Pass** (check the Ticket Prices section on www.wdwinfo.com).

When it comes to Universal Orlando, SeaWorld and Busch Gardens, the choice is a little simpler. Again, you have **1-Day Tickets** but, for Universal, it's cheaper to buy a **2- and 3-Day Ticket,** giving access to Universal Studios, Islands of Adventure and the clubs of CityWalk. There is also a clubs-only pass ($8.95 plus tax) or a clubs-plus-film ticket ($12), as CityWalk has a 20-screen cinema. Even better value (and highly recommended) are the 2-week **Orlando FlexTickets**. The 4-Park Ticket gives admission to Universal Studios, Islands of Adventure, SeaWorld and Wet 'n Wild, while the 5-Park Ticket adds Busch Gardens, and both are valid for 14 days from first use. There is even a **Universal Bonus Pass** if you order at www.universalorlando.com, for 5 consecutive days at Universal Studios, Islands of Adventure and CityWalk. Finally, SeaWorld and Busch Gardens have a 2-park **Combo Ticket** as well, but most people prefer the FlexTickets.

With price hikes every year, it is worth shopping around for tickets and buying as soon as possible. **Tour operators** tend to be ABOVE the gate price for the convenience of being able to pre-book and budget for your main costs at once. I recommend the **Keith Prowse**

BRIT TIP: Be wary of travel agent pressure to buy too many tickets. You may well find you can't fit everything in, plus, for some attractions, you can often buy cheaper in Orlando, even from the tour operators' reps.

GETTING AROUND ORLANDO

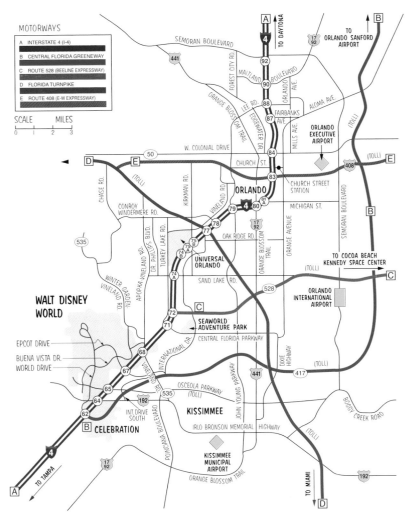

agency (02890 232425, website at www.keithprowsetickets.co.uk or see your travel agent) as one of the best for competitive prices AND pre-booking convenience, while they do several one-off tickets, excursions and 2-day trips especially for the UK market. They also supply the actual tickets as opposed to a voucher, which you have to exchange at the ticket booths.

A first word of warning: you don't want to try to do Disney's parks in one chunk. Apart from ending up with serious theme park indigestion, you'll probably also hit one of the parks on a busy day (check the Busy Day guide on page 280). The *Magic Kingdom Park* and *Epcot* can be particularly exhausting (especially with children) and you'll need a quiet day afterwards.

KEY TO ORLANDO – MAIN ATTRACTIONS

A1	Disney's Animal Kingdom Theme Park	M	Disney's Typhoon Lagoon Water Park
A	Magic Kingdom Park	N	Disney's Blizzard Beach Water Park
B	Epcot	O	Festival Bay
C	Disney-MGM Studios	P	Water Mania
D	Universal Orlando	Q	Wet 'n Wild
E	SeaWorld Adventure Park	R	Discovery Cove by SeaWorld
F	Busch Gardens	S	Holy Land Experience
G	Kennedy Space Center	T	Ripley's Believe It or Not
H	US Astronaut Hall of Fame	U	Hard Rock Vault
I	Splendid China	V	Orange County History Center
J	Cypress Gardens	W	Downtown Disney area
K	Silver Springs	X	Green Meadows Petting Farm
L	Gatorland	Y	Fantasy of Flight

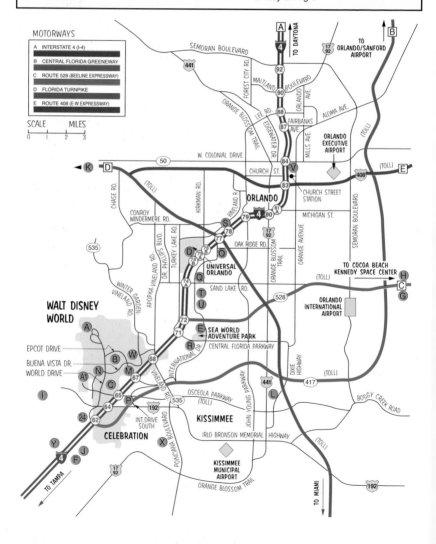

© Disney

Minnie meets mini-Minnie!

The others

If you think Orlando is all about Disney, you will be in for a pleasant surprise when you encounter some of the other attractions on offer.

Universal Orlando is the newest resort development that aims to rival Disney with its choice of two theme parks, water park, entertainment district and series of speciality hotels. **Universal Studios:** this features the state-of-the-art simulator ride Back to the Future, the mind-boggling Terminator 2 attraction, Jaws, Kongfrontation, Earthquake, Woody Woodpecker's KidZone and the Men In Black ride. **Islands of Adventure:** new in 1999, Universal's second park is a superb blend of thrill rides, family attractions, shows and awesome, eye-catching design, with some of the most technologically advanced hardware in the world. **Wet 'n Wild:** Although on International Drive (I-Drive), this water park is Universal-owned and offers plenty of fun rides and slides. **SeaWorld:** don't be put off thinking it's just another dolphin show, this is *the* place for the creatures of the deep, with killer whales being the main attraction, a bright, refreshing atmosphere and a pleasingly serious ecological approach, plus the 5-star thrill rides Journey to Atlantis and Kraken. SeaWorld also has an exclusive neighbour, **Discovery Cove,** that offers the chance to swim with dolphins, among other things.

Busch Gardens: the sister park to SeaWorld, here it's creatures of the land, with the highlights being the new Rhino Rally ride, Myombe Reserve, a close-up look at the endangered central African highland gorillas and the Edge of Africa safari experience. A real treat, plus a number of brain-numbing roller-coasters and other rides.

Cypress Gardens: a chance to slow down and take in the more scenic attractions of beautiful gardens, water-skiing shows and animal encounters.

Kennedy Space Center: the dramatically upgraded home of space exploration. **Silver Springs:** a close look at Florida's nature via jeep and boat safaris through real swampland, with several alligator displays.

Splendid China: a novel alternative attraction, a 5,000-mile journey through China with miniaturised reproductions of features like the Great Wall and the Terracotta Warriors, plus live shows, great shopping and food.

Jungle Cruise at Silver Springs

Fantasy of Flight: this aviation museum experience has the world's largest private collection of vintage aircraft, plus fighter-plane simulators.

> BRIT TIP: The humidity levels – up to 100% – and fierce daily rainstorms in summer take a lot of visitors by surprise, so take a lightweight, rainproof jacket or buy one of the cheap plastic ponchos available in local shops.

The climate

So that's just a taste of what's on offer, the next question is when to go? Florida's weather does vary a fair bit, from bright but cool winter days in November, December and January, with the odd drizzly spell, to furiously hot and humid summers punctuated by tropical downpours.

The most pleasant option is to go in between the two extremes in spring or autumn. You will also avoid the worst of the crowds. However, as most families are governed by school holidays, July to September remain the most popular months for Brit visitors, and so there will also be some advice on how to get one jump ahead of the high-season crush.

And now to business: it's big, brash and fun, but above all it's American, and that means everything is exceedingly well organised, with a tendency towards the raucous rather than the reserved. It's clean, well maintained and very anxious to please: Floridians generally are an affable bunch, but they take affability to new heights in the theme parks, where staff are almost painfully keen to make sure you 'have a nice day'.

Tipping

Also close to every American's heart is the custom of tipping. With the exception of petrol pump attendants and fast-food restaurant servers, just about everyone who offers you any sort of service in hotels, bars, restaurants, buses, taxis, airports and other public amenities will expect a tip. In bars, restaurants and taxis, 15% of the bill is the usual going rate while porters will expect $1 per bag. Brits are notoriously forgetful of this little habit but, as all service industry workers are automatically taxed on the assumption of receiving 15% in tips, you will be doing a major service to the local economy if you remember those few extra dollars each time.

It is also useful to know dollar travellers' cheques can be used as cash, so it is not necessary (as well as not being advisable) to carry large amounts of cash around. **Take note that all Orlando prices, both where indicated in this book and on every price tag you see, do not include the 6–7% Florida Sales Tax. There is also a 4–5% Resort Tax on hotel rooms.**

Having a credit card is pretty essential as they are accepted everywhere, are easy to carry and use and provide an extra degree of buying security. In some cases, notably car hire, you can't operate without your flexible friend, so don't leave your Visa or Mastercard at home!

> BRIT TIP:
> Tipping Guide
>
> | Bill | Suggested Tip |
> | --- | --- |
> | $15 | $2.25 |
> | $20 | $3.00 |
> | $25 | $3.75 |
> | $30 | $4.50 |
> | $40 | $6.00 |
> | $50 | $7.50 |

Visa requirements

Holiday visitors to America do not need a visa providing they hold a valid British passport showing they are a British citizen (and which does not expire before the end of your holiday). Instead, all you do is fill in a green visa waiver form (usually given out on your flight or when you check in) and hand it in with your passport to the US immigration official who checks you through after landing. However, British subjects do need a visa (£30), and you should apply at least a month in advance to the US Embassy.

In England, Scotland and Wales write to the Visa Office, US Embassy, 5 Upper Grosvenor Street, London, W1A 2JB (0891 200 290).

In Northern Ireland, write to US Consulate General, 3 Queens House, Belfast, BT1 6EQ.

Alternatively, call 0991 500 590 (£1.50/minute) for more detailed visa advice, or visit the website at www.usembassy.org.uk.

What's new in 2003

In keeping with Orlando's habit for providing an ever-changing profile of attractions, there are a host of developments in store for 2003.

Walt Disney World Resort in Florida will be aiming to boldly go where no theme park has gone before, hopefully in summer 2003, when they debut their latest and most advanced ride, **Mission: SPACE**. This promises to be a blockbuster attraction and a real highlight for the *Epcot* park as it prepares guests for a space mission and then slingshots them into space in the most realistic manner possible. It should be an awesome proposition and a ride like no other anywhere in the world. Watch out, too, for **Mickey's PhilharMagic**, an imaginative new 3-D giant-screen special effects film show which you can see at the *Magic Kingdom Park*.

Elsewhere in *Walt Disney World in Florida*, Disney is finally due to open its **Pop Century Resort** (delayed from 2002), the second of their massive, more budget-orientated value hotels. When complete, it will offer 5,760 rooms in colourful blocks representing the different decades of the 20th century.

Universal Orlando has two major new attractions in the Studios park, scheduled to be up and running by spring 2003. **Jimmy Neutron: Boy Genius** promises to be an engaging and amusing high-energy adventure with the TV and cinema hero, as well as being a state-of-the-art simulator ride. **Shrek 4-D** should be an equally fun multi-sensory show based on the hilarious Oscar-winning film, with a riot of gags – both visual and otherwise – taking up where the film left off.

Meanwhile, Universal has just announced plans to build two more on-site hotels (their fourth and fifth), following the grand opening in 2002 of the excellent and elegant **Royal Pacific Resort**. These are not due to open before 2004, but it shows Universal's intention to keep their resort development thriving.

I-Drive continues to thrive and develop as an entity in its own right, with two significant new elements. The **Festival Bay** shopping and entertainment complex should complete its major second phase in late Spring, following the opening of an eye-catching Ron Jon's Surf Shop and Vans Skate Park, while the **Hard Rock Vault** (a kind of Hall of Fame) is due to open in front of The Mercado, paying homage to the restaurant chain's immense collection of rock memorabilia. Meanwhile, **Dolly Parton's Dixie Stampede** promises to add another novel element to the variety of dinner shows available in the area from May 2003. That follows the recent opening of the **SoulFire**

Theatre & Dinner Experience, which provides more lively, interactive fun in various elaborate comedy stage shows.

Two superb upscale hotels are due to open their doors in 2003 in the Grande Lakes Resort, a 584-room **Ritz-Carlton** and a 1,000-room **JW Marriott**, in addition to an 18-hole Greg Norman-designed golf course and a huge luxury spa. Also destined to open is the 730-room **Omni Orlando Resort**, in the new golf-orientated Champions Gate area (just south of Disney), which will include a spa and six restaurants.

For shopping, the **Mall at Millenia** (just off I-4 north of Universal Orlando) should now be open (as of October 18, 2002), taking the retail experience seriously upmarket with a high-tech 150-shop spread highlighted by the three great American department stores of Bloomingdale's, Macy's (the first in Florida) and Neiman-Marcus. The **Florida Mall** is getting a 2-storey Nordstrom department store and a Lord & Taylor outlet, too.

Away from the parks, **Downtown Orlando** is experiencing a regeneration. While much of the rebuilding is for business or residential use, the addition of some smart new hotels, shops and the free Lymmo bus system is adding to the picture all the time and making it a highly enjoyable city in its own right. I believe that a major new theatre is also in the pipeline, which will put Orlando firmly on the cultural map as a performing arts centre, although it already has much to recommend it.

Orlando International Airport's fourth runway should be open later in 2003. And watch out for all the new numbering of the junctions on **Interstate 4 (I-4)**, the main motorway through central Florida.

As ever, there will be announcements that beat our deadline, so don't forget to check out www.wdwinfo.com for all the latest information.

Plan your visit

The next few chapters will help you plan your days and tell you everything you need to know to make your holiday perfect. Draw up a rough itinerary and then fine tune it with the help of the Discussion Boards on www.wdwinfo.com

Now read on and enjoy…

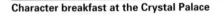

Character breakfast at the Crystal Palace

© Disney

Planning and Practicalities

(or, How to Almost Do It All and Live to Tell the Tale)

There is one simple rule once you have decided Orlando is the place for you. Sit down (preferably with this book) and PLAN what you want to do very carefully. This is not the type of holiday you can take in a freewheeling, carefree 'make it up as you go along' manner. Frustration and exhaustion lie in wait for all those who do not have at least a basic plan of campaign.

First of all work out WHEN you want to go, then decide WHERE in the vast resort is the best place for you. Then consider WHAT sort of holiday you are looking for, WHO you want to entrust your holiday with and finally HOW much you want to try to do.

> **BRIT TIP:** Thanksgiving is always the fourth Thursday in November; George Washington's birthday, or President's Day, is the third Monday in February. Try to avoid those weeks!

When to go

If you are looking to avoid the worst of the crowds, the best periods to choose are October to December (but not the week of the Thanksgiving holiday in November or between Christmas and New Year), early January up until 2 weeks before Easter (avoiding President's Day in February) and April (after Easter) to the end of May. Orlando gets down to some serious tourist business from Memorial Day (the last Monday in May, the official start of the summer season) to Labor Day (the first Monday in September and the last holiday of summer), peaking on the Fourth of July, a huge national holiday. The Easter holidays are similarly uncomfortable (although the weather is better), but easily the busiest is Christmas time, starting the week before December 25 and lasting until January 2. It is not unknown for some of the parks to close as their massive car parks become full by mid-morning.

The best combination of comfortable weather and smaller crowds is to be had in April (avoiding Easter) and October. However, few of the main attractions are affected by rain, although the roller-coasters and water rides will close if lightning threatens, and you will be one jump ahead if you have waterproofs, as the crowds noticeably thin out when it gets wet.

Disney's All-Star Sports Resort

© Disney

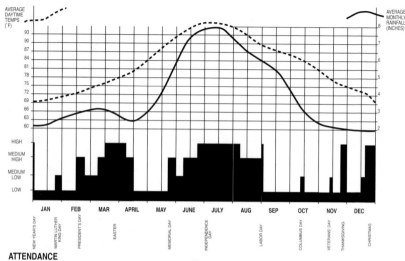

Temperature, rainfall and attendance figures

In any event, all the parks sell cheap, plastic ponchos (cheaper at Wal-Mart or other supermarkets). In the colder months, take a few lightweight but warm layers for early morning queues then, when it warms up later, leave them in the lockers provided in all the parks. If it's too hot, you can take advantage of the air-conditioned attractions and restaurants.

Where to stay

The choice of where to stay is equally important, especially if you have a family who will demand the swimming pools and games rooms. Having the use of a swimming pool is also a major plus for relaxing at the end of a busy day. Inevitably, there is a huge choice of accommodation areas and prices. As a guide, four main areas make up the greater Orlando tourist conglomeration:
Walt Disney World Resort in Florida: some of the most sophisticated, convenient and fun places to stay are to be found in Disney's great range of hotels. The same imagination that has gone into the creation of the theme parks has been at work on the likes of *Disney's Polynesian Resort* and *Disney's Animal Kingdom Lodge.* They all feature free, regular transport to all of the attractions, your own resort ID card (so you can charge meals and souvenirs to your room, and have your purchases delivered to the hotel), free parking and the Disney Character Caravan. This latter was a new feature in 2002, bringing a whole wagon-load of kids' favourites to each Disney hotel at breakfast time on selected days. Many resorts also have great kids' clubs and baby-sitting services. The drawbacks here are, with the exception of *Disney's All-Star Resorts* and the new *Pop Century Resort,* Disney hotels are among the most expensive, especially to eat in, and are a fair drive from the likes of Universal Orlando and Kennedy Space Center. For a 1-week holiday it takes some beating, though.
Lake Buena Vista: a loosely defined area around the eastern fringes of *Walt Disney World Resort in*

Florida and along Interstate 4 (I-4), this again features some upmarket hotels. It is also handy for all the Disney fun, with most hotels offering free transport to the parks, while there are excellent restaurants and shops. A bit pricey, but its proximity to I-4 makes it convenient for much of Orlando.

International Drive: this ribbon development lies midway between Disney and downtown Orlando and is therefore an excellent central location. Running parallel to I-4, it is about 15–20 minutes drive from the main theme parks, while it is also a well-developed tourist area in its own right, with some great shopping, restaurants and attractions like Wet 'n Wild, Ripley's Believe It Or Not, WonderWorks and Skull Kingdom. The down side is that it does get congested and occasionally chaotic with tourist traffic in peak periods, so you have to make a slightly earlier start in the morning. But it does represent good value for money and is one of the few areas with extensive pavements, making it easy to explore on foot. A sub-district off I-Drive is the Universal area of Kirkman Road and Major Boulevard, where new hotels are being developed all the time.

Kissimmee: budget holiday-makers can be found in their greatest numbers along the tourist sprawl of Highway 192, an almost unbroken 12-mile strip of hotels, motels, restaurants and shops. It offers some of the best economy accommodation in the area and is handy for all Disney's attractions, although it is furthest away from Universal Orlando and downtown Orlando. A car is most advisable here, although the completion of the first phase of the BeautiVacation project, which has enhanced the heavily built-up stretch of 192 – from Route 535 as far west as Splendid China – with pavements, landscaping, bus shelters, benches and water fountains, making it a much better location for getting around on foot or by bus.

Split holidays

It is fair to say you can't really go far wrong no matter what you're seeking from your holiday, as long as you plan well. The Atlantic coast and some great beaches are only an hour's drive away to the east, the magnificent Florida Everglades are little more than 3–4 hours to the south, and there are more wonderful beaches and pleasant coast roads to the west. Great shopping opportunities are to be found almost everywhere, while Orlando has some stunning golf courses, and there are plenty of opportunities to play or watch tennis, baseball and basketball.

A common choice nowadays is to split the holiday by having a week or two in Orlando as well as a week elsewhere in Florida like the Gulf Coast or Florida Keys. The main tour companies offer a huge variety of packages, with cruise-and-stay options increasingly popular.

If you can afford the time (and the expense), the best combination is to have 2 weeks in Orlando itself and then a week relaxing on one of Florida's many fabulous beaches. A 2-week, half-and-half split is a popular choice, but can tend to make your time in Orlando rather hectic, unless you pick your additional week on the Atlantic coast at somewhere like Cocoa Beach. This resort, near to Cape Canaveral and the Kennedy Space Center, is only an hour from Orlando and gives you the choice of being able to return to Disney for the day.

Several companies offer a good 10-day Orlando and 4-day coast split. Fly-drives obviously offer the greatest flexibility, but again there is a lot to tempt you in just 2 weeks and you may find it better to book a 1-centre package that includes a car

Liki Tiki Village

as well as your accommodation, so you can still travel around but avoid too much packing and unpacking.

Travel companies

There is some serious competition for your hard-earned holiday money and, in the last couple of years, the travel companies have worked hard to keep the cost of an Orlando holiday down, making it excellent value, whether you fly-drive, book your own flights or take a package.

Shop around to get the best value for your holiday £, but make sure your package is booked with an ABTA agent for security should anything go wrong. At the last count, there were more than 80 tour operators offering holidays to Florida, and here is a rundown of the biggest and best:

Virgin Holidays: the biggest operator to MCO (that's Orlando Airport in travel-agent speak), Virgin also has the biggest and most exhausting brochure. They offer the largest variety of combinations, including Miami, the Keys, New

York, Washington, Boston, the Bahamas, Mexico, nine Caribbean islands (including Cuba for the first time in 2003) and some tempting cruises, as well as the Florida coasts.

A strong selling point is Virgin's non-stop scheduled service to Orlando (from Manchester as well as Gatwick) with award-winning in-flight entertainment, free drinks, kids' packs, meals and games. They have a good, all-round choice of accommodation in the different areas and are popular for fly-drives, flying into Orlando and out from Miami.

Kids have fun on Virgin flights

Flight upgrades to their Premium Economy (extra leg room and bigger seats from just £175), Club Orlando (from Manchester only, from £110) or the wonderful Upper Class service (from £750), where the seats fully recline for a comfortable sleep, are all available and the service throughout is impeccable. You can pre-book seats (on 0871 222 0050) no more than 180 days before departure and even check in the evening before your flight at Gatwick.

Orlando is becoming increasingly popular as a wedding venue, and Virgin have their own wedding co-ordinators for ceremonies in *Walt Disney World Resort in Florida* or elsewhere in Florida. Other bonuses include single-parent discounts, extra help for passengers with disabilities, 'kids eat free' deals at selected hotels and some excellent

Fishing on Disney's Bay Lake

© Disney

Orlando's downtown

non-driver packages, including an Attraction Pass for 10 round-trip journeys to any of the main attractions or shopping malls. You can find more details on their website www.virginholidays.com or call 0870 000 0870 for a brochure.
Airline: Virgin Atlantic.
Airport: Orlando International.

Travel City: the UK's largest independent direct-sell Florida specialist, carrying around 130,000 customers a year, Travel City offers a wide range of holidays at ultra-competitive prices, including fly-drives, 1- and 2-centre holidays, private pool villas and Caribbean cruises. A sharp reservations team has excellent local knowledge and can advise you on where to stay, what to do and keep you up to date with what's new. You can also pre-book flight seats (for £20 return or £59 for a family of four), airport hotel and parking.

Flights in peak periods are now with their own direct charter service, using Boeing 747s and with one of the most generous seat pitches (31 and 32in of knee room) of any charter operator, plus free drinks and head-sets in all classes. There is an economy cabin (the Sunshine Cabin), the Sunshine Upper Deck (for adults only, economy-size seats but with a relaxation area and enhanced in-flight service for an extra £99) and Sunshine First (22 seats with a 50in pitch that recline almost flat, upgraded menus and free drinks, priority boarding and late check-in for £199 extra). They have a double baggage allowance offer (£15/person, or £79 for a family of four if buying their Value Pack, which includes pre-bookable seats) where you can increase your allowance from 20kg to 40kg.

Travel City has a dedicated arrivals centre at Orlando Sanford Airport and a user-friendly welcome centre at the Lake Buena Vista Factory Shops, open 7 days a week. Travel City can be found on Teletext page 298, for direct bookings on 08709 904 877 or online at www.travelcity.co.uk.
Airlines: EAL (European Aviation Ltd), plus various charters.
Airport: Orlando Sanford Airport.

Thomson: another of the largest, mass-market operators, Thomson

The Disney Cruise Line at Castaway Cay

© Disney

has an excellent reputation in Orlando, having a large team of reps and Service Centres on I-Drive, and offers six departure airports (including Birmingham, Newcastle and Glasgow). You can pre-book your flight seats (£17 per adult, £7 per child), and great in-flight entertainment and kids' packs are provided (with Britannia).

Thomson prices packages well for the family market, with special children's fares and bonuses like 'kids eat free' and 'extra value' hotels, while offering a decent selection of coastal resorts for 2-centre holidays and an increasing number of private villas (sleeping up to 10). They also organise wedding packages (from £519) at Cypress Gardens, Cypress Grove, the Wyndham Palace or the Wyndham Orlando hotels.

Flight upgrades cost £60 (for extra leg room) and £140 for Premium service (with complimentary drinks, wider seats, choice of meals and priority boarding). Call 0870 550 2567 or visit www.thomson.co.uk.
Airline: Britannia.
Airport: Orlando Sanford.

Airtours: also in the leading group who take around 100,000 British tourists to Orlando every year, they fly from eight UK airports, with good in-flight entertainment, children's fun packs and seat-back TVs. They offer an excellent Premiair Gold upgrade (extra leg room and baggage allowance, free bar, pre-selected menu, late UK check-in) for £149 or £179/person (see below).

Airtours has some novel 10- and 11-night packages (from Manchester and Gatwick only) for a more flexible choice and offers a 15-seater mini-van. There is an Airtours service desk at the huge McDonald's on I-Drive and Sand Lake Road (with special meal deals!) and Welcome Meetings are imaginatively held in Universal's

CityWalk (with free parking), so you're well placed to hit the fun straight away.

Airtours offers some good 2-centre combos, including a week at a *Walt Disney World Resort in Florida* hotel and a week at a Universal resort, both coasts, the Florida Keys and 4-, 7- and 14-night cruises to the Bahamas, Mexico and Caribbean. Villa accommodation is now a feature, with good quality pool homes available throughout Florida. Airtours fly-drives also have a range of 'Drive and Stay' holidays. Their flexible-price approach puts the onus on you to select the exact package for you, but it does mean you can be more price-conscious as you select from: *Holiday Plus*, which includes pre-booked flight seating, 90-minute latest check-in, in-flight refreshment voucher, choice of 10 meals, pre-departure pack, a reduced price Premiair Gold upgrade (£149) or extra leg-room seat (£50) and low deposit; *Economy Holidays*, with 2-hour check-in, 20kg luggage allowance, pre-bookable seating (£20), Premiair Gold upgrade option (£179) or extra leg-room seat (£70); *Sundeal Holidays*, the no-frills option, with accommodation assigned on arrival, a 2½-hour latest check-in, only 15kg luggage allowance and no optional upgrades or in-flight meal (it is £15 extra); and *Flight Only* (as Sundeal, but no accommodation). Non-drivers can buy coach transfer passes for all the theme parks of 3, 7 and 10 days (£33, £77 and £110). For a brochure, call 0870 191 3703 or visit www.airtours.co.uk.
Airline: My Travel.
Airport: Orlando Sanford.

First Choice: a comprehensive flight programme uses five UK airports (including Glasgow, Birmingham and Newcastle), plus a Classic Premium upgrade (extra leg room and in-flight services, plus special check-in facilities) for £159 and pre-bookable seats on their smart in-house Air 2000 airline (£14 per adult, £5 per child, at least 7 days in advance). They offer a choice of twin-centre Gulf Coast options (with coach transfers for non-drivers) and 4- and 7-night cruises.

First Choice has a family-friendly touch offering hotels (mainly the 3- and 4-star variety) with themed kids' suites and 'kids eat free' deals, plus villas and apartments (with their own reps). A new service desk at the Holiday Inn Resort is staffed every day by their reps. Their more luxurious Premier Choice properties provide 50 per cent discounts off VIP lounges in UK departure airports. You can also check in the day before departure (between noon and 10pm) at Gatwick, Birmingham and Manchester, but this costs £10 per booking (up to 6 people), £15 (7–10 people) or £20 (more than 11). Call 0870 757 2757.

Airlines: Air 2000, Britannia.
Airport: Orlando Sanford.

Four other First Choice brands also sell Florida – **First Choice Villas** (0870 750 0001), for a solely villa-based holiday, **Eclipse,** a direct-sell operator (08705 010203), and **Unijet** and **Sunstart** (see below). Look them up online at www.firstchoice.co.uk or request a brochure on 020 8880 8155.

Unijet: flying from five UK airports, Unijet favours more flexible options for more experienced and independent-minded travellers (although they still feature many family-friendly deals, including 'kids eat free' hotels). Holiday homes, which are great value for larger families or groups, are heavily featured, but there is also a full range of hotels, from budget choices to top of the range. Two-centre and tailor-made options include the Gulf Coast, south-east Florida and the Keys. Unijet's well-run wedding service offers Cypress Gardens and Leu Gardens, as well as *Disney's Wedding Pavilion*. Most flights offer

pre-bookable seats (£14 per adult, £5 per child), kids' meals and fun-packs, plus upgrades (from £159) to the Classic Premium service for greater comfort and choice. Call 08705 336 336 or visit www.unijet.co.uk.

Airlines: Air 2000 and Britannia.
Airport: Orlando Sanford.

Sunstart: this is the budget operator in the First Choice range, featuring mainly a handful of 2- and 3-star hotel types. One brochure covers all their destinations (mainly Europe), and their flights operate from four UK airports – Gatwick, Birmingham, Manchester and Newcastle. There are optional airport-hotel transfers and a 'rep on demand' service, in addition to the usual airport meet-and-greet and welcome meetings.

Airlines: Air 2000, Britannia.
Airport: Orlando Sanford.

British Airways Holidays: another company to benefit from its own direct, scheduled air service (kids' activity packs, etc), British Airways Holidays offers great flexibility with almost any duration and combination possible. Beach add-ons, twin centres – for example with the Bahamas, Antigua and Barbados – and an extensive selection of quality but great value private homes are all on offer. BAH also flies to Miami and Tampa which opens up plenty of fly-drive and multi-centre possibilities.

New for 2003 is a Disney tie-up, providing special in-flight entertainment and fun packs for the kids. British Airways flights also come with the option to upgrade to the luxurious Club World or the new World Traveller Plus (larger seats with more leg room), plus specially designed kids' meals and seat-back TVs. Call 0870 443 4439 or visit www.baholidays.co.uk.

Airline: British Airways.
Airport: Orlando International.

Thomas Cook: there are two main brands under the famous

Great shopping at Pointe*Orlando

Cook's banner here, a new mass-market *Thomas Cook* brochure and the more distinctive *Thomas Cook Holidays Signature* programme. The former is a fairly standard choice, broken down into three value ranges – Extra, Standard and Economy – with a variety of charter flights (optional upgrades available). The latter offers a more quality-conscious selection designed to suit repeat visitors. Bonuses include free night offers (stay 6 and get another free), kids eat free and free room upgrades at many hotels, while flights are with scheduled airlines and ticketing info is first class. Both brands feature good wedding options (from £1,500/couple at a Disney location, to just £399 in Winter Park) and some tempting twin-centre options and cruises.
Airlines: Various charters (Thomas Cook); Virgin Atlantic, British Airways and American (Signature).
Airports: Both.
Kuoni: as with all their holidays, Kuoni offers the upmarket version of Orlando, with some of the best hotels, a strong Disney tie-up, a comprehensive wedding and honeymoon service and a Price Watch guarantee (money back if you find an identical holiday for less). They have a range of twin-centre options, including the Florida Keys, exclusive Boca Raton and Marco Island, the Caribbean and even New

York and Las Vegas.

The average price reflects the more exclusive nature of many of their packages (plus their flexible, tailor-made choice facility), but there are some big child reductions, 'kids eat free' hotels, and Kuoni uses only scheduled airlines. Free airport-hotel transfers for non-drivers are provided, too. Call 087007 458664 for a brochure or visit their website at www.kuoni.co.uk.
Airlines: Virgin Atlantic, United (via Washington) and British Airways.
Airport: Orlando International or Miami Airport.

Funway Holidays: this is the sister company of America's largest tour operator and a leading specialist in holidays to the US, hence they offer a tailor-made service to match Orlando with any other option, making for total flexibility of choice from no less than 23 UK airports. Their private homes are a big feature of the Florida programme, but they also serve up some terrific-value deals, especially with low children's prices, if you book early, making them consistently among the best prices for a family of four. They also use only scheduled airlines (with an option to upgrade to Virgin's premium economy service for £169 each way).

A wide range of 2-centre choices include the Gulf Coast, Miami and the Keys, plus cruises to the Bahamas and Caribbean from Miami, Fort Lauderdale and Port

Universal's Incredible Hulk Coaster

Sunset over Clearwater

Canaveral. Other extras include 'kids eat free' hotels, free kids' clubs, free hotel nights at certain times and free shuttles at selected hotels for non-drivers. Look them up at www.funwayholidays.co.uk or call 020 8466 0222 for a brochure.

Airlines: various scheduled, including Virgin Atlantic, British Airways and Continental.

Airport: Orlando International.

Style Holidays: one of the UK's top self-catering specialists (and a Thomas Cook-owned company), they offer a huge selection of private-pool homes and hotel suites, with accommodation up to luxurious 5- and 6-bed varieties, as well as the usual range of hotel and *Walt Disney World Resort* options. All properties are in named, well-described situations and can be booked on an accommodation-only basis, leaving you free to book your flights. Their comprehensive brochure has an excellent range of Gulf Coast villas (all of which can be combined with Orlando), while they maintain a high standard of in-resort service. Transfers can be arranged for non-drivers (£15 per person each way). For a brochure, call 0870 444 4474 or e-mail brochures@style-holidays.co.uk. Or check out www.style-holidays.co.uk.

Airline: Various charters.
Airport: Orlando Sanford.

There are a number of other travel companies worth checking out, including: **Jetsave** (Florida specialists with a highly flexible approach; call 0870 160 7312 or visit www.jetsave.co.uk); **Trailfinders** (the UK's largest independent travel company and highly recommended by several readers; 020 7937 5400, or www.trailfinders.com); **USAirtours** (mainly villas; 020 8559 7799 or www.usairtours.co.uk); Travelbag (0870 890 1456, www.travelbag.co.uk); **Transolar Holidays** (also great for attraction ticket offers on 0151 630 3737 or www.transolarholidays.com) and **Premier Holidays** (01223 516688 or see their website at www.premierholidays.co.uk).

Flightbookers (020 7757 2000, www.ebookers.com) and the **Flight Centre** (08708 999888) feature keen flight-only services. **Teletext** (page 222, or www.teletext.co.uk) often reveals special deals, as do www.expedia.co.uk, www.lastminute.com and www.opodo.com

Finally, for those looking to book an independent package, but wanting help with Disney accommodation, meal reservations, etc, the excellent **Dreams Unlimited Travel** service is a must. Visit www.dreamsunlimitedtravel.com for the essential information on this no-cost service which can save time, money and hassle. Other Orlando hotels (with some serious discounts) feature on their DreamsRes on-line booking service plus a discount ticket agency, TicketRes.

Stormalong Bay at Disney's Yacht and Beach Club Resorts

The important thing is to establish a plan of what you want to do, then get a selection of brochures and compare the prices and attractions of each one.

What to see when

Once you arrive, the temptation is to head for the nearest theme park, then the next, and so on. Hold on! If there is such a thing as theme park indigestion, that's the best recipe for it. Some days at the parks are busier than others; it is simply not possible to cover more than one a day, and it may be inadvisable to attempt two of the main parks on successive days. So here's what you do.

With the aid of the Holiday Planner on pages 276–80, make a note of all the attractions you want to see and pencil them in over the length of your holiday.

The most sensible strategy is to plan around the eight 'must-see' parks of the *Magic Kingdom Park*, *Epcot*, *Disney-MGM Studios*, *Disney's Animal Kingdom Theme Park*, Universal Studios, and the Islands of Adventure theme park, SeaWorld and Busch Gardens. If you have only a week, consider dropping Busch Gardens (it's furthest away from Orlando and doesn't have quite the same magical appeal as the others) and concentrate on the Disney parks and Universal Studios, with SeaWorld as an extra if it fits into your plan. Space travel fans will be hard-pressed not to include the Kennedy Space Center, but it will probably bore small children.

As a basic rule, the *Magic Kingdom Park* is the biggest hit with children, and families often find it requires 2 days. The same can be said of *Epcot*, but there are fewer rides to amuse small children and the emphasis is as much on education as entertainment, although it all has Disney's slick, easily digestible coating. Only the most fleet of foot,

given the benefit of a relatively crowd-free period, will be able to negotiate *Epcot* in a day. *Disney's Animal Kingdom Theme Park* is also a little short on attractions for the youngest kids (unless they really love their animals, as mine do), but it still requires nearly all of its 9am–6pm opening hours.

Disney-MGM Studios is usually possible to do in a day (not forgetting the early evening Fantasmic! show), while SeaWorld occasionally needs rather longer and Universal Studios can be a 2-day park when Orlando is at its busiest. Islands of Adventure will almost certainly keep everyone, except possibly under-5s, busy all day, too. Busch Gardens, extremely popular with British families, is another full-day affair, especially as it is a 75–90 minutes' drive away in Tampa in the south-west. However, an early start to the Kennedy Space Center (an hour's drive away on the east coast) will mean you can be back in your hotel swimming pool by teatime, confident you have fully enjoyed One Small Step For Man.

All the attractions are described in detail in Chapters 5–8, so it's best to try to get an idea of the time requirements of them all before you pick up your pencil.

Smaller attractions

Of the other, smaller-scale attractions, the nature park of Silver Springs is a full day out as it also involves a near 2-hour drive to get there, but everything else can be fitted around your Big Eight Itinerary. The water parks are all a good way to spend a relaxing afternoon, while Cypress Gardens is another quieter place to while away half a day or so. There are also a number of smaller-scale attractions in Orlando which will probably keep the children amused for several hours (and often after the major theme parks have closed).

Gatorland is a unique look at some of Florida's oldest inhabitants and is a good combination with a ride at Boggy Creek or Cypress Glades Airboats. Ripley's Believe It Or Not museum and WonderWorks interactive house of fun are both good family centres for several hours. Add in the terrific haunted house attraction Skull Kingdom, the imaginative model railway set-up of Trainland, and the more old-fashioned lure of go-karts and other fairground-type rides at Fun Spot or Midway Magic (all on the I-Drive corridor), and you have a full day of alternative fun and frolics. Aviation fans must not miss a trip to Fantasy of Flight (further down I-4) or the Flying Tigers Warbird Air Museum in Kissimmee for a novel experience.

DisneyQuest, another part of the *Downtown Disney* area, is a hugely imaginative interactive 'arcade' that guarantees up to half a day's fun (especially for older children). Each main tourist area is also well served with imaginative mini-golf courses that will absorb any excess energy (if you are not already exhausted!) for an hour or two.

Evenings

Then, of course, there is the evening entertainment, with a similarly wide choice of extravagant fun-seeking. By far the best, and a must for at least one evening each, are *Downtown Disney, Pleasure Island*, Universal's CityWalk and the fast-developing Pointe*Orlando area. All will keep you fully entertained until the early hours. Another popular source of fun are the various dinner shows: a 2-hour cabaret based on themes like medieval knights, pirates, Arabian Nights and murder mysteries that all include a hearty meal. Then there are the huge variety of nightclubs and bars, many offering live music.

What to do when

There are a couple of handy general guidelines for avoiding the worst of the tourist hordes, even in high season. The vast majority of fun-seekers in town are American, and they tend to arrive at the weekends, get settled in their hotels, and then head for the main theme parks first. That means Mondays and Tuesdays are generally bad times to visit the *Magic Kingdom Park* and *Epcot*.

The following parks are best avoided on the following days: Sunday, *Disney-MGM Studios*; Monday, *Magic Kingdom Park*; Tuesday, *Epcot*; Wednesday, *Disney-MGM Studios*; Thursday, *Magic Kingdom Park*; Friday, *Epcot*; Saturday, *Magic Kingdom Park*. *Disney's Animal Kingdom Theme Park* tends to be busiest on Monday, Tuesday and Wednesday and is hard to get round when it's crowded. The popular water parks of *Disney's Blizzard Beach* and *Typhoon Lagoon* hit high tide at the weekend, and Thursday and Friday in summer.

> BRIT TIP: If your hotel is not far from the park take a couple of hours out to return for a siesta or a swim. Have your hand stamped for re-entry when you leave (your car park ticket will also be valid all day) and then enjoy the evening entertainment back at the park, which is often the most spectacular part of the day.

At Universal Orlando, the picture is different as there are no early entry days and the weekends are usually busiest as the locals tend to visit then. This often means Monday is quietest in both parks, getting busier through the week, with the Universal Studios park slightly the more crowded of the two.

If *Walt Disney World Resort in Florida* is humming in the early part of the week, that makes it a good time to visit SeaWorld, Busch Gardens, Cypress Gardens, Silver Springs or the Kennedy Space Center. Wet 'n Wild and Water Mania are best avoided at the weekends when the locals come out to play (see Busy Day Guide on page 280).

Making sure you get the most out of your days at the main theme parks is another art form, and there are a number of practical policies to pursue. The official opening times seldom vary from 9am but arriving early is highly advisable. Apart from the obvious advantage of being near the head of the queues (and you will encounter some SERIOUS queues, or lines as the Americans call them), the parks do sometimes open earlier than scheduled if the crowds build up quickly before the official hour. So, you can get a step ahead of the masses by arriving at least 30 minutes before the expected opening time, or an hour early during the main holiday periods. Apart from anything else, you will be better

placed to park in the vast, wide open spaces of the public car parks and catch the tram to the main gates (anything up to half a mile away!).

Once you've put yourself in pole position, don't waste time on the shops, scenery and other frippery which will lure the unprepared first-timer. Instead, head straight for some of the main rides and get a few big-time thrills under your belt before the main hordes arrive. You will quickly work out where the most popular attractions are as the majority of the other early birds will be flocking to them. Use Chapters 5 and 6 to help you plan your individual park strategies.

You can also benefit from doing the opposite of what the masses do after the initial rush has subsided.

Pace yourself

A word of warning: Disney's parks, notably the *Magic Kingdom Park*, stay open late in the evening during the main holiday periods, occasionally until 11pm, and that can be a long day for young children. Therefore, it is important to pace yourself, especially if you have been one of the first through the gates.

> BRIT TIP: The water IS safe to drink in the US but it may not taste great as they tend to put a lot of fluoride in it.

There are plenty of opportunities to take time off and stop for a drink or bite to eat, and you can take advantage of the American propensity to take meal-times seriously by avoiding lunchtime (12 noon–2pm) and dinnertime (5.30–7pm). So, after you've had a couple of hours of real adventure-mania, it pays to take an early lunch (i.e. before midday), plunge back

---

ORLANDO THEME PARK ATTENDANCES 2001
(As estimated by *Amusement Business* magazine)

1 Magic Kingdom, 14.7 million (down 4% on 2000)
2 Epcot, 9 million (down 15%)
3 Disney-MGM Studios, 8.3 million (down 6%)
4 Disney's Animal Kingdom, 7.7 million (down 7%)
5 Universal Studios, 7.2 million (down 10%)
6 Islands of Adventure, 5.5 million (down 8%)
7 SeaWorld, 5.1 million (down 2%)

2

into it all for another 3 hours or so, have another snack-sized meal in mid-afternoon and then return to the main rides, as the parks tend to quieten down a little in late afternoon.

Finally, a word about shopping in Orlando – it's world class. Your battle plan should also include at least half a day to visit one of the spectacular shopping malls, as well as some of the discount outlets and speciality centres like Old Town in Kissimmee, the excellent Orlando Premium Outlets, The Mercado and the Pointe*Orlando on I-Drive.

Clothing and comfort

The most important part of your holiday wardrobe is your footwear – you will spend a lot of time on your feet, even during the off-peak periods. The smallest of the parks covers 'only' 100 acres, but that is irrelevant to the amount of time you will spend queuing. Don't save those new sandals or trainers for when you're there! Comfortable, well-worn shoes or trainers are essential. Otherwise, you need dress only as the climate dictates. T-shirts and shorts are quite acceptable in all of the parks (but swimwear is not acceptable away from pool areas) and most restaurants and other eating establishments will happily accept informal dress.

If, after a long day, you feel the need for a change of clothes or a sweater for the evening, use the handy lockers which all the theme parks provide. All the main parks are also well equipped with pushchairs (or strollers) for a small charge, and baby services are freely located at regular intervals.

It is absolutely *vital* to use high-factor sun creams at all times, even during the winter months when the sun may not feel that strong but can still burn. Nothing is guaranteed to ruin your holiday in a hurry like severe sunburn. Orlando has a sub-tropical climate and requires higher-factor sun creams than even the Mediterranean. Use sun blocks on sensitive areas like your nose and ears, and splash on the after-sun cream liberally at the end of the day. Skincare products are widely available and usually inexpensive (especially at Wal-Mart or K-Mart).

> **BRIT TIP:** Don't be tempted to pack a lot of smart or formal clothing – you really won't need it in hot, informal Florida.

Don't forget a waterproof sun cream if you are swimming. Wear a hat if you are out in the hottest parts of the day, and try to avoid alcohol, coffee and fizzy drinks until the evening as they will all make you dehydrated and susceptible to heatstroke. You will need to increase your fluid intake *significantly* during the summer months in Orlando, but stick to still soft drinks (try Gatorade, a squash-like energy drink) or water.

Medical aid

Should you require medical treatment, whether it be for sunburn or other first aid, consult your tour company's information about local hospitals and surgeries. In the event of a medical, or other, emergency, dial 911 as you would 999 in Britain.

It cannot be over-stressed that you should have comprehensive travel

The Gaylord Palms Wedding Pavilion

BRIT TIP: The summer is mosquito time. Buy a spray-on insect repellent. Alternatively, try Avon's Skin So Soft which works wonders at keeping the bugs at bay.

and health insurance for any trip to America as there is NO National Health Service and ANY form of medical treatment will need to be paid for – and is usually expensive. Keep all the receipts and reclaim on your return home.

Emergency out-patients departments can be found with **Centra Care** at Florida Hospital Medical Center in five locations and can provide in-room services (407 238 2000) and free transport (407 239 6463). Open from 8am–5, 6, 7, 8 or 9pm, Centra Care can be found at 12139 South Apopka-Vineland Road, and 12500 Apopka-Vineland Road, next to Eckerd Drugs in The Shoppes at Buena Vista, and next to Turner Drugs, near the Crossroads shopping centre, at Lake Buena Vista (the latter open until midnight on weekdays – 407 239 7777 or 407 934 2273); 7848 West Irlo Bronson Memorial Highway, in Formosa Gardens Village near Splendid China (407 397 7032); 6001 Vineland Road, near Universal Studios (407 351 6682); and 4320 West Vine Street, near Medieval Times (407 390 1888). Sand Lake Hospital on 9400 Turkey Lake Road also has an emergency out-patients department.

The **East Coast Medical Network** (407 648 5252) and **House Med Inc** (407 239 1195) both make hotel 'house calls' 24 hours a day. House Med also operates **MediClinic**, a walk-in facility on 2901 Parkway Boulevard, Kissimmee (open daily 9am–9pm)

and Orlando Regional Healthcare System (operator of Sand Lake Hospital) has **Walk-In Medical Care** centres on I-Drive (407 351 3035 and 239 6679) open 8am–8pm.

A 24-hour tourist-orientated **dentist** can be found at J Antonellis on W Colonial Drive (407 292 8767).

The two largest **chemists** ('drug stores' in America) are Eckerd Drugs and Walgreens, and their branches at 908 Lee Road and 6201 I-Drive are both open 24 hours.

If you are taking regular prescription drugs, check with your doctor or pharmacist to see if they have a different name in the US. Many do (adrenaline is known as epinephrine) and it is worth finding out and carrying the drug with both names in case of an emergency. (Many thanks to Valerie Mulcare-Tivey for this advice.) Another reader points out the American term for paracetamol is acetaminophen.

Travel insurance

Having said you should not travel without good insurance, you should also not pay over the odds for it. Tour operators are notoriously expensive or may imply you need to buy their insurance policy when you don't. In all cases make sure your policy covers you in the USA for: **medical cover** of at least £2 million; **personal liability** up to £2 million (though this won't cover driving abroad; you would still need Supplementary Liability Insurance with your car-hire firm); **cancellation** or **curtailment** cover up to £3,000; **personal property** cover up to £1,500 (but check on expensive items, as most policies limit single articles to £250); **cash and document** cover, including your passport and tickets; and finally that the policy gives you a 24-hour **emergency helpline**. If you want to go bungee jumping or even horse riding, check your policy includes

2

dangerous sports cover.

Shop around at reputable dealers like **American Express** (0800 700 737), **AA** (0191 235 6513), **Bradford & Bingley** (0800 435642), **Club Direct** (0800 0744 558), **Columbus** (0207 375 0011), **Direct Travel** (01903 812345), **GA Direct** (0800 121007), **Options** (0870 848 0870), **Premier Direct** (0990 133218), **Primary Direct** (0870 444 3434), **Thomas Cook** (0845 600 5454), **Travel Insurance Direct** (0990 168113), **Worldcover Direct** (0800 365121) and **Worldwide Travel Insurance** (01892 833338).

> BRIT TIP: Avoid making phone calls from your hotel room – it's very expensive (see page 53). It's cheaper to buy a local phonecard and use a normal payphone.

Florida with children

I am often asked what I think is the right age to take children to Orlando, and there is no set answer, I'm afraid. Some toddlers take to it instantly, while some 6- or even 7-year-olds are left rather bemused. Quite often, the best attractions for young children are the hotel swimming pool or the tram ride to a park's front gates! Some love the Disney characters at first sight, while others find them quite frightening. There is simply no predicting how they will react, but I do know my oldest boy at 4½ loved just about every second of his first experience (apart from the fireworks – see below) and still talks about it. Yes, a 3-year-old may not remember much, but they WILL have fun and provide YOU with some great memories, photos and video.

Here are some top tips for travelling with youngsters – with thanks to the folks at wdwinfo.com

for chipping in! (Additional tips are given in the theme parks chapters.):

The flight: Try to look calm (even if you don't feel it) and relaxed. Small children soon pick up on any anxieties and make them worse! Pack a bag with plenty of little bits for them (comics, sweets, colouring books, small surprise toys, etc) and keep vital 'extras' like Calpol (in sachets, if possible), change of clothes, small first aid kit (plasters, antiseptic cream, baby wipes), sunglasses, hat and sunscreen in your hand luggage.

Once you're there: take things slowly and let your children dictate what pace you go at, to a large extent. The heat, in particular, can make for angsty children in no time flat, so take time-outs for drinks, splash zones or attractions with air-conditioning. Remember to carry your small first-aid kit with you. Things like baby wipes always come in handy, and it is a good idea to take spare clothes, which you can leave in the handy lockers at all the main parks. Going back to the hotel for an afternoon snooze is also well worthwhile – the late afternoon/early evening is usually the best time at the parks in terms of cooler temperatures, less crowds and pure fun.

In the sun: carry sun cream and sun block at all times and use it frequently, in queues, on buses, etc. A children's after sun cream is also a good idea. And please ensure you all drink a lot of water or non-fizzy drinks. Tiredness and irritability are often a result of mild dehydration.

Eating out: look for the 'kids eat free' deals in many places, as they can apply to children up to 12, and take advantage of the many buffet options (see Chapter 10, Eating Out) to fill the family up or for picky eaters. 'Many restaurants do Meals To Go if you want a quiet meal in your own accommodation without the worry of the kids playing up!'

says Lisag on wdwinfo.com. Try to let your children get used to the (size of the) characters before you go to one of the many fab Disney character meals.

Having fun: try to involve your children in some of the decision-making and be prepared to go with the flow if they find something unexpected they like (the many squirt fountains and splash zones in the main parks are an example – bring along swimsuits and/or a change of clothes!). The Orlando rule of 'You Can't Do It All' applies especially with children. And beware the evening fireworks at many of the parks – they are loud, and young children can get quite distressed (my oldest – then 4 – had to be taken out of Epcot in a hurry!). The resort hotels around the *Magic Kingdom Park* offer safer ways to view the fireworks – at a distance!

BRIT TIP: Pushchairs are essential, even if your children are a year or two out of them. The distances involved around the parks wear kids out quickly, and a pushchair can save a lot of discomfort (for dads especially!). You can take your own, hire them at the parks or even buy one there at a local supermarket for around £10.

Travellers with disabilities

The parks pay close attention to the needs of holiday-makers with disabilities. There are few rides that cannot cater for them, while wheelchair availability and access is almost always good. All Disney hotels have rooms accessible for guests with disabilities – call 407 939 7807 or visit www.disneyworld.com – and Disney publishes a *Guidebook for Disabled Guests* (as do Universal), available in all three main parks. Life-jackets are always on hand at the water parks, and there are special tape cassettes for blind visitors.

BRIT TIP: If you have a fridge in your hotel or holiday home, put drink cartons in the freezer overnight and they will be cool for much of the next day in your back-pack.

Disabled drivers should take their orange car badge with them as this is honoured in the US and there are designated parking areas at all theme parks. For more local assistance, **Walker Medical & Mobility Products** specialises in 3-wheeled electric scooters and wheelchair rentals, with free delivery and pick-up even from holiday homes. Call 407 331 9500 for more info. **Rainbow Wheels** (www.rainbowwheels.com) is another specialist company who rents full-size or mini vans equipped for wheelchair users. Call them on 407 365 8813.

Reader Les Willans confirms: 'Orlando is superb when it comes to accessibility for wheelchair users like myself, but Americans often use quite offensive language, such as the term "handicapped", when referring to the disabled.'

Another helpful website is www.accessibleverything.com which aims to provide detailed info to plan holidays for wheelchair, pram or walking stick users.

Orlando for grown-ups

It may sound daft to include something specifically for adults, but it is an often overlooked aspect here that you certainly don't need to have kids in tow to enjoy Orlando. I've often felt the place is actually too good for kids! There is so much clever detail and imagination which most youngsters miss that it is usually the grown-ups who get most out of the experience. In fact, there are just as many couples and single adults visiting the parks.

Certainly, when you look at some of the evening entertainment on offer at places like *Pleasure Island* and CityWalk, the downtown district and The Pointe*Orlando, the great range of bars and the proliferation of fine restaurants in recent years, with a good number of romantic offerings, it is easy to see the attraction for those 21 and over. As well as being a key honeymoon destination, the friendly, Floridian social atmosphere also makes for an ideal place for singles, while couples without children can also take full advantage of the late opening hours at the parks and clubs like Jellyrolls at Disney's Boardwalk Resort.

Orlando for Seniors

If it's true Orlando has just as much to offer grown-ups as kids, then the more mature traveller can also benefit from a healthy dose of the Sunshine State. And, if my parents (both in their 60s) are any guide, they will have just as much fun, within slightly different parameters. For the older person, staying on site in *Walt Disney World Resort Florida* is recommended as it removes the stress of driving. The extra cost is offset, my parents felt, by the beauty and convenience of their surroundings. In the parks, they found there was still plenty for them to do, even if they weren't keen on most of the thrill rides (although just watching can provide a good element of spectator entertainment!). *Epcot* and *Disney's Animal Kingdom*

Theme Park both have much to engage the older visitor, while the shows of *Disney-MGM Studios* make that a popular park, too, and the *Magic Kingdom Park*, while 'probably the noisiest of all the parks,' still represents an essential experience.

The *Downtown Disney* area can feel a bit frenetic for the senior crowd, but *Disney's Boardwalk Resort* is popular and the whole of the *Epcot* resort area offers much in the way of fine dining and relaxation. For my parents in particular, the highlights they recommend for their age group are: Jim Henson's Muppet Vision 3-D and Fantasmic! at *Disney-MGM Studios;* Kilimanjaro Safaris, the Maharajah Jungle Trek and Festival of the Lion King at *Disney's Animal Kingdom Theme Park;* Spaceship Earth, Universe of Energy, Test Track and IllumiNations at *Epcot* (plus the wonderful gardens and architecture); The Haunted Mansion, Jungle Cruise, Pirates Of The Caribbean and the monorail ride to the *Magic Kingdom Park;* watching the children at the many parades and character greetings; dinner at the California Grill in *Disney's Contemporary Resort;* shopping at Orlando Premium Outlets; most of Universal Studios,

Top 10 Romantic Restaurants	
1	Park Plaza Gardens, Winter Park
2	California Grill, Disney's Contemporary Resort
3	Delfino Riviera, Portofino Bay Hotel
4	The Boheme, Grand Bohemian Hotel
5	Emeril's, CityWalk
6	Old Hickory Steakhouse, Gaylord Palms Resort
7	Roy's, Sand Lake Road
8	Flying Fish, Disney's Boardwalk Resort
9	Arthur's 27, Wyndham Palace Resort
10	Palm, Hard Rock Hotel

but less of Islands of Adventure (although they were wowed – as most people are – by the Amazing Adventures of Spider-Man).

Weatherwise, March was just about ideal for them, but they wouldn't be keen to visit in the summer. Seniors can also take advantage of many discounts and special deals for their age group at the attractions and even many restaurants and hotels, or take up our special offer on page 93. The Official Visitor Center on I-Drive publishes a brochure of all the deals (www.orlandoinfo.com).

Measurements

American clothes sizes are smaller than ours, hence a US size 12 dress is a UK size 14, or an American jacket sized 42 is really a 44. Shoes are the opposite: a US 10 should fit a British size 9 foot. Their measuring system is also still imperial and NOT metric.

American-speak

Another thing to watch out for are words or phrases that have a different meaning across the Atlantic. For instance, when Americans say the first floor, they mean the ground floor, the second floor is really the first, and so on. (NB: NEVER ask for a packet of fags. Fag is a crude, slang term for homosexual.) See table opposite.

Wedding bells

Florida is increasingly sought after by couples looking to tie the knot (some 20,000 couples a year at the last count), and Orlando offers a terrific range of wedding services, from ceremony co-ordinators, photography and flowers to a wonderfully scenic range of venues like Cypress Gardens, Winter Park and Leu Gardens, plus more unusual venues like the pit-lane of the

Richard Petty Driving Experience at *Walt Disney World Resort in Florida* or even at 145mph around the speedway itself!

Walt Disney World's Wedding Pavilion offers true fairytale romance, with the backdrop of Cinderella Castle and Seven Seas Lagoon. You can opt for traditional elegance in this Victorian setting with up to 260 guests or the full Disney experience, arriving in Cinderella's glass coach with Mickey and Minnie among the guests. Disney's wedding organisers can tailor-make the occasion for individual requirements (407 828 3400). Universal have a wedding service based on their beautiful Portofino Bay Hotel. Call 407 503 1120 for their wedding specialist.

All the main **tour operators** feature wedding options and co-ordinated services, and offer ceremonies as varied as aboard a hot air balloon or helicopter, the beach or a luxury yacht. Prices vary from £595 per couple (Cypress Grove – Thomson) to £1,980 (Disney's Premium Intimate Wedding package – Virgin).

You can also **do it yourself** by calling at the Osceola County Administrative Building, 17 South Vernon Street, Room 231-A, Kissimmee between 8.30am–4.30pm, Mon–Fri (407 847 1424). In Orange County, apply to the Orange County Courthouse on 425 N Orange Avenue (407 836 2067) 8am–5pm, Mon–Fri. Both parties must be present to apply for the marriage licence, which costs

> **BRIT TIP:** if you shop at any Wal-Mart store in America, you can return any faulty or mis-size goods to your local Asda for a refund, provided you keep your receipts.

American	English	American	English
Check or Tab	Bill	Lines	Queues, so 'Stand in line' not 'Queue up')
Restroom	Public toilet		
Bathroom	Private toilet	Elevator	Lift
Eggs 'over easy'	Eggs fried both sides but soft	Underpass	Subway
		Subway	Underground
Eggs 'over hard'	Eggs fried both sides but hard!	Mailbox	Postbox
		Faucet	Tap
Eggs 'sunny side up'	Eggs fried on just one side (soft)	Collect call	Reverse charge phone call
French fries	Chips	Gas	Petrol
Chips	Crisps	Gas pedal	Accelerator
Cookie	Biscuit	Trunk	Car boot
Grits	Porridge-like breakfast dish made out of ground, boiled corn	Hood	Car bonnet
		Fender	Car bumper
		Antenna	Aerial
		Windshield	Windscreen
Biscuit	Savoury scone	Stickshift	Manual transmission
Hash browns	Grated, fried potato (delicious!)	Trailer	Caravan
Jelly	Jam	Freeway	Motorway
Silverware or		Divided highway	Dual carriageway
place-setting	Cutlery	Denver boot	Wheel clamp
Liquor	Spirits	Turn-out	Lay-by
Seltzer	Soda water	No standing	No parking OR stopping
Shot	Measure		
Liquor store	Off-licence	Parking lot	Car park
Broiled	Grilled	Semi	Articulated truck
Grilled	Flame-grilled	Ramp	Slip-road
Sub	Torpedo roll	Intersection	Junction
Shrimp	King prawn	Construction	Roadworks
Sherbet	Sorbet	Yield	Give way
Eggplant	Aubergine	Purse	Handbag
Appetiser	Starter	Fanny pack	Bumbag
Entree	Main course	Pants	Trousers
To go	Take-away (as in food)	Undershirt	Vest
		Vest	Waistcoat
Candy	Sweets	Pantyhose	Tights
Drug store	Chemist	Sneakers	Trainers
Bandaid	Plaster	Shorts	Underpants
Movie theater	Cinema	Facecloth/ washcloth	Flannel
Sidewalk	Pavement		
Pavement	Roadway	Quarter	25 cents
Bill	Note (as in $5 note)	Dime	10 cents
		Nickel	5 cents
Crib	Cot	Downtown	The city or town centre (not the rundown part!)
Cot or rollaway	Fold-up bed		
Diaper	Nappy		
Stroller	Pushchair	A/C	Air-conditioning

$88.50 (in cash) and is valid for 60 days, while the ceremony (equivalent to a British register office) can be performed at the same time by the clerk for an extra $20 (8–11am or 2–4pm, Mon to Fri). Passports and birth certificates are required and, after acquiring a marriage licence, a couple can get married anywhere in Florida. Witnesses to the marriage are not required, and blood tests are no longer required either.

The County's Marriage Department can also supply names of public notaries to conduct the ceremony if you want to marry elsewhere, like one of the more picturesque resort hotels. For more info, you can call the Orlando/Orange County Convention & Visitors' Bureau for an info pack (407 363 5872). You can also look up www.orlandoweddinglocations.com or call 407 876 6433.

Those looking for a church or other place of worship can visit the **Center of Light Church & Spiritual Center** on East Robinson Street (407 228 0101), the **First Baptist Church** on John Young Parkway (407 425 2555, www.fborlando.org), **St Nicholas Catholic Church** on Sand Lake Road (407 351 0133) or **Trinity Lutheran Church** on East Livingston Street downtown (407 422 5704, www.trinitydowntown.org).

The Disney Wedding Pavilion

© Disney

Safety first

While crime is not a serious issue in central Florida, this is still big-city America and, as with all big cities, you need to keep your wits about you. This is not the time to leave your common sense at home.

The area has its own Tourist Oriented Policing Service (or TOPS), centred on I-Drive, with more than 70 officers patrolling purely the main tourist areas, arranging crime prevention seminars with local hotels and generally ensuring Orlando takes good care of its visitors. You will often see the local police in these areas out on mountain bikes, and they are a polite, helpful bunch should you need their assistance or to ask them directions. Tourism is such a vital part of the local economy the authorities cannot afford not to be seen to be taking an active role against crime, hence the area has a highly safety-conscious attitude.

Having said that, it would be foolish to behave as if the villainous element did not exist and therefore there are a number of guidelines which all visitors to America in general, and Orlando in particular, should follow. Put simply, it is just a matter of being sensible and not throwing caution to the wind.

For example, just as it would be inadvisable to walk around the darker corners of London late at night alone, so it would be the same in parts of Florida.

Emergencies

General: in an emergency of any kind, for police, fire department or ambulance, dial 911 (9-911 from your hotel room). It is a good idea to make sure your children are aware of this number, while for smaller-scale crises (mislaid tickets or passports, rescheduled flights, etc) your holiday company should have an emergency contact number in the hotel reception. If you are travelling independently and run into passport or other problems that require the assistance of the British Consulate in Orlando, their office is located in Sun Bank Towers, 200 South Orange Avenue, with walk-in visitors' hours 9.30am–noon and 2–4pm, or phone 9.30am–4pm on 407 426 7855.

Hotel security

While in your hotel, motel or guest house, you should always use door peepholes and security chains whenever someone knocks at the door. DON'T open the doors to strangers without asking for identification, and check with the hotel desk if you are still not sure.

It is stating the obvious, but keep doors and windows locked at all times and always use deadlocks and security chains. It is still surprising how many people forget basic precautions when they are on holiday (the local police never cease to be amazed at how many people do leave their common sense behind when they leave home!). Always take your cash, credit cards, valuables and car keys when you go out (or use room safes, which are often provided), and don't leave the door open at any time, even if you are just popping down the corridor to the ice machine. And make a point of asking hotels about their safety precautions when you make a reservation. Do

they have electronic card-locks (which can't be duplicated) and do they have security staff?

Don't be afraid to ask reception staff for safety pointers in the surrounding areas or if you are travelling somewhere you are not sure about. Safety is a major issue for the Central Florida Hotel/Motel Association and hotel staff are usually well briefed to be helpful. Using a bumbag (the Americans call them fanny packs!) is a better bet than a shoulder bag or handbag.

Nothing is guaranteed to get the local police shaking their heads in disbelief than the tourist who goes round looking like an obvious tourist. The map over the steering wheel is a giveaway, but other no-nos are wearing large amounts of jewellery, carrying masses of photographic equipment or flashing wads of cash around. The biggest giveaway is leaving your camera or camcorder on view in the car.

Finally, and this is VERY strong police advice, in the unlikely event of being confronted by an assailant, DO NOT resist or 'have a go', as it more often than not will result in making the situation more serious.

Money and valuables

Following on from the advice about bumbags, it is inadvisable and unnecessary to carry large amounts of cash with you. US travellers' cheques are accepted almost everywhere as cash and can be readily replaced if lost or stolen, as can credit cards, which are another widespread form of currency. Visa,

BRIT TIP: If you want to be extra safety conscious, you can hire mobile phones, pagers and even two-way radios from as little as $20 a week from Airwave Communications (407 843 1166).

Mastercard and American Express are all widely accepted. The Sun Bank in *Disney's Magic Kingdom Park* and *Epcot* is open 7 days a week should you need extra help with any financial transactions. It is worth separating the larger notes from the smaller ones in your wallet to avoid flashing all your money in view. Losing £200 of travellers' cheques shouldn't ruin your holiday – but losing £200 in cash might.

Most hotels will offer the use of safes and deposit boxes for your valuables, and many rooms now come equipped with mini-safes in which it is a good idea to leave your passports, return tickets, cameras etc, when you don't need them. Always keep your valuables out of sight, whether in the hotel room or the car. Shut your jacket or camera in the boot.

Car crime

Car crime is one of the biggest forms of criminal activity in America and has led to some of the most lurid headlines, especially in the Miami area in the mid-1990s. Once again, it pays to make a number of basic safety checks before you set off anywhere. The first thing is to familiarise yourself with the car's controls BEFORE you drive out of the hire company's car park. Which button is the air-conditioning, which side of the steering wheel are the indicators and where are the windscreen wipers?

Also, make sure you know your route in advance, even if it is only a case of memorising the road numbers. Most car-hire firms now give good directions on how to get to your hotel from their car park, so read them before you set off.

One of the main items on the of local police list of Dos and Don'ts is to use your map BEFORE you set off – trying to drive with the map over the steering wheel is just asking for an accident.

BRIT TIP: Be forewarned all American banknotes are EXACTLY the same green colour and size. It is only the picture of the president and the denomination in each corner that change.

Check that the petrol tank is full and never let it get near empty. Running out of 'gas' in an unfamiliar area holds obvious hazards. If you stray off your pre-determined route, stick to well-lit areas and stop to ask directions only from official businesses like hotels and garages or better still, a police car or station. Always try to park close to your destination where there are plenty of street lights and DO NOT get out if there are any suspicious characters lurking around. Always keep your windows closed (you've got air-conditioning, remember?) and don't hesitate to lock the doors from the inside if you feel threatened (larger cars have doors that lock automatically as you drive off). And don't forget to lock the doors when you leave the car. Not many rental cars have central locking, so it's wise to double check.

Miami crooks developed the habit of trying to get cars to stop by trying to look official or deliberately bumping into hire cars from behind. The easily identified hire car plates have now been phased out, but still NEVER stop for a non-official request. Go instead to the nearest garage or police station, and always insist on identification before unlocking your car and getting out of it for an official.

It is comforting to know that a unique aspect of driving in Orlando is that none of the main tourist areas have any no-go areas. The nearest is the portion of the Orange Blossom Trail south of downtown Orlando. This houses a selection of strip clubs and 'adult bars' that are not particularly attractive and can be downright seedy at night.

For more information on safety contact the Community Affairs office of Orange County Police on 407 836 3720 or the TOPS office on 407 351 9368.

Know before you go

You can contact these organisations for advance information. Florida Tourism (www.flausa.com) have an info line on 0900 1600 555 (60p/minute) that lists all Florida destinations and gives other consumer lines in the UK, while they have a free information pack if you call 01737 644882 (plus some more great ideas on www.culturallyflausa.com). The Orlando Tourism Bureau in London has a 24-hour information line on 0800 018 6799, on which you can request their free *Destination Imagination* information pack or visit www.orlandoinfo.com/uk. The Orlando/Kissimmee information line is 09001 600 220 (calls 60p per min). You can also look up the Kissimmee Convention & Visitors Bureau on www.floridakiss.com.

When you arrive in the area, it is also worth checking out Orlando's ONLY official **Visitor Center** at

8723 International Drive (407 363 5872) for discounted attraction tickets, free brochures and accommodation advice and free information pamphlets and maps. The Kissimmee **Visitor Center** is at the eastern end of the Highway 192 tourist drag (407 847 5000 or 1-800 327 9159 in the States) and they have a toll-free accommodation line in the US of 1-800 333 KISS. Of course, THE website for all things Orlando and Disney is the fun and info-packed **www.wdwinfo.com**, to which I also contribute. The creation and maintenance of this independent site is a truly mind-boggling feat. It provides up-to-the-minute advice and assistance including the complete range of theme park info (right down to rides under refurbishment, park hours and ride height requirements), news, weather, facts, figures and tips, plus discount offers throughout Orlando, discussion boards and a chat forum.

The official sites are pretty good, too, with Disney's the pick of the bunch: www.disneyworld.co.uk (check opening hours, parades and book on-line). Then there is www.universalorlando.com, plus www.seaworld.com and www.buschgardens.com. The local newspaper has a Calendar 'what's on' section, (www.orlandosentinel.com) and the free *Orlando Weekly* (www.orlandoweekly.com) if full of helpful info.

Among the many unofficial and fan websites are www.wdwig.com (for restaurant info), www.wdwmagic.com (great for Disney trivia and rumours), the well-designed www.wdisneyw.co.uk (with more pages for UK visitors) and www.orlandorocks.com (for all theme park addicts).

Now, on to the real thing…

3 Driving and Car Hire
(or, The Secret of Getting Around on Interstate 4)

For the vast majority, introduction to Orlando proper comes immediately after clearing the airport via the potentially bewildering local road systems in a newly acquired, left-hand drive hire car. Yet driving here is a lot more simple and, on the whole, enjoyable than driving in the UK. In fact, anyone used to the M25 should find Orlando's motorways far less stressful.

Before you get to your hire car, however, a quick note about Orlando International Airport and the alternative Orlando Sanford Airport, mainly a British charter flight gateway 30 miles to the north of Orlando. Details of how both airports work are given in Chapter 12, but you need to be aware of a couple of quirks on arrival.

Orlando International – currently in the middle of a major expansion project – is one of the most modern and enjoyable airports you will encounter, but it does have a bewildering double baggage collection system. You disembark at one of four satellite terminals and have to collect your luggage straight after going through Immigration, then put it on another baggage carousel that takes it to the main

I-Ride trolley

BRIT TIP: Make sure you follow the correct instructions to collect your hire car. There are several different desks for each of the main hire companies and, if you do not check in at the right one, you will waste a lot of time.

terminal while you ride the passenger shuttle. Once in the main terminal you will be on Level Three and need to descend to Level Two for baggage reclaim. Porters will help you down to Level One for car pick-up (remember the $1 a bag tip), while the trolleys need $1 in change to operate. Taxis and limos are also found on Level One. Several tour operators – notably Virgin Holidays – have help desks here, too. The public bus system, Lynx (see opposite), operates from the A side of Level One, in spaces A32–34.

The Big Four hire companies with check-in desks at the airport are Dollar, National, Budget and Avis and all offer the most comprehensive hire services, if rather lacking in the

BRIT TIP: If you are hiring from one of the Big Four, save time and queuing by going to their desk to complete the paperwork BEFORE collecting your luggage again.

personal touch. However, there is also a telephone desk at Level One connecting you to another 15 hire companies who often work out better value (notably Alamo Rent A Car).

The off-airport rental firms will have a regular free shuttle outside on Level One to take you to their nearby depots, which will give you a preview of the roads before you take to them. Hertz and Avis are the biggest companies in the US, but Dollar and Alamo are tops for tourist business. Dollar is included in typical packages by Thomson, Airtours, Virgin, Style Holidays, Travel City and First Choice, while Alamo are the main clients for Unijet, Funway, Jetlife, Jetsave, Kuoni, British Airways Holidays and Thomas Cook Holidays, among others. Alamo's international tour centre, a 10-minute bus ride from the airport, features no less than 52 terminals, plus desks for the tour operator reps (handy for any paperwork wrangles), a changing area and a childcare area.

> BRIT TIP: Alamo is *A Brit's Guide* partner and can offer you a special rate with this book. It is my car rental company of choice, providing a quick and efficient service. *See inside front cover for details.*

Orlando without a car

Although being mobile is advisable, it is possible to survive without a car. However, few of the attractions are within walking distance of anywhere and taxis can be expensive. If you decide not to drive, your best base is either *Walt Disney World Resort in Florida* (free transport throughout, but harder to get to the rest of

The Orlando airport shuttle

Orlando) or International Drive (I-Drive) for its location, good pavements (or 'sidewalks') and the great I-Ride Trolley. Many hotels also have free shuttles to some of the main parks or a regular mini-bus service for a small charge.

There are basically three different transport routes. The reliable, cheap, but slightly plodding **Lynx bus system** covers much of Metro Orlando. For information visit www.golynx.com, or call 407 841 8240. Ask for a copy of their excellent System Map, which shows all their routes (or 'Links') and the main attractions. Worth noting are **Link 42** from the International Airport to I-Drive; **Links 56** and **304**, respectively from Kissimmee and the I-Drive area to *Walt Disney World Resort in Florida*; **Link 18** from Kissimmee to downtown Orlando; **Link 55**, which covers a large part of Highway 192 in Kissimmee from Osceola Square Mall all the way west past Splendid China to Secret Lake Drive; **Link 38**, I-Drive to downtown Orlando; and **Links 50** and **300**, which both operate from Disney to downtown Orlando. It costs $1 a ride (plus 10 cents for transfers) or $10 for a weekly pass (children 6 and under go free with a full-fare passenger). They average a bus every 30 minutes in the main areas, every 15 minutes from 6–9am and 3.30–6.30pm, but remember to have the right change. Lynx bus stops are marked by pink paw-print signs and all the buses are wheelchair accessible.

The I-Drive area also has the great-value **I-Ride trolley**, which operates two routes along a 14-mile stretch of this tourist corridor. The *Main Line* runs from the Universal Orlando resort area of Windhover Drive and Major Boulevard in the north, via Belz shopping centre at the top of I-Drive, to SeaWorld via Westwood Boulevard and Sea Harbor Drive, and on to Orlando Premium Outlets in the south. The *Green Line* basically covers Universal Boulevard, from the Orange County Convention Centre up to the junction of I-Drive and Kirkman Road (tel 407 354 5656, www.iridetrolley.com). Running every day, 7am–11.30pm at roughly 15-minute intervals (30 minutes on the Green Line), it costs 75cents per trip (25 cents for seniors) – please have the right change – or you can buy Unlimited Ride passes for 1, 3, 5, 7 or 14 days at $2, $3, $5, $7 or $14. If you need to transfer between routes, ask for a transfer coupon when you board (transfers are free with Unlimited Ride passes). Kids 12 and under go free with an adult, and all trolleys have hydraulic lifts for wheelchairs. Passes are sold at 75 locations along the I-Drive area, including most hotel service desks and visitor centres.

One other regular service worth noting is from SeaWorld to Busch Gardens in Tampa, with six departure points daily from 8.15 to 9.30am. Called the **Busch Shuttle Express**, it costs $5 a person but is free if you have bought Busch tickets in advance (included in the 5-Park Orlando FlexTicket). For more details, see page 160.

As an alternative to public transport, there is a raft of well-organised firms who offer **shuttle services** to the attractions for a set fee and excursions to places like Kennedy Space Center and Busch Gardens that pick up at the hotels.

The main firms are Mears (www.mearstransportation.com, or call 407 423 5566) and Coach USA (www.coachusa.com, or call 407 826 9999). Mears offers the most comprehensive service, from limousines to coaches, and typical round-trip shuttle fares would be: Airport–Walt Disney World, $28/person ($20/child); Airport–I-Drive, $24/person ($17/child); Airport–Highway 192 in Kissimmee $28–40/person ($20–31/child); *Walt Disney World*–Universal Orlando, $13/person; I-Drive–*Walt Disney World*, $13/person; I-Drive or *Walt Disney World*–Kennedy Space Center, $20/person. Mears also offers a SuperPass service of 3, 4, 5, 6, 7 days of unlimited service to and from the main area attractions (including airport transfers) from I-Drive or Walt Disney World for $59, $70, $81, $92, $103. You can book a Mears shuttle on arrival at one of their desks in the luggage halls, but it can be a long journey to your hotel if they have a full van.

> **BRIT TIP:** The boot size of American cars tends to be smaller than the British equivalent. And you will not get 7 people PLUS their luggage in a 7-seater people carrier!

Quick Transportation (407 354 2456) comes well recommended for its excellent Town Car and Limousine service. They offer a highly personal and efficient alternative to taxis and shuttles for airport transfers and can be more economical for larger families and groups. Town cars will cope with a family of four, while there are spacious vans for larger parties (plus the limos, of course). The driver meets you in the baggage hall and takes you directly to the hotel with no stops in between. Their website (www.quicktransportation.com) also offers a useful insight into arriving at Orlando International. Town car rates are $68.50 one way from the airport to anywhere in Greater Orlando and $136 round-trip, while stretch limos are $106 and $208.75. Larger parties may need a luggage trailer for $17.50 extra each way. You can also try **Florida Tours** (1-800 790 6290, www.fltours.com), who operates town cars, luxury vans – good for up to 10 people with luggage – and limousines, or **Tiffany Town Car** services at (www.tiffanytowncar.com), but Quick Transportation get the official *Brit's Guide* seal of approval.

Then there are the **excursion services** offered by the likes of Coach USA, Gray Line (303 433 9800, www.grayline.com), International Divers (407 352 5151, www.swimdolphins.com), and Keith Prowse (see page 10). Finally, for groups of four or five, **taxis** can be a convenient occasional option. The journey from Orlando International to I-Drive would cost around $45, plus tip (about $10 each for five), $12 from I-Drive to Universal Orlando and $23 from I-Drive to *Walt Disney World Resort in Florida*. Try Central Florida Taxi on 407 851 7523 (freephone 1-800 441 3276 in Florida) or Yellow Cab Co on 407 422 4561.

The car

Ultimately, having a car is the key to being in charge of your holiday and, on a weekly basis, it tends to work out quite reasonable pricewise, too.

Weekly rental rates can be as low as $60 for the smallest size of car, an **Economy** (or Sub-compact), usually a Corsa-sized hatchback; next up is the **Compact,** a small family saloon

like a Vauxhall Astra; the **Midsize** (or Intermediate) is a more spacious 4-door, 5-seater like a Vectra; and the **Fullsize** would be a large-style executive car like an Omega, and you can go up the scale still, with **Premium, Luxury** and **Convertible,** plus the **Minivan,** a Renault Espace or VW Sharan type.

But beware these low starting rates. There are a number of insurances, taxes and surcharges which are pretty much essential, and these can easily take the final weekly rate to $280 or more. However, all the big rental companies now offer all-inclusive rates, which can work out significantly cheaper if booked in advance in the UK. Rates can be as low as £161 a week, and you also benefit from easier processing at the Orlando end, making the whole business quicker. To book, call **Alamo** (see inside the front cover for our special readers' offer) or **Dollar** on 0800 252897. Or you could try **Avis** (0990 900 500); **Budget** (0880 181181); **Thrifty** (0990 168 238); **Hertz** (0990 906090); **National** (0345 222525); or **Suncars** (0990 005566).

> BRIT TIP: Be firm with the hire company check-in clerk as some can push you into taking extras, like car upgrades that you don't really need.

Once again, the scale of the car-hire operation is huge and, with as many as 400 tourists arriving at a time, it can be a pretty formidable business getting everyone off. The current practice of British holiday companies offering free car hire with their packages does not mean it won't cost you anything. It is only the *rental* cost that is free and you must still pay the insurance, taxes and other extras BEFORE you drive

Main Line Trolley Stops

1. Wellesley Inn Orlando
2. Best Western Universal Inn /Sleep Inn
3. Extended Stay America
   Delta Orlando Resort
4. AmeriSuites Orlando Universal
   Days Inn Universal Studios
5. Radisson Hotel Orlando
6. International Drive Center
7. International Corner Plaza
8. International Drive Value Center
   Festival Bay @ International Drive
9. Belz Designer Outlet Centre
   Festival Bay @ International Drive
10. Sweets Market Plaza / McDonald's
11. Belz Factory Outlet World
12. Orlando International Resort Club
13. Fun Spot Action Park
14. American Way @ Sheraton Studio City
    Ramada Inn
15. Visitors Circle @ Kentucky Fried Chicken
16. Best Western Movieland / Wet 'n Wild
17. Rodeway Inn / Ponderosa / Bennigan's
18. Holiday Inn Resort / MIC Plaza
19. Carrier Drive @ Pizza Hut / Magical Midway
20. Wild Jack's Steak & Ribs / Dowdy Plaza
21. Dunkin Donuts
22. Quality Inn International
    Olive Garden / IHOP / Burger King
23. HollywoodPlaza / Wyndham Orlando Resort
24. Jamaican Court @ Pizzeria Uno
    Goodings Plaza / Ripley's Believe It Or Not!
25. Jamaican Court @ Ran Getsu
    The Mercado Village
26. Austrian Court @ Summerfield Suites
27. Ponderosa / Bargain World
    OOCCVB Official Visitors Center
28. Embassy Suites / Race Rock
    Cattleman's Steak House
29. Quality Inn Plaza
    Pointe*Orlando / WonderWorks
30. Samoan Court @ Sizzler Restaurant
    Pointe*Orlando / FAO Schwarz
31. Rosen Plaza Hotel
32. Orange County Convention Center
    Peabody Hotel
33. Hawaiian Court @ Rosen Centre Hotel
    Future Orange County Conv. Ctr. Expansion
34. Hawaiian Court @ Red Lobster
    Canadian Court Parking Garage
35. Travelodge Orlando South Villager Premier
    Village Inn Restaurant
    Sheraton World Resort
36. Extended StayAmerica Orlando
    Hawthorn Suites
37. Hilton Garden Inn
38. Renaissance Orlando Resort @ SeaWorld
39. SeaWorld Adventure Park Orlando
40. Hilton Grand Vacations Club
41. Horizon's by Marriott/ Residence Inn
    MarriottCypress Harbor
42. Ramada Inn All Suites
43. Parc Corniche Orlando Resorts
44. Crowne Plaza Resort Orlando
45. Oasis Lakes Resort /Sheraton Vistana Villages
46. Orlando Premium Outlets

Green Line Trolley Stops

1. Clarion Hotel Universal / Wet 'n Wild
2. Ramada Inn
3. Howard Johnson / Hampton Inn
4. Republic Square / MidPoint Plaza
   Siam Orchid
5. Holiday Inn @ Mercado Village
6. La Quinta Inn & Suites
7. Spring HillSuites
8. Pointe*Orlando
9. Orange County Convention Center
   Peabody Hotel

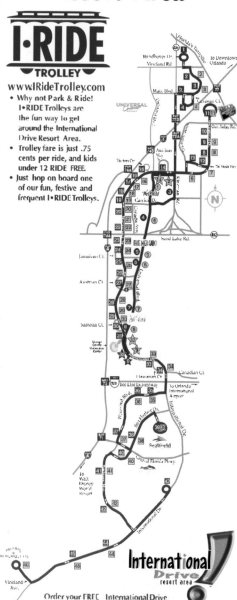

International Drive
Resort Area

I·RIDE
TROLLEY

www.IRideTrolley.com

- Why not Park & Ride!
  I·RIDE Trolleys are
  the fun way to get
  around the International
  Drive Resort Area.

- Trolley fare is just .75
  cents per ride, and kids
  under 12 RIDE FREE.

- Just hop on board one
  of our fun, festive and
  frequent I·RIDE Trolleys.

International
Drive
resort area

Order your FREE International Drive
Official Visitors Guide and I·RIDE Trolley
Map online at www.InternationalDriveOrlando.com

Map not to scale. 6/18/02
Map and I·RIDE Trolley Service Routes subject to change without notice.

away (which makes the all-inclusive packages even more attractive).

Having a credit card is essential, and there are two main kinds of insurance, the most important being the Loss or Collision Damage Waiver, LDW or CDW. This costs around $20 a day and covers you for any damage to your hire car. You can manage without it, but the hire company will insist on a huge deposit in the order of $1,500 on your credit card (and you are also liable for ANY damage).

You will also be offered Supplemental Liability Insurance (SLI) or Extended Protection at around $13 a day. This covers you against being sued for astronomical amounts by any court-happy American you may happen to bump into (not strictly essential, but good for your peace of mind). Relatively new and again optional is the Underinsured Motorists Protection (in case somebody with only minimal cover runs into you) at around $6 a day. Drivers under 25 have to pay an extra $15–20 a day, while all drivers must be at least 21. Other rental costs (which all mount up over a 2-week holiday) include local and Florida state taxes, which can add $6 a day to your final bill, and Airport Handling Tax and Access Fee at $6 or $7 a day and then there's petrol (or gas, in America), although this is still appreciably cheaper than in the UK (about $15–20 to fill up). Ask to return the tank full yourself, as this will save a few dollars on their fill-up option.

For those on a tight budget or happy to take the DIY route, you can cut costs by using travel insurance specialists like Extrasure (tel 020 7480 6871), whose Americasure policy offers both LDW and SLI at around £5 a day. You may still need to leave a credit card imprint with the hire firm, but they should accept these policies (but do still check in advance).

Drivers also please note: you may feel the effects of jet-lag for a day or two after arrival, but this can be reduced by avoiding alcohol and coffee in-flight and instead drinking plenty of water.

> **BRIT TIP:** You probably won't be able to take the keys out of the ignition unless you put the car in 'Park' first. This sometimes causes much consternation!

Most people soon find driving is a pleasure rather than a pain, mainly because nearly all hire cars are automatics and rarely more than a year old. And, because speed limits are lower than we're used to at home (and rigidly enforced), you won't often be rushed into taking the wrong turn. Keep your foot on the brake when you are stationary as automatics tend to creep forward, and always put the automatic gear lever in 'P' (for Park) after turning off the engine.

Controls

All cars are fitted with air-conditioning, which is essential for most of the year. The button to turn it on will be marked A/C, Air, or will just be a snowflake symbol. (Handy hint: to make it work, you also have to switch on the car's fan!) Don't be alarmed by a small pool of liquid under your car in summer – it's condensation off the A/C unit.

Power steering is also common on many hire cars, so be gentle around

Panoramic view of Universal Orlando

corners until you get the feel of it. Larger cars have cruise control, which lets you set the desired speed and take your foot off the accelerator (or gas pedal, in American-speak). There will be two buttons on the steering wheel, one to switch the cruise control on, the other to set the desired speed. To take the car off cruise control either press the first button again or simply touch the brake. The handbrake may also be different. Some cars have an extra foot pedal to the left of the brake, and you need to push this to engage the handbrake. There will then be a tab just above it which you pull to release it, or a second push on the pedal if there is no tab. The car probably won't start unless the gear lever is in 'P', which can be confusing at first. To put the car in 'D' for Drive, you also have to depress the main brake pedal. D1 and D2 are extra gears for steep hills (none in Florida!). Few cars have central locking, so make sure you lock ALL the doors.

> BRIT TIP: The Beeline Expressway (528) and Greeneway (417) are both toll roads, so remember to have some change in the car. Toll booths are reluctant to change more than $20 notes.

Getting around

Your car-hire company should provide you with a basic map of Orlando, plus directions to your hotel. Insist they give you these, as all the hire companies make a big point of this in their literature. Try to familiarise yourself with the main roads of the area in advance and learn to navigate by the road numbers (as those are mainly given

on the signposts) and the exit numbers of the main roads.

When you drive out of **Orlando International Airport** (or the hire company's off-airport depot) don't look for signs to 'Orlando' – the airport's new signage should be a big help here. The main tourist areas are all south and west of the city proper, so follow the appropriate signs for your hotel. For the International Drive area (or I-Drive as it is known locally), you want the Beeline Expressway (usually just listed as Route 528) all the way west until it crosses I-Drive just north of SeaWorld. The main hotel area of I-Drive is to the north, so keep right at the exit. For western Kissimmee and *Walt Disney World Resort*, go south out of the airport and take the Central Florida Greeneway (Highway 417) all the way west until it intersects with State Route 536 at Exit 6 (for *Animal Kingdom* resorts, stay on until Exit 3 and take Osceola Parkway). You can then follow 536 straight across into *Walt Disney World Resort in Florida* or take the Interstate 4 (I-4) west for one junction until it hits the main Kissimmee Routeway, Highway 192 (or the Irlo Bronson Memorial Highway). For eastern Kissimmee, come off Highway 417 at Exit 11 with the Orange Blossom Trail (Highway 441), where going south brings you on to Highway 192 at the other end of the main tourist drag.

> BRIT TIP: Watch out for one small hiccup on the Greeneway (417) heading south. Just after Exit 34 it appears to split into two where it meets Highway 408. Stay in the RIGHT lane to keep on the south-bound motorway.

Leaving **Orlando Sanford Airport** is also a straightforward affair, boosted by the airport's simple design. Dollar and Alamo have made a big impression here with their British-dedicated operations. There is no off-airport shuttle to your car to slow you down, just a quick walk from the airport's baggage reclaim hall to the car-hire office. But please remember to have your paperwork and especially your **driving licence** with you or you WILL find yourself either delayed or refused a car altogether (in the case of forgetting your licence, which many still do).

It may be further to the north and involve more driving, but you usually save time overall. You leave the airport on East Lake Mary Boulevard and quickly hit the junction with the Central Florida Greeneway (Highway 417) on which you head south. The slip-road on to this toll motorway is just under the fly-over on your LEFT, and you will need about $4.50 in total to reach Kissimmee or *Walt Disney World Resort in Florida* or $3.75 to reach I-Drive (via the Beeline Expressway, Route 528).

You can avoid the tolls by staying on Lake Mary Boulevard for 4 miles until you hit I-4, but you may well hit the 4–6pm snarl-up through the city centre. The Greeneway is an excellent, easy-driving introduction to Orlando roads, even if it does cost

BRIT TIP: The Osceola Parkway toll road which runs parallel to Highway 192 is a much easier route in to *Walt Disney World Resort in Florida* from much of Kissimmee and costs only $1.50. Use Sherberth Road for Disney access from west 192.

a few dollars (and no, no one receives any kick-backs for recommending it!).

For radio traffic news and reports, tune in to 1680AM.

Signs and road names

It's best to be aware that the system of signposting and road-naming can be confusing. For instance, you cannot fail to find the main attractions, but retracing your steps back to the hotel afterwards can prove tricky because they often take you out of the parks a different way. (Disney is notoriously poor at sign-posting to help find your way out. A good tip is to get a copy of their Transportation Guide/Map from Guest Services at any park to help navigation.) Here, it is vital to learn the main road numbers (and directions, either east-west or north-south) around the attractions so you know where you are heading, and whether you want I-4 east or west or 192 as you exit *Epcot* or *Disney-MGM Studios*.

Also, exits off the I-4 and other main roads can be on EITHER side of the carriageway, not just on the right. This potential worry is offset by the fact you can overtake in ANY lane on multi-lane highways, not just the outside ones. Therefore, you can happily sit in the middle lane until you see your exit. However, you don't get much advance notice of turn-offs. You get the sign and then the exit in quick succession. But, once again, the lower speeds tend to minimise the dangers of missing your turn-off.

Orlando has yet to come up with a comprehensive tourist map of its streets and the maps supplied by the car-rental companies tend to be simplified. It helps that none of the main attractions are off the beaten track, but the support of a front-seat navigator can be useful.

Around town, and in the main

tourist areas, you will come across another method of confusing the unwary in the way road names are displayed. At every junction you will see a road name hung underneath the traffic lights suspended ABOVE the road. This road name is NOT the road you are on, but the one you are CROSSING. Once again there is no advance notice of each junction and the road names can be difficult to read as you approach them, especially at night, so keep your speed down if you think you are close to your turn-off so you can get in the correct lane. If you do miss a turning, nearly all the roads are arranged in a simple grid system so it is usually easy to work your way back. Occasionally, you will meet a crossroads where no right of way is obvious. This is a **4-way stop,** and the priority goes in order of arrival, so when it's your turn you just indicate and pull out slowly (America doesn't have many roundabouts, so this is the closest you will get to one).

Tolls and traffic lights

For the toll roads, have some change handy in amounts from 25 cents to $1. They all give change (in the GREEN lanes), but you will get through much quicker if you have the correct money (in the BLUE lanes). On minor exits of Osceola Parkway and the Greeneway, there are auto-toll machines *only*, so try to keep some loose change in your car.

As well as the obvious difference of driving on the 'wrong' side of the road, there are also several differences in procedure. The most frequent British errors occur at traffic lights (which are hung above the road, not on posts – easy to miss occasionally). At a red light it is still possible to turn RIGHT, providing there is no traffic coming from the left and no pedestrians crossing, unless otherwise specified (signs will occasionally indicate 'No turn on red'). Turning left at the lights, you have the right of way with a green ARROW, but you have to give way to traffic from the other direction on a SOLID green.

The majority of accidents involving overseas visitors take place on left turns, so take extra care here. There is also no amber light from red to green, but there IS an amber light from green to red. A flashing amber light at a junction means proceed but watch for traffic joining the carriageway, while a flashing red light indicates it is okay to turn if the carriageway is clear.

Downtown Orlando

Restrictions

Speed limits are always well marked with black numbering on white signs and, again, the police are pretty hot on speeding and on-the-spot fines are steep. Limits vary from 55 to 70mph on the Interstates (and can change frequently), where there is also a 40mph *minimum* speed, to just 15 or 20mph in some built-up areas.

Flashing orange lights suspended over the road indicate a school zone so proceed with caution, while school buses cannot be overtaken in either direction when they are unloading and have their hazard lights on. U-turns are forbidden in built-up areas and where a solid line runs down the middle of the road.

It is illegal to park within 10ft of a fire hydrant or a lowered kerb, and never park in front of a yellow-painted kerb – they are stopping points for emergency vehicles and you will be towed away. Never park on a kerb, either. Seat belts are compulsory for all front-seat passengers, while child seats must be used for under 4s and can be hired from the car companies at around $5 a day (better still, bring your own). Children aged 4 or 5 must either use a seat belt, whether sitting in the front or back, or have a child seat fitted for them.

Additionally, you must put your lights on in the rain, and you must park bonnet first. Reverse parking is frowned upon because number plates are often found only on the rear of cars and patrolling police cars like to be able to read them without the officers having to stop and walk round the car. If you park parallel to the kerb you must be facing in the direction of the traffic. Disabled drivers should note their orange disabled badge IS recognised in Florida for parking in the well-provided disabled parking spaces.

Finally, don't drink and drive. Florida has strict laws, with penalties of up to 6 months in prison for first-time offenders. The legal blood-alcohol limit is lower than in Britain, so it is safer not to drink at all if you are driving. It is also illegal to carry open containers of alcohol in the car.

> BRIT TIP: The Kissimmee-St Cloud tourist information office on east Highway 192 has the best free map of the area, clearly indicating all the main routes and attractions.

Attention AA members – here is a bonus for you. Not only is your membership recognised by the equivalent AAA in the States, but you also benefit from several special deals, including area maps and ticket and hotel discounts. The Florida AAA centre is situated in Heathrow, north of Orlando, just off Exit 98 of I-4 (turn left on Lake Mary Boulevard, then first right on to International Parkway and the AAA is half a mile down on the left). For details (and decent discounts on attraction tickets and meals, plus special hotel rates) call the info number on the back of your AA card and ask for their USA pack, which gives you a special AAA card and their entitlements. It is even worth joining the AA (about £40) for the AAA discounts, which could add up to several hundred dollars if you take full advantage of them. Call the AA on 0870 544 4444.

Accidents

In the unlikely event of having an accident, no matter how minor, the police must be contacted before the cars can be moved (except on the busy I-4). Car-hire firms will insist on a full police report for the insurance paperwork. In the case of a breakdown, there should be an emergency number for the hire company among their essential literature, or, if you are on a major highway, raise the bonnet of your car to indicate a problem and wait for one of the frequent police patrol cars to stop for you (or, if you have a mobile phone, dial *FHP). Remember always to carry your driving licence and your hire agreement forms with you in case you are stopped by the police. Should you be pulled over, remain in your car with your hands on the wheel and be polite to the officer. Once they learn you are British, you *may* just get away with a ticking-off for a minor offence!

Key routes

As already mentioned, the main route through Orlando is **Interstate 4** (or I-4), a 4-, 6- or 8-lane motorway linking the two coasts. Interstates are always indicated on blue shield-shaped signs. For most of its length, I-4 travels east-west, but, around Orlando, it swings north-south, although directions are still given east (for north) or west (for south). All main motorways are prefixed I, the even numbers generally going east-west and the odd numbers north-south. Federal Highways are the next grade down and are all numbered with black numerals on white shields, while state roads are known as Routeways and prefixed SR (black numbers on white circular or oblong signs). All the attractions of *Walt Disney World Resort in Florida*, plus those of SeaWorld and Universal Orlando are well sign-posted from I-4. Cypress Gardens is a 45-minute drive from central Orlando (south) west on I-4 and Highway 27, while Busch Gardens is 75–90 minutes down I-4 to Tampa. The Kennedy Space

Center is a good hour's drive along the Beeline Expressway (Route 528), which intersects I-4 at junction 72.

Important note: The Florida Department of Transportation began re-numbering ALL the Interstate exits in early 2002 to a new mile-based system. And all the I-4 exits now have new numbers (although the old ones will also be shown, much smaller, until summer 2004). This is still catching the locals out, so repeat visitors should beware of this possible pitfall if they are used to navigating by the old junction numbers!

International Drive (or I-Drive) is the second key local roadway, linking as it does a 16-mile ribbon of hotels, shops, restaurants and attractions like Wet 'n Wild, The Mercado centre, Pointe*Orlando, Skull Kingdom, WonderWorks, Festival Bay and Belz Factory Outlet shopping malls. (Be aware that I-Drive South, from Highway 192 north to Route 535, is NOT the main stretch, although they will eventually link up.) From I-4, take exits 71, 72, 74A or 75A (the old 27A, 28, 29 or 30A) going (north) east, or 75B, 74A or 72 (the old 30B, 29A or 28) going (south) west. To the north, I-Drive runs into Oakridge Road and then the South Orange Blossom Trail, which leads into downtown Orlando (junctions 82C–84, the old 38–41, off I-4). I-Drive is also bisected by Sand Lake Road and runs away into Epcot Drive, via Route 536, to the south, which is also convenient for Disney's attractions.

I-Drive is a major tourist centre in its own right and makes an excellent base from which to operate, especially to the south of Sand Lake Road, near The Mercado, where you have the benefit of proper pavement. It's a 20-minute drive to Disney and 10 minutes from Universal. However, it can be congested at peak times, especially around Sand Lake

Road, so try to use Universal Boulevard instead.

The other main tourist area is the town of **Kissimmee** to the south of Orlando and the south-east of Disney. It's an attraction in its own right, being the home of Water Mania, the Old Town shopping complex, Gatorland, Green Meadows Petting Farm and the Medieval Times and Arabian Nights dinner shows, plus more hotels and restaurants. It is all grouped along a 19-mile stretch of the Irlo Bronson Memorial Highway, which intersects I-4 at junction 64B (the old 25B), and is only 10 minutes from *Walt Disney World Resort in Florida*, 20 from SeaWorld and 25 from Universal. The downtown area of Kissimmee is off Main Street, Broadway and Emmett Street and is ideal for walking.

A handy visual along **Highway 192** are the series of Markers from Splendid China (Number 4) to just past Medieval Times (Number 15). These highly visible numbered signs are good locators of many hotels, restaurants and attractions.

Fuel

Finally, a quick word about re-fuelling your car at an American gas station. You will often have a choice of attendant or self-service. You do not tip the attendant but you do pay a slightly higher price to cover the service. Most gas stations will also require you to pay in advance at night, before filling the car, and will require the exact amount in cash or your credit card. Some pumps also allow you to pay by credit card without having to go in to the cashier's office. The American gallon is smaller (by about a fifth) than the British version. Always use unleaded fuel and, to activate the petrol pump, you must first lift the lever underneath the pump nozzle.

RaceTrac petrol stations are usually the cheapest locally (even for soft drinks and cigarettes), although they don't take credit cards.

Local maps

The best and most up-to-date free maps are the bright orange Welcome Guide-Map (also full of discount coupons), available in the main tourist areas, and the pull-out map inside the Kissimmee-St Cloud Visitors' Guide (from the official Visitor Center on east Highway 192, call 407 847 5000). AA members are well catered for (see page 49), but the best paid-for maps are the Trakker series, with four products covering Orlando: the Pocket Map ($3.95) is almost as detailed as the AAA ones, while the City Slicker (a laminated fold-out of the main areas, $5.95) is useful in the car, and the Orlando/ Walt Disney Popout Map is a handy theme park reference. They also do a full Orlando Atlas ($16.95). You can contact them (and order maps) via www.trakkermaps.com or call 305 255 4485 in Florida.

Mobile phones and two-way radios are often useful here and another *Brit's Guide* partner provides a truly excellent service. Airwave Communications www.airwavef1.com are pioneering a state-of-the-art Nextel radio/phone/ wireless (with Internet access), which has built-in direct lines for things like taxis, dinner bookings, babysitters, doctors and film processing. Amazingly, this service is free, but it must be pre-booked on 407 843 1166 or e-mail rentals@airwavef1.com. They have service centres inside the business centres of various Orlando hotels and offer international phonecards at 7.9 cents/minute to the UK.

Now, on to your accommodation...

4 Accommodation
(or, *Making Sense of American Hotels, Motels and Condos*)

To list all the various hotels, motels, holiday homes, guesthouses, condominiums, campsites and other forms of accommodation available in the Orlando area would fill a book, so it is not the intention here to attempt a comprehensive guide. Metropolitan Orlando has the second highest concentration of hotels anywhere in the world and more are being built all the time, with the number of rooms approaching 110,000. Therefore, what follows is intended only as a general guide to the bigger, better or budget types.

Hotels

The first thing to be aware of is that American hotels, particularly in the largest tourist areas, tend towards the motel type, even among some of the bigger and more expensive ones. This doesn't mean you will be short-changed as far as facilities and service are concerned, but you won't necessarily be located in one main, internal building. The chances are your room will be in one of several blocks arranged around the other facilities such as the swimming pool, restaurant, etc. As well as the difference in style, this means it is more important to be security-conscious (see page 36). The size of rooms rarely alters, even between 2- and 4-star accommodation. It is generally the extra amenities and services that give a hotel extra star rating. A standard room usually features two double beds and will

comfortably accommodate a family of four.

The other feature of motel-type accommodation, which frequently takes British visitors by surprise, is the lack of a restaurant in some cases. This is because the American hotel scene operates purely on a room-only basis – meals are always extra, and hence dining facilities are not always provided. So you may have to drive to the nearest restaurant (of which there are a multitude – see Chapter 10) just for breakfast. Check the brochure to see what dining facilities the hotels provide before booking.

BRIT TIP: Few hotels have got round to providing hair-dryers as standard, although they can often be ordered from the front desk. If you bring your own, you will need a US plug adaptor (with two flat pins). Their voltage is also different, 110–120 AC, as opposed to our 220, so your hair-dryer/electric razor will work rather sluggishly.

As a general rule, hotels in Orlando are big, clean, efficient and great value for money. Another standard feature is the abundance of soft-drink and ice machines, with ice buckets in all the rooms (although you may find a can of Coke, or whatever, from the machine in your corridor more expensive).

All types of accommodation will be fully air-conditioned and, when it is really hot, you will have to live with the drone of the A/C unit at night. DON'T turn off the air-conditioning when you go out, even when it is cool in the morning because, by the time you return, the chances are your room will have turned into an oven.

Note that the most expensive place from which to make a telephone call is your hotel room! Nearly every hotel adds a 45–70% surcharge (Disney resorts add a $15 'connection fee') to every call (you can also be charged for a call even if no one answers, if it rings five or more times). It's best to buy a phonecard (see page 51).

Remember, too, that hotel prices (both in this book and in Orlando) are always *per room* and not *per person*. They will be cheaper out of the main holiday periods, but they are still likely to vary from month to month, with special deals offered at times. Always ask for rates if you book independently and check if any special rates apply during your visit (don't be afraid to ask for their 'best rate' at off-peak times which can be lower than any published rate). There may be an additional charge ($5–15 per person) as well for more than two adults sharing the same room. It often pays to book in advance because Orlando's popularity as a convention centre means it is busy much of the time.

If you've just arrived and are still looking for accommodation, head for one of the two official Visitor Centers in the area, one on International Drive (I-Drive) just south of The Mercado (on the corner of Austrian Court and open daily 8am–7pm) and the other on the eastern stretch of Highway 192 in Kissimmee (open 8am–5pm), where they keep brochures on all the hotels and the latest special deals.

Alternatively, if you are comfortable with the auction-type websites like www.priceline.com, you can pick up the occasional bargain.

However, for genuinely good deals – all with accommodation that is regularly checked for cleanliness and service – I recommend the online Dreams Unlimited Travel service, at www.dreamsunlimitedtravel.com/dreamsres

Disney's All-Star Music Resort

© Disney

The full-service tourist centres of **Know Before You Go** (407 396 5400 or 1-800 749 1993, www.knowbeforeugo.com) and **Vacation Works** (407 396 1844 or 1-800 396 1883, website at www.vacationworks.com) also deal in discounted accommodation as well as attraction tickets. Another new booking service to try is **Hotel Anywhere** on 01444 410555.

> BRIT TIP: Buy your soft drinks at the supermarket, and a neat polystyrene cooler for about $4 that you can fill with ice from your hotel ice machine to keep your drinks cold.

We have placed hotels, motels and holiday homes in four price bands to give you a rough and ready reckoner, although bear in mind no price is set in stone. These bands are:

$	=	up to $45 per night
$$	=	$46–$90
$$$	=	$91–$150
$$$$	=	$151–plus

Also, as there is no widely accepted star rating system for American hotels and bearing in mind there is little difference in the size of rooms (usually quite generous, with two double beds, TV and full en-suite facilities) we have our own C grades, based on the number of facilities and extra creature comforts. Hence, a CCCCC grading will include the highest level of hotel facilities and service, while a CC or C will be the more basic motel-type.

Resort hotels for Walt Disney World in Florida

In keeping with the rest of this guide, a review of Orlando's hotels starts with *Walt Disney World Resort in Florida*. With the convenience of being almost on the doorstep of the main attractions, and linked by an excellent free transport system of monorail, buses and boats, Disney's hotels, holiday homes and campsites are all magnificently appointed and maintained. They range from the futuristic appeal of *Disney's Contemporary Resort* (the monorail travels right through the main building) to the oversized fun of *Disney's All-Star Resorts*, and their landscaping, imagination and attention to detail are as good as the theme parks themselves.

In all, there are more than 25,000 rooms, while the 780-acre *Disney's Fort Wilderness Resort & Campground* has 1,190 sites.

Grandiose accommodation, naturally, comes at a price. A standard room at *Disney's Grand Floridian Resort & Spa* can cost $500 a night in high season (the suites can top $2,000!) and even the more modest *Disney's Caribbean Beach Resort* can be more than $150 a night. Dining at the hotels in the resorts is not cheap either, and you will find very few fast-food outlets on site.

> BRIT TIP: It is usual in American hotels to tip the housemaid by leaving $1/adult each day before your room is made up.

However, there is a budget choice for holiday-makers in the shape of *Disney's All-Star Sports, Music and Movies Resorts* and the new *Pop Century Resort*. This means that the convenience of staying right in the heart of the 'magic' is open to a wider range of holiday budgets, and it is worth a lot, especially in high season when the surrounding roads are packed.

BRIT TIP: For the smoothest entry to *Walt Disney World* Resort in Florida from Highway 192, take Seralago Boulevard opposite the Holiday Inn Hotel & Suites next to Old Town, turn left on to a non-toll stretch of Osceola Parkway and follow the signs to your chosen park.

Staying with the Mouse is one of the great thrills, for the style, service and the extras involved. The 21 resorts offer a superb array of facilities, and children especially love being a part of Disney full time. The benefits are: **resort ID card:** every guest can ask for a card with which to charge almost all your food, gifts and services while on site to your room account, plus have any purchases shipped to your room. **Free parking:** with your ID card, there is no charge for your car at any of the parks. **Free transport:** forget the car and use the monorail-bus-boat network to get around. **Dining priority:** guests can make Priority Seating arrangements for all restaurants, shows and special events between 60 and 120 days in advance (two years in the case of dinner shows). Call 407 939 3463. Note: a Priority Seating (or PS) is not strictly a reservation but a guarantee of the first available table when you turn up. **Priority golf:** the best tee times are reserved for Disney resort guests and can be booked 90 days in advance on 407 939 4653.

Children's services: all resorts have in-room or group baby-sitting (subject to availability; you can book in advance on 407 827 5444) and the eight Deluxe resorts have supervised activity centres and dinner clubs (around $7/child per hour), usually open until midnight. **E Nights:** periodically, resort guests get the chance to buy a $12 ticket for an extra 3 hours doing the main rides at one of the parks after official closing time (great value). **Mickey on call:** okay it's a bit twee, but what better way to wake up than with an alarm call from the Mouse himself?

Magic Kingdom Resorts

Around the *Magic Kingdom Park* are four of the grandest properties. The 15-storey **Disney's Contemporary Resort** has 1,030 rooms, a cavernous foyer, shops, restaurants, lounges, a real sandy beach, a marina, two swimming pools (with water-slide), six tennis courts, a video games centre and a health club – and magnificent views, especially from the superb, hotel-top California Grill restaurant (try to arrange a Priority Seating to coincide with the park's fireworks). Don't miss **Chef Mickey's** for a breakfast or dinner buffet with all your favourite characters. There is the Mouseketeer Club for 4–12s, while the monorail runs right *through* this hotel, and is an endless source of fascination for kids. As with all resort accommodation, rooms are large, scrupulously clean and well furnished. $$$$+, CCCCC.

Disney's Polynesian Resort is a South Seas tropical fantasy brought to life with modern sophistication and comfort. Beautiful sandy beaches, lush vegetation and architecture disguise the fact 853 rooms can be found here, built in

BRIT TIP: Dine in wonderful South Seas style at the 'Ohana restaurant, but don't ask for the salt – unless you want to spark an amazing reaction!

Disney's magnificent Animal Kingdom Lodge

film-set wooden longhouse style and all with balconies and wonderful views. There are excellent eating opportunities – **'Ohana** is a wonderful dinner venue, while it also offers character breakfasts – plus canoe rentals, a beautiful new pool area, a games room, shops and children's playground. The Neverland Club caters for 4–12s (4pm–midnight). $$$$+, CCCCC.

Disney's Wilderness Lodge opened in 1994, and is one of the most picturesque places to stay. It is an imposing re-creation of a National Park lodge in amazing detail, down to the stream running through the massive wooden balcony-lined atrium lobby and out into the gardens, past the swimming pool (with hot and cold spas) and ending in the resort's own Old Faithful geyser, which erupts faithfully every hour!

Offering authentic backwoods charm with true luxury, the resort is connected to the *Magic Kingdom Park* by boat and bus only. It also has two full-service restaurants: the outstanding **Artist's Point** and the **Whispering Canyon Café** (for a lively breakfast and huge all-you-can-eat buffets), a snack bar and a pool bar. The Cubs Den is for 4–12s (4.30pm–midnight). $$$$, CCCCC.

The Villas at Wilderness Lodge are a recent development of 136 studios and 1- and 2-bedroom villas. Facilities include fully-equipped kitchens, living room space, private balconies and whirlpool baths. There is also a quiet pool area, spa and health club.

Disney's Grand Floridian Resort & Spa, a hugely elaborate mock Victorian mansion with 867 rooms, an impressive domed and towered foyer and staff in Edwardian dress, completes the quartet of *Magic Kingdom* resort area hotels. The rooms are luxurious, hence the mega prices, and it is worth a look even if you are staying somewhere else. It also has six restaurants, including *Walt Disney World Resort* in Florida's top-of-the-range **Victoria and Albert's** (where their set, 6-course dinner with wine will set you back more than $110 per person) and the chic seafood-orientated **Narcoossee's** (one of my favourites), with its excellent view over Seven Seas

> **BRIT TIP:** *Disney's Grand Floridian, Contemporary* and *Polynesian Resorts* are situated on the monorail, the best system for getting into the *Magic Kingdom Park* and *Epco*t.

KEY TO WALT DISNEY WORLD AND LAKE BUENA VISTA ACCOMMODATIONS

1 Disney's Contemporary Resort
2 Disney's Polynesian Resort
3 Disney's Wilderness Lodge
4 Disney's Grand Floridian Resort & Spa
5 Walt Disney World Swan Hotel
6 Walt Disney World Dolphin Hotel
7 Disney's Caribbean Beach Resort
8 Disney's Yacht Club Resort
9 Disney's Beach Club Resort
10 Disney's Boardwalk Resort
11 Disney's All-Star Resorts
12 Disney's Port Orleans Resort (French Quarter)
13 Disney's Port Orleans Resort (Riverside)
14 Disney's Coronado Springs Resort
15 The Villas At The Disney Institute
16 Disney's Old Key West Resort
17 Disney's Fort Wilderness Resort and Campground
18 Disney's Animal Kingdom Lodge
19 Disney's Pop Century Resort (opening 2003)
20 Hilton At Walt Disney World
21 The Grosvenor
22 Wyndham Palace Resort and Spa
23 Doubletree Guest Suites Resort
24 Best Western At Walt Disney World
25 Hotel Royal Plaza
26 Courtyard By Marriott
27 Hyatt Regency Grand Cypress
28 Marriott's Orlando World Center
29 Embassy Suites Resort Lake Buena Vista
30 Sierra Suites Hotel
31 Radisson Inn Lake Buena Vista
32 Buena Vista Suites
33 Summerfield Suites At Lake Buena Vista
34 Vistana Resort
35 Sheraton Safari Resort
36 Holiday Inn Sunspree Resort
37 Marriott Village
38 Holiday Inn Family Suites
39 Gaylord Palms Resort

4

Lagoon and the nightly Electrical Water Pageant, plus four bars and a comprehensive array of sporting and relaxation facilities. A wonderful new pool area, complete with water-slide, has recently been added. The Mouseketeer Club caters for 4–12s (4.30pm–midnight) and the 1900 **Park Fare** restaurant is one of the most popular for character meals. $$$$+, CCCCC.

Epcot Resorts

The *Epcot* area features six hotels, including arguably the best value properties of them all. The unmistakable **Walt Disney World Swan** and **Dolphin** hotels are perfectly situated to be within walking distance of *Epcot* and *Disney-MGM Studios*, *Disney's Boardwalk Resort* entertainment district and the Fantasia Gardens Miniature Golf Courses. The 'entertainment architecture' style is fun and quite extensive, they have the full range of resort benefits, facilities and style, yet they are privately run and so come up a little cheaper than Disney's other deluxe hotels. The Swan features a 45-ft statue atop the hotel and has 758 large rooms (including 55 suites), while the Dolphin (1,509 rooms, with 136 suites) is crowned by two even bigger statues of dolphins. The duo effectively make up one mega-resort, with no less than 17 restaurants, four tennis courts, three pools (one, an amazing grotto pool with hidden alcoves and a water-slide), a kids'

> BRIT TIP: While the Yacht and Beach Clubs are firmly in the deluxe bracket, you can still visit to sample Beaches & Cream Soda Shop for arguably the best burgers in town.

pool and a white-sand beach, two health clubs, bike and paddle boat rentals, a great range of shops, video arcade and the Camp Dolphin centre for kids from 4–12 (1–4.30pm, 6–11pm, $12/hour). Even for non-guests, the Italian restaurant **Palio's** (Swan) and **Shula's Steak House** (Dolphin) are worth seeking out. The **Coral Café** (Dolphin) and **Garden Grove** (Swan) feature Disney character breakfasts, and some of their little touches for children are immensely thoughtful. And, at night, the whole resort looks magnificent. Visit www.swandolphin.com or call 407 934 3000 for more details on these perfectly situated gems. Transport is by boat (to *Epcot* and *Disney-MGM Studios*) and bus. $$$$, CCCCC.

The 45-acre **Disney's BoardWalk Inn and Villas Resort** is the most extravagant on-site property, featuring a 372-room inn, 520 villas, four themed restaurants, a TV sports club and two nightclubs, plus an impressive array of unique shops, sports facilities and a huge, free-form swimming pool with a 200-ft water-slide, all situated on a re-created semi-circular boardwalk around Crescent Lake. The overall effect is stunningly pretty, and the attention to detail in the rooms is excellent. Outstanding features are the summer-cottage style villas, Mediterranean restaurant **Spoodles** (tapas-style in the evening) and the **Big River Brewing Company** for a magnificent array of beers. Top of the range is the expensive but excellent seafood restaurant, the **Flying Fish**. Even if you are not staying here, it is a delightful resort to visit for a meal, the nightlife (especially **Jellyrolls** piano bar and the **ESPN Club**) or for just a wander along the boardwalk. The Harbor Club caters for 4–12s (4pm–midnight). $$$$+, CCCCC.

Disney's Caribbean Beach Resort has 2,112 rooms spread over five Caribbean islands (own bus service) and with the accent on moderate prices and value for money. The rooms tend to be a little plainer (although they still comfortably house a family of four), but the food court, main restaurant, **The Captain's Tavern,** and outdoor activities (including a lakeside recreation area with themed waterfalls and slides and the inevitable games arcade) are still a big hit with children. The six counter-service outlets in the food court at **Old Port Royale Center Town** (the hub of this pretty resort) can get busy in the morning, and the Trinidad South and Barbados 'islands' are a fair walk from the centre (hence the bus). However, it is an action-packed resort with some imaginative touches, like Parrot Cay Island Playground with its tropical birds and kids' play area. Transport to the theme parks is purely by bus. $$$, CCCC.

> BRIT TIP: To make a reservation at any *Walt Disney World* resort, call 407 934 7639. For information, don't forget www.disneyworld.co.uk and the best bookings service www.dreamsunlimitedtravel.com

Going upmarket again, the wonderfully refined, almost intimate, **Disney's Yacht Club Resort** has 630 rooms designed with nautical themes, all set around an ornamental lake. For dinner, the **Yachtsman Steakhouse** is another offering fine dining options and really underlines the resort's feeling of polished yet friendly elegance. Sister hotel **Disney's Beach Club Resort** completes the *Epcot* line-up. With 583 spacious rooms set along a man-made white-sand beach, it's like a tropical island paradise. **Cape May Café** is the lovely character breakfast opportunity and also offers a nightly New England-style clambake buffet. You can go boating or catch a water-shuttle service to Epcot, while other theme park transport is provided by bus. Water fun is 'on tap' for both Yacht and Beach Club resorts at the shared Stormalong Bay, a magnificent 2½-acre recreation area with water-slides and a sandy lagoon. The Sand Castle Club caters for 4–12s (4.30pm–midnight). Both $$$$+, CCCCC.

Disney's Animal Kingdom Resorts

Disney's All-Star Resorts were Disney's first serious venture into the budget hotel market in 1997. Here, for just $77–109 a night year-round, you can stay in one of the five sports-themed blocks (Surfing, Basketball, Tennis, Baseball and American Football) centred around a massive food court, two swimming pools, a games arcade and shops; the music-themed version (Jazz, Rock, Broadway, Calypso and Country); or the movies complex (Mighty Ducks, 101 Dalmatians, Fantasia, Love Bug and Toy Story). The latter is possibly the most imaginative, with its Fantasia pool and kids' play areas, and the most popular blocks are Toy Story and 101 Dalmatians (both of which are non-smoking only). All three centres, which total 5,760 rooms, have pool bars, shops, laundry facilities, video games rooms and a pizza delivery service and, while their bright, almost garish decor lacks the refined touches of other resorts, and rooms are smaller than their higher-priced counterparts, they are well designed for budget-conscious families who still want to enjoy all the Disney conveniences. Transport to the parks is provided by an extremely efficient bus schedule. $$–$$$, CCC.

Disney's Caribbean Beach Resort

Disney's Coronado Springs Resort is possibly the best value of the moderate resorts (Caribbean Beach and Port Orleans) as it's the newest and has slightly more in the way of facilities for its 1,921 rooms spread over 125 acres: four pools, including the beautiful – and massive – Lost City of Cibola feature pool, two games arcades, a boating marina, bike rentals, restaurant, food court and convenience store, lounge bar, gift shop, beauty salon and health club, business centre and two guest launderettes. Constructed in a wonderfully scenic Mexican/Spanish architectural theme in three 'villages' (Casitas, Ranchos and Cabanas), Coronado is an often-overlooked treasure. Check out the **Maya Grill** and its New Latino cuisine style for a memorable meal, the lovely 1-mile walk around the 15-acre central lagoon, and the main pool's changing facilities, which you can use once you've checked out of your room before your flight home. Coronado is also only 5 minutes from *Disney's Animal Kingdom Theme Park* and is well served by Disney's bus network. $$$, CCCC.

Disney's Animal Kingdom Lodge opened in 2001 and is a stunning example of architectural artistry. The basic premise is it is a private game lodge on the edge of a 33-acre animal-filled savannah, which many of the rooms overlook. The all-encompassing African theming – from the decor, to the shopping, cuisine, restaurant styling and even the musky, wood-laced smells – is almost overwhelming, and the effect of being able to open your curtains to a vista full of giraffes and zebras is immense. And all that wonderful creativity comes before you consider the actual amenities of this 1,293-room deluxe resort – two restaurants, a cafeteria, a bar, an elaborately themed 'watering-hole' main pool (with water-slide) and kids' pool, a massage and fitness centre, a large gift shop, children's play area and a 4-storey atrium lobby that makes you gasp. The main restaurant **Jiko** is spectacular enough, but then there is the buffet-style **Boma,** a 'marketplace' restaurant featuring African dishes from an exhibition

Disney's Coronado Springs Resort

wood-burning grill and rotisserie for both breakfast and dinner. Quite awesome.

Indeed, the lavishness and detail of the design are unmatched anywhere I have seen to date, and that's on top of the magnificent animal savannahs, inhabited by more than 200 mammals and birds. Guides are on hand to tell guests all about the animals and their habitats, while children can listen to African folklore stories around the outdoor firepit or become junior safari researchers while Mum and Dad do some wine-tasting (the hotel boasts the largest collection of South African wines in America). Rooms range from standard doubles (with the same slightly dated layout of the moderate resorts) to 1- and 2-bedroom suites, some with bunk beds for the kids. Simba's Cubhouse is for the 4–12s (4.30pm–midnight), and Disney transport is by bus. My one quibble is that some of the in-resort prices (in the bar and gift shop, for example) are a bit steep, but it is worth staying here, even only for a night, to experience an exercise in majesterial hotel design. $$$$, CCCCC.

Disney's Pop Century Resort is due to open in 2003 with at least half of its 5,760-room spread in similar vein to the *Disney's All-Star Resorts*. Its theme is the decades of the 20th century, hence there will be 10 different blocks with giant icons – like yo-yos, Rubik's cubes and juke-boxes – and a riot of period words, sayings and other visual gags that will either make you laugh or cringe! The Classic Years of the 1950s–90s feature a gigantic 10-pin bowling lane incorporating one of the three pools (the others are shaped like a flower and computer), a huge table football set-up and open air Twister mats. The five blocks are grouped around a main building which houses a spacious and surprisingly elegant check-in area (with large-screen TV showing

Disney's Pop Century Resort

Disney films to keep the kids amused during check-in), a large food court, a lounge (with quick-breakfast facility), a Disney store and games arcade. The 177-acre complex will also feature a central lake, while the Legendary Years section, the 1900s–40s, will have identical facilities and should be in operation by summer 2003. It should add significantly to Disney's more budget-orientated offerings and, like *Disney's All-Star Resort*, will have its own bus service to the parks. $$–$$$, CCC.

Downtown Disney Resorts

The other main accommodation centre within *Walt Disney World in Florida* is the *Downtown Disney* area. Here you will find: **Disney's Port Orleans Resort,** a 2-part complex (formerly the two distinct resorts of Port Orleans and Dixie Landings) split into the 2,048-room Riverside area – with a steamboat as a reception area, a wonderful cotton mill-style food court, a full-service Cajun-themed restaurant and an

Disney's Port Orleans Resort

old-fashioned general store (gift shop) – and the 1,008-room French Quarter, which has the **Sassagoula Floatworks and Food Factory** court, two bars, a games room and shopping arcade.

The Riverside includes **Ol' Man Island,** a magnificent 3½-acre playground, incorporating swimming pool, kids' area and a fishing hole, while the French Quarter has Doubloon Lagoon. Kids will especially enjoy the Mardi Gras dragon slide and alligator fountains, as well as their own play area. The eye-catching landscaping and architecture vary from rustic Bayou backwoods to turn-of-the-century New Orleans. Transport for both sections is provided by bus. $$$–$$$$, CCCC.

Disney's Old Key West Resort is partly a holiday ownership scheme of 5-star proportions, but the 1-, 2- or grand 3-bed studios in a magnificent Key West setting can also be rented on a nightly basis ($$$$+, CCCC) when not being used by club members. Facilities include swimming pools, tennis courts, games room, shops and fitness centre plus the lovely Olivia's restaurant (for superb Key Lime Pie!).

Camping Disney Style

Disney's Fort Wilderness Resort & Campground, on Bay Lake, opposite the *Magic Kingdom Park,* offers an impressive array of camping facilities and chalet-style homes that can house up to 6. Two 'trading posts' supply fresh groceries, while there are two bars and cafés and a range of on-site activities, including the thrice-nightly Hoop-Dee-Doo Musical Revue, campfire programme, films, sports, games and a prime position from which to view the nightly Electrical Water Pageant. Buses and boats link the campsites with other

Walt Disney World in Florida areas. $–$$$$, CCC.

Disney Hotel Plaza

In addition to the official *Walt Disney World* hotels, there are another seven 'guest' hotels inside *Walt Disney World Resort in Florida* itself at the **Disney Hotel Plaza** on the doorstep of the *Downtown Disney* area. These benefit from a free bus service to the attractions and guaranteed admission to the theme parks, and you can make reservations for shows and restaurants before the public, but they are almost all more expensive than similar hotels outside Disney property (although the convenience of being able to walk both to *Downtown Disney* and the nearby Crossroads shopping plaza is worth a lot).

Top of the list (for service, mod cons and price) is the 10-storey, 814-room Hilton (407 827 4000) $$$$+, CCCC.

Also fairly expensive are the **Grosvenor Resort** (626 excellently furnished rooms, exceptional service and colonial decor, 407 828 4444. $$$–$$$$, CCCC; **Wyndham Palace Resort & Spa** (a bustling, 27-storey cluster offering 1,014 rooms, many with a grandstand view of *Epcot's* Spaceship Earth, plus a European-style spa, three heated pools, tennis courts, a marina with boat rentals and the superb **Arthur's 27** restaurant which has stunning views from the top floor, 407 827 2727. $$$$, CCCC) and the contemporary **Doubletree Guest Suites** (229 family-sized suites offering every conceivable in-room convenience you can think of and great kids' facilities, 407 934 1000. $$$$, CCCC).

A major revelation on my last visit was the more modestly priced and tropically themed **Best Western Lake Buena Vista,** which had been extensively refurbished. Its 325 rooms provide good views over the Marketplace, while there are in-room coffee-makers and hair-dryers. The top-floor suites are truly huge and magnificently furnished. Garden-themed Traders restaurant is a pleasant choice for breakfast or dinner, while there is a lounge, bar and a full-scale nightclub on the 18th floor (Toppers, worth visiting during Disney firework shows!), plus a large pool and even a small gym room (www.orlandoresorthotel.com, or call 407 828 2424). The added convenience of this area marks the Best Western out as a real bargain. Like all the hotels in the Boulevard, it is well positioned for a stroll to *Downtown Disney's* attractions and features free bus transport and guaranteed access to the parks, plus preferred tee times at all five Disney golf courses. $$$, CCC.

The **Courtyard by Marriott** (323 rooms in a 14-storey tower and 6-storey annex featuring glass-walled lifts, three swimming pools and wonderful gardens, 407 828 8888, $$$, CCC) is another good choice.

Finally, the lovely **Hotel Royal Plaza** has a pleasant, welcoming aspect and accommodates 372 spacious and well-equipped rooms and 22 suites, along with a neat, full-service diner-restaurant and relaxing lounge bar, a landscaped pool area, four tennis courts, a health club and a Disney gift shop (407 828 2828). $$$, CCCC.

As you move further away from *Walt Disney World Resort in Florida*

> **BRIT TIP:** You can often save time from the Hotel Plaza properties by walking to *Downtown Disney* Marketplace and catching the free bus service to the parks from there.

the prices tend to moderate. Here's a round-up…

Lake Buena Vista

You can still spend a small fortune, however, at the **Hyatt Regency Grand Cypress,** reckoned to be Orlando's top hotel. This 1,500-acre resort offers three nine-hole and one 18-hole golf course (all designed by Jack Nicklaus), a swimming pool with waterfalls and slide, 21-acre boating lake, tennis complex, health club and equestrian centre. Rates START around $200, but the 750 rooms and suites are magnificently appointed and the resort is wonderfully picturesque (it also has five restaurants, three lounges and a poolside bar), 407 239 1234. $$$$+, CCCCC.

Nearby is **Orlando World Center Marriott** another personal favourite and an impressive landmark on Disney's outskirts, set as it is in 200 landscaped acres and surrounded by another golf course. An elaborate lobby, Chinese antiques and the sheer size of the hotel (2,003 rooms, including 110 suites, after a recent expansion, seven restaurants, four pools, tennis courts and a health club) put it in the expensive range, but it is conveniently situated and possesses one of the most picturesque pool areas, complete with waterfalls and palm trees, plus the whizziest glass-fronted lifts anywhere! It does, however, get busy, especially with convention business. 'Try their Christmas Day Buffet,' says reader Roy Carlisle. 'Pricey but brilliant.' (www.orlando.com/owcm or call 407 239 4200). $$$$, CCCCC.

Similarly, but on more budget lines, the **Holiday Inn Sunspree Resort** at Lake Buena Vista (507 rooms) is excellent for children's facilities, featuring a highly rated supervised childcare programme, a good range of pools, restaurants and

KEY TO HIGHWAY 192 ACCOMMODATIONS

1 Orlando World Center Marriott
2 Buena Vista Suites
3 Caribe Royale Resort Suites
4 Radisson Resort Parkway
5 Renaissance World Gate Hotel
6 Casa Rosa Hotel
7 Park Inn International
8 Magic Castle Inn & Suites Maingate
9 Holiday Inn Hotel & Suites Maingate East
10 Holiday Inn Maingate West
11 Holiday Inn Nikki Bird Resort
12 Four Points Hotel by Sheraton Lakeside
13 Celebration Hotel
14 Gaylord Palms Resort
15 Comfort Suites Maingate
16 Tropical Palms Funsuites
17 Holiday Inn Family Suites
18 Orange Lake Resort
19 Villages at Mango Key
20 Liki Tiki Village
21 Wonderland Inn
22 Comfort Suites Resort Maingate East
23 Hampton Inn Maingate West
24 Buenaventura Lakes

Sheraton Sand Key Hotel, Clearwater

other facilities. All rooms have mini-kitchenettes. It also features the trademark 'Kidsuites' which offers an attractive novelty for families – a private playhouse/bedroom built into the hotel room, equipped with its own TV, cassette player, video game player, clock, fun phone, table and chairs. They offer a refreshing alternative to normal hotel accommodation, right down to the separate check-in for the youngsters. Sunspree, perfectly situated for Disney and with free transport, also has a 2,100sq ft Cyber Arcade, with access to the Internet and other high-tech elements, while it has the extra option of 50 two-room suites for more family comfort. Kids 12 and under eat free. (www.kidsuites.com or call 407 239 4500). $$$, CCCC.

A novel choice is the African-themed **Sheraton Safari Hotel,** which sports the Python water-slide, a heated pool and kids' pool, with free transport to Disney parks and kids eat free with parents at **Casablanca's** restaurant. Rooms are well equipped, with hair-dryers, coffee-makers and ironing boards, and all within walking distance of the Crossroads shopping centre, a good selection of neighbouring shops and restaurants, and close to *Downtown Disney* Marketplace. There are 489 rooms, including 96 huge suites, all with an exotic safari theme, and the breakfast buffet at Casablanca's (highly recommended) is worth checking out. With its great

location and expansive style, the Sheraton Safari is an ideal mid-range family choice. Visit their website at www.sheratonsafari.com or call 407 239 0444. $$$, CCC.

Some of the big hotel chains also have one or two of their smartest properties in this area, notably the **Radisson Inn Lake Buena Vista,** which has 200 rooms (407 239 8400; $$$, CCC) and the recently refurbished **Doubletree Club Hotel** with 246 rooms (407 239 4646; $$$, CCC½).

There are hotels with some excellent suites here (see page 75), such as the **Embassy Suites Resort Lake Buena Vista** ($$$$, CCCC), the **Sierra Suites Hotel Lake Buena Vista** ($$$, CCC) and the extensive **Buena Vista Suites** ($$$, CCC½), which all offer great value for larger families.

Kissimmee

Moving out along Highway 192 (the Irlo Bronson Memorial Highway) into Kissimmee, you will find the biggest choice of budget accommodation in the area. Facilities generally vary little and what you see is what you get. All the big hotel chains can be found along this great tourist sprawl, and rates can be as low as $25 per room off-peak, or $35 for a room with a kitchenette (what the Americans call an 'efficiency'). Be prepared to shop

Wyndham I-Drive Resort

around for a good rate (discounts may be available at off-peak times), especially if you cruise along Highway 192, where so many hotels advertise their rates on large neon signs. As a general rule, prices drop the further you go from Disney. Don't be afraid to ask to see inside rooms before you settle on your holiday base (some of the smaller motels can be pretty ordinary).

Chains

Among the leading chain hotels are **Best Western** (all with pools, family orientated but large, in the budget $–$$ range), **Days Inn** (rather characterless and some without restaurants, but the newer properties are still good value – $$ in most cases – and convenient, with some rooms available with kitchenettes), **EconoLodge** (see under Best Western, but slightly more expensive), **Howard Johnson** (also a bit dearer, but with more spacious rooms and some with free continental breakfast), **Quality Inn** (sound, popular chain, and in $–$$ range), **Ramada** (rates can vary more widely between hotels in the $$–$$$ range, some offer free continental breakfast) and **TraveLodge** (another identikit group, but also on the budget $–$$ side). The **Fairfield Inns** are the budget version of the impressive Marriott chain (in the $$ range).

Doubletree hotels and suites are another upmarket chain with excellent facilities, as are the **Radisson** group (both in the $$$ range). The Marriott chain has three

> BRIT TIP: When booking one of the chain hotels, make sure you have its full address – it is easy to end up at the wrong Holiday Inn or Howard Johnson!

other family-friendly brands, the **Residence Inn by Marriott, SpringHill Suites** and **Courtyard by Marriott** (both $$$). Their smart new Lake Buena Vista complex at the junction of I-4 and Route 535 features a Fairfield Inn, Courtyard and Springhill Suites (www.marriott-village.com), with 24-hour gated security, free *Walt Disney World* transport and some great shared facilities.

The **Renaissance World Gate Hotel** (577 rooms; 407 496 1400; $$$, CCCC) scores highly in value-for-money terms with its oversized rooms, excellent facilities and pleasingly good service. In pure budget territory, the motel-type **Inns of America, Knights Inn, Motel 6, Comfort Inn** and **Super 8 Motel** brands all deliver a basic $ service, but the **Hampton Inn** and **Red Roof** groups seem to manage a more quality-conscious approach in the same price category. **The La Quinta Inn and Suites** series, in the $$–$$$ range, has half a dozen well-equipped new properties in the area, notably two on I-Drive.

Independent organisations

There are literally dozens of smaller, independent outfits who offer special rates from time to time in order to compete with the big boys. Look out in particular for offers of 'kids eat free' as this can save you quite a bit. Of the non-chain operators, the **Casa Rosa Hotel** offers simple, relatively peaceful Mediterranean-style hospitality (on west Highway 192; 407 396 1060; $–$$$, CC). The **Park Inn International** (same place; 407 396 1376) also has one of the better lake-front locations to go with its budget rates ($–$$, CCC); some rooms have kitchenettes.

For pure budget price, the **Magic Castle Inn and Suites Maingate** take some beating with their range of amenities – free continental breakfast, free Disney transport to the parks, fridges in all rooms, kids' playground, guest laundry and picnic area (107 rooms and 15 suites; 407 396 2212 or 1-800 446 5669; $–$$, CC½).

> BRIT TIP: Hotels designated Maingate East or Maingate West should be close to Disney's main entrance on Highway 192, although it is wise to check.

A firm personal choice is the **Holiday Inn Hotel and Suites Maingate East,** which also boasts Kidsuites rooms and Camp Holiday children's programmes, making it an outstanding family resort. Good attention to detail (hair-dryers, coffee-makers, microwaves and fridges even in standard rooms), free Disney transport and its proximity next door to Old Town make for great flexibility and value for money (614 rooms and 110 suites; 407 396 4488; $$–$$$, CCC½). Children get their own check-in area too, which is a neat touch, and under-13s eat free, as they do at the smart **Holiday Inn Maingate West,** with its tropical courtyard, free-form heated pool and kiddie pool (287 rooms; 407 396 1100; $$, CCC).

The **Holiday Inn Nikki Bird Resort,** just west of Disney's Highway 192 entrance, is another good family location with its 23-acre tropical setting, three pools, basketball and volleyball courts and children's entertainment (529 rooms; 407 396 7300; $$, CCC). **Angel's Diner,** the hotel's outstanding restaurant, offers some fabulous breakfast and dinner buffets.

The **Four Points Hotel by Sheraton Lakeside** on west Highway 192, is surprisingly good value (and has a great reputation with its guests) for a big-name group, especially with three pools, tennis courts, kids' playgrounds, mini-golf, paddleboats and two restaurants. Kids 10 and under eat breakfast and dinner free with paying adults and there is free Disney transport (651 rooms; 407 396 2222; $$–$$$, CCC½).

Equally, the **Radisson Resort Parkway** is above average in terms of its facilities and service after recent renovations. Just 1½ miles from Disney – and with free transport – the resort boasts an elaborate freeform pool, with waterfall, and lovely rooms, while kids stay and eat free (718 rooms; 407 396 7000; $$$, CCCC).

Slightly off the beaten track but with extra charm is the **Celebration Hotel** in the Disney-inspired town of Celebration. Just off Highway 192, the Central Florida Greeneway and I-4, this unique hotel is still well-situated, yet offers a small-town America style. With only 115 rooms in its 1920s' wood-frame design, the Celebration has a classy ambience, a long way from the usual tourist hurly-burly. Rooms come in a choice of an attic-like Retreat, Traditional (with either 1 king or 2 queen-size beds), Studio or a 2-room Suite and are all beautifully furnished. Lovely artwork, unhurried, courteous staff and a good array of facilities – pool, jacuzzi and fitness centre, plus the superb **Plantation Restaurant** (for buffet breakfast and new-Florida cuisine dinners Tues–Sat) – mark this out as a real gem. It is also within a short stroll of the town's shops, restaurants and peaceful walks. A shuttle service to the parks is available for a small fee. For those after a quieter or more romantic retreat, this member of the Grand Theme Hotels group (the Sheraton Safari, Doubletree Castle, Sheraton Studio City and Westin Grand Bohemian), is an ideal choice (407 566 6000,

KEY TO INTERNATIONAL DRIVE ACCOMMODATION

1 Peabody Orlando
2 Wyndham Orlando Resort
3 Renaissance Orlando Resort
4 Sheraton Studio City
5 Delta Orlando Resort
6 Days Inn Lakeside
7 Holiday Inn Express
8 Quality Inn International
9 Quality Inn Plaza
10 Embassy Suites Jamaica Court
11 Howard Johnson Plaza
12 Howard Johnson Inn
13 Rosen Plaza Hotel
14 Las Palmas Hotel
15 Enclave Suites
16 Quality Suites At Parc Corniche
17 Wynfield Inn

18 Summerfield Suites Hotel
19 Comfort Suites
20 The Doubletree Castle
21 Rosen Center Hotel
22 Hawthorn Suites
23 Holiday Inn & Suites At Universal
24 Best Western Plaza
25 Embassy Suites I-Drive/Conv. Center
26 Radisson Hotel Universal Orlando
27 Portofino Bay Hotel
28 Hard Rock Hotel
29 Amerisuites Convention Center
30 Sheraton World Resort
31 Sierra Suites
32 Homewood Suites
33 Country Inn & Suites
34 Royal Pacific Resort

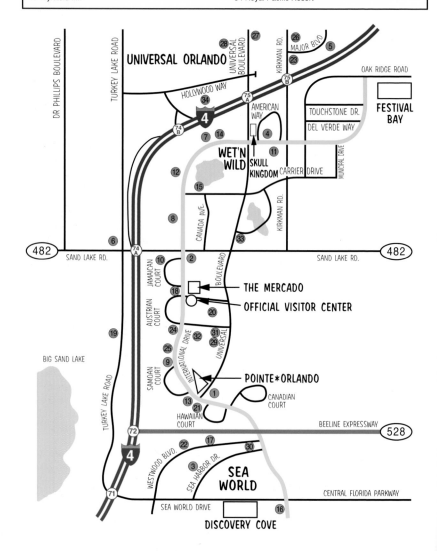

The superb Everglades Atrium at the Gaylord Palms Resort

www.celebrationhotel.com) $$$$, CCC).

The newest – and possibly most dramatic – property of them all is the 1,406-room **Gaylord Palms Resort** on the junction of I-Drive South and Osceola Parkway (hence very convenient for Disney). A cross between a convention centre and a vast turn-of-the-century Florida mansion, it features 4½ ACRES of indoor gardens, fountains and landscaped waters under a glass dome. Three intricately themed areas bear witness to a Disney-like creativity, and the resort offers just about every creature comfort you can imagine, with an array of restaurants and bars, an adults-only pool, family activity pool and beach (with octopus water-slide), a full-service spa, children's day care centre and a wide selection of shops.

Standard rooms are some of the smartest and most spacious in the area, while their suites are enormous, and there is even a hotel-within-a-hotel, as the central Emerald Tower offers an even more upmarket room choice and concierge facilities.

It is the internal architecture, though, which marks this hotel out as one of the most ambitious in Florida. One area is landscaped like the Everglades, complete with native plants, trees and atmospheric effects (watch out for the gators!), another

copies the old world charm of St Augustine – complete with replica Spanish Fort – while the third reproduces the style and eclecticism of Key West, with a mock-up marina and sailboat, and the rooms are also themed after each area as well. To walk into the resort, with its marbled lobby area and cavernous interior, at night is like walking into another world.

The elaborate settings add to the resort's signature fine dining experiences of the **Old Hickory Steakhouse** (naturally aged Black Angus beef a speciality, along with an artisanal cheese course), **Sunset Sam's** (for seafood hailed by the local press as some of the best in Florida) and the Spanish-style **Villa de Flora** (with six show kitchens). The Canyon Ranch SpaClub is the largest in central Florida and features a state-of-the-art spa, fitness facilities and a full-service beauty salon. There are no less than 13 stores sprinkled through the resort, plus their Planet Java coffee shop, while Auggie's Jammin' Piano Bar, the Gaylord Yacht Bar and the St Augustine Piazza all add to the entertainment opportunities. The kids' facilities and organised activities are amazing, too (407 586 0315, www.gaylordpalms.com). $$$$, CCCCC.

International Drive

Further away from *Walt Disney World Resort in Florida*, but handy for Universal Orlando, SeaWorld and closer to downtown Orlando is the final main tourist area. For overall

Sheraton Studio City Hotel lobby

location and value for money, I-Drive is hard to beat. It is more thoughtfully laid out, some attractions are within walking distance, and it is a good base for non-drivers.

BRIT TIP: For an attraction with a difference, don't miss the Peabody's twice-daily Duck March, which sees their trademark ducks take up residence 11am–4pm in the huge lobby fountain. It's a fascinating sight and a great place for afternoon tea. Just sit and watch them roll out the red carpet for the resident mallards!

Top of the range for quality is the **Peabody Orlando,** a luxurious, 891-room tower block, including an Olympic-size pool, health club, four tennis courts and some of the best restaurants in Orlando, notably the gourmet cuisine of **Dux** and the amazing **B-Line Diner** (see Eating Out, Chapter 10). Service is superb and the whole style is a cut above normal tourist fare. Check out the Royal Duck Palace if you don't believe me. However, rates are suitably impressive and the convention business can make it a hectic proposition. The hotel has also begun a massive expansion project to add 1,000 rooms in a 42-storey tower block (the tallest in central Florida), plus more restaurants, shops and a spa (407 352 4000, www.peabodyorlando.com). $$$$+, CCCCC.

The recently refurbished (at a cost of some $53 million) **Wyndham Orlando Resort** (1,052 rooms) is similarly extravagant but with less of the price tag. It boasts a formidable line-up of facilities – three swimming pools, a full service restaurant and bar, a deli and an ice cream shop, two pool bars, a pool restaurant, tennis courts, a kids' club and game arcade, and even a health club – in its beautifully landscaped grounds and is well situated at the junction of I-Drive and Sand Lake Road. Rooms are all spacious and scrupulously clean, and there is the choice of deluxe kings, deluxe doubles and family fun suites. The whole resort is spread out over 42 acres, which takes some getting around, but it represents one of the best all-round hotels for the money (407 351 2420, www.wyndham.com). $$$, CCCC.

Going upscale again, the magnificent **Renaissance Orlando Resort** (on Sea Harbor Drive, 778 rooms), claims the world's largest atrium lobby and boasts some equally enormous rooms and suites, an Olympic-size pool, tennis courts, fitness centre, including sauna and steam room, and special kids' play areas and activities. The Renaissance also has some magnificent restaurants (all with children's menus), including the seafood-themed **Atlantis,** the Asian cuisine of **Haifeng** and a stupendous Sunday buffet. All the rooms have recently been renovated to a high standard, and there is now a 24-hour health club and a self-serve laundry. As the closest hotel to SeaWorld, the Renaissance also offers some great packages in conjunction with the park and its sister, Discovery Cove. Well worth checking out (407 351 5555, www.renaissancehotels.com). $$$, CCCCC)

On slightly more budget lines but still in a grand style, the remodelled 21-storey **Sheraton Studio City Hotel** (formerly Universal Tower) is an I-Drive landmark at the entrance to Universal Orlando and features a full art deco film-theme design, from the shower curtains and mirrors to the large-scale architecture and landscaping. Facilities include a heated outdoor pool and a paddling pool, games room, fitness room, **Starlight Grille** restaurant and free shuttle service to Universal, Wet 'n Wild (within walking distance) and SeaWorld. The clever 1950s' film styling is truly startling and even the staff add to the theme, which makes you feel like you are 'on set'. Check out www.sheratonstudiocity.com for more details. All rooms have hair-dryers, coffee-makers and Nintendo games (302 rooms; tel 497 321 2100). $$$, CCCC.

The **Quality Inn International** (728 rooms, in the heart of I-Drive, kids under 12 eat free, 407 996 1600; $$, CCC), and **Quality Inn Plaza** (a massive 1,020 rooms in multiple blocks with multiple pools and another 'kids eat free' restaurant, 407 345 8585; $–$$, CCC), are both firmly in budget territory but make excellent bases in this area.

Another I-Drive landmark (next door to The Mercado) is the **Doubletree Castle Hotel,** a 9-storey fantasy modelled on Cinderella's castle at the *Magic Kingdom Park*. It features tower and turret rooms, a grand outdoor heated pool, hot tub, pool bar and grill, fitness centre, gift shop and a kids' play area. Rooms are immaculately furnished and there is a free shuttle to *Walt Disney World*, SeaWorld and Universal (216 rooms; 407 345 1511). $$$–$$$$, CCCC.

The other eye-catching property on I-Drive is the **Rosen Center Hotel,** the third largest hotel in Orlando, right next to the Beeline Expressway. It caters primarily for the convention trade (it is right next door to the massive Convention Center), but also offers excellent tourist facilities with 1,334 rooms and 80 suites. It features a huge swimming grotto, an exercise centre, tennis courts, two top-quality restaurants (including the seafood-based **Everglades**) and two bars (407 354 9840). $$$, CCCC.

Universal Orlando

With the expansion of Universal as a major resort destination has come the development of the locale around it on Kirkman Road and Major Boulevard. It is highlighted by Universal's own resort hotels, and these are easily some of the best in the area. The **Portofino Bay Hotel** is the jewel in the crown, a splendid re-creation of the famous Italian port and a stunning resort in its own right, with every possible facility and a little bit more. The elaborate porticos, the genuine *trompe l'oeil* (false 3-D) painting, the lovely harbourside piazza and the faithful ornamentation of the waterfront make it one of the most memorable settings of any hotel in Florida, and the 750 rooms are all impeccably appointed, with lashings of Italian style. The standard rooms are truly deluxe, with huge beds (and proper duvets, a first for an Orlando hotel), spacious bathrooms, mini-bar and coffee facilities, ironing board and hair-dryer, while the exclusive Villa rooms feature butler service, fax facility, CD and video players and separate showers, plus their own private pool area. There are also 18 elaborate Kidsuites for extra family fun, with separate themed rooms that include TV, Sony Playstation, CD player and a play area.

The resort facilities are equally breathtaking – a Roman aqueduct-style pool with water-slide, a completely enclosed kids' play area and wading pool, a separate quiet pool, jacuzzis, a full (if expensive) health spa, business centre, gift shops (check out Galleria Portofino for some magnificent artwork and jewellery) and video games room. There is also the Campo Portofino activity centre for kids 4–14, from 5–11.30pm every day ($45 for the first child and $35 for each additional child).

For wining and dining, the

Italian Piazza at Portofino Bay Hotel

Portofino boasts eight restaurants and lounges, including the 5-star (and wonderfully romantic) **Delfino Riviera,** the boisterous **Trattoria del Porto, Mama Della's,** an authentic Italian family dining experience (watch out for Mama herself!), an aromatic deli, a pizzeria and gelateria. All in all, it is a spectacular choice. $$$$+, CCCCC.

New in 2001 was the **Hard Rock Hotel,** very possibly the 'coolest' hotel in Orlando. This is the home of rock chic (it is actually themed as a former rock star's home that has been converted into a hotel!), 650 rooms and suites in the architectural style of a Californian mission, with public areas decorated with pieces from the Hard Rock group's extensive collection of rock 'n roll memorabilia. High ceilings, wooden beams, marble floors and eclectic artwork give a unique genre of decor that is both eye-catching and elegant, while the rock star theme is maintained through most of the public areas, from the black-suited foyer staff to the music that plays fairly constantly (not to everyone's taste, but those who like it will just love it).

The 14-acre site includes three bars (the ultra-cool Velvet Bar, Lobby Lounge and Beach Club poolside bar and grill), two restaurants (the full-service **Sunset Grill** and the 5-star, dinner-only **Palm Restaurant**), a fitness centre, Hard Rock gift shop (with live TV links to other HR Cafes around the world), Camp Lil' Rock (for the

Hard Rock Hotel

4–14s, like Campo Portofino) and games room. The pool area which is the hotel's focus is just terrific, with a large, free-form pool and 240-ft water-slide, two Jacuzzis, a sand beach and volleyball court, shuffleboard, and life-size chess and checkers. There is even a sound system under water in the pool! The rooms (including 14 Kidsuites) are another outstanding feature: big, modish, beautifully furnished in the hotel's trademark cool, chic style and wonderfully comfortable, they feature a radio/CD player (and you are given a free Hard Rock CD when you check in), mini-bar, coffee maker, in-room safe and either a king-size or two queen-size beds. It all adds up to another awesome package from the Universal designers. $$$$, CCCC.

The 53-acre, 1,000-room **Royal Pacific Resort** opened in June 2002, adding an exotic South Seas touch to the Universal portfolio, and bags more style. The basic theme aims to transport you back to a 1930s-era luxury hotel in the tropics (but with all mod cons), and you really do feel as if you have stepped into another world as you cross the bamboo bridge, over the rice terraces, into the elegant lobby, which is faced by the splendidly colourful Orchid Garden courtyard. The extensive use of rich, dark woods, cool stone floors and masses of greenery (some 58,000 plants and 2,500 trees – including 1,200 palms – were used around the resort) give the place an opulent, colonial feel, while the rooms and range of facilities are equally impressive. The spacious standard rooms all feature hand-carved Balinese wood furniture, among many refined touches, and there is also a Club level of accommodation, with separate lounge and extended facilities, and some superlative suites.

The Islands Dining Room offers breakfast, lunch and dinner in a setting of oriental simplicity (children also have their own buffet area, with TV screen), while fine dining is due to be added in November 2003 with a new restaurant by top American chef Emeril Lagasse called Tchoup Chop. Then there is a pool snack bar, lobby lounge and Luau garden party area (with barbecue buffet). The huge freeform pool is ideal for kids, with zero-depth entry at one end and a whole boat-shaped interactive water play area of squirting fountains, water jets and canons, paddling pool, sandcastle pit and a 'lifeboat' that fills with water and tips up at regular intervals. Add in a health club (including large jacuzzi, sauna and gym), elaborate kids' club (complete with computer games, TVs and organised activities), video games room and two shops, and it is hard to imagine anything they've missed! $$$$, CCCC.

Finally, all Universal resort guests benefit from a number of exclusive privileges: **resort ID card** (for buying food, merchandise and other items throughout Universal Orlando), **free water taxi** transport; **priority seating** at most restaurants (just show your room key card); **package delivery** to your room; the chance to buy a special **Length of Stay pass** (for unlimited access to the parks while you are at the resort); and, most importantly, **Universal Express** no-wait access to all the rides all day (just by showing your room key card).

For all Universal hotels, call 407 224 7117 or visit their website at www.universalorlando.com.

Mid-range hotels

The choice around Universal is also growing. There are recent examples of the budget **Days Inn, Hampton Inn, TraveLodge** and **Country Inn** chains, plus the **Extended Stay**

America group (good, clean efficiency studios, but few other amenities), but there are also two excellent mid-range properties.

The **Radisson Hotel Universal Orlando** is a twin-tower, 742-room complex which has a smart resort feel, with spacious, tropical-themed rooms, a large pool, kids' playground and jacuzzi, pool bar, video games room, hair salon, gym and sauna, plus a sports bar, full-service restaurant and food court. It also offers a free shuttle to Universal (right across the road), SeaWorld and Wet 'n Wild (407 351 1000; $$, CCC). The **Holiday Inn Hotel & Suites** is a similar proposition, with 256 rooms and 134 one- and two-bedroom suites for greater flexibility, a large heated outdoor pool and on-site TGI Friday's restaurant (407 351 3333, $$–$$$, CCC).

A recent trend to provide more deluxe accommodation has also added a true touch of class to the downtown scene with the **Westin Grand Bohemian**. Part of the Grand Theme Hotels group, it features an early 20th-century Austrian theme, with the accent on fine art, fine dining and fine service. Its 14 storeys make it a major landmark, and it also boasts a sensational restaurant (**The Boheme**), one of the most stylish bars I have been to (the Bosendorfer Lounge), and a 14th-floor concierge suite, plus an in-hotel **Starbucks** coffee lounge, a heated pool, spa and fitness centre. The rooms are superbly appointed with high-speed Internet access, mini-bars, radio/CD players and huge interactive TVs, while there are 36 sumptuous suites. All rooms feature the Westin Heavenly Bed, one of the most luxurious sleeping experiences in the known world!

The art collection, both classical and modern, liberally sprinkled through the public rooms, makes it more reminiscent of an art gallery than a hotel (407 313 9000, www.grandbohemianhotel.com). $$$$, CCCC.

This element of quality will take a turn for the even more luxurious in July 2003 with the opening of the **Grande Lakes Resort**, a combination of a 584-room, 5-star Ritz-Carlton Hotel, a 1,000-room JW Marriott Hotel, a 40,000sq ft health spa, an 18-hole Greg Norman-designed golf course and a rich spread of shops and restaurants. The Ritz-Carlton should be the most upscale resort in central Florida, and the scale and detail of their plans are truly staggering. Lush natural gardens, abundant lakes and streams, Italian-inspired architecture and a wealth of genuine antiques put this 500-acre development on a different level to anything else hereabouts. The JW Marriott also promises to be the most upscale property in Florida to bear the Marriott name, with Spanish-Moorish design, a formal Italian restaurant, French brasserie and a pool bar and grill. And there is a mini water-park of awesome complexity. Situated on the junction of Central Florida Parkway and John Young Parkway (10 miles from Disney, 7 from Universal and 2 from SeaWorld), it should provide the kind of hotel opulence usually seen only in the great cities of the world (1-800 241 3333, www.ritzcarlton.com).

Suites and holiday homes

A fast-growing area of accommodation in Orlando, suites hotels and holiday homes are a valuable way of larger family groups or friends staying together and cutting costs by self-catering. The homes, whether individual houses, collections of houses, resorts or condominiums (holiday apartment blocks), all usually have access to excellent facilities, such as swimming pools and recreation areas, and are fully equipped with microwaves,

TVs and washer-dryers. For these, a hire car is just about essential, but the savings for, say, a group of 8 staying together are obvious.

Suite things

Suites hotels seek to provide extra value for larger families or groups. Typically, a suites room gives you a living room and mini-kitchen, including microwave, coffee-maker, fridge, cutlery and crockery, while many offer a complimentary continental breakfast (or better). All have swimming pools and grocery stores or snack bars. They vary only in the number of bedrooms and can usually sleep 6 to 10 people.

They include the **Comfort Suites** on west Highway 192 near Splendid China (407 390 9888), on Turkey Lake Road (407 351 5050), adjacent to I-4 and I-Drive, plus their smart new 198-room development behind Old Town in Kissimmee, which even offers a fitness centre (407 397 7848; $$–$$$, CCC); the **Tropical Palms Funsuites,** on Holiday Trail, next to Old Town (407 396 4595; $$–$$$, CCC½) with well-equipped studio and two-bedroom suites; the two-bedroom, two-bath studios of **Enclave Suites** (on Carrier Drive, just off Kirkman Road, $$–$$$, CCC½) where kids eat free with their parents; or the new **AmeriSuites** (on I-Drive, in Lake Buena Vista and by the airport, tel 1-800 833 1516; $$–$$$, CCC), which have a heated pool, fitness centre and a free breakfast.

The most remarkable property is the **Holiday Inn Family Suites Resort** at Lake Buena Vista (almost opposite Orlando World Center Marriott, on I-Drive South). From the lobby, themed as a turn-of-the-century railway station, through the amazing range of facilities (food court, general store, Club Car casual dining, lounge bar, toddlers' play area, video games room, fitness centre, mini-golf, swimming pool and elaborate kiddie pool), to the choice of six different 1-and 2-bedroom suites, here is a dazzling family choice, especially with their Camp Holiday activity programme and separate check-in for kids. The Kidsuites feature a semi-private bedroom with bunk beds (additional fold-out child's sleeper available), TV, video and CD/cassette player, video game system, activity table and chairs, plus, of course, the private adult king bedroom. The **Club Car Restaurant** has an excellent free buffet breakfast daily, and there is free transport to all the Disney parks. The zero-depth-entry water playground with its array of squirty fountains will keep the young 'uns happy! (407 387 5437, www.hifamilysuites.com). $$$, CCCC.

Other one-off suites properties worthy of note include the well-appointed **Buena Vista Suites** (407 239 8588, $$$, CCC) and the massively eye-catching **Caribe Royale Resort Suites** (407 238 8000, $$$$, CCCC½), both at the lower end of I-Drive, with their choice of 1-bedroom suites and 2-bedroom villas, super pool area with water-slide and one of the best free breakfast buffets in town. Equally, the **Hawthorn Suites** (three properties in Orlando), **Homewood Suites** (two in Lake Buena Vista and one on I-Drive) and the **Sierra Suites** (Lake Buena Vista and I-Drive) offer a more up-market feel with mid-range pricing ($$–$$$, facilities vary). The two **Summerfield Suites** (on I-Drive, 407 352 2400, and Lake Buena Vista, 407 238 0777, www.summerfield-orlando.com) are another fine example, with suites sleeping up to 8, free breakfast, convenience store and fresh, inviting ambience ($$$, CCC). The **Embassy Suites** on I-Drive (407 345 8250, $$$, CCC½)

4

is the most prominent of their eight Orlando properties and consistently gets good reader feedback. 'I would strongly recommend the Embassy Suites,' says Gary Baldwin. 'It includes an "all you can eat" buffet breakfast, which is great when you're planning a day at a theme park. Also, there are free drinks and snacks from 5.30–7.30 every evening.'

One of the newest offerings is the **Country Inn & Suites** on Universal Boulevard (also in Lake Buena Vista and Kissimmee). Nicely situated just off the main I-Drive drag, it gives great value with large, clean rooms, free continental breakfast, local phone calls and Disney transport, plus pool and fitness centre. The 170 standard rooms feature an in-room safe, coffee-maker, hair-dryer and iron/ironing board, while the 48 king suites also include microwave and fridge. It is little more than a mile from Universal Orlando and half a mile from Wet 'n Wild, yet in a much quieter location than many of the I-Drive hotels (407 313 4200, www.jaytelhotels.com). $$–$$$, CCC.

Holiday resorts

Another accommodation type, which combines the best of hotels, suites and private villas, is the handful of genuine resort-style, purpose-built complexes, some of which double as timeshare resorts. A kind of cross between condominiums and motels, they have the advantage of great in-resort facilities. The best include the **Orange Lake Resort** (4½ miles west of Maingate on Highway 192, 407 239 0000; $$$–$$$$, CCCC), with a

Holiday Inn Family Suites

Boulevard, 4 miles west of Maingate, 407 239 7100; $$$, CCC), a collection of smart, new 2- and 3-bedroom townhouses, with pool, jacuzzi, tennis and volleyball.

Liki Tiki Village on the western fringe of Highway 192 is a timeshare set-up that often has good-value apartments to rent on a weekly basis. Their newest blocks offer huge 2-bedroom flats, with well-equipped kitchens (down to coffee-makers and ice-makers), while the complex itself has two pools plus the Liki Tiki Lagoon mini water park, tennis courts, paddle boats, bikes, poolside bar and grill and a free continental breakfast Mon–Fri (when timeshare presentations are held). You don't have to attend any timeshare hard-sell, just enjoy the great facilities of this resort (407 239 5000, www.islandone.com). $$$, CCCC.

Top of the range in this category, though, is the **Vistana Resort,** just off the lower end of I-Drive in Lake Buena Vista, where facilities include fitness centres with steam and sauna rooms, five pools and 13 tennis courts, to back up their luxurious 2-bedroom villas that sleep up to 8 (407 239 3100). $$$–$$$$, CCCCC.

Holiday homes

There are now dozens of companies offering private homes with pools throughout central Florida, some more reliable than others, so here are just a select few who pass the *Brit's Guide* credibility test.

Welcome Homes USA have condos, villas and private homes in the Kissimmee area, with some smart properties at a broad range of prices. Their full-size houses (3–5 bedrooms) come with communal or private pools. Homes are only 10 or 15 minutes' drive from Walt Disney World, in residential areas, and feature everything from dishwashers to teaspoons (but not hair-dryers).

$$–$$$$, CC. For more details, call 407 933 2233 for their holiday homes and 407 933 2889 for their well-equipped condo complex, or visit www.welcome-homes.com.

For similar great value and excellent properties **Alexander Holiday Homes,** also in Kissimmee, manage some 260 properties, from standard condo villas to ultra-luxury large executive homes sleeping up to 10, all with pools and immaculately furnished, within 15 minutes of *Walt Disney World Resort*. From fully fitted kitchens to walk-in wardrobes and private pools, these are a great way to enjoy a bit of Florida freedom. This company was the first of its kind in Orlando, and still offers a friendly, efficient service in keeping with the Sunshine State. Their excellent website www.floridasunshine.com features nearly all their properties, (407 932 3683). $$–$$$, CC.

Premier Vacation Homes offers a great range of spacious properties with 2 to 6 bedrooms, sleeping up to 14, all in secure residential communities within a 15-minute drive of *Walt Disney World Resort*. The homes are privately owned and have been purchased and furnished as a 'vacation' home, with screened pools, two TVs, fully equipped kitchens (including dishwasher, washer-dryer, microwave and coffee-maker), at least one king or queen bed, and free local phone calls. Maid service can be provided for an additional fee. The **Luxury homes** (2 to 4 bedrooms) are their standard accommodation, while the **Executive homes** (3 to 6 bedrooms) are bigger still, with an extra TV, VCR and gas barbecue grill (407 396 2401, or 0500 892634 in the UK, or visit www.premier-vacation-homes.com). $$$, CC.

A company I have got to know recently and can recommend is **Florida Leisure,** British-owned and with great attention to detail. With some 90 homes – from 2 to 6 and even 7 bedrooms – in the Kissimmee area (and most of them barely a year old), they pride themselves on a real personal touch. Many of their properties are in the Executive range, which means the fullest range of amenities in addition to their large, private, screened pools, and often in a secure, gated community. You can see ALL their homes on their website, and what you see is most definitely what you get. Call Nigel or Marion on 407 870 1600 or look up www.floridaleisure.com. $$–$$$$, CCC.

By the way, for all holiday homes, it is usually necessary to request a Welcome Pack if you would like some basic groceries provided in advance (about $35), but homes are seldom more than 10 minutes' drive from a supermarket.

Bed and breakfast

Bed and breakfast in Orlando is some way removed from a traditional British B&B as they tend to go for a more upscale, almost boutique style. Principle among them is the **Wonderland Inn** in Kissimmee, an 11-room, restored Historic Registry property off the beaten track but only 10 minutes from the Highway 192 area. Each room has a delightful, individual touch, and several are designed for singles as well as doubles, plus one honeymoon suite. The attentiveness of the staff is wonderful and even the gardens – with orange trees (freshly squeezed juice for breakfast), begonias and jasmine – have an old-fashioned charm light years from the hectic tourist whirl elsewhere (tel: 1-877 847 2477, www.wonderlandinn.com). $$$, CC.

The pretty Lake Eola district downtown also has two fine properties. **The Veranda** has 12 intimate, cottage-style rooms, ranging from Queen Studio and

King Suites to a lovely honeymoon suite, set in landscaped gardens with a private courtyard, swimming pool and spa area. Breakfast features fresh pastries, seasonal fruits, juices, tea and coffee, and the quiet setting is another bonus, although there are some good restaurants and shops within easy walking distance (407 849 0321). $$$–$$$$, CCC.

The nearby **Eo Inn** is another little gem, a genuine boutique hotel and spa (with a huge range of treatments, from massage to pedicures), featuring 17 deluxe rooms. The lush grounds, rooftop terrace and lake vistas provide a refreshing alternative to the usual hotel experience. Breakfast is not usually included, but the excellent bakery café **Panera Bread** is part of the complex (407 481 8485, www.eoinn.com). $$$–$$$$, CC.

Babysitting

For folks who want an evening off from parenthood to take advantage of Orlando's nightlife, babysitting is a ready option. The two most relied-upon, fully trained and licensed companies are KinderCare (also contracted to *Walt Disney World Resort in Florida* and Airtours, 407 846 2027) and Anny's Nannies (407 826 8949). Both will visit hotels, motels, condos and homes, while KinderCare also organises group events and activities.

Right, that's enough planning and preparation for now, it's time to HIT THE THEME PARKS...

Buying a holiday home

Many tourists are tempted by the idea of buying a house after a holiday here, but there are many pitfalls. Apart from the fact it is easy to be starry-eyed about such a serious business after a wonderful holiday, there are companies willing to exploit the naivety of tourists. Therefore, you need to do your homework, especially when it comes to understanding American property buying as the terminology is completely different. That means you need help from someone who has built up an unimpeachable reputation over a good deal of time. In this instance, **Greater Homes of Orlando** get the *Brit's Guide* seal of approval, a family-run company who have been building in Central Florida since 1965 and have sold 2,000 homes to British owners. Not only are they a reliable and quality-conscious firm, their website carries essential info for anyone thinking of stepping into home ownership here. Look up www.greaterhomes.com (especially for their pages on the different terminologies involved) or call 407 869 0300. You will also find useful info on the websites of Alexander Holiday Homes and Florida Leisure (click on the Real Estate links).

Yes, owning a piece of the Magic is tempting, but you must get all the facts first. *Bob's Buying Tips:* 1) ask for references from other UK owners; 2) check the management company for references – and look up the Better Business Bureau for Central Florida; 3) ensure product has a warranty; 4) walk through the community where you're thinking of buying and talk to people there; 5) ensure the documentation allows you to let it on a short-term basis; 6) make sure you have all the proper fees, registrations and taxes in the US (with thanks to Bob Mandell, Chairman of Greater Homes).

The Theme Parks – Disney's Fab Four

(or, Spending the Day with Mickey Mouse and Co.)

By now you should be prepared to deal with the main business of any visit to Orlando: *Walt Disney World Resort* in Florida and the other main theme parks of Universal Orlando, SeaWorld and Busch Gardens.

If you have only a week in the area this is where you should concentrate your attention but even then you may decide Busch Gardens is a bridge too far. If you have less than a week, you should focus on seeing as much of *Walt Disney World Resort* as possible. There is SO much packed into every park and the main tourist areas, even 2 weeks is scarcely enough to give first-timers more than an outline of central Florida.

> BRIT TIP: Beware offers of free tickets for theme parks as they are used as inducements to visit timeshare firms (see below). And never buy a ticket from an unofficial source as it may be stolen or non-transferable.

Firstly, you can save money off many attractions if you shop around. Disney tickets are available at *The Disney Stores* in the UK, and through Keith Prowse (see page 00) and most of the tour operators. But try not to buy ALL your tickets in advance as you may find you don't have enough time for them all. You will also find **discount coupons** in tourist publications distributed in Orlando (or from the Guest Services desk at your hotel – it's worth asking – and see our fantastic offer on page 93), while the **tour operators'** welcome meetings usually have special offers and tickets for the latest excursions.

The official **Visitor Center** at 8723 International Drive (in the Gala Center on the corner of Austrian Row; 407 363 5871, www.orlandoinfo.com) is also worth checking out for discounts. Equally, the **Universal Attractions** booths at several shopping malls (notably Orlando Premium Outlets) have some great deals (3 days for the price of 2, 2-for-1 drinks, etc) on a huge range of attractions. It is possible to pick up free tickets for attending timeshare presentations but they can take up half a day of your precious holiday. Other sites worth visiting for discounts are www.ticketmania.com, www.discountorlandovacation.com and www.go2orlando.com (the latter is also useful for a whole range of info and features).

> BRIT TIP: If you DO want to check out timeshare options, look first at *Disney Vacation Club* for the guaranteed way to secure memorable holidays. Call 407 566 3300 or visit http://disney.go.com

Ratings

All the rides and shows are judged on a unique rating system that splits them into the **thrill rides** and **scenic rides**. Thrill rides earn T ratings out of five (hence a TTTTT is as exciting as they get) and scenic rides get A ratings out of five (an AA ride is likely to be over-cute and missable). Obviously, it is a matter of opinion to a certain extent, but you can be sure a T or A ride is not worth your time, a TT or AA is worth seeing only if there is no queue, a TTT or AAA should be seen if you have time, but you won't miss much if you don't, a TTTT or AAAA ride is a big-time attraction that should be high on your list of things to do, and finally a TTTTT or AAAAA attraction should not be missed! The latter will have the longest queues and so you should plan your visit around them. Some rides are restricted to children over a certain height and are not advisable for people with back, neck or heart problems, or for pregnant women. Where this is the case I have just noted 'Restrictions: 3ft 6in', and so on. Height restrictions (strictly enforced) are based on the average

Beauty and the Beast

5-year-old being 3ft 6in tall, 6s being 3ft 9in and 9s being 4ft 4in.

Where families have small children, but Mum and Dad still want to try a ride, you DON'T have to queue twice. When you get to the front of the queue, tell the operator you want to do a 'baby swap'. This means Mum can ride while Dad looks after junior and, on her return, Dad can have his go. Many children also get a big thrill from collecting autographs from the various Disney characters they meet, and most shops sell some neat **autograph books** for that purpose.

SpectroMagic Parade

Magic Kingdom Park

The starting point for any visit has to be the *Magic Kingdom*, the park that best embodies the spirit of delight that Disney bestows on its visitors. It's the original development that sparked the tourist boom in Orlando back in 1971. In comparative terms, the *Magic Kingdom Park* is similar to the *Disneyland Park* at *Disneyland Paris®️ Resort* and *Disneyland Park* in Los Angeles. Outside those, it has no equal as an enchanting and exciting

Barnstormer at Goofy's Wiseacre Farm

The Magic Kingdom Park at a glance

Location	Off World Drive, Walt Disney World		
Size	107 acres in 7 'lands'		
Hours	9am–7pm off peak; 9am–10pm Washington's birthday (see page 17), spring school holidays; 9am–11pm high season (Easter, summer holidays, Thanksgiving and Christmas)		
Admission	Under 3 free; 3–9 $38 (1-day ticket), $152 (4-Day Park Hopper), $197 (5-Day Park Hopper Plus); adult (10+) $48, $192, $247. Prices do not include tax.		
Parking	$6		
Lockers	Yes; under Main Street Railroad Station; $7 ($2 refund)		
Pushchairs	$8 and $15 (Stroller Shop to right of main entrance, $1 deposit refunded)		
Wheelchairs	$8 ($1 deposit refunded) or $40 ($10 deposit refunded) (Main Ticket Centre or Stroller Shop)		
Top Attractions	Splash Mountain, Space Mountain, The ExtraTERRORestrial Alien Encounter		
Don't Miss	Share A Dream Come True Parade, SpectroMagic Parade (high season and weekends) and Fantasy in the Sky fireworks		
Hidden Costs	**Meals**	Burger, chips and coke $7.48 3-course dinner $35 (Cinderella's Table)	
	Kids' meal	$3.49	
	T-shirts	$19–32	
	Souvenirs	$1–895	
	Sundries	Spray Fan (handy when it's hot) $16.04	

day out for all the family. All Disney employees are known as Cast Members and they are almost unfailingly cheerful and keen to help. It is also worth pointing out that while, superficially, some rides are the same as those in Paris or LA, there are key differences, notably on Pirates of the Caribbean, Big Thunder Mountain Railroad and the Haunted Mansion. And Space Mountain here is a completely different ride.

I will now attempt to steer you through a typical day at the parks, with a guide to the main rides, shows and places to eat, how to park, how to avoid the worst of the crowds and how much you should expect to pay.

This essential park takes up just 107 of Disney's near 31,000 acres but attracts almost as many visitors as the rest put together! It has seven separate 'lands', like slices of a large cake, centred on Florida's most famous landmark, Cinderella Castle. More than 40 attractions are packed in, not to mention numerous shops and restaurants (although the eating opportunities are less impressive than *Epcot* and *Disney-MGM Studios*).

It's easy to get overwhelmed by it all, especially as it does get so busy (even the fast-food restaurants have serious queues in high season), so study the notes and plan your visit around what most takes your fancy.

BRIT TIP: Reader Roy Williams says: 'We bought a bright, 3-in plastic ball that we fixed to our car aerial in the car park, enabling us to find it easily on our return.' You could also leave a familiar, non-valuable item in the window for extra help.

Disney's FASTPASS Service

Another essential aid to queuing here is *Disney's FASTPASS Service*. A number of the main attractions at the parks now have this wonderful service that allows you to roam while you wait for your allotted time to ride. How it works: insert your main park entrance ticket into the FASTPASS (FP) turnstile (to the side of the attraction's entrance) and you get another ticket giving you a period in which to return for your ride with only a minimal wait. You can hold only one FP ticket per 2-hour period but once you've used it you can get another one. If you start by going to one of the FP rides, collecting your ticket and returning later, you can by-pass a lot of standing in line. You can then get another FP as soon as your 'window' opens – if your time slot for Space Mountain is 10–11am, you could get another FP for, say, Buzz Lightyear's Space Ranger Spin at 10.05am and then go and ride Space Mountain! Many people still miss this, but it is FREE (FASTPASS rides are indicated by FP in the description of each attraction).

BRIT TIP: If you have pre-paid vouchers for park entrance rather than the actual tickets, you have to exchange them at a ticket booth. Go to the Guest Relations window and you will avoid the queues.

Location

The *Magic Kingdom Park* is situated at the innermost end of the vacation kingdom, with its entrance toll plaza three-quarters of the way along World Drive, the main entrance road off Highway 192. World Drive runs north-south through *Walt*

Disney World Resort in Florida, while the Interstate 4 (I-4) entrance, Epcot Drive, runs basically east-west. Unless you are staying at one of *Walt Disney World Resort* hotels, you will have to pay your $6 parking fee at the toll plaza and that brings you to the car park (or 'parking lot' in American-speak) that can accommodate more than 10,000 cars.

The majority arrive between 9.30 and 11.30am, so the car parks can become pretty jammed then, which is another good reason to get here EARLY. If you can't make it by 9am during peak periods, you might want to wait until after 1pm, or even later when the park is open late into the evenings (as late as 11pm in high summer and Christmas). Remember to note on your parking ticket exactly what area you are parked in and the row number, eg Mickey, Row 30. You will struggle to remember otherwise, and all hire cars look exactly the same!

> BRIT TIP: You can sometimes get to ride up front on the monorail (and get a special 'driver' certificate!) if you ask a Cast Member when you get on to the platform.

A system of motorised trams carries you from the car park to the Transportation and Ticket Center at the heart of the operation. Unless you already have your ticket (which will save you valuable time), you will have to queue up at the ticket booths to go any further. From here, the monorail or a ferryboat will bring you to the doorstep of the *Magic Kingdom Park* itself. The monorail (dead ahead of you) is quicker, if there isn't a long queue, otherwise, it is usually better to bear left and take a slower ferryboat. Of course, if you are staying at a Disney hotel, one of

the free resort buses will deliver you to the park's front door (or the monorail or boat if you are at one of the *Magic Kingdom Resorts*).

One final note, in all the main theme parks you may well find one or two attractions closed for refurbishment to mark the constant process of keeping everything fresh. However, you will never be short of things to do!

Main Street, USA

Right, we've finally reached the park itself... but not quite. Hopefully you've arrived early and are among the leading hordes aiming to swarm through the main entrance. The published opening times may say 9am, but the gates to the *Magic Kingdom Park* are likely to open up to 45 minutes before then.

You will find yourself in **Main Street, USA,** the first of the seven lands. Immediately on your right is **Exposition Hall,** a photographic centre featuring archive film material, a mini cinema showing Disney classics and a series of interactive games, plus some cartoon photo opportunities. On your left is **City Hall,** where you can pick up a park map and daily schedule (if you haven't been given one at the toll plaza) and make reservations for the main restaurants (highly advisable at peak periods). Ahead of you is **Town Square,** where you can take a one-way ride down Main Street, USA on a horse-drawn bus or fire engine and visit the **Car Barn** mini museum or shop at the **Main Street Gallery** for

> BRIT TIP: Save paying up to three times more for your drinks by bringing your own bottled water in a back-pack to all the parks and use the many drinking fountains for refills.

5

ADVENTURELAND
1 Swiss Family Treehouse
2 Jungle Cruise
3 Pirates Of The Caribbean
4 The Enchanted Tiki Birds (under new management)
5 Magic Carpets of Aladdin

FRONTIERLAND
6 Splash Mountain
7 Big Thunder Mountain Railroad
8 Country Bear Jamboree
9 Raft To Tom Sawyer Island

LIBERTY SQUARE
10 Diamond Horseshoe Saloon Revue
11 Liberty Square Riverboat
12 The Haunted Mansion
13 The Hall of Presidents

FANTASYLAND
14 'It's a Small World'
15 Dumbo The Flying Elephant
16 Mad Tea Party
17 The Many Adventures Of Winnie The Pooh
18 Snow White's Scary Adventures
19 Cinderella's Golden Carousel
20 Mickey's PhilharMagic (opening 2003)
21 Peter Pan's Flight
22 Castle Forecourt Stage
23 Fantasyland Character Festival
24 Ariel's Grotto

MICKEY'S TOONTOWN FAIR
25 Mickey's Country House
26 Minnie's Country House
27 Toontown Hall of Fame
28 The Barnstormer at Goofy's Wiseacre Farm
29 Donald's Boat

TOMORROWLAND
30 Space Mountain
31 Tomorrowland Indy Speedway
32 Astro Orbiter
33 Walt Disney's Carousel of Progress
34 Tomorrowland Transit Authority
35 The ExtraTERRORestrial Alien Encounter
36 Buzz Lightyear's Space Ranger Spin
37 Galaxy Palace Theater

TRANSPORT
38 Walt Disney World Railroad
39 Boat Dock
40 Monorail Station
41 Bus Station

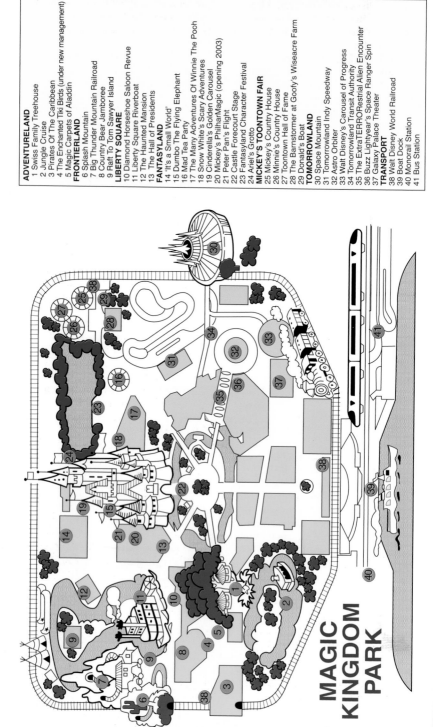

MAGIC
KINGDOM
PARK

exclusive Disney collectables. The Street itself houses some of the best shopping in the *Magic Kingdom Park* (check out the massive Emporium), plus the **Walt Disney World Railroad,** a Western-themed steam train that circles the park and is one of the better attractions when the queues are long elsewhere (although – be warned – the Town Square station is often the busiest).

For dining, you have breakfast, lunch and dinner at **Tony's Town Square Restaurant,** specialising in Italian meals, **The Plaza Restaurant** (lunch and dinner, sandwiches, salads and sundaes) and **The Crystal Palace** (breakfast, lunch and dinner, buffet-style food with Winnie the Pooh, Tigger and Co). Quick bites can be bought from **Casey's Corner** (hot dogs, chips and soft drinks), **Main Street Bakery** (coffee and pastries) and the **Plaza Ice Cream Parlor.** Disney characters also appear periodically outside Exposition Hall.

Look out for the **Guest Information Board** at the top of Main Street, USA (on the left) that gives waiting times for all the attractions through the day.

Unless you are a late arrival, give Main Street no more than a passing glance for the moment and head for the end of the street where you will find the real entrance to the park. This is where you must await the official opening hour for the famous 'Rope drop', and you should adopt one of three tactics here, each aimed at doing one or two of the most popular rides before the queues become substantial (an hour for Splash Mountain is not unknown).

One: if you fancy heading straight for the 5-star, log-flume ride Splash Mountain, keep left in front of the Crystal Palace with the majority of the crowd who will be heading for the same place.

Two: if you have young children who can't wait to ride on Cinderella's Golden Carousel or the other Fantasyland rides, stay in the middle and head directly through the castle.

Three: if the thrills of the ExtraTERRORestrial Alien Encounter and the indoor roller-coaster Space Mountain appeal to you first, move to the right by the Plaza Restaurant and you'll get straight into Tomorrowland. Now you will be in pole position for the opening rush (and it will be a rush, believe me; take care if you're here with small children).

Adventureland

If you head to the left (effectively going clockwise around the park – always a good idea), you will enter Adventureland. If you're going to Splash Mountain first, you pass the Swiss Family Treehouse on your left and bear right through an archway (with toilets/restrooms on your right) into Frontierland, where you turn left and Splash Mountain is dead ahead. Stopping in Adventureland, however, these are the attractions you encounter:

Main Street, USA

© Disney

5

Swiss Family Treehouse: this imitation Banyan tree is a clever replica of the treehouse from Disney's 1960 film *Swiss Family Robinson*. It's a walk-through attraction where the queues (rarely long) move steadily if not quickly, providing a fascinating glimpse of the ultimate treehouse, complete with kitchen, rope bridges and running water! AAA.

Jungle Cruise: it's not so much the scenic, geographically suspect boat ride (where the Nile suddenly becomes the Amazon) that is so amusing here as the patter of your boat's captain, who spins a non-stop yarn about your adventure that features wild animals, tropical plants, hidden temples and sudden waterfalls. Great detail but long queues, so visit either early morning or late afternoon (evening queues are shortest, but you'll miss some of the detail in the dark). AAAA (FP).

Pirates of the Caribbean: one of Disney's most impressive attractions that involves their pioneering work in audio-animatronics, life-size figures that move, talk and, in this instance, lay siege to a Caribbean island! Your underground boat ride takes you through a typical pirate adventure and the wizardry of the special effects is truly amazing. This is worth several rides, although it may be a bit spooky for very young children. Queues are rarely long and almost non-existent late in the day. AAAAA.

The Enchanted Tiki Birds – Under New Management: this bird-laden, audio-animatronics

> BRIT TIP: When you are faced by more than one queue for an attraction, head for the left-hand one. Almost invariably this will move slightly quicker than that on the right.

venture features Iago (from *Aladdin*) and Zazu (*The Lion King*) at the head of a colourful, 16-minute revue that will appeal especially to younger children. Queues are rare here. AAA.

Magic Carpets of Aladdin: here, in a new, Agrabah-themed area styled after the animated film, the latest ride spins you up, down and around as you try to dodge the spitting camel! Your 'flying carpet' tilts as well as levitates, but it is basically simple stuff geared towards younger children (and virtually identical to the Magic Carpets of Agrabah in the new Walt Disney Studios in *Disneyland Resort Paris®*). TT (TTTT for under 5s).

Disney characters also turn up outside Pirates of the Caribbean and the Magic Carpets of Aladdin, while the best of the shopping is in the **House of Treasure** here and **Agrabah Bazaar**. For food, you have **Aloha Isle** (yoghurt and ice cream) and **Sunshine Tree Terrace** (fruit, snacks, yoghurt, tea and coffee).

Frontierland

Passing through Adventureland brings you to the target for many of the early birds. This Western-themed area is one of the busiest and is best avoided from late morning to late afternoon.

Splash Mountain: based on the 1946 classic Disney cartoon *Song of the South*, this is a watery journey into the world of Brer Rabbit, Brer Fox and Brer Bear. The first part is all jolly cartoon scenery and fun with the main characters and a couple of minor swoops in your 8-passenger log-boat. The conclusion, a 5-storey plummet at 45 degrees into a mist-shrouded pool, will seem like you are falling off the edge of the world! A huge adrenalin rush, but busy almost all day (try it first thing or during one of the parades to avoid the longest queues). You will also get VERY wet!

Restrictions: 3ft 4in. TTTTT (FP).

Big Thunder Mountain Railroad: when Disney does a roller-coaster you can be sure it will be one of the classiest, and here it is, a runaway mine train that swoops, tilts and plunges through a mock abandoned mine filled with clever scenery. You should ride at least twice to appreciate all the detail, but again queues are heavy, so go first thing (after Splash Mountain) or late in the day. Restrictions: 3ft 4in. TTTT (FP).

Country Bear Jamboree: now here's a novelty, a 16-minute musical revue presented by audio-animatronic bears! It's great family fun with plenty of novel touches (watch for the talking moose-head). Again, you'll need to beat the crowds by going early morning or early evening. It's possibly also the first theme park attraction to inspire a film, rather than vice versa, with the 2002 movie *The Country Bears*. AAAA.

Frontierland Shootin' Arcade: this is the only other attraction to cost extra (50 cents), as you shoot the animated targets. TT.

Tom Sawyer Island: take a raft over to this overgrown playground, with mysterious caves, grottos and mazes, rope bridges and Fort Sam Clemens, where you can fire air guns at passing boats. A good get-away in the early afternoon when the crowds are at their biggest, while **Aunt Polly's Dockside Inn** is a refuge within a refuge for snacks and soft drinks. TT.

Frontierland shops sell cowboy hats, guns and badges as well as Native American and Mexican handicrafts. For food, try **Pecos Bill Café** (salads, sandwiches and burgers), **Frontierland Fries** (McDonald's fries and drinks) or the **Turkey Leg Cart** (massive, smoke-grilled turkey legs).

Liberty Square

Continuing the clockwise tour brings you next to a homage to post-Independence America. A lot of the historical content will go over the heads of British visitors, but it still has some great attractions.

The Diamond Horseshoe Saloon Revue: after all the audio-animatronic gadgetry, this is an honest-to-goodness saloon show performed by real people. If you fancy a slapstick song-and-dance routine featuring can-can girls, corny comedy and audience participation, this is for you. Snacks are available before the show. AAA.

Liberty Square Riverboat: cruise America's 'rivers' on an authentic paddle steamer, be menaced by Indians and thrill to the tales of the Old West. This is also a good ride to take at the busiest times of the day, especially early afternoon. AAA.

The Haunted Mansion: a clever delve into the world of ghost train rides that is neither too scary for kids nor too twee for adults. Not so much a thrill ride as a scenic adventure. Watch out for the neat touch at the end when your car picks up an extra 'passenger'. Longish queues during much of the day, however (so a good one for a FASTPASS). AAAA or TTTT for under 6s (FP).

The Hall of Presidents: this is the attraction that is likely to mean least to us, a 2-part show that is first a film about the history of the Constitution and then an audio-animatronic parade of all 43 American presidents. Technically it's impressive, but dull for young children, although it is another air-conditioned haven. AAA.

Shopping here includes **Ye Olde Christmas Shoppe** and **The Yankee Trader,** while eating opportunities consist of the full-service **Liberty Tree Tavern** (serving hearty soups, steaks and

5

The Magic Carpets of Aladdin

traditional dishes like meatloaf and pot roast, plus dinner with Mickey and Co), **Columbia Harbour House** (for counter-service fried chicken or shrimp, fish and salads) and **Sleepy Hollow** (a picnic area serving snacks, fresh fruit and drinks).

Fantasyland

Leaving Liberty Square, you walk past Cinderella Castle and come into the park's spiritual heart, the area with which young children are most enchanted. The attractions are designed with kids in mind, but some of the shops are quite sophisticated.

'It's a Small World': this could almost be Disney's theme ride, a family boat trip through the different continents, each represented by hundreds of dancing, singing audio-animatronic dolls in delightful set-piece pageants. It sounds twee, but it actually creates a surprisingly striking effect, accompanied by an annoyingly catchy theme song which young children adore. Crowds peak in early afternoon. AAAA.

Dumbo the Flying Elephant: parents hate it but kids love it and all want to do this 2-minute ride on the back of a flying elephant that swoops in best Dumbo style (even if the ears do not flap). Do this one early or expect a long queue. TT (TTTT under 5s).

Mad Tea Party: again the kids will insist you take them in these spinning, oversized tea cups that have their own 'steering wheel' to add to the whirling effect. Actually, they're just a heavily disguised fairground ride. Again, go early or expect serious crowds. Characters from *Alice In Wonderland* also visit from time to time. TT (TTTT under 5s).

The Many Adventures of Winnie the Pooh: building on the timeless popularity of Pooh, Tigger and Co, this family ride offers a fairly predictable jaunt through Hundred Acre Wood with several notable special effects and another original soundtrack. AAA (AAAAA under 5s) (FP).

Snow White's Scary Adventures: this lively, fast-paced ride tells the cartoon story of Snow White with a few ghost train effects that may scare small children. Good fun, though, for parents and kids. Again, you will need to go early or late (or during the main afternoon parade) to beat the queues. TTT (TTTTT under 5s).

Cinderella's Golden Carousel: the centrepiece of Fantasyland shouldn't need any more explanation other than it is a vintage carousel ride which kids adore. Long queues during the main part of the day. T (TTT under 5s).

Disney's Agrabah Bazaar

Mickey's PhilharMagic: opening provisionally in early summer 2003, this 3-D film show (replacing *Legend of the Lion King*) aims to present Mickey and Co in a whole new way. Set in the PhilharMagic Concert Hall, it will feature a massive 150ft-wide screen and various 'live' special effects to immerse guests in the richly animated world of Disney characters, including the Little Mermaid, Aladdin and the Lion King. AAAAA (expected).

Peter Pan's Flight: don't be fooled by the long queues at this one, it is a rather tame ride by *Magic Kingdom Park* standards, although it is still a big hit with kids. Its novel effect of flying up, up and away with Peter Pan quickly wears off, but there is still a lot of clever detail as your 'sailing ship' journeys over the heart of London to Neverland. AA (AAAA under 5s) (FP).

In addition to the rides, there are different musical shows daily on the **Castle Forecourt Stage** in front of the castle, while the *Sword In The Stone* show is re-enacted several times a day near Cinderella's Golden Carousel.

Cinderella's Surprise Celebration: this new show on the castle stage is superb for character interaction, a 20-minute fantasy featuring Cinderella, Mickey and the gang, and various Disney villains, with the action extending to the castle ramparts and featuring some clever special effects. Stay afterwards for a lovely character meet-and-greet. AAAA.

Fantasyland Character Festival behind Dumbo allows you to meet some more Disney characters, as does **Ariel's Grotto** (where children frequently get very wet in the squirt ponds!), which draws quite a queue at peak periods. At the **Fairytale Garden,** on the corner of the Castle facing Tomorrowland, youngsters can enjoy Storytime with Belle.

Eating opportunities are at The **Pinocchio Village Haus** (salads, burgers and hot dogs), the **Enchanted Grove** (ice drinks and juices), **Scuttle's Landing** and **Mrs Potts' Cupboard** (for ice creams and sundaes). **Cinderella's Royal Table** is a fine setting for a meal, be it lunch, dinner or the standout character breakfast (but you must book well in advance for the latter – 407 939 3463, and give a credit card deposit). The majestic hall, waitresses in costume and well-presented food – salads, seafood, roast beef, prime rib and chicken – make for a memorable experience. It's a touch pricey for dinner, though. Shopping is provided by **Tinkerbell's Treasures** and the excellent **Sir Mickey's**.

Mickey's Toontown Fair

In the top corner of Fantasyland (just past the Mad Tea Party) is the shrub-lined entrance to **Mickey's Toontown Fair.** It is easy to miss, but it does have its own station on the railroad. Its primary appeal is to young children, and they won't want to miss the chance to meet their favourite Disney characters. It is exceptionally kid-friendly and well landscaped, and features a huge merchandising area, the **County Bounty** – wallets beware!

Mickey's Country House: here is a walk-through opportunity to see Mickey at home and have your

Buzz Lightyear's Space Ranger Spin

© Disney

> **BRIT TIP:** Not many people think to watch the fireworks from Mickey's Toontown Fair, but you get a great view from here.

picture taken with him in the Judge's Tent. AAAA (plus TTTTT for the photo opportunity. Just watch those awed young faces!).

Minnie's Country House: this is a chance to view Minnie's home and 'unique memorabilia', all designed in a Country and Western style. AAA.

Mickey's Toontown Fair Hall of Fame: three opportunities to meet a host of other Disney favourites. The Villains Room features the likes of Captain Hook and Jafar; Mickey's Pals allows you to meet Goofy, Pluto, Minnie and Co; and Famous Faces introduces Cinderella, Belle, Snow White and Pocahontas. TTTTT (for kids!).

The Barnstormer at Goofy's Wiseacre Farm: a mini roller-coaster just for the young 'uns (although possibly a bit too much for the under 5s) and is another masterpiece of design as it swoops through the barn, even if it is a pretty short ride after all the queuing. TTT (TTTTT for 5–9s). Restrictions: 3ft.

Donald's Boat: parents beware, your youngsters could get seriously wet here. If you've seen the dancing fountains at *Epcot* between Future World and World Showcase (see page 100), prepare for more watery delights as this boat-themed fountain spouts off in all sorts of wonderful ways. Ideally, bring a change of clothes or swimsuit for your offspring. It's a great place to revitalise tired or irritable children. AAAA (under 10s).

Tomorrowland

Coming on round from Fantasyland finally brings you into the last of the seven lands. It has a cartoon-like space-age appearance guaranteed to appeal to youngsters and some of the park's more original shops.

Space Mountain: this is one of the three most popular attractions, and its reputation is deserved. It is a fast, tight-turning roller-coaster completely in the dark save for occasional flashes as you whiz through 'the galaxy'. Don't do this after eating! The only way to beat the crowds is to go either first thing, late in the day or during one of the parades (or, of course, get a FASTPASS). Restrictions: 3ft 8in. TTTTT (FP).

Tomorrowland Indy Speedway: despite the long queues, this is a rather tame ride on supposed race tracks that just putt-putts along on rails with little real steering required. Restrictions: children must be 4ft 4in to drive alone. T (TTTT under 6s).

Astro Orbiter: this is a jazzed-up version of the Dumbo in Fantasyland, just a bit faster, higher and on 'rockets'. Large, slow-moving queues are another reason to give this a miss unless you have children. TT (TTTT under 10s).

Walt Disney's Carousel of Progress: this one will surprise, entertain and amuse. It is a 100-year journey through modern technology with audio-animatronics and a revolving theatre that reveals different stages in that development. Its 22-minute duration is rarely threatened by crowds. AAA. (Note: this attraction opened only at peak periods in 2002)

Tomorrowland Transit Authority: a neat 'future transport system', the TTA gives an elevated view of the area, with a glimpse inside Space Mountain, in electro-magnetically powered cars. If the queues are short, which they usually are, give it a go. AAA.

ExtraTERRORestrial Alien Encounter: this draws some HUGE queues (so go early) to its clever, high-tech preamble and scary show: a 'teleportation' demonstration that goes wrong and brings an alien to life in the middle of the audience. The fear factor adds a new dimension to the park, but it will be too much for most under 9s and anyone scared of the dark! Restrictions: 3ft 8in. TTTT.

Buzz Lightyear's Space Ranger Spin: kids will not want to miss this chance to join the great *Toy Story* character in his battle against the evil Emperor Zurg. Ride into action against the robot army – and shoot them with laser cannons! A sure-fire family winner, especially as you get to keep score. AAAA (FP).

The Galaxy Palace Theater hosts live musical productions, featuring Disney characters and talent shows, at various times of the day. For food, **Cosmic Ray's Starlight Café** has burgers, chicken and salads, **The Plaza Pavilion** does pizza, subs and salads, **Auntie Gravity's** (ouch!) **Galactic Goodies**

> BRIT TIP: Try to sit on the left side of Main Street, USA (as you face the castle) to stay in the shade if it's hot. People start staking out the best spots here up to an hour in advance.

serves ice cream and juices, the **Lunching Pad** (double ouch!) offers smoked turkey legs, snacks and drinks, and the **Cool Ship** provides various drinks.

Having come full circle you are now back at Main Street, USA and it's best to return here in early afternoon to avoid the crowds and look at the impressive array of shops.

The afternoon highlight, however, is the **Share A Dream Come True** parade every day at 3pm, originally part of the 100 Years of Magic celebration. This 6-part extravaganza, along Main Street and through Frontierland, is designed as a flurry of classic Disney moments frozen inside giant snow globes full of special effects. All the favourite characters are featured, along with a new musical score, plus some lighting tricks along the parade route. Watch out for the chance to be a part of the parade as it stops at intervals to allow characters to select people to dance and play act with. The globes themselves feature some outstanding effects, with Aladdin taking to the air on his flying carpet, the Wicked Queen turning into the evil old hag, and snow in the leading globes. It is a dazzling parade for all ages, but is especially popular with children. Don't miss it. AAAAA.

There's more

If you think the park looks good during the day, prepare to be amazed at how wonderful it appears at night – some of the lighting effects are astounding. When the park is open in the evenings (during the main holiday periods and weekends), there is the **SpectroMagic parade** (when there are two, the second one is less crowded), which is a mind-boggling light and sound festival full of glitter

> BRIT TIP: After the fireworks crowd exits, you are often allowed to take the Resort Only monorail back to the Transportation & Ticket Center, rather than stand in the LONG queues for the main monorail.

and razzamatazz, with the Disney characters at the centre of a multitude of sparkling lights and fibre-optic effects. It is difficult to do it justice in words, so make sure you see it. Evening hours are also highlighted by the **Fantasy in the Sky** firework show over the castle which is sparked off most nights in peak periods by Tinkerbell (seeing is believing!).

At Easter and Christmas, the daily parade takes on extra seasonal charm with appearances by the Easter Bunny and Father Christmas.

Character meals

You can breakfast with Disney characters at Cinderella's Royal Table ($15.99 for adults, $8.99 for 3–11s; 8–10am and have dinner with them at the **Liberty Tree Tavern** ($19.99 and $9.99; 4pm–park close). Or visit the **Crystal Palace** for buffet breakfast ($15.99 and $8.99; 8–10.30am), lunch ($16.99 and $9.29; 11.30am–2.45pm) and dinner ($20.99 and $9.99; 4pm–park close)

Mickey opens the SpectroMagic parade

© Disney

with Pooh, Tigger and Co. You can book a Disney character meal at the *Magic Kingdom Park* up to 60 days in advance on 407 939 3463.

Halloween and Christmas

Two additional annual events in the *Magic Kingdom Park* are **Mickey's Not So Scary Halloween Party** (on selected dates in October) and **Mickey's Very Merry Christmas Party** (late November and December) which provide a separate, party-style ticketed event from 7pm–midnight, with most of the rides open and extra themed fun and games (and snow on Main Street with the Christmas party, plus free hot chocolate and cookies, which all makes for an utterly enchanting atmosphere), plus a parade and more fireworks. Tickets cost $33.95 and can be booked on 407 939 7671.

If the crowds get too heavy, you CAN escape by leaving the park in early afternoon (get a hand-stamp for re-admission and keep your car park ticket which is valid all day) and returning to your hotel for a few hours' rest or a dip in the pool.

Finally, one of the park's little-known 'secrets' is the **Keys to the Kingdom**, a 4–5-hour guided tour of many backstage areas, including the service tunnel under the park, and entertainment production buildings. It costs an extra $58 (including lunch; not available for under 16s). Call 407 939 8687 for more information. **Disney's Family Magic Tour** is a 2-hour guided adventure that takes you on a search for clues throughout the park, at $25, or you can experience **Disney's The Magic Behind Our Steam Trains** tour ($30/person; no under 10s) as you join the crew who prepares the park's steam trains each day.

MORE SAVINGS WITH A BRIT'S GUIDE

We have a special deal for YOU to save lots of $$$s on restaurants, hotels, shops and attractions throughout Orlando. The *Entertainment Book* is usually available only to local residents, but we have arranged for our readers to benefit from the pages of discounts if you visit one of the area's Goodings supermarkets.

The *Entertainment Book* costs $35, but the total discounts are worth more than $6,000 over a full year, so you should easily be able to save $100–200 in 2 or 3 weeks, more if you plan around the many places which have money-off coupons in this book. There are some 110 restaurant deals alone, of which several dozen are in the I-Drive area, with savings of $15 or more at most of them.

All you have to do (ideally, as soon as you arrive in Orlando) is take this copy of *A Brit's Guide* to the guest services counter of the Goodings supermarket either at the Crossroads Plaza, Lake Buena Vista, or on International Drive, next to The Mercado, and ask to buy a copy of the *Entertainment Book* – and start saving! The local Red Cross receives a donation for each copy sold. Visit www.entertainment.com for the full saving available with this great book.

5

MAGIC KINGDOM PARK with children

Here is a rough guide to the rides which appeal to different age groups. Obviously, children vary enormously in their likes and dislikes but, as a general rule, you can be fairly sure the following will have most appeal to the ages concerned (height restrictions have been taken into account):

Under 5s
Walt Disney World Railroad, Main Street Vehicles, Jungle Cruise, The Enchanted Tiki Birds – Under New Management, Country Bear Jamboree, Liberty Square Riverboat, 'It's a Small World', Peter Pan's Flight, Mickey's PhilharMagic, Cinderella's Carousel, Dumbo The Flying Elephant, Many Adventures of Winnie The Pooh, Mickey's Country House, Donald's Boat, Tomorrowland Indy Speedway (with a parent), Buzz Lightyear's Space Ranger Spin, Tomorrowland Transit Authority.

5–8s
Walt Disney World Railroad, Pirates of the Caribbean, Jungle Cruise, Swiss Family Treehouse, Magic Carpets of Aladdin, The Enchanted Tiki Birds – Under New Management, Country Bear Jamboree, Liberty Square Riverboat, Tom Sawyer Island, Big Thunder Mountain Railroad, Splash Mountain, Haunted Mansion, Mickey's PhilharMagic, Snow White's Scary Adventures, Mad Tea Party, Many Adventures of Winnie The Pooh, Mickey's Country House, Donald's Boat, The Barnstormer at Goofy's Wiseacre Farm, Tomorrowland Indy Speedway (with parent), Tomorrowland Transit Authority, Buzz Lightyear's Space Ranger Spin, Walt Disney's Carousel of Progress, Astro Orbiter, Space Mountain (with parental discretion).

9–12s
Pirates of the Caribbean, Big Thunder Mountain Railroad, Splash Mountain, Diamond Horseshoe Saloon Revue, The Haunted Mansion, Mad Tea Party, Mickey's PhilharMagic, The Barnstormer at Goofy's Wiseacre Farm, Tomorrowland Indy Speedway (without parent), Buzz Lightyear's Space Ranger Spin, ExtraTERRORestrial Alien Encounter, Walt Disney's Carousel of Progress, Astro Orbiter, Space Mountain.

Over 12s
Big Thunder Mountain Railroad, Splash Mountain, Haunted Mansion, ExtraTERRORestrial Alien Encounter, Astro Orbiter, Space Mountain.

Epcot

Amaze and annoy your friends by revealing *Epcot* stands for 'Experimental Prototype Community Of Tomorrow' (or the visitor's version: Every Person Comes Out Tired!), once you have marvelled at the magnificent entertainment value of this 300-acre playground. Actually, it is not so much a vision of the future as a look at the world of today, with a strong educational and environmental message which children in particular are quick to pick up on.

At more than twice the size of the *Magic Kingdom Park*, it is more likely to require a 2-day visit (although under 5s might find it less entertaining) and your feet in particular will notice the difference!

Location

Epcot is located on Epcot Drive and the parking fee is again $6 as you drive into its main entrance (there is a separate entrance for guests at the Epcot resort hotels, called International Gateway). It opened in October 1982 and its giant parking lot is big enough for 12,000 vehicles, so again a tram takes you from your car to the main entrance (although if you are staying at a Disney hotel you can catch the monorail, boat or bus service to its gates). Once you have your ticket, you wait by the turnstiles for the opening moment (often accompanied by a Disney character or two) and are then admitted to the central plaza, between the Innoventions centres.

Epcot is divided into two distinct parts arranged in a figure of eight and there are two tactics to avoid the worst of the early morning crowds. The first or lower half of the '8' consists of **Future World,** with six different pavilions arranged around Spaceship Earth (the giant 'golfball' that dominates the *Epcot* skyline) and

Innoventions. The second part, or the top of the '8', is **World Showcase,** a potted journey around the world via 11 internationally presented pavilions that feature a taste of their culture, history, shopping, entertainment and cuisine.

Once you are through the gates, start by heading for the Future World pavilions to your left (Universe of Energy, Wonders of Life and Test Track) and then continue up into World Showcase. This way you will visit some of the best rides in *Epcot* ahead of the main crowds. Alternatively, if the rides don't appeal quite so much as a visit to such diverse cultures as Japan and Morocco, spend your first couple of hours in the Innoventions centres (busy from mid-morning), then head into World Showcase as soon as it opens at 11am and you will be ahead of the crowds for several hours. If you time your journey around the Showcase (which is a 1¼-mile walk) to arrive back in Future World by late afternoon, you will find the worst of the milling throng will have passed through (except from Test Track).

The other thing you should do early on is book lunch or dinner at one of the many fine restaurants around World Showcase (Mexico, Morocco, Canada and Japan are all highly recommended). The best reservations go fast, but check in at Guest Relations (immediately on the left as you enter the Innoventions Plaza) and they will be able to give you advice and make a Priority Seating (never just a reservation at Disney, remember – see page 55).

Future World

Here is what you will find in the first part of your *Epcot* adventure:

Universe of Energy: there is just the one attraction here but it is a stunner. The 45-minute show-and-ride with comedienne Ellen

Epcot at a glance

Location	Off *Epcot* Drive, *Walt Disney World*
Size	300 acres in Future World and World Showcase
Hours	9am–8pm (Future World; except Test Track, Innoventions, Spaceship Earth, Honey I Shrunk the Audience, 9am–9pm), 11am–9pm (World Showcase)
Admission	Under 3 free; 3–9, $38 (one-day ticket), $152 (4-Day Park Hopper), $197 (5-Day Park Hopper Plus); adult (10+) $48, $192, $247. Prices do not include tax.
Parking	$6
Lockers	Yes; to left underneath Spaceship Earth and International Gateway; $7 ($2 refund)
Pushchairs	$8 and $15 ($1 deposit refunded); to the right underneath Spaceship Earth and International Gateway
Wheelchairs	$7 ($1 deposit refunded) or $40 ($10 deposit refunded) (same location as pushchairs)
Top Attractions	Test Track, Spaceship Earth, 'Honey, I Shrunk the Audience', Maelstrom, Universe of Energy, American Adventure
Don't Miss	IllumiNations, Tapestry of Dreams Parade, live entertainment (including Off Kilter in Canada) and dinner at any of the World Showcase pavilions.

Hidden Costs	**Meals**	Burger, chips and coke $7.58 3-course dinner $33 (Le Cellier, Canada)
	Kids' meal	$3.49
	T-shirts	$19–32
	Souvenirs	$1–1,100
	Sundries	Disney character imposed photo $12.95

DeGeneres explores the creation of fuels from the age of dinosaurs to their modern day usages. The film elements convince you that you are in a conventional theatre, but then your seats rearrange themselves into 96-person solar-powered cars and you are off on a journey through the sights, sounds and even smells of the prehistoric era, with some realistic dinosaurs! Queues are steady but not overwhelming throughout the day from mid-morning. AAAAA.

Wonders of Life: this is one of Future World's most popular pavilions, hence you need to be here either early or late in the day. **Body Wars** is a terrific simulator ride through the human body as in the film *Fantastic Voyage*. It is quite a violent adventure, too, hence it is not recommended for people who suffer from motion sickness, anyone with neck or back injuries, or pregnant women. Restrictions: 3ft 4in. TTTT.

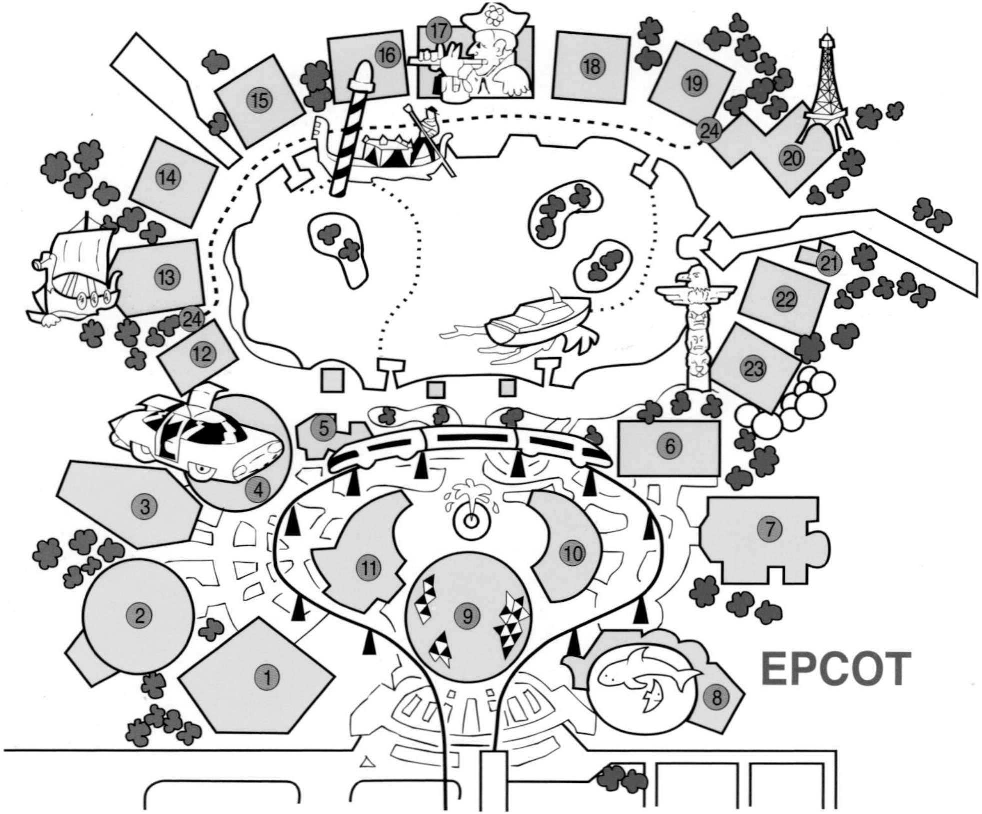

FUTURE WORLD

1 Universe Of Energy
2 Wonders Of Life
3 Mission: SPACE (2003)
4 Test Track
5 Odyssey Center
6 Imagination!
7 The Land
8 The Living Seas
9 Spaceship Earth
10 Innoventions West
11 Innoventions East

WORLD SHOWCASE

12 Mexico
13 Norway
14 China
15 Germany
16 Italy
17 The American Adventure
18 Japan
19 Morocco
20 France
21 International Gateway (To Epcot Resort Hotels)
22 United Kingdom
23 Canada
24 Tapestry Of Dreams parade route

EPCOT

Spaceship Earth

Cranium Command is a hilarious theatre show set in the brain of a 12-year-old boy, showing how he negotiates a typical day. It is both audio-animatronic and film-based. See how many famous TV and film stars you can name in the 'cast'. AAAA. **The Making of Me** is a sensitive film on the creation of human life and will therefore require parental discretion for children as it has its explicit moments, although not without humour. AAA.

The Fitness Fairground, with hands-on exhibits like exercise bikes, gives you the chance to see just how far all the holiday fun has taken its toll on your body! The **Pure and Simple** restaurant serves breakfast until 11am and then a range of snacks thereafter. Hot tip: this is a good pavilion in which to spend time if you need to cool down!

Mission: SPACE: the old Horizons pavilion has been pulled down and in its place is the building for Mission: SPACE, a dramatic new high-tech attraction which will feature a simulated shuttle launch and 'weightless' space travel, among other things. The idea is set decades into the future, with guests transported to an International Space Training Centre to encounter challenges faced by real astronauts. Disney promises it will boast the most advanced ride technology to date 'with a rare glimpse into a world where the possibilities for computers and space flight are

endless'. Story Musgrave, who has been a NASA Space Shuttle astronaut six times, is a consultant on the ride, which indicates the level of realism they aim to reproduce. All in all, it sounds dazzling and is sure to raise the thrill-ride stakes to new levels, but it is not due to open until at least the summer of 2003. TTTTT (expected; FP).

Test Track: this is a big production, 5½-minute whirl along Disney's longest and fastest track to date. It starts with a pre-show into the world of General Motors' quality and safety techniques to prepare riders for a taste of vehicle testing. The way the cars whiz around the outside of the building (at up to 60mph) provides a glimpse of what's in store. The reality is pretty good, too, as you are taken on a tour of a GM proving ground, including a hill climb test, suspension test (hold on to those fillings!), brake test, environment chamber, barrier test (beware the crash test dummies!) and the steeply banked, high-speed finale. For those who manage to regain their breath, there is a post-

Test Track in Future World

show area with a multimedia film and the chance to view the latest GM models. Along with a smart gift store and photo opportunity, it all makes for an extremely involved exhibit (although a bit technical for youngsters). The downside is the HUGE queues it attracts, topping 2 hours at times, while the available FASTPASS service often runs out. Head straight here after opening or return in the evening to keep your queuing to bearable levels. If you are on your own, you can save time by using the Singles Queue here. Restrictions: 3ft 4in. TTTT (TTT for teens) (FP).

The next door **Odyssey Center** offers baby-care and first-aid facilities, telephones and restrooms.

Imagination!: The 2-part attraction here starts with **Journey Into Imagination with Figment,** a recently revamped ride into experiments with imagination, in the company of Eric Idle (as Dr Nigel Channing of the Imagination Institute) and the cartoon dragon, Figment. The sight laboratory sees Figment having fun with a vision chart, the sound lab is a symphony of imaginative melodies and Figment's house is a truly topsy-turvy world (and watch out for the skunk in the smell lab!). It is gentle fun and rarely draws much of a crowd. AAA. (For fans of the original Dreamfinder ride here, Figment is highly prominent once again, while the ride's theme song, *One Little Spark*, has made a welcome return).

You exit into **Image Works – The Kodak 'What If' Labs,** an interactive playground of unusual sights and sounds, which will probably amuse children more than adults (although you are also tempted here to part with more money on various cartoon images and select-your-own CDs).

Come out of the building and turn right for the fabulous 3-D experience of '**Honey, I Shrunk The Audience**', as Rick Moranis reprises his hapless inventor character Wayne Szalinski. A neat 8-minute pre-show is the perfect prelude to the fun and games in store. If you have seen Jim Henson's Muppet*Vision 3-D at *Disney-MGM Studios* you might have an idea what to expect. Special effects and moving seats add to the feeling you have been miniaturised. And beware the sneezing dog! AAAAA (FP). Outside, kids are always fascinated by the Jellyfish and Serpentine Fountains that send water squirting from pond to pond, and there is always one who tries to stand in the way and 'catch' one of the streams of water. Have your cameras and camcorders ready!

The Land: this pavilion features four elements that combine to make a highly entertaining but educational experience on food production and nutrition. **Living with the Land** is an informative 14-minute boat ride that is worth the usually long queue. This journey through various types of food production sounds a dull idea, and it may not appeal much to younger children, but adults and school-age kids will sit up and take notice of the three ecological communities, especially the greenhouse finale. AAAA (FP).

Having ridden the ride you can also walk the walk on the **Behind The Seeds** guided tour through the greenhouse complex and learn even more about Disney's horticultural projects. It takes an hour ($6 for adults, $4 for 3–9s), but you have to book up in person at the desk near the Green Thumb Emporium. **Food Rocks,** just to the right as you exit the ride, is easy to overlook, but don't! This musical tribute to nutrition, presented by Fud Rappa (what a great name!) and featuring Pita Gabriel (ouch!) is a hilarious 12-minute skit that will amuse kids and adults alike. AAAA. **The Circle of Life** is a 15-minute live-action/

animated story, featuring characters from the film *The Lion King*, that explains environmental concerns and is easily digestible for kids. Queues not a problem here, either. AAA.

The **Sunshine Season Food Fair** offers the chance to eat some of Disney's home-grown produce, and there are healthy alternatives to the usual fast-food fare, while the **Garden Grill** restaurant is a slowly revolving platform that offers more traditional food, including pasta, seafood and delicious rotisserie chicken. Mickey and friends stage character meals here at lunch (11.30am–4.20pm; $17.95 for adults, $10.95 for children) and dinner (4.30pm–8pm; $19.95 and $10.95), but book early.

The Living Seas: this pavilion does for the sea what The Land Pavilion does for the land. A 7-minute film pre-show leads on to a short journey to Sea Base Alpha by 'Hydrolator' (imagine an undersea lift simulator) and an elaborate marine research facility centred around a 5.7 million-gallon aquarium. This 2-level development takes visitors through six modules that present stories of undersea exploration and marine life, including a research centre that provides a close-up encounter with the endangered manatee. Plenty of interactive elements and educational touch-screens are on offer, plus additional fish tanks displaying Caribbean reef fish, jellyfish and the curious cuttlefish, while there is also an excellent real-life demonstration of a diving chamber. Crowds build up steadily through the day, but queues rarely get too long. AAA.

The pavilion also includes the highly recommended **Coral Reef Restaurant** that serves magnificent seafood, as well as providing diners with a grandstand view of the massive aquarium. Dinner for two will cost around $65, which isn't cheap, but the food is first class.

Spaceship Earth: this ride spirals up the 18 storeys in the 'golfball', telling the story of communication from early cave drawings to modern satellite technology. This is one of the most popular rides in the park, largely because of its visibility and location, hence you need to do it either first thing or late afternoon when the crowds have moved on from Future World into World Showcase. The highlight is the depiction of Michelangelo's painting of the Sistine Chapel, which will be lost on small kids, but it's an entertaining 15-minute journey all along. AAAA.

As you leave, you come into the Global Activity Center, presented by AT&T, with a host of interactive educational exhibits.

Innoventions East and West: these two centres of hands-on exhibits and computer games – subtitled **The Road to Tomorrow** – were revamped for the Millennium celebrations. They include a glimpse of Disney's latest investigations into virtual reality entertainment and other demonstrations of current and future technologies, especially the Internet and computers, by companies like IBM, Xerox, Compaq, Motorola and General Motors. The kids will gravitate to the free **Video Games of Tomorrow** selection presented by Sega and they may take a bit of moving along! Both sides are routed like a journey into the future and will reward the enquiring mind in areas like People At Play and Mouse House Jnr. Worth waiting for are the **Ultimate Home Theater Experience** (West) and the opportunity to send a video e-mail to friends in the **Internet Zone** (East). The Internet Zone is also home to the **Mission: SPACE Launch Center,** which features several hands-on challenges and displays that preview the blockbuster new ride in Future World.

5

Musical entertainment is provided periodically in the Innoventions Plaza, along with other innovative live acts, while the majestic fountains are choreographed to an hourly music performance. Food outlets include the self-service **Electric Umbrella Restaurant** for lunch and dinner (sandwiches, pizza, burgers and salads) and the **Fountain View Espresso and Bakery** for tea, coffee and pastries. At **Ice Station Cool,** presented by Coca-Cola™, you'll be given some free product samples and the chance to encounter real snow! You'll also find the huge gift shop Mouse Gear in Innoventions East, featuring stacks of quality Epcot and Disney souvenirs (and some wonderfully wacky ceiling architecture!).

World Showcase

If you found Future World a huge experience, prepare to be amazed also by the more down-to-earth but equally imaginative pavilions around the World Showcase Lagoon. Each features a glimpse of a different country in dramatic settings. Several have either amusing rides or films that show off the tourist features of their country, while in nearly every case the restaurants offering national fare are some of the best in Orlando. **Mexico:** starting at the bottom left of the circular tour of the lagoon and moving clockwise, your first encounter is the spectacular pyramid

that houses Mexico. Here you will find the amusing boat ride along **El Rio del Tiempo,** the River of Time, which gives you a potted 9-minute journey through the people and history of the country. Queues here tend to be surprisingly long from mid-morning to late afternoon. AAA. The rest of the pavilion is given over to a range of shops in the **Plaza de los Amigos,** which vary from pretty tacky to sophisticated, and the **San Angel Inn,** a dimly lit and romantic full-service diner offering traditional and tempting Mexican fare. Outside, on the lagoon, is the **Cantina de San Angel,** a fast-food counter for tacos, chilli and burgers. In addition, as with all World Showcase pavilions, there is live entertainment and music.

> BRIT TIP: The Cantina is a great spot from which to watch the nightly IllumiNations fireworks and laser show, but you need to arrive at least an hour early.

Norway: next up is Norway, which probably has the best ride in World Showcase, the Viking-themed **Maelstrom.** This 10-minute longboat journey through the history and scenery of the Scandinavian country features a short waterfall drop and a North Sea storm. It attracts longish queues during the day, so the best tactic is to go soon after World Showcase's 11am opening. TTT (FP). There are periodical Norwegian-themed exhibits in the reconstructed **Stave Church** and twice-daily guided tours (sign up at the Tourism desk), while kids can play on the Viking boat. The pavilion also contains a clever reproduction of Oslo's Akershus Fortress. The popular **Restaurant Akershus** offers lunch and dinner buffets and the **Kringla**

The Coral Reef Restaurant

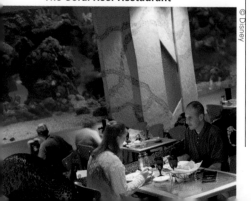

© Disney

Bakeri Og Kafé serves open sandwiches, pastries and drinks. Brand new here is the Princess Storybook Breakfast (8.30–10.30am), which features various Disney princesses and friends. Can't get a seat at Cinderella's in the *Magic Kingdom Park*? Try here instead, as you can book up to 120 days in advance ($15.99 adults, $8.99 children 3–11). **NB:** this was being tested in late Summer 2002 and I'm hopeful it will become permanent.

China: the spectacular architecture of China is well served by the pavilion's main attraction, the stunning **Wonders of China,** a 20-minute, 360-degree film in the circular Temple of Heaven. Here you are surrounded by the sights and sounds of one of the world's most mysterious countries in a special cinematic production, the technology of which alone will leave you breathless. Queues build up to half an hour during the main part of the day. AAAA.

Land of Many Faces is an exhibit introducing China's ethnic peoples. Two restaurants, the **Nine Dragons** (table service, decent if unremarkable food) and the **Lotus Blossom Café** (self-service, fairly predictable spring rolls and stir-fries), offer tastes of the Orient, while the **Yong Feng Shangdian Department Store** is a virtual warehouse of Chinese gifts and artefacts. Don't miss the periodic shows of Oriental music and acrobatic acts on the plaza in front of the temple.

The **Outpost** between China and Germany features hut-style shops and snacks, with entertainment from Africa and the Caribbean.

Germany: this provides more in the way of shopping and eating than entertainment, although you still find strolling players and a magnificent recreation of a Bavarian **Biergarten,** with lively Oktoberfest shows featuring the resident brass band at regular intervals. It also offers hearty portions of German sausage, sauerkraut and rotisserie chicken. The **Sommerfest** is fast food German-style (bratwurst and strudel). This pavilion has the highest number of shops of any *Epcot* pavilion, including chocolates, wines, porcelain, crystal, toys and cuckoo clocks. An elaborate outdoor model railway adds some more interest for children.

Italy: similarly, Italy has pretty, authentic architecture (including a superb reproduction of St Mark's Square in Venice), lively music and amusing Italian folk stories, three tempting gift shops (including wine, Perugina chocolates, Armani collectables, fine crystal, porcelain and Venetian masks), and a restaurant, **L'Originale Alfredo di Roma Ristorante**. It's a touch expensive, but the atmosphere, decor and singing waiters (!) add extra zest to the meals, which include fettucine, chicken, veal and seafood. Expect a 3-course meal to cost about $38.

> BRIT TIP: Kids, to get the best autographs from your Disney favourites, use a thick pen or pencil, as some characters have trouble writing otherwise!

America: at the top of the lagoon and dominating World Showcase is **The American Adventure,** not so much a pavilion as a celebration of the country's history and constitution. A colonial fife and drum band and wonderful *a cappella* group (Voices Of Liberty) add authentic sounds to the 18th-century setting, overlooked by a faithful reproduction of Philadelphia's Liberty Hall. Inside you have the spectacular American Adventure show, a magnificent film and audio-animatronic production lasting half an hour, which details the country's struggles and triumphs, its presidents, statesmen and heroes. It's a glossy, patriotic performance, featuring outstanding audio-animatronic effects and, while some of it will leave foreign visitors fairly cold, it is difficult not to be impressed by the sense of pride and achievement inherent in so much American history. Avoid at midday for the queues. AAAA.

Outside, handcarts offer touches of American nostalgia and antiques, along with the Heritage Manor Gifts store, while the **Liberty Inn** offers fast-food fare for lunch and dinner. **The America Gardens Theater,** facing the lagoon, presents musical performances from worldwide artists and Disney characters.

Japan: next up on the clockwise tour, you will be introduced to typical Japanese gardens and architecture, including the breathtaking Chi Nien Tien, a round building one-half scale reproduction of a temple, some magnificent art exhibits (notably the Bijutsu-kan Gallery), musical shows and dazzling live entertainment. For one of the most entertaining meals in *Epcot*, the **Teppanyaki Dining** rooms and **Tempura Kiku** both offer a full, table-service introduction to Japanese cuisine while **Yakitori House** is the fast-food equivalent and the **Matsu No Ma Lounge** features sushi and cocktails. The restaurants are run by Mitsukoshi, as is the superb department store. Periodic live music features the Matsuriza traditional drummers.

Morocco: as you would expect, this is a real shopping experience, with bazaars, alleyways and stalls selling a well-priced array of carpets, leather goods, clothing, brass ornaments, pottery and antiques (seek out that Magic Lamp!). All of the building materials were faithfully imported for the pavilion, which was hand-built to give Morocco a great degree of authenticity, even by the World Showcase's high standards. You'll be unable to keep your eyes off the clever detail around the winding alleyways and gardens, which can be enjoyed on daily guided walking tours. The **Gallery of Arts and History** offers more historical and cultural insight into the country.

Restaurant Marrakesh provides a full Moroccan dining experience, complete with traditional musicians and a belly dancer. It's slightly pricey ($55 for the Moroccan feast for two) but the atmosphere is lively and entertaining. **Tangerine Café** offers Mediterranean-style foods (hummus, tabouleh, couscous, roast lamb, lentil salad and Moroccan breads) at more down-to-earth prices ($5.95–10.95). Watch out, too, for characters from Disney's *Aladdin.*

France: France is predictably overlooked by a replica Eiffel Tower, but the smart streets, buildings and the sheer cleanliness of France is a long way from modern-day Paris! This is pre-World War One France, with official buskers and comedy street theatre acts adding to the rather dreamy atmosphere. Don't miss **Impressions de France,** another stunning big-film production that serves up all the grandest sights of the country to the accompaniment of the music of Offenbach, Debussy, Saint-Saëns and Satie. Crowds get quite heavy from late morning but it is a stunning performance (although kids might feel left out). AAAA.

This is also the pavilion for a gastronomic experience, with three restaurants, of which **Chefs de France** and **Bistro de Paris** are major discoveries. The former is an award-winning, full-service, and therefore expensive, establishment featuring top quality cuisine created by French chefs on a daily basis, while the latter offers more intimate bistro dining, still with an individual touch and plenty of style (starters from $9–20, main courses $28–35). Alternatively, the **Boulangerie Patisserie** is a sidewalk café offering more modest fare at a more modest price. Shopping is also suitably chic, with a Guerlain perfumery, wine shop and patisserie.

United Kingdom: the least inspired of all 11 international pavilions, and certainly with little to entertain those who have been inside a traditional pub before or shopped for Royal Doulton or Burberry goods. It is partly offset by some good street entertainers and the excellent Beatles tribute band, the British Invasion, but that really is the sum total here. The **Rose and Crown Pub** is antiseptically authentic, but you can get far better elsewhere for these prices (ploughman's $9.99, cottage pie $12.99, fish and chips $13.99, and a pint of Bass, Harp Lager or Guinness for a whopping $6.65). There is also a takeaway **Harry Ramsden's** fish and chippie. Other shops are the Tea Caddy, the Magic of Wales, the Queen's Table, Crown And Crest (perfumes, heraldry) and the Toy Soldier (traditional games and Disney toys). It's all terribly twee, though.

BRIT TIP: The Rose & Crown dining room is actually a great place from which to see the nightly IllumiNations fireworks spectacular, especially if you can manage to get a table on the Terrace.

Canada: completing the World Showcase circle, the main features here are **Victoria Gardens,** based on the world-famous Butchart Gardens on Vancouver Island, some spectacular Rocky Mountain scenery, a replica French gothic mansion, the Hôtel du Canada, and another stunning 360-degree film, **O Canada!** As with China and France, this showcases the country's sights and scenery in a terrific, 17-minute advert for the Canadian Tourist Board. It gets busiest from late morning to late afternoon. AAA. Resident band **Off Kilter** are also one of the most entertaining acts I've seen anywhere. Want to hear rock 'n roll bagpipes? This is the group for you! **Le Cellier Steakhouse** is a modestly priced dining room offering steaks, prime rib, seafood, chicken and several vegetarian dishes for lunch and dinner.

Around World Showcase are 11 **Kidcot Fun Stop** activity centres, at which children can play games and collect a special 11-point Star Medallion to get stamped at each of the pavilions as they visit them. The Medallion has a pop-out disc centre, the use for which will become apparent at the Tapestry of Dreams parade (see page 104).

Disney characters put on a show several times a day at **Showcase Plaza,** just across the bridge from Future World to World Showcase, and you can take their sight-seeing bus on tour to several locations in World Showcase, so have those autograph books handy!

Planning your visit

If you plan a 2-day visit, it makes sense to spend the first day in World Showcase, arriving early and heading there while most of the rest of the morning crowds linger in Future World, booking your evening meal around 5.30pm, and then lingering around the lagoon for the evening entertainment.

For your second visit, try arriving in mid afternoon and then doing

Future World in more leisurely fashion than it would be earlier. Queues at most of the pavilions are almost non-existent for rides like Universe of Energy, Body Wars and The Land, although Test Track stays busy nearly all day (except for the evening, when everyone is around the lagoon for the firework finale). Make best use of the FASTPASS service by grabbing a pass for Test Track early on and then riding Universe of Energy or Body Wars. You CAN do *Epcot* in a day – if you arrive early, put in some speedy legwork and give some of the detail a miss. But, of all the parks, it is a shame to hurry this one. In the shops (almost 70 in all), try to save your browsing for when most people are on the rides. The Innoventions centres are also busiest from mid morning to mid afternoon, and crowd-free in the evening.

Tapestry of Dreams

Epcot's twice-daily parade (usually 6.30 and 8.10pm) is one of the most colourful and exhilarating in any Disney park. **Tapestry of Dreams** is a development of the Tapestry of Nations parade which was such a feature of Disney's Millennium celebrations. It takes the basic premise of a series of large, elaborate puppet-like figures and rolling percussion units and adds four new floats, known as Dream Catchers, with characters called Dream Spinners.

The parade is geared towards children's dreams for the future and is narrated in suitable fashion, with magnificent music by Hans Zimmer and British composer Gavin Greenaway (prepare to have your heart-strings severely tugged!). At strategic points, children are invited to pull out the centre disc of their Star Medallion (from the World Showcase Kidcot centres – see page 103) and deposit a Magic Dream Wish into the net carried by the Dream Spinners. It's a vibrant and colourful street festival that should not be missed!

IllumiNations: Reflections of Earth

The day's big finale is another absolute show-stopper. **IllumiNations: Reflections of Earth,** is a firework and special-effect extravaganza, awesome even by Disney standards. Again, Greenaway provides original music for a 15-minute performance of vivid brilliance. Some 2,800 firework shells are launched as a celestial backdrop to a series of fire-and-water effects on the World Showcase lagoon. The central icon is a 28-ft video globe of Earth that opens in a spectacular climax of choreographed pyrotechnics. Magnificent. However, people do start staking out the best lagoon-side spots up to 2 hours in advance.

The ultimate way to view IllumiNations is by private boat on one of three **speciality cruises** from

---

The Tapestry of Dreams parade

© Disney

Disney's Boardwalk or Yacht/Beach Club resorts (for non-residents, too). They vary from $130–290 per boat (holding 4–12 guests) and can be used for special celebrations. The basic cruise costs $130 and the pontoon boat holds up to 12. The level-1 cruise adds soda, sandwiches, water and snacks and costs $210 for up to 4 guests and $20 for each additional person. The level-2 cruise adds fruit, cheese and dessert, costing $290 for 4 and $35 for each additional guest. Call 407 939 7529 up to 90 days in advance to book. Be aware that cruises launch regardless of whether fireworks are taking place.

Epcot also has some special behind-the-scenes tours (but not for under-16s). **Dolphins In Depth** ($140, including souvenir video, T-shirt and refreshments) is a 3½-hour delve into the backstage and research areas of the Living Seas pavilion, including a chance to meet the resident dolphins. **Gardens of the World** ($59) is a 3-hour botanical tour of the gardens in *Epcot*, and includes tips for your own garden. **Hidden Treasures** is a 3-hour ($59) tour of the 11 countries of World Showcase. **Undiscovered Future World** is a 4½-hour journey into the creation of *Epcot*, Walt's vision for the resort and backstage areas like IllumiNations ($49). **Backstage Magic** ($199) goes behind the scenes of *Epcot*, *Magic Kingdom Park* and *Disney-MGM Studios* on a 7-hour tour into little-seen aspects, like animators at work in *Disney-MGM Studios* and tunnels below the *Magic Kingdom Park*. These tours must be booked on 407 939 8687.

Two other *Epcot* specialities are the wonderful free **International Flower and Garden Festival** (mid April to June), and the **Food and Wine Festival** (late October to November), which showcases national and regional cuisines, wines and beers, with the chance to attend grand Winemakers Dinners and Tasting Events, or just sample the inexpensive offerings of more than 20 food booths around World Showcase.

5

EPCOT with children

Here is our rough guide to the rides which appeal to different age groups in this park:

Under 5s
Spaceship Earth, Universe of Energy, Journey Into Your Imagination, The Living Seas, Living with the Land, Circle of Life, El Rio del Tiempo.

5–8s
All the above, plus Body Wars, Cranium Command, Test Track, Innoventions, 'Honey, I Shrunk The Audience' (with parental discretion), Image Works, Food Rocks, Maelstrom, The American Adventure.

9–12s
All the above, plus Behind the Seeds tour, Treasures of Morocco tour, Impressions de France, Wonders of China, O Canada!

Over 12s
All the above, plus Land of Many Faces (China), Bijutsu-kan Gallery, Norway guided tours, Off Kilter, British Invasion.

Disney-MGM Studios

Welcome to Hollywood! Well, the *Walt Disney World Resort in Florida* version of it. When it opened in May 1989, Michael Eisner, chairman of the Walt Disney Company, insisted it was 'the Hollywood that never was and always will be'. Sounds double Dutch? Don't worry, all will be revealed in your day-long tour of this real-life combination of theme park and working TV and film studio. The most common question about *Disney-MGM Studios* is 'Are they really working studios?', and yes, there really are film and TV productions going on even while you're riding around the park peering into the backstage areas.

In 2002, *Disney-MGM Studios* was also the focus of the *100 Years of Magic* celebration, when the awesome grand icon – a 12-storey **Sorcerer Mickey** hat – was added at the centre of the park, a gigantic, shimmering symbol of the Disney magic.

Rather bigger than the *Magic Kingdom Park* at 154 acres but substantially smaller than *Epcot*, *Disney-MGM Studios* is a different experience yet again with its combination of rides, spectacular shows (including the unmissable Fantasmic!), street entertainment, film sets and smart gift shops. Like the *Magic Kingdom Park*, the food on offer at the park may not win awards, but some of the restaurants (notably the **Sci-Fi Dine-in Theater** and **50s Prime Time Café**) have superbly imaginative settings to keep everyone amused while they are eating.

Disney-MGM Studios also has rather more to occupy smaller children than *Epcot*, but you can still easily see all of it in a day unless the crowds are really heavy.

Location

The entrance arrangements will be fairly familiar if you have already visited any of the other parks. *Disney-MGM Studios* is located on Buena Vista Drive (which runs between World Drive and Epcot Drive) and the parking fee is $6. Again, make a note of where you park before you catch your tram to the main gates, where you must wait for the official opening hour. If the queues build up quickly, the gates will again open early, so be ready to get a running start.

Once through the gates, you are into Hollywood Boulevard, a street of mainly gift shops, and you have to decide which of the main attractions to head for first, as these are the ones where the queues will be heavy nearly all day. Try to ignore the lure of the shops as it is better to browse in the early afternoon when the queues build up at the rides. Incidentally, if you thought Disney had elevated queuing to an art form in their other two parks, wait until you see the clever ways they are arranged here. Just when you think you have got to the ride itself, there is another twist to the queue you hadn't seen or an extra element to the ride which holds you up. The latter are called 'holding pens' and are an ingenious way of making it seem like you are being entertained instead of queuing. Look out for them in particular at the Great Movie Ride, Twilight Zone™ Tower of Terror and Jim Henson's Muppet*Vision 3-D. An up-to-the-minute check on queue times at all the main attractions is kept on a **Guest Information Board** on Hollywood Boulevard, just past its junction with Sunset Boulevard, where you can also book for the restaurants.

Disney-MGM Studios at a glance

Location	Off Buena Vista Drive or World Drive, Walt Disney World
Size	154 acres
Hours	9am–7pm off peak; 9am–10pm high season (Easter, summer holidays, Thanksgiving and Christmas)
Admission	Under 3 free; 3–9 $38 (one-day ticket), $152 (4-Day Park Hopper), $197 (5-Day Park Hopper Plus); adult (10+) $48, $192, $247. Prices do not include tax.
Parking	$6
Lockers	Yes; next to Oscar's Super Service, to right of main entrance; $7 ($2 refundable)
Pushchairs	$8 and $15 ($1 deposit refunded) from Oscar's Super Service
Wheelchairs	$8 ($1 deposit refunded) or $40 ($10 deposit refunded); same location as pushchairs
Top Attractions	Twilight Zone™ Tower of Terror, Rock 'n Roller Coaster Starring Aerosmith, Star Tours, The Great Movie Ride, Who Wants To Be A Millionaire – Play It!, Voyage of the Little Mermaid, Jim Henson's Muppet*Vision 3-D
Don't Miss	Disney Stars and Motor Cars Parade, Indiana Jones™ Epic Stunt Spectacular!, Fantasmic!

Hidden Costs	**Meals**	Burger, chips and coke $7.48 3-course lunch $23 (Prime Time Café)
	Kids' meal	$3.49 and $4.99
	T-shirts	$19–32
	Souvenirs	$1.25–385
	Sundries	Rock 'n Roller Coaster Starring Aerosmith photo $16.95

Disney-MGM Studios is laid out in a rather more confusing fashion than its counterparts, which have neatly packaged 'lands', so you need to consult your map frequently to ensure you're going in the right direction.

The main attractions

The opening-gate crowds will all surge in one of four directions, which will give you a pretty good idea of where you want to go. By far the 'biggest' attraction in *Disney-MGM Studios* is the **Twilight Zone™ Tower of Terror,** a magnificent haunted hotel ride that culminates in a 13-storey drop in a lift, where queues build to 2 hours at peak periods. Consequently, if the Tower appeals to you, do it first! Head up Hollywood Boulevard then turn right into Sunset Boulevard and it is at the end of the street, looming ominously over the park. **Rock 'n**

DISNEY-MGM STUDIOS

1 Parade Route ... Disney Stars And Motor Cars Parade

2 100 Years Of Magic Icon

3 Indiana Jones™ Epic Stunt Spectacular!

4 ABC Sound Studio 'Sounds Dangerous' Starring Drew Carey

5 Star Tours

6 Disney's Hunchback Of Notre Dame – A Musical Adventure

7 Jim Henson's Muppet*Vision 3-D

8 Honey, I Shrunk The Kids Movie Set Adventure

9 Catastrophe Canyon On Disney-MGM Studios Backlot Tour

10 Disney-MGM Studios Backlot Tour

11 Meet Mickey Mouse

12 The Great Movie Ride

13 Voyage Of The Little Mermaid

14 Who Wants To Be A Millionaire – Play It!

15 The Magic Of Disney Animation

16 The Twilight Zone™ Tower Of Terror

17 Beauty and the Beast – Live On Stage

18 Guest Information Board

19 Toy Story Pizza Planet

20 Fantasmic!

21 Rock 'n Roller Coaster Starring Aerosmith

22 Playhouse Disney – Live On Stage!

23 Walt Disney: One Man's Dream

DISNEY-MGM STUDIOS

The Wicked Witch in Fantasmic!

Roller Coaster Starring Aerosmith, at the end of Sunset Boulevard on the left, is another huge draw but is also a FASTPASS (FP) ride (see page 82) like Tower of Terror, so you can get a pass for one and ride the other if you head here first.

Star Tours, the great Star Wars™ simulator ride, and **Voyage of the Little Mermaid** are also serious queue-builders and FP attractions. If you are not up for the really big thrills, grab a pass for Mermaid (straight up Hollywood Boulevard, past Sunset, turn right into Animation Courtyard) then head for Star Tours (back across the main square past the Indiana Jones™ show). Finally, the new **Who Wants To Be A Millionaire – Play It!** attraction is a major success, but has only 10 shows (accommodating 1,600 people a time) a day, hence FPs can run out quickly. So, if this appeals to you, head here first (past the Little Mermaid and along Mickey Avenue).

Here's a full rundown of the attractions, in a clockwise direction:

The Great Movie Ride: this faces you (behind the new hat icon) as you walk in along Hollywood Boulevard and is a good place to start if the crowds are not too serious. An all-star audio-animatronics cast recreates a number of box office smashes, including Jimmy Cagney's *Public Enemy*, Julie Andrews in *Mary Poppins*, Gene Kelly in *Singing in the Rain* and many more masterful set pieces as you ride through on your conducted tour. Small children may find the menace of *The Alien* too strong, but otherwise it has fairly universal appeal and features some clever live twists that I won't reveal. AAAA.

ABC Sound Studio 'Sounds Dangerous' Starring Drew Carey: this sound FX special features American comedian Drew Carey in an instalment of a spoof undercover police show *Sounds Dangerous*. Most of the 12-minute show is in the dark – which upsets some children – and is centred on your special headphones as Carey's stakeout goes wrong. Clever and amusing – if a bit tame for older children – you exit into the Sound Works Studio to try out some well-known sound effects. AAA.

Indiana Jones™ Epic Stunt Spectacular!: consult your park map for the various times for when this rip-roaring stunt cavalcade will hit

The Twilight Zone™ Tower of Terror

the stage. A specially made movie set creates three different backdrops for Indiana Jones'™ stunt people to put on a dazzling array of clever stunts, scenes and special effects from the Harrison Ford film epics. Audience participation is an element and there are some amusing sub-plots. Queues for the 30-minute show begin to form up to half an hour beforehand, but the auditorium holds more than 2,000 so everyone usually gets in. TTTT (FP).

Star Tours: anyone remotely amused by the *Star Wars*™ films will enjoy just queuing for one of my personal favourites, a breathtaking 7-minute spin in a Star Speeder. The elaborate walk-in area is full of *Star Wars*™ gadgets and gizmos that will make the long wait (often up to an hour) pass quickly. From arguing robots C-3PO and R-2D2 to your robotic 'pilot', everything has a brilliant sense of space travel, and the ride won't disappoint! Restrictions: 3ft 4in, no children under 3. TTTT (plus AAAAA) (FP).

Jim Henson's Muppet*Vision 3-D: the 3-D is crossed out here and 4-D substituted in its place, so be warned that strange things will be happening! A wonderful 10-minute holding-pen pre-show takes you into the Muppet Theater for a 20-minute experience with all of the Muppets, 3-D special effects and more – when Fozzie Bear points his squirty flower at you, prepare to get wet! It's a gem, and children in particular will love it. Queues build up through the main parts of the day, but Disney's queuing expertise makes them seem shorter than they actually are. AAAAA (FP).

Disney's Hunchback of Notre Dame – A Musical Adventure: this clever 32-minute musical and animated puppet show highlights the key elements of the Disney film and is staged 4 or 5 times a day in the Backlot Theater. It features a wonderfully elaborate setting, too.

AAA. Have your cameras handy here for the Backlot, a collection of clever façades that look like city scenery, which you can wander around on foot. There is also a recreation of Al's Toy Barn from the *Toy Story* films, and children can meet Buzz Lightyear, Woody and Jessie here at various times.

Honey, I Shrunk the Kids Movie Set Adventure: this adventure playground gives youngsters the chance to tackle gigantic blades of grass that turn out to be slides, crawl through caves, investigate giant mushrooms and more. However, some may turn round and say 'Yeah. A giant ant. So what?' and head back for the rides. There can be long queues here, too, so arrive early if the kids demand it (and bring plenty of film). TT (TTTT under 9s).

The Disney-MGM Studios Backlot Tour: this 35-minutes walk-and ride tour starts with some special effects (involving a clever and funny water tank with a mock Pearl Harbor attack!) before you board the special trams for a look at the off-limits part of the studios. You are introduced to the production backlot, famous film and TV 'houses' and props before visiting **Catastrophe Canyon** for a demonstration of special effects that try both to drown you and blow you up! AAA (plus TTTT!). You exit into the **American Film Institute Showcase** of costumes and props from recent films. Nearby, Goofy's Prop Stop is a neat photo opportunity with various Disney images ($12.95 and $16.95).

Who Wants To Be A Millionaire – Play It!: Disney's live version of the hit TV show is based on the US programme (presented by Regis Philbin rather than our Chris Tarrant), but is still effectively the same show. The great twist is EVERYONE gets to play – all 1,600 members of the audience. Whoever is fastest with the put-them-in-order question starts in the hot seat and, as you play along, you build up a score, with the top 10 shown on screen at various stages. Then, when a contestant loses out, the person with the highest score in the audience is next up! The hosts do a terrific job of maintaining the TV 'illusion' and there are the usual rules and lifelines, which add to the sense of reality here (although you play for Disney points, not money, which add up to some great souvenirs and prizes). One difference is there can be no Phone A Friend lifeline. Instead, you have Phone A Complete Stranger, when a passer-by is grabbed off the street outside! It is addictive fun, and the only drawback is it has become so popular the FASTPASS tickets run out quickly, so try to get here early in the day. AAAAA (FP).

Walt Disney: One Man's Dream: as part of the *100 Years Of Magic celebration,* Disney's Imagineers came up with this attraction, an interactive show-and-tell chronicle of Walt himself and his accomplishments. From archive school records to a model of the submarine Nautilus from *20,000 Leagues Under The Sea,* the story of the man behind the Mouse comes to vivid life with a number of hands-on elements. The homage to the creator of the magic concludes with a preview of Disney's future developments, plus a 10-minute film encapsulating everything Walt has achieved and dreamed about. AAAA.

Voyage of the Little Mermaid: this 17-minute live performance is primarily for children who have seen and enjoyed the Disney cartoon. It brings together a creative mix of live actors, animation and puppetry to recreate the highlights of the film. Parents will still enjoy the special effects, but queues tend to be surprisingly long so go either early or late. Those in the first few rows

> BRIT TIP: Try to sit at least half-way back in the Mermaid Theatre, especially with young children, as the stage front is a bit high for little 'uns.

may also get a little wet. AAA (AAAAA under 9s) (FP).

The Magic of Disney Animation: an amusing and entertaining 35-minute tour through the making of cartoons. It's up to you how you pace it, but don't miss Robin Williams in a special cartoon, *Back to Neverland,* with Walter Cronkite, and the fascinating view of some of Disney's animators at work. It concludes with a film of some of the highlights of Disney's many animated classics, and you will be amazed at how much you have learned by the end (although small children might be a bit lost by it all). Queues are rarely serious here, so it's a good one for the afternoon. AAAA.

Playhouse Disney – Live On Stage!: straight out of several popular kids' TV series comes this 20-minute live show with such pre-school favourites as *Bear in the Big Blue House* and *Rolie Polie Olie,* plus others like the *Book of Pooh* and *Stanley.* Much of this can be seen only on cable or satellite TV in the UK, so it is doubtful how much it will mean to the kids it is aimed at, but it is still a colourful and entertaining offering. AAA (AAAAA under 5s).

The Twilight Zone™ Tower of Terror: the tallest landmark in *Walt Disney World Resort in Florida* (at 199ft) invites you to experience another dimension in this mysterious Hollywood Tower Hotel that time forgot. The exterior is intriguing, the interior is fascinating, the ride is scintillating and the queues are mind-blowing! The only unfortunate aspect of this thrilling

5

Hollywood Brown Derby

attraction, which is so much more than just the advertised 13-storey free-fall, is the fact that much of the queuing is outside in the sun, and, when it is hot, you are almost

melting by the time you reach the air-conditioned, spooky hotel. Typically, just when you think you are through to the ride itself, there is another queue, but the inner detail is so clever you can spend the time inspecting how realistic it all is. You have been warned! Restrictions: 3ft 4in. TTTTT (FP).

Rock 'n Roller Coaster Starring Aerosmith: Disney's first big-thrill inverted coaster is a sure-fire draw for the high-energy ride addicts, with a magnificent indoor setting and nerve-jangling ride. It features a clever 3-D film show starring rock group Aerosmith in their recording studio. That preamble leads to the real fun, set to specially recorded tracks from the band itself and with outrageous speaker systems, as riders climb aboard Cadillac 'cars' for this memorable whiz through a mock Los Angeles setting (watch out for a

Playhouse Disney – Live on Stage!

A meeting with the characters from Monsters Inc.

> **BRIT TIP:** Beat the crowds by booking a Fantasmic! dinner package when you enter the park (or in advance on 407 939 3463). Just make an early-evening Priority Seating for the Hollywood Brown Derby or Mama Melrose's, and you get no-wait VIP seating later for the show.

close encounter with the 'Hollywood' sign!). The high-speed launch and inversions ensure an up-to-the-minute coaster experience. Go first thing or expect serious queues. Restrictions: 4ft 1in TTTTT (FP).

Beauty and the Beast – Live on Stage: an enchanting live performance of the highlights of this Disney classic will entertain the whole family for 20 minutes in the nearby Theater of the Stars. Check the daily schedule for showtimes. AAA.

BRIT TIP: I always recommend the Sci-Fi diner or '50s Prime Time Café for a main meal with a difference.

Fantasmic!: this epic special-effects spectacular is simply not to be missed. Staged every night in a 6,900-seat amphitheatre behind the Tower of Terror™, it features the 'dreams' of Mr M Mouse, portrayed as the Sorcerer's Apprentice, through films such as *Pocahontas*, *The Lion King* and *Snow White*, but hijacked by various Disney villains, leading to a tumultuous battle, with Our Hero emerging triumphant. Dancing waters, shooting comets, animated fountains, swirling stars, balls of fire and more combine in a truly breathtaking presentation – just watch out for the giant, fire-breathing dragon! The 25-minute show begins seating up to 90 minutes in advance and it is advisable to head there at least half an hour beforehand (watch out for the splash zones!). AAAAA.

Daily parade

In keeping with the park's movie-star style, the daily parade (another designed for the *100 Years of Magic* celebration) is **Disney Stars and Motor Cars,** and is one of the highlights. The theme is a film premier in 1930s and 1940s Hollywood, with a series of genuine vintage cars and clever replicas being used to mount a riotous cavalcade of Disney showbiz favourites. It kicks off with motorcycle police outriders and continues with some 15 crazily customised cars – including a 1929 Cadillac – that provide the likes of *Aladdin*, *Mary Poppins*, *Mulan*, the *Muppets* and new films like *Atlantis* and *Monsters Inc* with a chance to

show off in larger-than-life fashion. Watch out for the *Star Wars*™ 'Land Speeder' with a radio-controlled R-2D2 in the largest parade ever staged in *Disney-MGM Studios*. The lead car also features any special guests at the Studios that day – or a visiting family or two instead! AAAA

Disney characters are out and about along Mickey Avenue (including Sorcerer Mickey) as are performing 'actors and actresses' in Hollywood Boulevard.

Food and shops

While the choice of food may not be wide, there is plenty of it and at reasonable prices. **The Hollywood Brown Derby** offers a full-service restaurant in fine Hollywood style (reservations necessary – special Early Evening Value meals 4–6pm), while **Mama Melrose's Ristorante Italiano** is a wonderful table-service Italian option (one of my favourites). The **Sci-Fi Dine-In Theater Restaurant** is a big hit with kids as you dine in a mock drive-in cinema, with cars as 'tables', waitresses on roller skates and a big film screen showing corny old black-and-white science fiction clips. The **'50s Prime Time Café** is another hilarious experience as you sit in mock stage sets from American 1950s' TV sitcoms and eat meals 'just like Mom used to make'. (The waiters all claim to be your brother and warn you to take your elbows off the table, etc. Hilarious!) Priority Seatings are also necessary.

The fast-food eateries consist of the **ABC Commissary** (breakfast to 10.30am, then burger, fish and chips, chicken yakitori and vegetable wraps), **Backlot Express** (excellent burgers and hot dogs), **Rosie's All-American Café** (chicken, burgers, salads) and the **Toy Story Pizza Planet** (pizza, salads and drinks). Disney character meals are available at **Hollywood & Vine Cafeteria of the Stars** for breakfast and lunch ($15.99 and $17.50 for adults, $8.99 and $9.95 for 3–11s; 8.30–11.30am and 11.30am–3pm) but you need to book first thing for these (or call 407 939 3463).

There are also 21 gift and speciality shops, six of them along Hollywood Boulevard, which are worth checking out in early afternoon. **Sid Caheunga's One-of-a-Kind** (just to the left of the main gates as you enter) stocks rare movie and TV items, including many celebrity autographs. Try the **Legends of Hollywood** (on Sunset Boulevard) for a rather different range of souvenirs and **It's a Wonderful Shop** (in the Backlot) for Christmas gifts and collectables. **Keystone Clothiers** (at the top of Hollywood Boulevard) offers some of the best Disney apparel in any of the parks. All the main rides and attractions have their own shops.

Disney at Christmas

At Christmas, don't miss the incredible **Osborne Family Lights,** switched on in the evening in the Backlot Tour area.

5

DISNEY-MGM STUDIOS with children

Here is our general guide to the rides which appeal to the different age groups in this park (and it is, possibly, the best spread of all):

Under 5s
Playhouse Disney – Live On Stage!, Voyage of the Little Mermaid, Beauty and the Beast – Live on Stage, Disney's Hunchback of Notre Dame – A Musical Adventure.

5–8s
Voyage of the Little Mermaid, Beauty and the Beast – Live On Stage, Honey I Shrunk the Kids Movie Set Adventure, Sounds Dangerous Starring Drew Carey, Jim Henson's Muppet*Vision 3-D, Disney's Hunchback of Notre Dame – A Musical Adventure, *Disney-MGM Studios* Backlot Tour, Star Tours (with parental discretion), Fantasmic!

9–12s
Sounds Dangerous Starring Drew Carey, Indiana Jones™ Epic Stunt Spectacular!, The Great Movie Ride, Star Tours, Jim Henson's Muppet*Vision 3-D, Disney's Hunchback of Notre Dame – A Musical Adventure, *Disney-MGM Studios* Backlot Tour, The Magic of Disney Animation, Beauty and the Beast – Live On Stage, Rock 'n Roller Coaster Starring Aerosmith, Twilight Zone™ Tower of Terror, Fantasmic!

Over 12s
Indiana Jones™ Epic Stunt Spectacular, Star Tours, The Great Movie Ride, Jim Henson's Muppet*Vision 3-D, *Disney-MGM Studios* Backlot Tour, Who Wants To Be A Millionaire – Play It!, The Magic of Disney Animation, Rock 'n Roller Coaster Starring Aerosmith, Twilight Zone™ Tower of Terror, Fantasmic!

Disney's Animal Kingdom Theme Park

The newest, smartest and most radical theme park at *Walt Disney World Resort in Florida* opened in 1998 and represents a completely different park experience. With an emphasis on nature and conservation, it largely eschews the non-stop thrills and attractions, which mark out the other parks, and instead offers a change of pace, a more relaxing motif, as well as Disney's usual seamless entertainment style – plus two excellent thrill rides.

The attractions are relatively few, just five out-and-out rides, plus two scenic journeys, two nature trails, five shows (including the hilarious 3-D film *It's Tough to Be a Bug!* and the full-blown theatre of *Festival of The Lion King*), an elaborate adventure playground, conservation station and petting zoo, and a Disney character greeting area. It's a far cry from the hustle-bustle of the *Magic Kingdom Park*, and it carries a strong environmental message that aims to create a greater understanding of the world's ecological problems. School-age children should find it quite educational, though under 5s may be a little left out. It is outrageously scenic, notably with the 145-ft Tree of Life and the Kilimanjaro Safaris, but it won't overwhelm you with Disney's usual sense of grand fantasy. Rather, it is a chance to experience a part of the world that is both threatened and threatening in a safe, secure manner. It is obviously not the Real Thing but it provides a genuine glimpse of some of the world's most majestic areas in a manner that allows ecology and the commercial world to co-exist happily and meaningfully.

The most conclusive word on Disney's first full-blown animal adventure goes to Professor David Bellamy, who told me: 'This park has been designed and looked after by the best animal welfare people you can think of. Bad zoos are bad news and should be closed down, but good zoos are good news and the only hope for keeping about 500 species of animal alive in the future.' The park does get horribly crowded, however, and the walkways can be very congested. There are also fewer areas to cool down. It is definitely a good idea to be here on time and use FASTPASS (FP) to minimise queuing.

Getting there

If you are staying in the Kissimmee area, *Disney's Animal Kingdom Theme Park* is the easiest to find. Just get on the (toll) Osceola Parkway and follow it all the way to the toll booths, where parking costs $6. Alternatively, coming down I-4, take the new Exit 65 which puts you on Osceola Parkway. From western Highway 192, come in on Sherberth Road (turn right at the first traffic lights).

The majestic Tree of Life

© Disney

THE OASIS
1 The Oasis Tropical Garden

DISCOVERY ISLAND
2 The Tree Of Life
3 It's Tough to Be a Bug!
4 Discovery Island Trails

CAMP MINNIE-MICKEY
5 Character Greeting Trails
6 Pocahontas And Her Forest Friends
7 Festival Of The Lion King

DINOLAND USA
8 DINOSAUR!
9 The Boneyard
10 Tarzan™ Rocks!
11 Chester & Hester's Dino-Rama!
12 TriceraTOP Spin
13 Primeval Whirl

AFRICA
14 Harambe
15 Kilimanjaro Safaris
16 Pangani Forest Exploration Trail
17 Rafiki's Planet Watch

ASIA
18 Flights Of Wonder
19 Kali River Rapids
20 Maharajah Jungle Trek

21 Rainforest Café

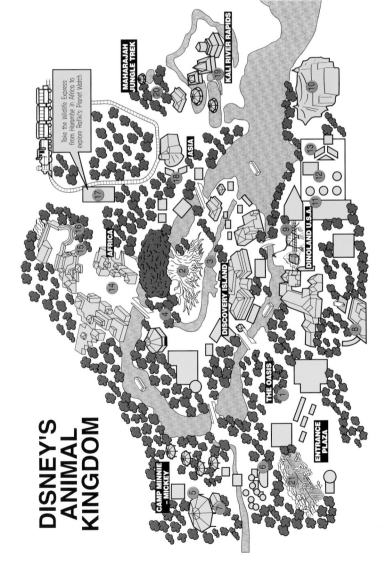

DISNEY'S ANIMAL KINGDOM

Take the Wildlife Express from Harambe in Africa to explore Rafiki's Planet Watch

Disney's Animal Kingdom Theme Park at a glance

Location	Directly off Osceola Parkway, also via World Drive and Buena Vista Drive
Size	500 acres divided into 6 'lands'
Hours	9am to 5 or 6pm
Admission	Under 3 free; 3–9 $38 (one-day ticket), $152 (4-Day Park Hopper), $197 (5-Day Park Hopper Plus); adult (10+) $48, $192, $247. Prices do not include tax.
Parking	$6
Lockers	Yes; either side of Entrance Plaza; $7 ($2 refundable)
Pushchairs	$8 and $15 ($1 refundable) at Garden Gate Gifts, through entrance on right
Wheelchairs	$8 ($1 refund) and $40 ($10 refund); with pushchairs
Top Attractions	DINOSAUR!, Kilimanjaro Safaris, It's Tough to Be a Bug!, Kali River Rapids, Festival of the Lion King
Don't Miss	Pangani Forest Exploration Trail, Maharajah Jungle Trek, Conservation Station, dining at Rainforest Café

Hidden Costs	**Meals**	Burger, chips and coke $7.48
	Kids' meal	$3.79
	T-shirts	$19–32
	Souvenirs	$1.99–275
	Sundries	Caricature drawings $15–28

If you arrive early (which is advisable), you can walk up to the Entrance Plaza. Otherwise, the usual tram system will take you in, so make a note of the area in which you park (e.g. Unicorn, row 67). The Plaza is overlooked by the mountainous **Rainforest Café,** with its 65-ft waterfall, which is a must for an early lunch or dinner (rarely busy). With Orlando so hot through the summer months, you need to be here as early as possible to see the animals before they seek shade.

For the early birds, here is your best plan of campaign. Once through the gates, animal lovers should head first for Kilimanjaro Safaris, through the Oasis, Discovery Island and into Africa. After the Safari, go straight to Pangani Forest Exploration Trail and you will have experienced two of the park's best animal encounters. Alternatively, thrill-seekers should turn right in Discovery Island for DinoLand USA, where the DINOSAUR! ride (formerly Countdown to Extinction) is the big attraction. With that one safely

BRIT TIP: The early start is especially advised for Kilimanjaro Safaris. You will see far more in the first few hours of the day than during the afternoon.

under your belt before the serious crowds arrive, head back through the Island to Asia and Kali River Rapids raft ride, followed by the scenic Maharajah Jungle Trek. The best combination for the first arrivals is to get a FASTPASS (FP) for DINOSAUR! then head straight for Kilimanjaro Safaris, and, once you have done that (and depending on your FP time), either do your DINOSAUR! ride (followed by a Kali River Rapids FP) or go straight to the Rapids. Check your show schedule for the *Legend of The Lion King* and try to catch one of the first two performances as the later ones draw sizeable queues. The 'wait time' board at the entrance to Discovery Island is also helpful.

Right, those are your main tactics, here is the full rundown.

The Oasis

The Oasis Tropical Garden is a gentle, walk-through introduction to the park, a rocky, tree-covered area featuring several animal habitats, studded with streams, waterfalls and lush plant life. Here you will meet miniature deer, macaws, parrots, iguanas, sloths and tree kangaroos in a wonderfully understated environment that leads you across a stone bridge to the main open park area. AAA.

Discovery Island

This hugely colourful 'village' is the hub of the park. Its theme is a tropical artists' colony, with animal-inspired artwork everywhere, four main shops and two eateries.

The Tree of Life: this 145-ft high arboreal edifice is the park centrepiece, an awesome creation that seems to give off a different perspective from wherever you view it. The 'trunk' and 'roots' are covered in 325 animal carvings representing the Circle of Life, from the dolphin to the lion. Trails lead round the tree, interspersed with more natural animal habitats that showcase flamingos, otters, ring-tailed lemurs, macaws, axis deer, cranes, storks, ducks and tortoises. For statistics lovers, the tree canopy spreads 160ft, the trunk is 50ft wide and the roots spread out 170ft in diameter. There are 103,000 leaves (all attached by hand) on more than 8,000 branches! AAAA.

It's Tough to Be a Bug!: winding down among the Tree's roots brings you 'underground' to a 430-seat theatre and another example of Disney's artistry in 3-D films and special effects. This hysterically funny 10-minute show, in the company of Flick from the Disney/Pixar hit film *A Bug's Life*, is a homage to 80% of the animal world, featuring grasshoppers, beetles, spiders, stink bugs and termites (beware the 'acid' spray!) as well as a number of tricks I couldn't possibly reveal. Sit towards the back in the middle of a row (allow a good number of people in first as the rows are filled up from the far side) to get the best of the 3-D effects. Queues build up from midday onwards, but they do move quite steadily. Don't miss the 'forthcoming attractions' posters in the foyer for some excruciating bug puns on well-known films. AAAAA (FP).

> BRIT TIP: The dark, special effects and creepy-crawlies often scare young ones in this show.

Shopping is at its best here, with a huge range of merchandise, souvenirs and gifts (notably in **Disney Outfitters** and **Island Mercantile**), while the two counter-service restaurants, **Pizzafari** and **Flame Tree Barbecue,** are both good choices. Indeed, provided it is not too hot, the Flame Tree is a relaxing and picturesque option, set among some pretty gardens, pools and fountains on the edge of Discovery River.

Camp Minnie-Mickey

A woodland retreat featuring gently winding paths and more of Disney's clever scenery – the benches, lighting and the gurgling stream, with Donald Duck and his nephews hiking down the side, that develops into a series of kid-friendly squirt fountains.

Character Greeting Trails: here, four trails lead to a series of jungle encounters with Disney characters like Mickey and Minnie (naturally), Winnie the Pooh and Tigger, Chip 'n Dale, Baloo and King Louie, Timon and Rafiki. AAAAA (for kids).

Pocahontas and Her Forest Friends: based on characters from the Disney film *Pocahontas*, this 15-minute show sees various animals – racoons, rabbits, cranes, a skunk, armadillo and porcupine – interacting with the central actress and Mother Willow in the question of 'Who can save the forest?' It doesn't seem to do much for small children, there is not much shade in summer and it is standing room only once the 350 seats have been filled. AAA.

The amazing Festival of the Lion King

Festival of the Lion King: not to be missed, this high-powered 40-minute production brings the hit film to life in spectacular fashion with giant moving stages, huge animated figures, singers, dancers, acrobats and stilt-walkers. All the well-known songs are given an airing in a coruscation of colour and sound, and it serves to underline the quality Disney brings to live shows. This is matched only by its popularity – people begin queuing 30 minutes in advance for the 1,000-seater theatre, so try to take in one of the earlier shows of the day. AAAAA.

DinoLand USA

Rather at odds with the natural theming of the rest of the park, DinoLand USA is a full-scale palaeontology exercise, with this mock 'town' taken over by a university fossil dig. Energetically tongue-in-cheek (the 'students' who work in the area have the motto 'Been there, dug that', while you enter under a mock brachiosaurus skeleton, the 'Oldengate Bridge' – groan!), it still features some glimpses into dinosaur research and artefacts.

Some of the cast at Disney's Animal Kingdom Theme Park

© Disney

Primeval Whirl

DINOSAUR!: this was renamed after Disney's big animated film and its original fast, jerky ride has been toned down a little for a more family-friendly experience (although the dinosaur menace is still too scary for many children). It is a wonderfully realistic journey back to the end of the Cretaceous period and the giant meteor that put paid to dinosaur life. You enter the high-tech Dino Institute, 'a discovery center and research lab dedicated to uncovering the mysteries of the past', for a multimedia show of dino history that leads to a briefing room for your 'mission' 65 million years in the past to view Cretaceous life.

> BRIT TIP: Try to ride at the front left of your Time Rover car for maximum effect of the twists and turns and the dinosaur menace.

However, one of the Institute's scientists 'hijacks' your journey for his own project, to capture a dinosaur before the fateful meteor's arrival, and you go careering back to a prehistoric jungle in your 12-passenger Time Rover. The threat of a carnivorous carnotaurus and the impending doom of the meteor add

up to a breathtaking whiz through a stunning environment. You will need to ride it at least twice to appreciate all the clever detail, but queues build up quickly, so go either first thing or late in the day. Restrictions: 3ft 4in. TTTT plus AAAA (FP).

The Boneyard: a hugely imaginative adventure playground, it offers kids the chance to slip, slide and climb through the 'fossilised' remains of triceratops and brontosaurs, explore caves, dig for bones and splash through a mini-waterfall. The amusing signage will go over the heads of most kids, but it is ideal for parents to let their young 'uns loose for up to an hour (although not just after the neighbouring Tarzan show has finished). TTTT (kids only).

Tarzan™ Rocks!: and he really does. This amazing show is basically a 30-minute rock concert showcasing the songs from the animated film, with special effects provided by dancers, acrobats and roller bladers, all in wonderful costumes and superbly choreographed. Tarzan and Jane make only a brief appearance, and then mainly as acrobats (ladies – no staring at that loincloth!). Its loud, high-energy style may not be

Chester and Hester's Dino-Rama!

© Disney

everyone's cup of tea (especially for sensitive young ears) but it is visually stunning and the quality of the performers leaves you gasping. AAAA.

Chester & Hester's Dino-Rama!: this new mini-land of rides, fairground games and stalls opened as part of the *100 Years of Magic* festivities and adds a rather garish element to DinoLand USA. It's main icon is a towering Concretosaurus (!), and it is designed to have a quirky, tongue-in-cheek style reminiscent of 1950s' American roadside attractions. The top rides are:

TriceraTOP Spin: another version of the Dumbo/Aladdin rides in the *Magic Kingdom Park*, a flying, twirling, spinning top bounces you around, up and down (watch for the surprise dino appearance at the top!). AA (or TTTT for under 5s).

Primeval Whirl: coaster fans will definitely get a laugh out of this wacky offering that sends its riders through a maze of curves, hills and (quite sharp) drops that make it seem much faster than it actually is. It is basically a fairground lampoon of the DINOSAUR! ride, a mock journey 'Way back' in time, with plenty of cartoon frippery. The extra fun is provided by the cars being free-spinning, which means an extra, unpredictable element to each 3-minute ride (plunging through the jaws of a skeleton dino at one point!). The queuing area alone is a riot of visual gags, but the ride itself is not recommended for anyone with back or neck problems (especially neck problems). Height restriction 4ft. TTTT (FP).

There are then six fairground-type games (each costing $2 extra) to tempt you into trying to win a large cuddly dinosaur, all with the larger-than-life Dino-Rama trademark. Dining options include the **Restaurantosaurus,** counter-service burgers and hot dogs (presented by McDonald's, so you get McDonald's

fries, Chicken McNuggets and Happy Meals but no Big Macs) and a snack bar, while shopping is centred on the huge **Chester and Hester's Dino-Rama! – Dinosaur Treasures,** the 'Fossiliferous Gift Store' with groan-inducing slogans like Merchandise of Extinction, Prehistoric Prices and Last Stop for 65 Million Years!

Africa

The largest land in the park, it re-creates magnificently the forests, grasslands and rocky homelands of equatorial Africa's most fascinating residents in a richly landscaped setting that is part rundown port town setting and part endless savannah. In here the outside world seems thousands of miles away and there is hardly a glimpse of this great resort anywhere (there is one, but I'm not telling!).

Harambe, a reconstruction Kenyan port village, complete with white coral walls and thatched roofs, is the starting point of your adventure. The Arab-influenced Swahili culture is depicted in the native tribal costumes and architecture. Here you will find two more shops, including the **Mombasa Marketplace/Ziwani Traders,** where you can suit up safari-style, and the counter-service **Tusker House Restaurant** for rotisserie chicken, fresh fish, salads, vegetarian sandwiches and a special African dish (a slightly healthier offering than most, but a touch expensive, I find), as well as four snack and drink bars. The splendid **Karuka Acrobats** also perform here on select days.

Kilimanjaro Safaris: the queuing area alone earns high marks for authenticity, preparing you for the sights and sounds of the 110-acre savannah beyond. You board a 32-passenger truck, with your driver/guide relaying information about the flora and fauna on view and a bush pilot overhead relaying facts and figures on the wildlife, including the dangers threatening them in the real world. Hundreds of animals are carefully spread out in various habitats, with no fences in sight – the ditches and barriers are all well concealed – as you splash through fords and cross rickety bridges, and you are likely to get a close-up of rhinos, elephants, giraffes, zebras, lions, baboons, antelope, ostriches and hippos.

BRIT TIP: The best (that is most jolting) ride is at the back of the truck, while the Safari is best avoided from midday to late afternoon when many animals take a siesta.

Halfway round, your journey becomes a race to stop elephant poachers, though the outcome is fairly obvious. Once again, the authentic nature of all you see (okay, some of the tyre 'ruts' and termite mounds are concrete and the baobab trees are fake) is quite awesome with the spread of the vegetation and the landscaping, and the only drawback is the lack of photo stops along the way (and the ride can be pretty bumpy). The animals can also roam over a wide area and disappear from view. Not recommended for expectant mothers or anyone with

back or neck problems. AAAAA (FP).

Pangani Forest Exploration Trail: as you leave the Safari you turn into an overgrown nature trail that showcases gorillas, hippos, meerkats and rare tropical birds. You wander the trail at your own pace and visit several research stations to learn more about the animals on display, including the underwater view of the hippos (check out the size of a hippo skull and those teeth!) and the savannah overlook, where giraffe and antelope graze and the amusing meerkats frolic. The walk-through aviary gives you the chance to meet the carmine bee-eater, pygmy goose, African green pigeon, ibis and brimstone canary, among others, but the real centrepiece is the silverback gorilla habitat, in fact, two of them. The family group are often just inches away from the plate-glass window, while the bachelor group further along can prove more elusive. Again, the natural aspect of the trail is breathtaking and it provides a host of photo opportunities. It is best to visit early on to see the animals at their most active (and because it quickly becomes quite crowded). AAAAA.

Rafiki's Planet Watch: the little train journey here, with its peek into some of the backstage areas, is just the preamble to the park's interactive and educational exhibits. The 3-part journey starts with **Habitat Habit!,** where you can see cotton-top tamarins and learn how conservation begins in your own back garden. **Conservation Station** is next up, a series of exhibits, shows and hands-on information stations about the environment and its ecological dangers, aimed primarily at children. Look out for *Song of the Rain Forest*, the story of endangered species at the **Mermaid Tales Theater** and the Eco-Heroes trying to redress the balance (who can be quizzed on screen), then take a self-guided tour of the park's backstage areas such as

5

Kilimanjaro Safaris

the veterinary treatment centre, the hatchery and neo-natal care. You can easily spend an hour absorbing the environmental message here, along with that of Disney's Wildlife Conservation Fund. Plus, youngsters can also meet Rafiki and some of his animal chums at various times. The **Affection Section,** a petting zoo of lambs, goats, donkeys, sheep and guinea pigs, completes the Planet Watch line-up.

Asia

The final land of the park is elaborately themed as the gateway to the imaginary south-east Asian city of Anandapur, with temples, ruined forts, landscape and wildlife.

Flights of Wonder: another wildlife show, this portrays the talents and traits of a host of birds, built into a production of mythical proportions, as a treasure-seeking student encounters Phoenix, the birds' guardian, in a crumbling, fortified town. Vultures, eagles, toucans, macaws and many other feathered friends take a bow as Phoenix reveals the treasures of the avian world. Unfortunately, the Caravan Stage is not air-conditioned and is fiendishly hot in summer, so be warned. AAA.

Kali River Rapids: part thrill-ride, part scenic journey, this

bouncy, raft-ride journey will get you pretty wet (not great for early morning in winter unless you bring a change of clothes). It starts out in tropical forest territory before launching into a scene of logging devastation, warning of the dangers of clear-cut burning. Your raft then plunges down a waterfall (and one unlucky soul – usually the rider with their back to the drop – gets seriously damp) before you finish the journey more sedately, albeit with a few more watery encounters. Queues can be quite long through the main part of the day, so make good use of the FastPass here, and you will probably want to ride at least twice to appreciate all the clever detail. Restrictions: 3ft 6in (although a few rafts have adult-and-child seats allowing smaller children to ride). TTT (plus AAAA) (FP).

Maharajah Jungle Trek: Asia's version of the Pangani Forest Trail, this is another picturesque walk-through journey past decaying temple ruins and various animal encounters. Playful gibbons, tapirs, Komodo dragons and a bat enclosure (including the flying fox-bat, the world's largest variety) lead up to the main viewing area, the 5-acre Tiger Range, which includes a pool and fountains and is a popular playground early in the day for these magnificent big cats. An antelope enclosure and walk-through aviary complete this breathtaking trek (which rarely draws heavy crowds) in fine style. AAAAA.

Kali River Rapids

Finally, returning to the front entrance gives you the chance to sample or just visit (and shop at) the **Rainforest Café,** the second on Disney property. If you haven't seen the one at *Downtown Disney* Marketplace, you should definitely call in to witness the amazing jungle interior with its audio-animatronic animals, waterfalls, thunderstorms and aquariums. A 3-course meal will set you back about $28 (kids' meals at $6.99), but the setting alone is worth it and the food is above average.

Jammin' Jungle Parade

Following on from the park's *100 Years of Magic* offerings is the new daily (about 4pm) parade, a tour de force called **Mickey's Jammin' Jungle Parade.** Here, the Imagineers have created a series of fanciful, individually designed 'Expedition Rovers' that give various Disney characters the chance to celebrate all the animals who live here. The parade is enhanced by stilt-walkers, puppets, mobile sculptures, Disney characters and different 'party animals', plus live percussionists atop some of the sculptures, as it snakes down a narrow path from Harambe, around Discovery Island and back. Set to a memorable musical backing, it sounds truly delightful, while 25 park guests are chosen to take part each day, travelling on the back of amusingly designed rickshaws which follow each of the character jeeps.

Finally, for a behind-the-scenes look at the park, the **Backstage Safari** is a wonderful 3-hour journey into the handling and care of all the animals ($65, not for under 16s. Call 407 939 8687 to book).

Mickey's toe-tapping Jammin' Jungle Parade

© Disney

DISNEY'S ANIMAL KINGDOM PARK with children

Here is our general guide to the rides which appeal to the different children's ages in this park:

Under 5s
Character Greetings Trails, Festival of the Lion King, Discovery Island Trails, Kilimanjaro Safaris, Pangani Forest Exploration Trail, Affection Section, Maharajah Jungle Trek, TriceraTOP Spin, The Boneyard.

5–8s
All the above, plus Pocahontas and Her Forest Friends, Habitat Habit!, Conservation Station, Kali River Rapids, Flights of Wonder and It's Tough To Be a Bug! and DINOSAUR! with parental discretion.

9–12s
All the above, plus Primeval Whirl and Tarzan™ Rocks!

Over 12s
Festival of the Lion King, It's Tough To Be a Bug!, Kilimanjaro Safaris, Pangani Forest Exploration Trail, Kali River Rapids, Maharajah Jungle Trek, Flights of Wonder, DINOSAUR!, Tarzan™ Rocks!, Primeval Whirl.

Walt Disney World Resort in Florida at Christmas

If you can visit prior to the seriously busy days from just before Christmas Day to New Year's Day, you get the benefit of all the added decorations and atmosphere and none of the overwhelming crowds. Each of the parks takes on a festive character, with the addition of artistic artificial snow, Christmas lights and a huge, magnificently decorated fir tree.

Magic Kingdom Park features an eye-popping extravaganza of exterior house decorations on the Backlot Tour with over 2 million lights! Donated by the Osborne family, they open up as a walk-through attraction every evening. Main Street is transformed into a Christmas extravaganza, with a 60-ft tree dominating the scene. The unmissable **Mickey's Very Merry Xmas Parade** replaces the main 3pm parade in December and is a positive delight for its lively music and eye-catching costumes. Another seasonal extra is the lively *Twas the Night before Xmas* show at the Galaxy Palace Theater.

Epcot is the jewel in the Christmas crown, though, with two outstanding features. At 6pm, the daily Christmas tree lighting ceremony is quite breathtaking as the rest of the park lights go out and then the World Showcase bridge and the tree itself are illuminated in dramatic stages to some grand musical accompaniment. The nightly **Candlelight Processional** also draws a crowd, with a guest narrator telling the story of Christmas to the backdrop of a large choir and elaborate candle parade. It is tasteful, dramatic and eye-catching, but you should arrive early as people start queuing almost 3 HOURS in advance. However, you can get a reserved seat if you buy the *Candlelight Processional Dinner Package* (variously $25.95, $32.95 or $39.95, plus tax, depending on which World Showcase restaurant you select, and $10.95 for children 3–11), by calling well in advance on 407 939 3463.

Five More of the Best
(or, Expanding Orlando's Universe)

It is time to leave the wonderful world of Disney and venture out into the rest of central Florida's great attractions. And, believe me, there is still a terrific amount in store.

For a start, they don't come much more ambitious than Universal Orlando. The area that used to consist of just the one theme park, Universal Studios Florida®, is fast developing into a fully fledged resort of similar scope to Disney's. A second dynamic theme park, Universal's Islands of Adventure, opened in 1999, hot on the heels of the 30-acre CityWalk entertainment district. The first resort hotel, the Portofino Bay, made its debut in 1999, followed by the Hard Rock Hotel in 2000, and the Royal Pacific Resort in 2002.

A waterway network connects the hotels to the CityWalk hub, while the multi-storey car parks, handling more than 20,000 vehicles, have done away with the need for any other transport system, and it is quite convenient to move from park to park.

The marketing tie-up with SeaWorld and Busch Gardens, plus their purchase of the Wet 'n Wild water park, has also proved a success, with the 14-day Orlando FlexTickets giving excellent value. The opening of Islands of Adventure has added 2- and 3-Day Tickets (which include a CityWalk Party Pass) allowing movement between both Universal parks. They have also introduced their **Universal Express** system for most of their rides. Similar to Disney's FastPass, it allows all park guests to 'reserve' one ride at a time and then another once you have done that attraction, and so on. You just present your park entry ticket at the Distribution Center next to the Universal Express ride or show of your choice, then return at the allotted time for what should be no more than a 15-minute wait (instead of an hour or more at peak periods). Universal hotel guests also benefit from Express ride priority ALL DAY by producing their room key.

Additionally, many rides have **Single Rider** queues which can save time if you are the only one in your group who wants to do, say, Dr Doom's Fearfall, or if you don't mind being split up. Once again, any height restriction is noted and Universal Express attractions are indicated by UE.

> BRIT TIP: Reader Tom Burton advises, 'If you buy an Orlando FlexTicket giving you 14 consecutive days at Universal, etc, try going to their parks a couple of times in the evenings only. There are virtually no queues this late in the day and I went on The Hulk Coaster five times in an hour!'

Universal Studios Florida®

Universal opened its Florida park in June 1990 (its original Los Angeles site has been open to the public since before World War Two) and quickly became a serious competitor to Disney. For the visitor, it means a consistently high standard and good value in everything on offer (although the choice is beginning to be utterly bewildering!). Also, if you have already been to the LA Universal Studios, this one is better.

The obvious question to ask here is if you need to do *Disney-MGM Studios* as well as Universal, and the answer is an emphatic YES! Universal is a very different kettle of fish to Disney, with a more in-your-face style of entertainment that goes down well with older kids and younger adults. Younger children are also well catered for in Woody Woodpecker's KidZone. Universal can require more than a full day in

Universal Studios Florida® at a glance

Location	Off Exits 75A and 74B from I-4; Universal Boulevard and Kirkman Road
Size	110 acres in 7 themed areas
Hours	9am–7pm off peak; 9am–10pm high season (Washington's birthday, Easter, summer holidays, Thanksgiving, Christmas)
Admission	Under 3 free; 3–9 $40.95 (1-Day Ticket), $81.95 (2-Day Ticket), $96.95 (3-Day Ticket), $134.95 (4-Park FlexTicket), $164.95 (5-Park FlexTicket); adult (10+) $49.95, $94.95, $109.95, $169.95, $202.95; Universal Bonus Pass (5 consecutive days, online sales only) $76.95 and $89.95.
Parking	$8
Lockers	Yes; immediately to left in Front Lot; $5 ($2 refundable)
Pushchairs	$8 and $14, next to locker hire
Wheelchairs	$7 and $35, same location as pushchairs
Top Attractions	Men In Black, Jaws, Back to the Future, ET, Earthquake, Kongfrontation, Terminator 2
Don't Miss	Curious George Playground (for kids), The Blues Brothers

Hidden Costs		
	Meals	Burger, chips and coke $7.48 3-course dinner $25 (Finnigan's)
	Kids' meal	$4.95–6.95 (Finnigan's and Lombard's Landing only)
	T-shirts	$17–30
	Souvenirs	$1.50–199
	Sundries	Portrait studio photo $24.95 and $26.95

PRODUCTION CENTRAL
1 Guest Services
2 Shrek 4-D (opening 2003)
3 Nickelodeon Studio Tour
4 Jimmy Neutron: Boy Genius (opening 2003)

NEW YORK
5 Twister
6 Kongfrontation
7 The Blues Brothers
8 Finnegan's Bar and Grill

SAN FRANCISCO/AMITY
9 Earthquake – The Big One
10 Jaws
11 All-New Beetlejuice Revue
12 The Wild, Wild, Wild West Stunt Show
13 Lombard's Landing

EXPO CENTER
14 Back To The Future… The Ride
15 Men In Black: Alien Attack

WOODY WOODPECKER'S KIDZONE
16 Animal Planet Live!
17 Fievel's Playland
18 A Day In The Park With Barney
19 ET Adventure
20 Woody Woodpecker's Nuthouse Coaster
21 Curious George Playground

HOLLYWOOD
22 Universal's Horror Make-Up Show
23 Terminator 2: 3-D
24 Lucy: A Tribute

UNIVERSAL STUDIOS FLORIDA

6

high season. As with Disney's parks, the strategies for a successful visit are the same. Arrive EARLY (up to 30 minutes before the official opening time), do the big rides first, avoid main meal times, and step out for a few hours in the afternoon (try shopping or dining at CityWalk) if it gets too crowded.

Location

Universal Studios Florida® is sub-divided into six main areas, set around a huge, manmade lagoon, but there are no great distinguishing features, so keep the map handy to steer yourself around. The main entrance is found just off the new exit to Interstate 4 (I-4) or by the Universal Boulevard link from International Drive (I-Drive) by Wet 'n Wild. Parking costs $8 in their massive multi-storey car park and there is quite a walk (with some moving walkways) to the front gates.

Once through with the madding crowd, your best bet is to turn right on to Rodeo Drive, along Hollywood Boulevard and Sunset Boulevard and into World Expo for Back To The Future... The Ride and Men In Black. From there, head across the bridge to Jaws, then go back along the Embarcadero for Earthquake and into New York for Twister and Kongfrontation. This will get most of the main rides under your belt before the crowds build up, and you can then take it a bit easier by putting your feet up for a while at one of the shows or taking advantage of Universal Express. Alternatively, try to be among the early birds flocking to the blockbuster Terminator show on Hollywood Boulevard to avoid the queues that build up here, then use Universal Express for the likes of Back To The Future and Men In Black.

Additionally, two major new attractions open in the Production Central area in spring 2003 that could well become major crowd draws, so if the **Shrek 4-D** show and the **Jimmy Neutron: Boy Genius** (simulator) rocket ride appeal to you, head here first.

Here's a full blow-by-blow guide to the Studios. For the rundown on CityWalk, see Chapter 9.

Production Central

Coming straight through the gates brings you immediately into the administrative centre, with a couple of large gift stores (have a look at these in mid afternoon) plus The Fudge Shoppe. Call at **Guest Services** here for guides for disabled visitors, TDD and assisted listening devices, and to make restaurant bookings. If you are here early, you can sign up to be in the audience for one of Universal's TV shows at the **Studio Audience Center**. First aid is available here (and on Canal Street between New York and San Francisco), while there are facilities for nursing mothers at Family Services by the bank through the gates on the right. Coming to the top of Plaza of the Stars brings you eventually to the business end of the park.

Shrek 4-D: replacing the old Alfred Hitchcock Theater in spring 2003 will be one of Universal's newest features, a '4-D' film show with the original cast of the hilarious Oscar-winning film *Shrek*. Continuing the saga of the swamp-dwelling 700lb ogre, this 15-minute show should be a riot of both 3-D screen-induced hilarity and new levels in live special effects all around you as Shrek (Michael Myers) goes on honeymoon with Princess Fiona (Cameron Diaz) and persistent companion Donkey (Eddie Murphy). There will also be a 5-minute pre-show with the 'ghost' of Lord Farquaad in one of his dreaded dungeons! AAAAA (expected; UE).

Nickelodeon Studios: a lot of this American kids' TV series will be lost on us (although it's on satellite TV in Britain) as visitors go behind the scenes into the production set. Most kids will welcome the chance to get gunged in green slime by the Gakmeister! And they'll love the restrooms which feature green slime 'soap' and sirens when you flush the loo. Long queues build up quickly. AAAA (for children only) (UE).

Jimmy Neutron: Boy Genius: also scheduled to open in spring 2003, this will be the latest of Universal's scintillating simulator rides, with the cartoon star and his amazing inventions (many of which go awry with suitably amusing results!). Replacing the Funtastic World of Hanna-Barbera, it will also feature various Nickelodeon characters like the Rugrats and Wild Thornberrys on a wild rocket ride with state-of-the-art technology and computer graphics. Guests are invited to take part in Jimmy's latest invention only to learn the sinister (but hapless) Yokians are again threatening Earth, and it is up to YOU to save the day. So rev up for a real gadget-filled blast of a ride that promises to be truly comical, in a thrilling kind of way. There is sure to be a height restriction, though, plus warnings for expectant mothers and anyone with heart, neck or back problems. TTTT (expected; UE).

The main eating outlet here is the magnificently themed **Monsters Café,** specialising in salads, pasta, pizza and chicken. The counter-service area is done up like Frankenstein's lab, with the dining areas sub-divided into Swamp, Space, Crypt and Mansion Dining, all to the accompaniment of old black and white horror film clips on the many video screens. There is also monster face painting for kids ($8–$17). Shopping includes the **Bates Motel Gift Shop** and the main **Universal Studios Store**.

New York

From Production Central you head on to New York and some great scene-setting in the architecture and detail of the buildings and streets. It's far too clean to be authentic, but the façades are first class.

Twister: this experience, based on the hit film, brings audiences 'up close and personal' with the awesome destructive forces of a tornado. The 5-storey terror will shatter everything in its path (okay, so it's pretty tame compared with the real thing), building up to a shattering crescendo of destruction (watch out for the flying cow!). The noise is stunning, but it's a bit much for young children (parental discretion advised for under 13s). The pre-show area is almost a work of art but, unless you can get here early, save this for late in the day. TTT (UE)

Kongfrontation: Universal's engineers have really gone to town on this attraction, a full-scale encounter with the giant ape on a replica of the Roosevelt Island tram. The startlingly real special effects (King Kong even has banana breath!) and clever spiel of your tram driver all add up to a breathtaking experience that will have you convinced you have met King Kong and lived to tell the tale. It's only a 5-minute ride and queues regularly top an hour, so going early (or using UE) is the best plan here. Restrictions: 4ft (but smaller children can ride with an adult). TTTT (UE).

The Blues Brothers: fans of the film will not want to miss this live show as Jake and Elwood Blues (well, pretty good doubles, anyway) put on a stormin' performance on New York's Delancey Street 4–5 times a day. They cruise up in their Bluesmobile and go through a selection of the film's hits before heading off into the sunset, stopping

6

The 5-storey tornado at Twister

only to sign a few autographs. Terrific entertainment. AAAA.

For dining, you have the choice of two contrasting restaurants. **Finnegan's Bar and Grill** offers the likes of shepherd's pie, fish and chips, corned beef and cabbage along with more traditional New York fare like prime rib, burgers, fries and a good range of beers, as well as live Irish-tinged entertainment and Happy Hour from 3–5pm (half-price beer and wine). **Louie's Italian Restaurant** has counter-service pizza and pasta, Italian ice cream and tiramisu. For shops you have **Safari Outfitters Ltd** (and the chance to have your picture taken in the grip of King Kong!), **The Aftermath** for Twister souvenirs, and **Second Hand Rose** for Coca-Cola™ merchandise and sweets. New York also boasts a noisy – and therefore kid-friendly – amusement arcade.

San Francisco/Amity

Crossing Canal Street brings you all the way across America to San Francisco/Amity and two of the biggest queues in the park.

Earthquake – The Big One: this 3-part adventure has them lining up from first thing in the morning until late. Go behind the scenes first to two stage sets where, with audience help, some of the special effects of the Charlton Heston film are explained. Then you enter the Bay Area Rapid Transit underground and arrive in the middle of a full-scale earthquake that shakes you to your boots. Tremble as the walls and ceilings collapse, trains collide, cars fall in on you and fire erupts all around, followed by a seeming tidal wave of water. It's not for the faint-hearted (or small children), while those who have bad backs or necks, or are pregnant, are advised not to ride. Restrictions: 4ft (unless accompanied by an adult, with parental discretion). TTTT (UE).

Jaws: the technological wizardry alone will leave you gasping here, where queues of more than an hour are commonplace. The man-made lagoon holds 5 million gallons of water; nearly 2,000 miles of wire run throughout the 7-acre site, which required 10,000 cubic yards of concrete and 7,500 tons of steel; and the 32-ft monster shark attacks with a thrust equal to a Boeing 727 jet engine! Yes, this is no ordinary ride,

Back to the Future

Men In Black – Alien Attack

and its 6-minute duration will seem a lot longer as your hapless boat guide steers you through an ever more spectacular series of stunts, explosions and menace from the Great White. Yes, of course it's only a model, but I defy you not to be impressed – and just a little scared! TTTT (UE).

All-New Beetlejuice Revue: *Disney-MGM Studios* has *Beauty and the Beast* and *The Little Mermaid*, Universal goes for *Dracula*, *Frankenstein*, *The Wolfman* and *Frankenstein's Bride* in this recently revamped, 20-minute shock 'n roll extravaganza, compered by Beetlejuice himself. It eschews the twee prettiness of Disney's attractions yet still comes up with a fun family show with lots of laughs, as the 'Graveyard' characters perform versions of hits like *Wild Thing* and *Great Balls Of Fire* in a spectacular setting. AAAA (UE).

The Wild, Wild, Wild West Stunt Show: corny gags, fistfights, explosions, high-level falls and dramatic shootouts all add up to 15 minutes of rootin', tootin' Wild West adventure, Universal Studios

style. A hilarious finale and some very loud bangs (not good for small children) are accompanied by large crowds, but the auditorium seats almost 2,000 so there is usually no serious queuing here (provided you arrive at least 15 minutes early). AAAA (UE).

San Francisco also has the park's best dining choice, with **Lombard's Landing** the highlight (reservations accepted). Great seafood, pasta and sandwiches are accompanied by a good view over the main lagoon, and there's a separate pastry shop for desserts and coffee. **Richter's Burger Co** offers a few interesting burger variations, while the **Midway Grill** serves smoked and Italian sausage hoagies. For a quick snack, **Chez Alcatraz** provides shrimp cocktails, clam chowder and speciality hot sandwiches, while **Boardwalk Snacks** does corn dogs, chicken fingers, candy floss and frozen yoghurt.

For shopping, try **Quint's Nautical Treasures** (seaside gifts) and **Shaiken's Souvenirs** for more upmarket mementoes and apparel. The added attraction of this area is a boardwalk of fairground games (which cost an extra few dollars to play), including a Guess Your Weight stall which usually attracts a good crowd for the fun patter of the person in charge.

The Terminator 2 experience

6

Expo Center

Crossing the bridge from Amity brings you to Expo Center and the park's other 5-star thrill attraction.

Back To The Future… The Ride: simulators just do not come more realistic than this journey through space and time in Dr Emmit Brown's time-travelling De Lorean. The queues are immense, but a lot of the time is taken up by some attention-grabbing pre-ride info on the TV screens above your head. Once you reach the front, there is still more information to digest and clever surroundings to convince you of the scientific nature of it all. Then it's into your time-travelling car and off in hot pursuit of baddie Biff, who has stolen another time-car. The huge, wraparound screen and violent movements of your vehicle bring the realism of the ride to a peak, and it all adds up to a huge experience. Restrictions: 3ft 4in. TTTTT (UE).

Men In Black – Alien Attack: new in 2000 and huge fun (especially for kids) is this combination thrill/scenic ride which takes up where the original hit film, starring Will Smith, left off. Visitors are secretly introduced to the MIB Institute in a wonderfully inventive mock-futuristic setting and enrolled as trainees for a battle around the streets of New York with a horde of escaped aliens. Your 6-person car is equipped with laser zappers for an interactive shoot-out that is like a real-life arcade game, as the aliens can also shoot back and send your car spinning out of control. The finale features a close encounter with a 30-ft bug that is all mouth – will you survive? Only your collective shooting skills can save the day, and there are numerous ride variations according to your accuracy as each rider's score is totted up. Will Smith and Rip Torn are your on-screen hosts, and Will returns at the end to reveal if your score makes you Galaxy Defenders, Cosmically Average or Bug Bait! Fast, frantic and a bit confusing, this will have you coming back for more until you can score more than 250,000 (Defender status). Restrictions: 3ft 6in. TTTT. (Beat my best score – 265,550)

The **International Food and Film Festival** here is a food court-style indoor diner offering burgers, sandwiches, meatball subs and salads (and in air-conditioned comfort).

Woody Woodpecker's KidZone

Animal Planet Live!: new in 2001, replacing the old Animal Actors Stage, is this highly amusing show version of the Animal Planet satellite TV channel. Several children are invited to take part as your hosts and present a series of unlikely feats and stunts featuring a whole range of fairly tame wildlife, from a racoon to a python, and on to domestic cats and dogs. Many have been rescued from animal shelters and have gone on to feature in films before finding a home at Universal. It's a big theatre, too, and is handy for avoiding the afternoon crowds. AAAA (UE).

BRIT TIP: Along the lagoon in the World Expo/ KidZone area is Central Park, a quiet area where you can escape the theme park whirl for a while.

Fievel's Playland: strictly for kids but also a big hit with parents for taking them off their hands for a good half-hour or so, this playground, based on the enlarged world of the cartoon mouse, offers youngsters the chance to bounce under a 1,000-gallon hat, crawl through a giant cowboy boot, climb a 30-ft spider's web and shoot the rapids (a 200-ft water slide) in Fievel's sardine can. TTTT (young 'uns only!).

A Day in the Park with Barney: again, this is strictly for the younger set (ages 2–5) as the purple dinosaur from the popular kids' TV show is brought to Super-Dee-Duper life on stage in a 65,000 sq-ft arena that features a pre-show before the 15-minute main event, plus an interactive post-show area. Guaranteed to make parents cringe, but the youngsters love it. Note: check out the amazing state-of-the-art restrooms! AAA (AAAAA under 5s) (UE).

ET Adventure: this is as glorious as scenic rides come, with a picturesque queuing area like the pine woods from the film and then a spectacular leap on the trademark flying bicycles to save ET's home planet. Steven Spielberg (Universal's creative consultant) has added some special effects and characters, and the whole experience is a huge hit with all the family (especially for your individual ET greeting at the end!). Queues here touch 2 hours at peak periods, so try to do this one either early or late (or, again, through UE). There is a height restriction of 4ft, but smaller children can ride with parents. AAAAA (UE).

Woody Woodpecker's Nuthouse Coaster: anchoring this excellent under 10s' adventure land is this child-sized but still quite racy roller-coaster. The brilliant red 800-ft track reaches only 28-ft high and 22mph, but it seems the real deal to youngsters. There is still a height restriction of 3ft, however, for the ride. TTTT (juniors only).

Curious George Goes to Town: this American children's book character means little to me, but kids of all ages just love this amazing adventure playground with its huge range of activities – and plenty of opportunities to get wet (bring swimsuits or a change of clothing for them here). It combines toddler play, water-based play stations and a hands-on interactive ball area, and adds up to a real boon to harassed parents. The town theme, on which Curious George has wreaked havoc, includes buildings to climb, pumps and hoses to spray water, a ball factory in which to shoot, dump and blast thousands of foam balls and – the tour de force – two 500-gallon buckets of water on the clock tower balconies which regularly dump their contents in spectacular fashion on the street below. TTTTT (under 12s).

Curious George himself roams the KidZone from time to time. For snacks, **Animal Crackers** offers hotdogs, chicken fingers, smoked sausage hoagies and frozen yoghurt. Shop at the **Cartoon Store, Barney Store** or **ET's Toy Closet** and **Photo Spot.**

Hollywood

Finally, your circular tour of Universal brings you back towards the main entrance via **Hollywood** (where else?). Here, you'll find **Universal's Horror Make-Up Show** (not recommended for under 12s) which demonstrates some of the often amusing ways in which films have attempted to terrorise us. It's a 20-minute show, queues are rarely long and the secrets of the special effects are well worth finding out about. AAA (UE).

Terminator 2: 3-D Battle Across Time: another first-of-its-kind attraction, this is hard to describe. Part film, part show, part experience but all action, it cost a staggering $60 million to produce and is guaranteed to leave its audience stunned and awed. The

'Wow!' factor works overtime as you go through a 10-minute pre-show that represents a trip into the workshops of the Cyberdyne Systems, from the *Terminator* films, and then into a 700-seater auditorium for a 'presentation' on their latest robot creations.

Needless to say, nothing runs to plan and the audience is subjected to a mind-boggling array of (loud) special effects, including indoor pyrotechnics, real actors interacting with the screen and the audience, and a climactic 3-D film finale that takes the *Terminator* story a step further. The original cast, including Arnold Schwarzenegger and director James Cameron, all collaborated on the 12-minute movie (which, at $24 million, is some of the most expensive frame-for-frame film ever made) and the overall effect of this technological marvel is quite dazzling. However, you do need to arrive early or expect queues well in excess of an hour all day (parental discretion for under 12s). TTTTT (UE).

The last attraction (or first, depending on which way you go round the park) is **Lucy: A Tribute,** which will mean little to all but devoted fans of the late Lucille Ball and her 1960s' TV comedy *The Lucy Show*. Classic shows, home movies, costumes and scripts are all paraded

for close viewing, but youngsters will find it tedious. AA.

If you haven't eaten by now there is a choice of four contrasting but highly enjoyable eateries. **Mel's Drive-In,** a re-creation from the film *American Graffiti*, serves all manner of burgers, hot dogs and milkshakes, while **Café La Bamba,** offers rotisserie chicken, ribs, salad and burgers, plus margaritas and beer (Happy Hour 3–5pm). **Schwab's Pharmacy** provides sandwiches, old-fashioned milkshakes, sundaes and ice cream and the **Beverly Hills Boulangerie** does baked breakfast treats, pastries, juices and coffee. Shop for hats in the **Brown Derby,** for *Terminator* gifts and clothing in **Cyber Image,** for movie memorabilia (especially Lucille Ball) at **Silver Screen Collectibles** and for some of the smartest gear at **Studio Styles**.

Street Entertainment

In addition to all the set-piece action, watch out for a new series of interactive street shows around the park. Check out **The Swashbucklers,** who engage in some amusing swordplay and stunts (eventually including the guests); **Extreme Ghostbusters: The Great Fright Way,** starring

Curious George Goes to Town

Beetlejuice and the Ghostbusters in a clever song and dance act; **Lucy and Ricky,** the 'stars' of a 7-piece Latin band who insist on starting a conga line (with you, of course!); and **Sarita and Rico,** who are another over-the-top Latin duo. Then there is more entertainment with the **MIB Agents** show (enrolling YOU in a humorous screen test), the **Street Breaks** dancers, and *a capella* group **Double Date.**

Special programmes

The park also features some brilliant extra seasonal entertainment for **Mardi Gras** (a major parade, plus music, street entertainment and authentic New Orleans food each night at 6pm from mid February to April 1), as well as a major party for **New Year's Eve** and the **4th of July,** when the park gets in full fiesta mode. Note, Universal's trademark Halloween Horror Nights programme has now moved from the Studios to Islands of Adventure.

Sadly, as part of their ongoing updating process, Universal have closed down their Dynamite Nights water stunt show which used to be the evening finale and there is no news of a replacement for the central lagoon area. The Hercules and Xena show (which replaced the original Murder She Wrote Mystery Theater) has also bitten the theatrical dust and we await developments with interest, as this has left the park with a couple of 'dead' spots. And don't forget to check out their website at www.universalorlando.com for more info.

UNIVERSAL STUDIOS with children

Our guide to the rides which generally appeal to the different age groups:

Under 5s
Nickelodeon Studios, Animal Planet Live!, A Day In The Park With Barney, Curious George Goes To Town, Fievel's Playland, ET Adventure.

5–8s
Nickelodeon Studios, Animal Planet Live!, Curious George Goes To Town, Fievel's Playland, ET Adventure, Woody Woodpecker's Nuthouse Coaster, Jimmy Neutron: Boy Genius, Wild, Wild, Wild West Stunt Show, Shrek 4-D, Men In Black, plus Earthquake – The Big One and Kongfrontation (with parental discretion).

9–12s
Jimmy Neutron: Boy Genius, Shrek 4-D, Terminator 2, Twister, Kongfrontation, Earthquake – The Big One, Animal Planet Live!, Curious George Goes to Town, Woody Woodpecker's Nuthouse Coaster, Wild, Wild, Wild West Stunt Show, ET Adventure, All-New Beetlejuice Revue, Jaws, Men In Black, Back To The Future… The Ride.

Over 12s
Terminator 2, Universal's Horror Make-Up Show, Jimmy Neutron: Boy Genius, Shrek 4-D, Twister, Kongfrontation, Earthquake – The Big One, The Blues Brothers, ET Adventure, All-New Beetlejuice Revue, Jaws, Wild, Wild, Wild West Stunt Show, Men In Black, Back To The Future… The Ride.

Islands of Adventure

In May 1999, Universal's creative consultant Steven Spielberg officially opened the £1 billion Islands of Adventure, or IoA as the park is known, with the words: 'These are not just theme park rides, these are entertainment achievements beyond anything I have ever seen anywhere else in the world.'

And that's only the beginning. Here is the most complete and thrilling theme park on offer. Complete, because the park is a genuinely rounded and consistent concept that has been carried through to the full extent of its designers' aims. And thrilling because it contains more T-rides (and the first TTTTT+ ratings) per square inch than almost all the other parks combined.

It has a full range of attractions from the real adrenalin overloads to pure family entertainment. The shopping and eating opportunities are above average and it sounds good as well – with some 40 pieces of original music, you can even buy the CD of the theme park!.

Okay, so they are not really islands (the six themed 'lands' form a chain around the central lagoon), but that's the only illusion. And you get a lot for your money here, unless you have extremely timid children or under 5s, in which case the *Magic Kingdom* is still your best bet. However, Seuss Landing will keep them amused for several hours, while Camp Jurassic is a clever adventure playground for the 5–12s, but the rest of the park, with its seven 5-star thrill rides and other standout attractions, is primarily geared to kids of 8-plus, their parents and especially teenagers. There are five elements that look truly alarming (two of which produce moments of supreme

terror), but don't be put off – they all deliver immense fun. There is also great spectator value in many attractions!

If there is one ride that sums up IoA, it is the Amazing Adventures of Spider-Man, the world's first moving 3-D simulator ride. It is sure to leave you in awe of its technological wizardry and imagination, and it is the only ride I have seen where people applaud at the end!

Port of Entry

You arrive for IoA as you do for Universal Studios Florida® in the big multi-storey car parks ($8) off Universal Boulevard and either walk or ride the moving walkways into CityWalk, where you continue through to the entrance plaza (head for the 130ft-high Pharos Lighthouse).

Once through the gates, the lockers, pushchair and wheelchair hire are all immediately to your left as the **Port of Entry** opens up before you. This elaborate 'village' consists of shops and eateries, so push straight on until you hit the main lagoon. Later in the day you can return here to check out the fully themed retail experience at places like the **IoA Trading Company** and **Ocean Trader Market.** Enjoy a snack from **Spice Island Wings & Fries** or the **Croissant Moon Bakery** or chill out with a soft drink or ice cream from **Arctic Express.** Alternatively, sit down for lunch or dinner (great steak, pasta, burgers and salads) at **Confisco Grille** or grab a beverage at the **Backwater Bar** (Happy Hour 3–5pm). Above all, take a closer look at the wonderful architecture, which borrows from Middle East, Far East and African themes and includes odd

Islands of Adventure at a glance

Location	Off Exits 75A and 74B from I-4; Universal Boulevard and Kirkman Road
Size	110 acres in 6 'islands'
Hours	9am–7pm off peak; 9am–10pm high season (Washington's Birthday, Easter, summer holidays, Thanksgiving, Christmas)
Admission	Under 3 free; 3–9 $40.95 (1-Day Ticket), $81.95 (2-Day Ticket), $96.95 (3-Day Ticket), $134.95 (4-Park FlexTicket), $164.95 (5-Park FlexTicket); adult (10+) $49.95, $95.95, $109.95, $169.95, $202.95; Universal Bonus Pass (5 consecutive days, online sales only) $76.95 and $89.95.
Parking	$8
Lockers	Yes; immediately to left through main gates; $5 ($2 refundable)
Pushchairs	$8 and $14; next to locker hire
Wheelchairs	$7 and $35; same location as pushchairs
Top Attractions	Amazing Adventures of Spider-Man, Dueling Dragons, Incredible Hulk Coaster, Jurassic Park River Adventure, Dudley Do-Right's Ripsaw Falls
Don't Miss	Eighth Voyage of Sindbad, Poseidon's Fury, Jurassic Park Discovery Centre, If I Ran the Zoo playground (for kids), Firework Finale (high season only)

Hidden Costs	**Meals**	Burger, chips and coke $7.58 3-course dinner $30 (Mythos Restaurant)
	Kids' meal	$5.99
	T-shirts	$18–30
	Souvenirs	$2.50–310
	Sundries	Dr Seuss character photos $12.95 and $17.95

bits of bric-a-brac from all over the world.

When you come to the end of the Port thoroughfare, you are faced with three choices, and this is where you need a plan of campaign. There are five attractions where the queues build up quickly and remain that way. If you are here for the big thrill rides, turn left into Marvel Super-Hero Island and head straight to Spider-Man, then do Dr Doom's Fearfall and the Incredible Hulk Coaster, taking advantage of the Universal Express (UE) system.

Alternatively, dinosaur fans should jump in one of the **Island Skipper boats** for the trip across the lagoon to Jurassic Park, where you should be able to do the TriceraTOPS Encounter and River Adventure before the majority arrive. Once you

PORT OF ENTRY
1 Island Skipper Tours
2 Confisco Grille

MARVEL SUPER-HERO ISLAND
3 Incredible Hulk Coaster
4 Café 4
5 Doctor Doom's Fearfall
6 The Amazing Adventures Of Spider-Man
7 Captain America Diner
8 Storm Force Accelatron

TOON LAGOON
9 Comic Strip Café
10 Popeye & Bluto's Bilge-Rat Barges
11 Me Ship, The Olive
12 Dudley Do-Right's Ripsaw Falls
13 Toon Lagoon Beach Bash

JURASSIC PARK
14 Jurassic Park River Adventure
15 Thunder Falls Terrace
16 Camp Jurassic
17 Pteranodon Flyers
18 Triceratops Encounter
19 Discovery Center

THE LOST CONTINENT
20 Dueling Dragons
21 The Enchanted Oak Tavern (and Alchemy Bar)
22 The Flying Unicorn
23 The Eighth Voyage of Sindbad
24 Poseidon's Fury
25 Mythos Restaurant
26 The Mystic Fountain

SEUSS LANDING
27 Caro-Seuss-el
28 One Fish, Two Fish, Red Fish, Blue Fish
29 The Cat In The Hat
30 If I Ran The Zoo
31 Circus McGurkus Café Stoo-pendous
32 Green Eggs and Ham Café
33 Guest Services

ISLANDS OF ADVENTURE

are nice and wet, you might as well go straight to Toon Lagoon and get Ripsaw Falls and the Bilge-Rat Barges under your belt. If you have younger children, turn right into the amazing multi-coloured world of Seuss Landing and enjoy the Cat In The Hat and other family-type rides prior to the crowd build-up.

Marvel Super-Hero Island

Taking the journey clockwise, you arrive first in the elaborate comic-book pages of the super-heroes. As with all the Islands, the experience is total immersion. The amazing façades of this world surround you with an utterly credible alternative reality that is one of the park's triumphs – and that's before you have tried the rides.

The Incredible Hulk Coaster: roller-coasters don't come any more dramatic than this giant green edifice that soars over the lagoon, blasting 0–40mph in 2 seconds and reaching a top speed of 65mph. It looks awesome, sounds stunning and rides like a demon as you enter the gamma-ray world of Dr David Banner, aka the Incredible Hulk.

> **BRIT TIP:** Keep left where the queue splits up and you will be in line for the front car for an even more extreme Hulk experience.

You zoom straight into a weightless inversion 100ft up, and it keeps getting better!

Just watching is quite mind-boggling, and the after-effects are distinctly brain-scrambling. You will need to deposit ANY loose articles (sunglasses, cameras, coins, etc) in the lockers at the front of the building as the ride is guaranteed to shake just about anything free. Crowds build up rapidly, but the queues seem to move quite quickly. Restrictions: 4ft 6in. TTTTT+ (UE).

Dr Doom's Fearfall: stand by for one of those two moments of supreme terror I mentioned earlier. This is where, O hapless visitor, you wander into the lair of the evil Dr Doom – arch-enemy of the Fantastic Four – and his sinister cohorts. His latest creation is the Fearfall, a

Night lights at Islands of Adventure

device for sucking every ounce of fear out of its victims, and YOU are about to test it. Four riders at a time are strapped into chairs at the bottom of a 200-ft tower, the dry ice rolls, and whoooosh! Up you go at breakneck speed, only to plummet back seemingly even faster, with an amazing split second in between when you feel suspended in mid air. Summon up the courage to do this and I promise a truly astonishing (if brief!) experience. Queues are also substantial during the main part of the day. Restrictions: 4ft 4in, and I reckon this is way too scary for under 10s. TTTTT+ (UE).

You exit Fearfall into the inevitable high-energy video arcade, or you may prefer to calm your nerves with a meal at the Italian buffeteria **Café 4** (pizza, spaghetti, sandwiches and salads) or a burger at the **Captain America Diner.** For shopping, each of the rides has its own character merchandise, while the **Comics Shop** and **Marvel Alterniverse** sell other souvenirs.

The Amazing Adventures of Spider-Man: just queuing is a novel experience as your visit to the Daily Bugle, home of ace reporter Peter Parker (or Spider-Man to his enemies), unravels into a reporting secondment in one of the 'Scoop' vehicles. Prepare for an audio-visual extravaganza as the combination of 3-D and motion simulator takes you into a battle between Spidey and arch-villains like Dr Octopus with his anti-gravity gun, culminating in a 400-ft sensory drop off a skyscraper, as the contest literally hots up. There are numerous jaw-dropping special effects and you will probably need to ride at least twice to appreciate it all. In fact, you'll see it and you still won't believe it. Ride early on or expect queues to top an hour. Restrictions: 3ft 4in. TTTTT+ (UE).

Storm Force Accelatron: this ride, aimed primarily at youngsters, puts you in the middle of a whirling, twirling battle between X-Men super-heroine Storm and arch-nemesis Magneto, with a range of special effects. It is basically an updated version of a fairground spinning-cup ride, but with some neat twists (there is a 3-way rotation and the cars look set to collide at any moment!). TTT (TTTTT under 12s) (UE).

You can also meet the **Marvel Super-Heroes** for autographs several times a day as they patrol the island.

Toon Lagoon

The thrills continue here with a watery theme and more comic-book elements as the newspaper cartoon characters take a bow. Children will love the chance to play with the fountains, squirt pools and overflowing fire hydrants, plus a purpose-built playland **Me Ship, The Olive,** a 3-storey boat full of interactive fun and games, including slides, bells and water cannons (with which to squirt riders on the Bilge-Rat Barges below) in best Popeye style. TTTT (youngsters only).

Popeye and Bluto's Bilge-Rat Barges: every park seems to have a variation on the white-water raft ride, but none is so outrageously themed and downright wet as this. It's fast, bouncy and unpredictable, with water coming at you from every direction, a couple of sizeable drops and a whirl through the Octoplus Grotto that adds to the fun. If you don't want to get wet, don't ride,

> BRIT TIP: A change of clothes is often advisable after riding the Barges, unless it's so hot you need to cool down in a hurry. Bring a waterproof bag for your valuables, too.

because there is no escaping the deluge here. This is also one of the top five rides for queues, but it's worth the wait. Restrictions: 4ft. TTTTT (UE).

Dudley Do-Right's Ripsaw Falls: Universal's designers have again taken an existing ride concept and given it a new spin as this becomes the first flume ride to send its passengers through the water surface and out the other side at high speed. You join guileless mountie Dudley Do-Right in a bid to save girlfriend Nell from the evil Snidely Whiplash. The action builds to an 'explosive' showdown at the top of a 60-ft precipice that drops you through the roof of a ramshackle dynamite shack and into the lagoon below. Just awesome – as are the queues from mid morning to late afternoon. Wet? You bet! Restrictions: 3ft 8in. TTTTT (UE)

After you have dried off, take a walk along **Comic Strip Lane** to meet up with characters like Beetle Bailey, Hagar the Horrible, Krazy Kat and Blondie (some of whom will mean little to a British audience). There is the usual array of character shopping outlets, like **Gasoline Alley** and **Toon Extra,** while you can grab a truly humongous sandwich at **Blondie's: Home of the Dagwood,** a trademark hamburger or hot dog at **Wimpy's,** sample the **Comic Strip Café** food court (Mexican, Chinese, American and Italian) or tuck into something colder at **Cathy's Ice Cream.** Watch out for appearances of the **Toon Lagoon Beach Bash** for a meet-and-greet with the characters.

Jurassic Park

Leaving the comic-book lands behind, you travel back in time to the Cretaceous age and the credible make-believe dinosaur film world. Again, the immersive experience is first class and the lavish scenery will have you looking over your shoulder for dinos.

Jurassic Park River Adventure: the mood change from scenic splendour to hidden menace is startling as your journey into this magnificent waterborne realm brings you up close and personal with the most realistic dinosaurs created to date. Inevitably, your passage is diverted from the safe to the hazardous, and the danger increases as the 16-person raft climbs into the heights of the main building – with raptors loose everywhere. You are aware of something large lurking in the shadows – will you fall prey to the T-Rex, or will your boat take the 85-ft plunge to safety (with a good soaking for all concerned)? Queues usually move quite briskly here. Restrictions: 3ft 6in. TTTTT (UE).

Triceratops Encounter: a face-to-face meeting with the park's resident 4-ton, 24ft-long 'living' dinosaur, which reacts to both its handler and visitors. The spiel is amusing and educational and the 'Trike' pretty convincing, especially for children. It also draws a crowd and there is little shade (one of the few minus points), but the queues move steadily. AAAA. (UE).

Pteranodon Flyers: the slow-moving queues are a major turn-off, especially for a fairly average ride, which glides gently over much of Jurassic Park. It is designed mainly for kids, though, and the height range of 3–4ft 8in requires anyone OVER the upper limit (usually 11 or older) to be accompanied by a child of the right height! TT (TTTT under 9s).

Camp Jurassic: more excellent kids' fare here with the mountainous jungle giving way to an 'active' volcano for youngsters to explore, climb over and slide down. Squirt guns and 'Spitter' dinosaurs add to the fun. TTTT (children first, but parents may explore).

6

Dr Doom's Fearfall

Discovery Center: the designers' imagination has gone into overdrive here with terrific results. Interactive opportunities include creating a dinosaur through DNA sequencing, mixing your own DNA with a dino via a computer touchscreen, seeing through the eyes of various large reptiles and even watching a baby raptor hatch, plus a host of other hands-on exhibits that are fun and educational. Air-conditioned, this is a good place to visit in the hotter part of the day. AAAA.

Dueling Dragons roller-coaster

Best of the shopping is in the Discovery Center itself, while you can chow down at the **Burger Digs** there, visit the **Pizza Predattoria** or the **Watering Hole,** or go for the rotisserie chicken at the rustic **ThunderFalls Terrace** (counter service), which boasts a great view of the River Adventure.

The Lost Continent

This is one of my favourite lands for its theming, gentle contrast after Jurassic Park, superb attractions, great eating options and a few amusing 'extras'.

One Fish, Two Fish

Dueling Dragons: there is no disguising the intense nature of this magnificent double coaster, with its 100-ft drop, multiple loops, twists and three near-miss encounters. There is a lot more, too, as the queuing area is a real mind-boggler – 1,060yds, most of it along a dark tortuous path through the ancient castle that is the domain of the dragons, Fire and Ice. You are given their story while you stand in line, and Merlin arrives in time to cast a spell to ensure you survive. You choose which dragon to ride (the tracks differ slightly), and you can join an additional queue for the front seats. Unlike the Hulk, this is a suspended coaster, so your legs dangle free, and the initial drop is like going into free-fall (Supreme

The Flying Unicorn

Terror moment Number 2!). Coaster aficionados reckon the best ride is in the back of the Ice (Blue) dragon, but it's all pretty amazing. Restrictions: 4ft 6in, and you will need to leave all your loose belongings in the lockers provided to the left of the entrance. TTTTT+ (UE).

The Flying Unicorn: this junior-sized coaster is aimed primarily at youngsters and features a wizard's workshop, hidden in an enchanted wood, which is the gateway to a magical journey inspired by the Unicorn. There are no big drops, but it delivers a surprisingly fast-paced whirl for its size. TTTTT (for 6–12s) (UE).

The Eighth Voyage of Sindbad: this stunt and special effects show is another marvel, as much for its elaborate staging as its performance. Mythical adventurer Sindbad and his sidekick Kabob (a name that's the cue for a truly awful pun) tackle the evil witch Miseria in a bid to rescue Princess Amoura, and the action springs up in surprising places. There are several loud bangs which could scare young children, but otherwise it is good, family fun. At peak times, arrive 15 minutes before showtime, but everyone usually gets in. TTT/AAAA (UE).

Poseidon's Fury: this is a walk-through show that puts its audience at the heart of the action as you journey in the company of a hapless young archaeologist (who ignores all the various 'warnings') beneath the sea to the lost temple of Poseidon, passing through an amazing water vortex en route, with your 'expedition' taking a wrong turn and awakening an ancient demon. Again, there is a terrific element of suspense, so I won't reveal any surprises, but the showdown between Poseidon and the evil demon is amazing as the arena seems to explode in water and fire around you. Queuing is a bit slow and tedious, but at least you are inside in the summer. TTT (UE).

Check out **Metal Smiths** for unusual trinkets, **Treasures of Poseidon** and **Shop of Wonders** for more upmarket gifts and the **Psychic Readings** tent in Sindbad's Village for something new. The **Fire-Eater's Grill** (sausages, fries and drinks) and **Frozen Desert** (sundaes and sodas) provide the

Popeye and Bluto's Bilge-Rat Barges

snacks, while there is the magnificent **Enchanted Oak Tavern** (in the dark, cool interior of a vast, sculpted oak tree) and Alchemy Bar for counter-service meals (hickory-smoked chicken, ribs and salads) which has to be seen to be believed. The elaborate **Mythos Restaurant** provides the best dining in IoA, though. Not only is the food first class (seafood, grills, pizza and pasta), but the setting, inside a dormant volcano with streams, fountains and clever lighting, is an attraction in its own right.

Finally, watch out for **The Mystic Fountain** in Sindbad's Village – it has the ability to get you very wet when you least expect it!

Seuss Landing

There is not a straight line to be seen in this vivid 3-D working of the books of Dr Seuss. The characters may not mean much to those unfamiliar with the children's stories, but everyone can relate to the fun here (although queues build up quickly). There is so much clever detail packed into the area, from squirt ponds to beach scenes, it is easy to miss something, so take your time.

Caro-Seuss-el: this intricate carousel ride on some of the Seuss characters – like cowfish, elephant-birds and dog-a-lopes – has rider-activated features that are a big hit with the young ones. AAA (AAAA under 5s) (UE).

One Fish, Two Fish, Red Fish, Blue Fish: another fairground ride is given a twist as you pilot these Seussian fish up and down according to the rhyme that plays while you ride. Get it wrong and you get squirted! More guaranteed fun for the younger kids. TTT (TTTTT under 5s) (UE).

The Cat In The Hat: prepare for a ride with a difference as you board these crazy 6-passenger 'couches' to meet the world's most adventurous cat and his friends, Thing One and Thing Two. You literally go for a spin through this storybook world, and it may be a bit too much for very young children. The slow-moving queues are a bit of a drag, so try to get here early or leave it until much later in the day (or use the UE system). AAAA/TTT (UE).

If I Ran The Zoo: interactive playgrounds don't get much more fun for the pre-school brigade than with the 19 different Seuss character scenarios, most of which can get them quite wet. Hugely imaginative and great fun just to watch. TTTTT (young 'uns only).

The Circus McGurkus Seussian Sing-a-Long: especially for the youngsters inside the Circus McGurkus Café (see below) is this 20-minute musical performance as Ringmaster McGurkus introduces The Cat In The Hat and his friends, with interruptions from The Grinch. AA (AAAA under 5s).

If you have been captivated by the land, you can buy the book at **Dr Seuss' All the Books You Can Read** store, or visit the **Mulberry Street Store** for all the characters. **Snookers & Snookers Sweet Candy Cookers** is a super sweet shop, while snacks and drinks can be had at **Hop on Pop Ice Cream Shop** and **Moose Juice Goose Juice**. The **Circus McGurkus Café Stoo-pendous** is a mind-boggling cafeteria for fried chicken, lasagne, pizza and spaghetti, complete with clowns and pipe organs (and the Sing-a-Long show – plus special birthday celebrations every afternoon at 2.45), while **Green Eggs and Ham Café** is a must for all Seuss fans to try the meal of the same name (and the eggs ARE green!).

Private nursing facilities, an open area for feeding and resting (with high-chairs) and nappy-changing stations can be found at the **Family Service Facility** at guest services (to the right inside the main gates), while ALL restrooms throughout the park are equipped with **nappy-changing** facilities. **First aid** is provided in Sindbad's Village in the Lost Continent, just across from Oasis Coolers.

In high season, there is even a nightly **firework show** on the Lagoon that provides a fitting and spectacular finale to the day.

Halloween Horror Nights

Moving over from the Studios park is Universal's massively popular Halloween celebration throughout October each year. The Horror Nights have become a real trademark hereabouts and add a wonderfully bloodthirsty touch (although there is an extra charge – about $46, or an extra $19–25 if you upgrade your park ticket on the day). The Islands are transformed with some highly imaginative re-creations and set-pieces from various horror movies, with a parade and shows that include live (terrifyingly so, in some cases!) character interaction. The rides are also all open (anyone for The Hulk and Dueling Dragons in the dark?!), adding more novelty to the park experience, but this over-the-top (and occasionally downright grisly) extravaganza is definitely not for kids. It goes down a treat with adults with the right sense of humour, though, and begins each evening at 7.30pm.

And that, folks, is the full low-down on arguably the world's best theme park to date. Miss it at your peril.

6

ISLANDS OF ADVENTURE with children

Our guide to the rides which generally appeal to the different age groups:

Under 5s
Caro-Seuss-el, If I Ran The Zoo, The Cat In The Hat, One Fish, Two Fish, Red Fish, Blue Fish, Circus McGurkus Sing-a-Long, Eighth Voyage of Sindbad, Jurassic Park Discovery Center, Me Ship, The Olive.

5–8s
All the above, plus Flying Unicorn, Triceratops Encounter, Pteranodon Flyers, Camp Jurassic, Amazing Adventures of Spider-Man, Storm Force Accelatron, and Jurassic Park River Adventure (with parental discretion).

9–12s
The Cat In The Hat, Flying Unicorn, Dueling Dragons, Eighth Voyage of Sindbad, Camp Jurassic, Pteranodon Flyers, Jurassic Park River Adventure, Triceratops Encounter, Jurassic Park Discovery Center, Dudley Do-Right's Ripsaw Falls, Popeye and Bluto's Bilge – Rat Barges, Amazing Adventures of Spider-Man, Dr Doom's Fearfall, Storm Force Accelatron, Incredible Hulk Coaster.

Over 12s
Dueling Dragons, Eighth Voyage of Sindbad, Jurassic Park River Adventure, Jurassic Park Discovery Center, Dudley Do-Right's Ripsaw Falls, Popeye and Bluto's Bilge – Rat Barges, Amazing Adventures of Spider-Man, Dr Doom's Fearfall, Storm Force Accelatron, Incredible Hulk Coaster.

SeaWorld Adventure Park

SeaWorld has quickly become one of the most popular parks with British visitors for its more peaceful and naturalistic aspect, the change of pace it offers and the general lack of substantial queues. It is a big hit with families in particular, but also possesses some pretty dramatic rides and attractions.

An extensive development programme by owners Anheuser-Busch has given SeaWorld the big-park treatment in recent years, with an impressive 12-acre entrance plaza and rebranding as an Adventure Park, and it now demands a full day's attention. The opening, in summer 2000, of an exclusive sister park – Discovery Cove, an exotic tropical island with dolphin, stingray and snorkelling adventures – has added even more.

Happily, the queues and crowds have yet to reach the monster proportions of elsewhere, so this is a park where you can still proceed at a relatively leisurely pace, see what you want without too much jostling and yet feel you have been superbly entertained (even if mealtimes do get rather crowded in the restaurants).

SeaWorld is also a good starting point if this is your first visit to Orlando as it will give you the hang of negotiating the vast areas, navigating by the various maps and learning to plan your visit around the showtimes. There is also a strong educational and environmental message, plus three hour-long, behind-the-scenes tours (book up as soon as you enter), which provide you with a greater insight into SeaWorld's marine conservation, rescue and research programme, as well as their entertainment resources.

The **Polar Expedition** provides a close-up of the penguin and polar bear environments, **To the Rescue** showcases the park's animal rescue and rehabilitation programme, and **Predators!** offers a backstage view of Terrors of the Deep. You have to pay

SeaWorld's dramatic main entrance

1 Information
2 Wild Arctic
3 Shamu Stadium
4 Dine with Shamu
5 Sea Lion and Otter Stadium
6 Key West Dolphin Fest
7 Atlantis Bayside Stadium
8 SeaWorld Theater
9 Nautilus Theater
10 Clydesdale Hamlet
11 Anheuser-Busch Hospitality Center
12 Manatees: The Last Generation?
13 Pacific Point Preserve
14 Shamu's Happy Harbor
15 Terrors Of The Deep
16 Tropical Reef
17 Penguin Encounter
18 Key West At SeaWorld
19 Stingray Lagoon
20 Turtle Point
21 Dolphin Cove
22 Journey To Atlantis
23 Kraken
24 Dolphin Nursery
25 Tide Pool
26 Polynesian Luau

SEA WORLD

6

an extra $8.95 ($7.95 for 3–9s) for these tours, but they are worth it and, if you take one of them early on, they will increase your appreciation of the rest of the park. You can also SAVE 10% on single-day park tickets if you book online at www.seaworld.com, which also allows you to print your own tickets and save waiting in line.

There are four additional programmes which all provide unique insights into the park's activities. The 6-hour **Adventure Express Tour** offers visitors their own guide to tour the park, with back-door access to the rides, reserved seating at shows and animal feeding opportunities (an extra $57 for adults, $51 for 3–9s; book up first thing at the Guided Tours counter or call 1-800 406 2244); **Trainer For A Day** is an 8-hour programme open to just 3 people (at least 13 years old and in good physical condition) each day, which shows how SeaWorld trainers care for and train their animals (cost is $349, including T-shirt, waterproof disposable camera and lunch with trainers; for reservations, call 407 370 1382); the new **False Killer Whale Interaction** programme, a 2-hour opportunity for 4 people

SeaWorld Adventure Park at a glance

Location	7007 SeaWorld Drive, off Central Florida Parkway (Junctions 71 and 72 off I-4)
Size	More than 200 acres, incorporating 25 attractions
Hours	9am–7pm off peak; 9am–10pm high season (Easter, summer holidays, Thanksgiving, Christmas)
Admission	Under 3 free; 3–9 $40.95 (1-Day Ticket), $134.95 (4-Park Orlando FlexTicket), $164.95 (5-Park FlexTicket), $67.95 (SeaWorld/Busch Gardens Combo ticket); adult (10+) $49.95, $169.95, $202.95, $82.95.
Parking	$7
Lockers	Yes, by main entrance; $1.50
Pushchairs	$11 and $15 ($2 refundable; from Information Centre, to left of main entrance)
Wheelchairs	$9 ($2 refundable) and $35 ($5 refundable); with pushchairs
Top Attractions	Shamu Stadium, Terrors of the Deep, Journey to Atlantis, Kraken, Wild Arctic
Don't Miss	Red Bright 'n Blue Spectacular, Manatees: The Last Generation?, Behind-the-Scenes Tours, Cirque de la Mer

Hidden Costs	**Meals**	Burger, chips and coke $8.08
	Kids' meal	$4.99
		3-course lunch (Sharks Grill) $22
	T-shirts	$12.99–26.95
	Souvenirs	99 cents–$1,500
	Sundries	Caricature Drawings $12.95–22.95

(must be at least 13 and 4ft 4in tall) daily to join the trainers at the Whale and Dolphin Stadium to help feed their wonderful animals and learn some of the training techniques (including lunch, T-shirt and souvenir photo PLUS a 7-day SeaWorld ticket; $200/person); and the **Animal Care Experience,** which is another new option for 4 visitors daily (aged 13 or above) to find out about the intensive care necessary to rehabilitate injured manatees, plus bottle-feed some of them, meet the seals and walruses and prepare meals for the beluga whales. It starts at 6.30am and lasts around 8 hours for $389/person (including lunch, T-shirt, special book, souvenir photo and 7-day SeaWorld pass).

Location

SeaWorld is located off Central Florida Parkway, between I-4 (exit 71 going east or 72 heading west) and I-Drive, and the parking fee is $7. It is still a good idea to arrive a bit before the officially scheduled opening time so you're in good position to book one of the backstage tours at a time convenient to you or scamper off to one of the few attractions that does draw crowds, like Journey to Atlantis.

The park covers in excess of 200 acres, with nine shows (10 with the nightly **Aloha Polynesian Luau Dinner Show** which costs $37.95 for adults, $27.95 for 8–12s and $16.96 for 3–7s, and for which you don't necessarily need park admission; nightly 6.30–8.45pm, call 407 351 3600 to book), nine large-scale continuous viewing attractions and nine smaller ones, plus relaxing gardens, a kids' play area and a smart range of shops (a noticeable feature of Anheuser-Busch parks). Their hire pushchairs (strollers) are also the most amusing – shaped like baby

dolphins. Be warned, though, the size of the park will take you by surprise and requires a lot of to-ing and fro-ing to catch the various shows, which can be wearing. Keep a close grip on your map and entertainment schedule and try to establish your own programme that gives you regular breaks to sit and enjoy some of the quieter spots.

For something different, you can sign up for the free 35-minute Anheuser-Busch **Beer School** at the Hospitality Center for a glimpse into beer-making (and tasting!).

Wild Arctic: this interactive ride-and-view experience provides a realistic environment that is both educational and thrilling. It consists of an exciting simulator jet helicopter journey into the Arctic wilderness arriving at a clever research base, Base Station Wild Arctic, where the 'passengers' are disgorged into a frozen wonderland to meet polar bears, beluga whales and walruses. The imaginative detail includes a replica sunken galleon and other nautical touches, as well as some scientific research. This one is not to be missed (but not just after a Shamu show when the hordes descend). Restrictions: 3ft 6in. TTTT plus AAAAA.

Shamu Stadium: SeaWorld has long since outgrown its tag as just the place to see killer whales, but the Shamu show is still one of its most amazing experiences. See the killer whales and their trainers pull off some spectacular stunts, as well as hearing everything you need to know about these majestic creatures.

> BRIT TIP: Reader David Snelling from Cheshire, warns, 'Gentlemen, do not volunteer to participate in the Shamu display – it will be chauvinistically humiliating.'

6

There are two distinct shows, the more humorous *Shamu Adventure* during the day (25 minutes) and the louder *Shamu Rocks America* at night (20 minutes). Both are worth seeing, and are easily the park's most popular events, so do make an effort to arrive early (especially as there is an amusing pre-show). Also, the first 14 rows get VERY wet (watch out for your cameras) – when a killer whale leaps into the air in front of you, it displaces a LOT of water on landing! AAAAA.

Dine with Shamu: this new offering gives guests a VIP experience 'backstage' with the killer whales and their trainers. An all-you-can-eat buffet on a covered terrace right alongside the main whale pool is accompanied by the chance to ask questions of the trainers and watch some of the training sessions. It costs $28 for adults and $14 for children, there are two seatings daily (at 4.45 and 7.30pm) and it's advisable to book in advance on 407 351 3600.

All guests can take advantage of the **Underwater Viewing** area for the wonderful whales.

Sea Lion and Otter Stadium: the venue to a wonderful show, *Clyde and Seamore Take Treasure Island*, it features the resident sea lions who, with their pals the otter and walrus (plus a couple of humans as the fall guys!), put on a hilarious 25-minute performance of watery stunts and gags. Arrive early for some first-class

Shamu the killer whale

audience mickey-taking from the resident pirate mimic. AAAA.

Key West Dolphin Fest: more breathtaking marine mammal stunts and tricks in a funky beach theme, with the accent again on informing and educating in a gentle manner on the current state of research into dolphins and false killer whales and the dangers they face. The show lasts almost 20 minutes and is rarely over-subscribed, but once again the first few rows face a soaking. AAAA.

BRIT TIP: The weather may occasionally mean the outdoor entertainment is cancelled, but don't let it stop you enjoying yourself. Cheap, plastic ponchos will appear in the shops at the first sign of rain!

Atlantis Bayside Stadium: this arena showcases the half-hour *Intensity Games Water Ski Show*, with an explosion of high-energy action in water stunts, featuring some breathtaking water-skiing, wake-boarding, plus jet skis and much more. AAAA.

SeaWorld Theater: an air-conditioned haven during the hottest part of the day, *Pets Ahoy!* is the show here, a genuinely cute 25-minute giggle featuring the

Beluga whales at Wild Arctic

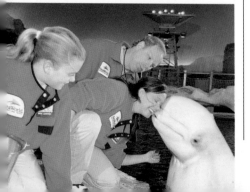

The touch pool at Stingray Lagoon

unlikely talents of a menagerie of dogs, cats, birds, rats, pot-bellied pigs and others, the majority of which were rescued from animal shelters. AAA.

Nautilus Theater: here is where the spectacular Cirque de la Mer show is staged, a unique 35-minute adventure of athleticism, acrobatics, modern dance, music and special effects. The South American cast exhibit a terrific élan as they illustrate the story of the *Flight of the Condor.* The theatre is air-conditioned, too. AAAAA.

Clydesdale Hamlet: these massive stables are home to the Anheuser-Busch trademark Clydesdale dray horses. They make great photo opportunities when fully harnessed, and there is a life-size statue outside on which to sit the kids to take their picture. The Hitching Barn shows how the horses are prepared for the twice-daily parade, including washing, grooming and braiding. AA.

Anheuser-Busch Hospitality Center: adjoining Clydesdale Hamlet, this offers the chance to sample the company's most famous product, beer (in fact, the world's No 1 bottled beer, Budweiser, and its cousins). Sadly, it's only three small samples per visitor aged over 21, but it still makes a nice gesture, and you can take your free drink and sit on the outdoor terrace which makes for a pleasant break from all the usual theme park hustle and bustle. AAA. You'll also find the Beer School, here, while **The Deli** restaurant is an attractive proposition, serving fresh-carved turkey and beef, German sausage, sauerkraut, fresh-baked breads and delicious desserts.

Manatees: The Last Generation?: here is an exhibit that will really tug at your heartstrings as you learn of the tragic plight of this endangered species of Florida's waterways. Watch these lazy-looking creatures (half walrus, half hippo?) lounge around their manmade lagoon from above, then walk down the ramp to the special circular theatre where a 5-minute film with amazing 3-D effects will reveal the full dangers facing the harmless manatee. Then pass into the underwater viewing section, with hands-on TV screens offering more information about them. It's a magnificent exhibit and often provokes a few tears at the animals' uncertain future. It is also right behind the Key West Dolphin Fest, so DON'T go just after one of the shows there. AAAAA.

Pacific Point Preserve: another SeaWorld first, this carefully

Journey to Atlantis

re-created rocky coast habitat shows the park's seals and sea lions at their most natural. A hidden wave-making machine adds the perfect touch of reality, while park attendants are on hand at intervals to provide informative talks. You can also buy small packs of smelt from two stalls to throw to the ever-hungry sea mammals. AAAA.

Shamu's Happy Harbor: 3 acres of brilliantly designed adventure playground await youngsters of all ages here, with all things climbable or crawlable. Activities include a 4-storey net climb, two tented 'ball rooms' to wade through, and a giant 'trampoline' tent. It does get busy in mid afternoon, but the kids seem to love it at any time. Next door is the clever **Shamu Splash Attack** (water-balloon catapults), the inevitable video arcade and some funfair games for a few extra dollars. TTTTT.

Terrors of the Deep: the world's largest collection of dangerous sea creatures can be found here, brought vividly and dramatically to life by the walk-through tubes that surround you with prowling sharks, barracudas and moray eels. It's an eerie experience (and perhaps too intense for small children), but brilliantly presented and, again, highly informative. Queues do build up here at peak times, though. AAAA or TTTT (take your pick!). Due to open in late summer 2002 was the **Sharks Underwater Grill,** for a chance to dine alongside some of these fearsome denizens of the deep. An upscale, full-service restaurant, it features a 'Floribbean'-style menu blending both local and Caribbean fare.

Tropical Reef: after the dramas and amusements elsewhere, this may seem a little tame, but stick with it. Literally thousands of colourful fish inhabit the centrepiece 160,000-gallon tropical reef, while smaller tanks show off other intriguing species. AAA.

Penguin Encounter: always a hit with all the family (and hence one of the more crowded exhibits at peak periods), the eternally comical penguins are in this brilliantly presented (if decidedly chilly) showpiece. You have the choice of going close and using the moving walkway along the whole of the display or standing back and watching from a non-moving position. Both positions afford views of how the 17 different species are so breathtaking under water. Feeding time is the most popular time for visitors, so arrive early if you want a prime position. There is also a special question-and-answer session at 2pm every day – the winner gets to pet a penguin. AAAA.

> BRIT TIP: Touching the rays and dolphins is an experience at SeaWorld you won't easily forget.

Key West at SeaWorld is a whole collection of exhibits grouped under the clever Key West theme. **Stingray Lagoon,** where you can feed and touch fully grown rays, includes a nursery for newborn rays, while the park's rescued and rehabilitated sea turtles can be seen at **Turtle Point,** which helps to explain the dangers to these saltwater reptiles. The centrepiece exhibit, the 2.1-acre **Dolphin Cove,** is a more spectacular, naturalistic development and offers visitors the chance to get right up close and feed this friendly community of frisky Atlantic bottlenose dolphins. There is an excellent underwater viewing area to the 700,000-gallon lagoon, which features waves, a sandy beach and a reproduced coral reef. The park's photographers also patrol here, ready to snap you at play with the dolphins, and a 2-photo package (in a 5 x 7in stand-up frame) will set you back $19.99.

The whole area is designed in the tropical, seaside flavour of America's southernmost city, Key West, with beach huts, lifeguard chairs, dune buggies, themed shops and other eclectic lookalike elements, but it also underlines the environmental message of conservation through a series of interactive graphics and video displays adjacent to the animal habitats, and children of all ages will find it a fun, educational experience. The shops here are above average, too. AAAA.

Journey to Atlantis: unique in Orlando, this terrific 'water-coaster' gave SeaWorld its first 5-star thrill attraction in 1998. The combination of extra elements here ultimately makes it unique, with a series of illusionary special effects giving way to a high-speed water ride that becomes a runaway roller-coaster. An amusing TV show preamble about the 'discovery' of Atlantis opens the way to your 8-passenger Greek fishing boat, which sets off gently through the lost city. The evil spirit Allura takes over and riders plunge into a dash through Atlantis, dodging gushing fountains and water cannons, with hundreds of dazzling holographic and laser-generated illusions, before the heart-stopping 60-ft drop, which is merely the entry to the roller-coaster finale back in the candle-filled catacombs. An amazing creation. Once again, be prepared to get seriously wet (soaked) in the course of the ride, which is great in the heat of the summer but not so clever first thing in the morning in winter. Restrictions: 3ft 6in. TTTTT. Riders exit into the **Sea Aquarium Gallery,** a combination gift shop and 25,000-gallon aquarium full of sharks, stingrays and tropical fish (don't forget to look up!).

Kraken: brand new in 2000, this outrageous addition to the coaster family is the longest, fastest and highest in central Florida. Based on the mythical sea monster, Kraken is an innovative pedestal ride (you are effectively sitting in a chair without a floor – pretty exposed!) that plunges an initial 144ft, tops speeds of 65mph, dives underground three times, adds seven inversions (including a 119-ft vertical loop, a 101-ft diving loop, a zero-gravity roll and a cobra roll) and a flat spin before riders escape the beast's lair. The ride from the front row, especially down that opening drop at an angle that can best be described as ludicrous, is positively blood-curdling, and the rear seats are pretty amazing, too. Restrictions: 4ft 6in. TTTTT+.

SeaWorld Specials

In addition to the **Shamu Rocks America** show, night-time at SeaWorld is marked by an end-of-evening pyrotechnic extravaganza, the **Red Bright 'n Blue Spectacular,** in front of the Atlantis Bayside Stadium. This 15-minute curtain call features lasers, fountains and pyrotechnics and is well worth staying for. AAAAA.

There is also live entertainment daily around the Key West attractions, including the trademark **Sunset Celebration** street party.

Through the summer, when the park tends to stay open until at least 9pm, the theme becomes **Every Night's the 4th of July,** with outdoor DJs, live music, dancers and games, plus a teens' music scene, Club Shamu, next to Kraken. The programme includes the *Shamu Rocks America* show, leading up to the nightly firework spectacular.

As well as all the main set-pieces, there are several smaller ones which can be equally rewarding for their more personal touch. The **Dolphin Nursery** provides more close encounters with the park's (younger) dolphins, and then there are the **Flamingo, Pelican and Spoonbill Exhibits.** The **Tide Pool** is another hands-on experience with starfish and sea anemones and, for an extra $3, you can ascend the **Sky Tower** for a lofty overview of the park (and I-Drive). The flamingo pedal-boats, which rent for $6 per half-hour (for 2 people) in one corner of the lagoon, are also fun to do. Look out, too, for the best photo opportunity of the day as a big, cuddly Shamu will greet the kids just inside the main entrance.

You can choose to eat from 10 different places, with the **Dockside Cafe** (barbecued, mesquite-grilled chicken and beef, chicken fingers and hot dogs), **The Deli** (see above, in the Anheuser-Busch Hospitality Center), **Mama Stella's Italian Kitchen** (pizza, pasta and salads), **Bimini Bay Café** (for a relaxing buffet lunch or dinner), **Smoky Creek Grill** (a Texas-style barbecue) and **Mango Joe's Café** (delicious grilled fajitas, speciality salads and sandwiches) the best of the bunch. As in the other main parks, try to eat before midday or after 2.30pm for a crowd-free lunch, and before 5.30pm if you want a leisurely dinner.

Your wallet will also be in severe peril in any of the 24 shops and photo-opportunity kiosks. Make sure you visit at least **Shamu's Emporium** (for a full range of cuddly Shamu toys and souvenirs), **Manatee Cove** (more cuddlies), **Friends of the Wild** (dedicated to animal lovers everywhere) and **The Label Stable** for Anheuser-Busch gifts and merchandise (some of it extremely smart). Your purchases can be forwarded to Package Pick-up in Shamu's Emporium, to collect on your way out of the park, provided you leave at least an hour for this service to work.

Finally, non-drivers will want to make a note of the special daily bus service from SeaWorld (and other points on I-Drive) direct to sister park Busch Gardens (see page 160).

SEAWORLD with children

The following gives a general idea of the appeal of SeaWorld's attractions to the different age groups:

Under 5s
Shamu Adventure Show, Key West Dolphin Fest, Clyde & Seamore Take Treasure Island, Pets Ahoy!, Wild Arctic (without the ride), Manatees: Last Generation?, Penguin Encounter, Tropical Reef, Pacific Point Preserve, Clydesdale Hamlet.

5–8s
All the above, plus Wild Arctic (with the ride), Intensity Games Water Ski Show, Cirque de la Mer, Red Bright 'n Blue Spectacular, Terrors of the Deep, Shamu's Happy Harbor.

9–12s
All the above, plus Kraken.

Over 12s
Kraken, Journey to Atlantis, Wild Arctic, Terrors of the Deep, Shamu Adventure Show, Intensity Games Water Ski Show, Clyde & Seamore Take Treasure Island, Cirque de la Mer, Red Bright 'n Blue Spectacular.

Discovery Cove

The author at Discovery Cove

Fancy a day in your own tropical paradise, with the chance to swim with dolphins, encounter sharks, snorkel in a coral reef and dive through a waterfall into a tropical aviary? Well, Discovery Cove is all that and more. The only drawback is the price. This mini theme park comes at a premium because it is restricted to just 1,000 guests a day, making for an exclusive experience, and the admission fee reflects that. The flat rate entrance fee is $219 (rising to $229 in March 2003) and the only reduction is to $119 (up to $129 in March) for those not wishing to do the Dolphin Swim and for 3–5s; under 3s are free.

A new **Trainer For A Day** programme adds the exciting opportunity to go behind the scenes into the training, feeding, health and welfare of the park's animals. You get to work side by side with the experts as they interact with dolphins, birds, sloths, anteaters, sharks, stingrays and tropical fish. The experience includes a behavioural training class, souvenir shirt, dolphin book and waterproof camera and participants, must be at least aged 6 and in good health. You need to book well in advance either online at www.discoverycove.com or 0208 668 4218. The cost? A healthy $399, including the main entrance fee, plus tax.

The famous dolphin encounter

So, just what do you get for your money? Well, as you would expect, it is a supremely personal park. You check in as you would for a hotel rather than a theme park (the entrance lobby is wonderfully impressive), and you have a guide to take you in and get you set for the day. All your basic requirements – towel, mask, snorkel, wet-jacket, lockers, beach umbrellas, lunch and soft drinks – are included in the price, and the level of service is excellent. A valuable 7-day pass for

Snorkelling in the Coral Reef

6

SeaWorld is also included. The lunch provided at the buffet-style **Laguna Grill** is pretty good, but you have to pay for any further snacks and any alcoholic drinks, while the gift shop and photographic prices reflect the entrance fee – expensive.

Located on Central Florida Parkway, almost opposite the SeaWorld entrance (open year-round from 8.30am–5.30pm. Parking is free), the whole of the 30-acre park is magnificently landscaped, with lovely thatched buildings, palm trees, lush vegetation, brilliant white-sand beaches, gurgling streams and even hammocks. The overall effect is as if you have been transported to some Caribbean or South Seas oasis.

The usual tourist hurly-burly is left far behind. The 5-star resort feel is enhanced by the high staff-to-guest ratio (the lifeguards can outnumber the guests at times, it seems). There should be no queues for anything (okay, the buffet-service restaurant may get a little busy at lunchtime) and the highlight dolphin encounter is unquestionably world class. The ultimate effect is of total relaxation, a holiday from your holiday, and a real feeling of escape.

Visitors with disabilities are also well catered for, with special wheelchairs that can move across the sand and into shallow water and an area of the Dolphin Lagoon designed to allow those who can't enter the water still to be able to touch the dolphins.

The essence of a day spent at Discovery Cove involves close encounters with all the animals – although not too close in the case of the sharks – with a strong underlying conservation message. The main attractions include:

Coral Reef: a huge rocky pool, filled with several thousand tropical fish, offers the most amazing manmade snorkelling experience you'll find. The water teems with silverjacks, angelfish and yellowtail snapper and, even if the 'coral' is hand-painted concrete, it is a clever environment. Some of the larger stingrays inhabit the bottom of the reef and they are fascinating to watch. Swimmers also come within inches of sharks and barracuda – all safely behind a Plexiglass partition – which adds another novel element. If you stay reasonably still in the water, many of the fish will crowd around you to inspect their latest pool-mate! AAAAA/TTTT.

Ray Lagoon: another carefully sculpted pool provides the opportunity to paddle among several dozen southern and cownose rays, quite harmless, but with just a hint of menace to the fascination. AAAA.

Tropical River: this 800-yd circuit of gently flowing bath-warm water is a variation on the lazy river feature of many of the water parks, although with a far more naturalistic aspect and none of the inner-tubes. It is primarily designed for snorkellers and features rocky lagoons, caves, a beach section, a tropical forest segment, sunken ruins and an underwater viewing window into the Coral Reef. The lack of fish makes it seem a bit bland after the Tropical Reef and Ray Lagoon, but again, it is as much about relaxing as about having fun. AAA.

Aviary: this recently enhanced 3-part adventure is both an area in its own right and a 40-yd section of the Tropical River. You can walk in off the beach or swim in through one of the two impressive waterfalls which guard each end, a beautifully scenic touch and fun for snorkellers. Some 200 tropical birds fill the main 30ft-high enclosure and, if you stand still for a while, they are likely to use you for a perch. An expansion in 2002 effectively doubled the size of the aviary by adding a small-bird sanctuary – full of finches, honeycreepers and hummingbirds –

and a large-bird enclosure, featuring toucans and the red-legged seriema. Guides will introduce you to specific birds (which you can also hand-feed) and tell you about their habits, habitats and conservation issues. AAAAA.

Animal Encounters: a minor additional touch, but a big hit with children in particular, is the chance to meet some of the cove's lesser lights, such as the macaws, tree sloths and anteaters, on an individual basis at various points as you go around the park. AAA.

Dolphin Swim: the headline attraction at Discovery Cove is the encounter with the park's Atlantic bottlenose dolphin community. A 15-minute orientation programme in one of the four thatched beach cabanas, with a film and instruction from two of the animal trainers, sets you up for this deeply thrilling experience. Groups of 12–20 go into the huge lagoon with careful supervision from the trainers and, starting off by standing in the waist-deep (and slightly chilly) water as one of the dolphins comes to you, you gradually become more adventurous until you are swimming next to them. Timid swimmers are catered for and there are life-jackets for those who feel they need them, but the lagoon is up to 12ft deep so there is a feeling of really being in the dolphins' environment. You will learn how the trainers use hand-signals and positive reinforcement to communicate with them, and get the chance to stroke, feed and even kiss (!) your dolphin. The encounter comes to a dramatic conclusion as you are towed back to shore by one of these awesome animals, which can weigh from 300–600lb (although the activities can vary according to the dolphins' own attention span). You spend around 30 minutes in the water and it is genuinely unforgettable. Under 6s are not allowed into the dolphin lagoon). TTTTT+.

Truly, Discovery Park is an attraction with huge style and appeal – not to mention the stuff of which cherished memories are made – but it will take a big bite out of your holiday budget. A family of four, with children of 6 or older who want to do the Dolphin Swim, would pay **$928.56** (including tax; **$970.96** after March) for the day and that's not including the Trainer for a Day programme. Even with the 7-day SeaWorld pass included, it is a massive outlay. The charge for 3- to 5-year-olds is also pretty steep, in my opinion. Your sundries are likely to add up quickly, too. A 5 x 7in photo is $15.99 and an 8 x 10in is $28.99. Then there are various photo packages at $29.99, $59.99 and $99.99, while the video of your experience (which includes 30 minutes of highlights of the whole park) costs $59.99.

The weather can get distinctly cool in the winter months, but the water is always heated (apart from the dolphin lagoon, which remains at a sea-water 72°F) and full wetsuits are also available to keep out the chill. In the winter of 2000/2001, when the temperature in Florida hit freak lows (almost freezing at night), Discovery Cove came to its visitors' aid by installing temporary heaters around the park and providing complimentary coffee and hot chocolate! Their attention to detail is really that good, and the guest satisfaction ratings remained extremely high (it is hugely popular with British visitors – up to 40% of the daily attendance at times!). However, if any element falls below expectations, it is worth bringing it to the attention of the park managers as they are always keen to rectify any apparent oversights.

For more details, look up www.discoverycove.com. You can book online or call 407 370 1280.

6

Busch Gardens

Question: when is a zoo not a zoo? Answer: when it is also a theme park like 335-acre Busch Gardens in nearby Tampa.

Busch Gardens, the second big Anheuser-Busch park in the area, started life as a mini-menagerie for the wildlife collection of the brewery-owning Busch family. In 1959, they opened a small, tropical-themed hospitality centre next to the brewery and things have mushroomed ever since. Now, it is a major, multi-faceted family attraction, the biggest on Florida's west coast and a little more than an hour from Orlando.

Busch Gardens is rated among the top four zoos in America, with more than 2,700 animals representing more than 320 species of mammals, birds, reptiles, amphibians and spiders. But that's just the start. It boasts a safari-like section of Africa spread over 65 acres of grassy veldt, with special tours to hand-feed some of the animals.

Interspersed among the animals are more than 20 bona fide theme park rides, including the mind-numbing roller-coasters **Kumba, Montu** and **Gwazi,** which guarantee a new experience for coaster addicts, and yet another in the series of simulator rides, the amusing and novel **Akbar's Adventure Tours;** plus animal shows, comedians, musicians, strolling players and a family show extravaganza in the impressive Moroccan Palace Theater, *World Rhythms on Ice.*

The overall theme is Africa, hence the park is subdivided into areas like Nairobi and the Congo, and the dining and shopping facilities are equal to most of the other theme parks. It doesn't quite have the pizzazz of an *Epcot* or Universal, and the staff are a bit more laid back. In a way, it is like the big brother of the Chessington World of Adventures in Surrey, although admittedly on a much grander scale (and in a better climate). But it has guaranteed, 5-star family appeal, especially with its selection of rides just for kids, and it is a big hit with the Brits.

Location

Busch Gardens is the hardest place to locate on the sketchy local maps and the signposting is not as sharp as it could be but, from Orlando, the directions are pretty simple. Head west on I-4 for almost an hour (it is 55 miles from I-4's junction with Highway 192) until you hit the intersecting motorway I-75. Take I-75 north for 3½ miles until you see the exit for Fowler Avenue (Highway 582). Continue west on Fowler for another 3½ miles, then just past the University of South Florida on your right, turn LEFT into McKinley Drive. A mile down McKinley Drive, Busch Gardens' car park entrance will be on your left, where it costs $7 to park.

Those without a car can use the brilliant daily **Busch Gardens Shuttle Express** bus service, which makes several round-trips a day from Orlando at $5 a time (free if you have a 5-Park FlexTicket). You board the Shuttle at SeaWorld, The Mercado, Orlando Premium

The breathtaking Montu roller-coaster

MOROCCO
1 Zagora Café
2 Marrakesh Theater
3 Moroccan Palace Theater
CROWN COLONY
4 Skyride Station
5 Clydesdale Hamlet
6 Crown Colony Restaurant and
  Hospitality Center
SERENGETI PLAIN
7 Edge of Africa
NAIROBI
8 Myombe Reserve
9 Rhino Rally
TIMBUKTU
10 Scorpion
11 Das Festhaus
12 Dolphin Theater
CONGO
13 Kumba
14 Congo River Rapids
15 Python
STANLEYVILLE
16 Stanley Falls Log ïume
17 Tanganyika Tidal Wave
18 Stanleyville Theater
LAND OF THE DRAGONS
19 Dragon's Table Theater
BIRD GARDENS
20 Bird Show Theater
21 Lory Landing
22 Koala Display
23 Hospitality House/Beer School
24 Gwazi
EGYPT
25 Montu
26 Akbar's Adventure Tours
27 Tut's Tomb
28 Train Stations

BUSCH GARDENS

6

Busch Gardens at a glance

Location	Busch Boulevard, Tampa; 75–90 minutes drive from Orlando
Size	335 acres in 11 themed areas
Hours	9.30 or 10am–6pm off peak; 9am–9pm high season (Easter, summer holidays, Thanksgiving, Christmas)
Admission	Under 3 free; 3–9 $40.95 (1-Day Ticket), $67.95 (Busch/SeaWorld Combo ticket), $164.95 (5-Park FlexTicket, including Universal Studios, SeaWorld and Wet 'n Wild); adults (10+) $49.95, $82.95, $202.95
Parking	$7
Lockers	Yes; in Morocco, Congo, Egypt and Stanleyville; $1
Pushchairs	$9 and $15 ($2 refundable; in Morocco)
Wheelchairs	$9 ($2 refundable) and $35 ($5 refundable) with pushchairs
Top Attractions	Rhino Rally, Kumba, Congo River Rapids, Edge of Africa, Elephant Wash, Mystic Sheikhs Band
Don't Miss	*World Rhythms on Ice*, Myombe Reserve, Edge of Africa, Elephant Wash, Mystic Sheikhs band

Hidden Costs	**Meals**	Burger, chips and coke $7.68 3-course meal $15–21 (Crown Colony House)
	Kids' meal	$3.99 ($4.95 Crown Colony House)
	T-shirts	$9.99–27.99
	Souvenirs	99 cents–$599
	Sundries	Ride photos $8.99

Outlets, Universal Studios or Old Town in Kissimmee and pick-up times range from 8–10.15am, returning at 6 or 7pm. Book at the **Guest Services** window at SeaWorld or call 1-800 211 1339.

You may think you have left the crowds behind in Orlando, but, unfortunately, in high season you'd be wrong. It is still advisable to be here in time for opening, if only to be first in line to ride the amazing new Rhino Rally or the dazzling roller-coasters Gwazi, Kumba and Montu, which all draw queues of up to an hour. The Congo River Rapids, Stanley Falls Log Flume ride and Tanganyika Tidal Wave (all opportunities to get wet!) are also prime rides, as is Akbar's Adventure Tours and the other two roller-coasters, Python and Scorpion. The queues take longer to build up here, so for the first few hours you can enjoy a relatively crowd-free experience, even in high season.

Busch Gardens is divided into 11 main sections, with the major rides all a bit of a hike from the main entrance. **Rhino Rally**, which opened in summer 2001, is one of the prime attractions, so I would definitely head here first (especially as the animals are more visible early in the day). Bear right through Morocco, turn left into Nairobi, pass the train station and the Rally entrance is opposite the elephant habitat. **Gwazi,** the fabulous wooden double-coaster, is another to draw a crowd relatively quickly, so, if you are tempted by this first, bear left through Morocco past the Zagora Café and you will soon arrive in its own purpose-built area. Then go through Stanleyville to Congo for **Kumba,** and retrace your steps to do **Congo River Rapids,** the **Python** and the other two water rides. Alternatively, turn right through the main entrance and visit Egypt for **Montu** and **Akbar's**. Here is the full 335-acre layout:

Morocco

Coming through the main gates brings you first into **Morocco,** home of all the main guest services and a lot of the best shops. *Epcot's* Moroccan pavilion sets the scene rather better, but the architecture is still impressive and this version won't overtax your wallet quite as much as Disney does! For a quick meal try the **Zagora Café,** especially at breakfast when the marching, dancing, 8-piece brass band **Mystic Sheikhs** swings into action to entertain the early crowds. Alternatively, the wonderfully enticing **Sultan's Sweets** serves coffee and pastries. Watch out, too, for the strolling Men of Note, a scintillating 4-piece *a cappella* group, and the costumed characters like TJ the Tiger and Hilda Hippo. The **Sultan's Tent** provides a first animal encounter in the form of a resident snake charmer, while turning the corner brings you to the alligator pen. Morocco is also home to two of the park's biggest shows. The **Marrakesh Theater** offers the 25-minute *Moroccan Roll* song and dance show, with live musicians, top-

notch singers and energetic dancers all in an amusing pastiche of pop and rock with a desert theme (hence songs like *Midnight At The Oasis* and *Rock The Casbah*). AAA.

Moroccan Palace Theater: the award-winning and unmissable *World Rhythms on Ice* show is performed here. Even if the thought of an ice show doesn't immediately appeal to you, think again, because this is a surprising and highly entertaining 30-minute spectacular celebrating different cultures around the world. The costumes (some 95 of them) are terrific, the music is vibrant and enhanced by video screens to either side of the stage, and some breathtaking special effects sum up a brilliant concept here. It is also air-conditioned, a welcome relief in summer. AAAAA.

Crown Colony

This area sits in the park's bottom right corner and has five distinct components. Here, you can take the **Skyride** cablecar (AAA) on a 1-way trip to The Congo (and providing a great look at Rhino Rally). The **Clydesdale Hamlet** is also here, but if you've seen the massive dray horses and their stables at SeaWorld, the set-up is pretty similar (AA). The **Showjumping Hall of Fame** will interest equine devotees.

The **Crown Colony Restaurant and Hospitality Center** is a large Victorian-styled building overlooking the Serengeti Plain. It offers counter-service salads, sandwiches and pizzas (downstairs) or a full-service restaurant upstairs with magnificent views of the animals roaming the plain. For a memorable lunch, book here early in the day or, better still, come back for dinner in the early evening and see the animals come down to drink at the water hole.

Serengeti Plain

The Serengeti Plain itself is a 49-acre spread of African savannah that is home to buffalo, antelope, zebra, giraffe, wildebeest, ostriches, hippos, rhinos and many exotic birds, and can be viewed for much of the journey on the **Serengeti Express Railway,** a full-size, open-car steam train that chugs slowly from its main station in Nairobi to Egypt and all the way round to Congo, Stanleyville and back (AAA). It is a good ride to take during the main part of the day when queues build up at the thrill rides.

    Edge of Africa: a 15-acre safari experience that guarantees a close-up encounter almost as good as the real thing. The walk-through attraction puts you in an authentic setting of natural wilds and native villages (right down to the imported plants and even the smells), from which you can view giraffes, lions, baboons, meerkats, crocodiles, hyenas, vultures and even get an

> BRIT TIP: Edge of Africa offers some wonderful photo opportunities, but, in the hot months, come here early in the day as many animals seek refuge from the heat later in the day.

Rhino Rally

underwater view of a specially designed hippopotamus habitat. Look out for the abandoned jeep – you can sit in the front cab while lions lounge in the back! Wandering 'safari guides' and naturalists offer informal talks, and the attention to detail is wonderful. AAAAA. You can also sign up here for the Serengeti Safari by truck (see page 169).

Nairobi

Nairobi is home to the awesome **Myombe Reserve,** one of the largest and most realistic habitats for the threatened highland gorillas and chimpanzees of central Africa. This 3-acre walk-through has a superb tropical setting where the temperature is kept artificially high and convincing with the aid of lush forest landscaping and hidden water mist sprays. Take your time, especially as there are good, seated vantage points, and be patient to

Edge of Africa

Land of the Dragons

twist in store, which opens the way to part two of the ride and the thrilling raging river section that is unlike any attraction to date. Check this out (but get here early to beat the queues). Height restriction is just 3ft. TTTT and AAAAA.

Back at **JR's Gorilla Hut** you can buy your own cuddly baby gorilla (a toy, of course!) and you can get a snack or soft drink at the **Myombe Outpost**. This is also the place to see the Gardens' Asian elephants (check the advertised times for the **Elephant Wash**) and the **Animal Nursery**, which houses all manner of rehabilitating and hand-reared creatures. Continuing round the Nursery brings you to the **Reptile House** and **Tortoise Habitat.** The **Curiosity Caverns,** just to the left of the Nursery, are easy to miss but don't if you want to catch a glimpse of nocturnal and rarely seen creatures in a clever, cave-like setting.

Timbuktu

Passing through Nairobi brings you to the more ride-dominated area of the park, starting with Timbuktu. Here in a North African desert setting you will find many of the elements of a traditional funfair, with a couple of brain-scrambling rides and two good shows.

catch these magnificent creatures going about their daily routine. It is also highly informative, with attendants usually on hand to answer any questions. AAAAA.

Rhino Rally: new in summer 2001, this wonderfully dramatic and scenic ride starts out as an off-road jeep safari and changes into an innovative raft adventure as your 17-passenger vehicle gets caught up in a flash flood. The blockbuster 8-minute whirl through the wilds of Africa includes encounters with elephants, rhinos, crocodiles, antelope and more, as the off-road part of the ride is just about as 'real' as they can make it. Your driver adds to the fun with some amusing spiel about the rally and your purpose-built (by Land-Rover) vehicle, but it soon becomes clear your 'navigator' (the front seat passenger) has led you up the garden path into a blind gully. An unused pontoon bridge is your only way out, but 'fate' has a unique

Lory Landing

Scorpion: a 50mph roller-coaster, this features a 62-ft drop and a 360-degree loop that is guaranteed to dial D for Dizzy for a while! The ride lasts just 120 seconds, but it seems longer! The queues build up here from late morning to mid afternoon, and you have to be at least 3ft 6in tall to ride. TTTT.

Other rides include **The Phoenix,** a positively evil invention, that involves sitting in a gigantic, boat-shaped swing which eventually performs a 360-degree rotation in dramatic, slow-motion style. Don't eat just before this one! TTTT. **Sandstorm** is a fairly routine whirligig contraption that spins and levitates at fairly high speed (hold on to your stomach). TTT. The **Crazy Camel** is an odd sort of ride resembling a giant sombrero that spins and tilts its riders into a state of dizziness. TT.

Then there are a series of scaled-down **Kiddie Rides** that always seem popular with the under 10s (and give Mum and Dad a break as well). The **Carousel Caravan** offers the chance to ride a genuine Mary Poppins-type carousel, while there is also the inevitable **Electronic Arcade** and a **Games Area** of side shows and stalls that require a few extra dollars to play.

Das Festhaus is a combined German Bierfest and entertainment hall, offering a mixture of German and Italian food. It's a jolly, rather raucous establishment, with the 25-minute *International Celebration* show featuring singers, dancers and musicians four or five times a day (AAA). The final element is the **Dolphin Theater,** complete with an aluminium sculpture outside that is a homage to the value of recycling. The 25-minute *Dolphins of the Deep* show borrows heavily from SeaWorld's education-orientated dolphin offering, but still comes up with some terrific leaps, stunts and tricks. AAAA.

Congo

You're into serious ride territory here, with the unmistakable giant turquoise structure of **Kumba** looming over the area. First of all, it's one of the largest and fastest roller-coasters in the south-east United States and, at 60mph, it features three unique elements: a diving loop which plunges the riders a full 110ft, a camelback, with a 360-degree spiral that induces a weightless feeling for three seconds, and a 108-ft vertical loop. For good measure, it dives underground at one point! It looks terrifying close up, but it is absolutely exhilarating, even for non-coaster fans. Restrictions: 4ft 6in. TTTTT.

The **Congo River Rapids** look pretty tame after that, but don't be fooled. These giant rubber tyres will bounce you down some of the most convincing rapids outside of the Rockies, and you will end up with a fair soaking for good measure. TTTT. The **Ubanga-Banga Bumper Cars** are just that, typical fairground dodgems (TT), and you won't miss anything by passing them by for the more daring **Python,** the fourth of Busch Gardens' roller-coasters, with this one featuring a double spiral corkscrew at 50mph from a 70-ft drop. Height restriction is 4ft, and the whole ride lasts just 70 seconds, but it's a blast. TTTT.

More **Kiddie Rides** are available for the smaller visitors. The **Vivi Storehouse Restaurant** offers chicken fajitas, club sandwiches, salads and desserts, and there are two gift shops, including the **Tiger's Den.**

Stanleyville

You pass over Claw Island, home to the park's spectacular rare white Bengal tigers, to get to Stanleyville, which all rather merges into one area from the Congo. Here there are more watery rides, with the popular

BRIT TIP: Don't stand on the bridge into Orchid Canyon unless you want to catch the full weight of the Tidal Wave!

Stanley Falls Log Flume ride (almost identical to the ones at Chessington, Legoland, Thorpe Park and Alton Towers), which guarantees a good soaking at the final drop (TTT) and the distinctly cleverer **Tanganyika Tidal Wave,** which takes you on a scenic ride along 'uncharted' African waters before tipping you down a 2-stage drop that really does land with tidal-wave force. TTTT.

Stanleyville Theater is a good place to relax and put your feet up for a while as you are entertained by the unusual *Jungle Fantasy* show, a mix of circus and acrobatics (direct from St Petersburg, Russia) which provides 30 minutes of offbeat entertainment (AAA).

For a hearty, if messy, meal visit the **Stanleyville Smokehouse** – their wood-smoked ribs platter is a delight. As you leave Stanleyville behind, say hello to the muntjac deer and orang-utans (who are rarely active during the day) in the large pens either side of the **Train Station**.

Land of the Dragons

Parents will want to know about this large, wonderfully clever area of activities, entertainment, rides and attractions purely for the young 'uns. It features a 3-storey treehouse complete with towers and maze-like stairways, a rope climb, ball crawl and outdoor **Dragon's Tale Theater,** which features the 15-minute show with *Captain Kangaroo's Roo Crew* – fun, friendship and ping-pong balls! It is all good, knockabout, well-supervised stuff,

and some of the kiddie rides are superbly inventive, as well as offering plenty of opportunity to get wet. TTTTT (youngsters only – but mums and dads can watch!).

Bird Gardens

Your anti-clockwise route now brings you to the most peaceful area, the **Bird Gardens**. Here it is possible to unwind from the usual theme park hurly-burly. The exhibits and shows are all family-orientated, too, with the 30-minute *For The Birds* presented in the **Bird Show Theater** (part of the original park attraction in 1959; AAA) and the **Hospitality Patio,** where the resident band plays a mix of musical favourites, past and present. **Lory Landing** is a desert island-themed walk-through bird encounter featuring lorikeets, hornbills, parrots and more, with the chance to become a human perch and feed the friendly lorikeets (or have your ear nibbled!). A cup of nectar costs $1, but is a great investment for a memorable photo. Take a slow walk round to appreciate the lush, tropical foliage, and special displays such as the walk-through **Aviary, Flamingo Island, Eagle Canyon** and the emus. AAA.

The highlight of the Bird Gardens, confusingly enough, is the **Koala Display,** in the bottom corner, where these natives of Australia happily sit around and seemingly do nothing all day in front of large crowds. A moving walkway takes you through this gentle exhibit, which also showcases kangaroos and some ring-tailed lemurs. AAA.

A free taste of Anheuser-Busch products is on offer in **Hospitality House,** where you can enroll for **Beer School,** a 40-minute session in the process of beer-making. It offers a fascinating glimpse into the brewery world, and is excellently

6

explained, with the bonus of some tasting! You will also be presented with a Brewery Master certificate. AAA (21 and over only).

Gwazi: now included as part of the Bird Gardens, although it started life as an area in its own right, Busch's most recent roller-coaster is a massive 'duelling' wooden creation in the classic mould (i.e. no going upside down). The two sets of cars, the Gwazi Lion and Gwazi Tiger, each top 50mph and generate a G-force of up to 3.5 as they career around nearly 7,000ft of track with six fly-by encounters. You get to choose your ride in the intricately themed 8-acre village plaza and then you are off up the 90-ft lift for a breathtaking 2½ minutes. The shake, rattle 'n roll effect of a classic coaster is cleverly re-created and the Lion and Tiger rides are slightly different, so you need to do both. Even if you don't like coasters, try this one. Height restrictions: 4ft. TTTTT.

Next door is the **River Rumble** game for kids, a series of catapults that fire water-filled balloons guaranteed to get everyone wet. TTTT (for under 12s). This actually costs an extra $3 for a bucket of 9 balloons (or $5 for two buckets).

Egypt

The final area of Busch Gardens is tucked away through the Crown Colony, so it is best visited either first thing or late in the day. **Egypt** is 8 acres of carefully re-created pharaoh country, dominated by the

Serengeti Safari

Congo River Rapids

trademark roller-coaster **Montu,** named after an ancient Egyptian warrior god. It is a truly breathtaking creation, one of the world's tallest and longest inverted coasters, covering nearly 4,000ft of track at speeds topping 60mph and peaking with a G-force of 3.85! Like Kumba, it looks terrifying, but in reality it is an absolute 5-star thrill as it leaves your legs dangling and swoops and plunges (underground at two points) for almost 3 minutes of brain-scrambling fun. Restrictions: 4ft 6in. TTTTT.

Akbar's Adventure Tours is actually located in Crown Colony because it replaced the Questor ride in 1998. Another in the array of simulator rides, it relies as much on fun as thrills. The TV pre-show leads its audience into the world of down-at-heel Akbar (brilliantly played by comedian Martin Short) and his home-made (and untried) excursion machine. It explores, in unconventional fashion, the secrets and treasures of ancient Egypt, but don't expect a smooth ride – a mysterious force takes control in the forbidden tomb and the trip takes a high-speed turn for the unexpected! It is not recommended for anyone with back or neck problems or expectant mothers, while the height restriction is 3ft 6in. TTTT.

You can travel back in time on a tour of **Tut's Tomb,** as it was discovered by archaeologist Howard

Carter, with clever lighting, audio and even aroma effects. AAA. There is also a neat **Sand Pit** that invites youngsters to undertake their own excavations (with some little 'treasures' to be found!), while the shopping here takes on a high-quality air with its hand-blown glass items, elaborate sculptures and authentic cartouche paintings.

You should finally return to Morocco for a spot of shopping in the area's tempting bazaars. Middle Eastern brass, pottery and carpets will all tempt you into opening your wallet yet again, while there is a full range of Anheuser-Busch products and gift ideas if you haven't already fallen prey to the array of shops and cuddly-toy emporiums around the park.

In addition…

You can take the **Serengeti Safari** tour, a 30-minute excursion (five times a day, taking 20 people at a time) aboard flat-bed trucks to meet the Serengeti Plain's giraffes, zebras, ostriches and rhinos close up and learn more about the park's environmental efforts. You book up at the entrance to Edge of Africa (see page 164) for an extra $29.95, and places fill up very quickly (children must be at least 5 to take part, and 5–15s must be accompanied by a parent).

The **Guided Adventure Tours** take 15 at a time on a VIP park trek, with your own guide, reserved seating at *World Rhythms on Ice* and *Dolphins of the Deep*, front-of-line access for a number of rides and an up-close animal encounter with many of the animals and their staff. It costs $50 in advance (or $60 on the day) in addition to park entry. Finally, the 2-hour **Animal Adventures Tour** is a personal animal experience for 7–10 people a day. The next best thing to

becoming a park zookeeper, it provides close encounters with the Budweiser Clydesdales, black rhinos, hippos, giraffes and elephants, plus participation in various animal behavioural sessions. It is $75 per person in addition to daily admission. All Busch gardens tours can be booked in advance via email at bgt.viptours@buschgardens.com or call 813 984 4043.

For a full family day out, you can combine Busch Gardens with next-door water park **Adventure Island** (on McKinley Drive) which is particularly welcome when it hots up (provided you plaster on the sun cream). The 25 acres of watery fun, in a Key West theme, offer a full range of slides and rides, like the **Wahoo Run** adventure ride, the 76-ft free-fall plunge of the **Tampa Typhoon** and the spiralling **Calypso Coaster,** kids' playground, cafés, gift shops, arcades and volleyball, plus the wonderful **Splash Attack** adventure, a water activity maze culminating in a 1,000-gallon bucket dump on the unwary! Adventure Island is open from mid Feb to late Oct (weekends only Feb to Mar and Sept to Oct) 10am–5pm (later in high season) and a combined Busch Gardens ticket costs $62.95 for adults and $52.95 for 3–9s.

Well, that's the full low-down on all the main theme parks now, but there are still plenty of other attractions…

Montu at Busch Gardens

7

The Other Attractions
(or, One Giant Leap for Tourist Kind)

If you think you have seen everything Orlando has to offer by simply sticking to the theme parks, in the words of the song, 'You ain't seen nothin' yet'. It would be relatively easy to add the Kennedy Space Center to Chapter 6 because, although it's not strictly a theme park, it is adding new attractions all the time and is fast becoming a full day's excursion from Orlando to the east or 'space' coast.

Cypress Gardens and Silver Springs will give you a taste of the more natural things Florida has to offer. The Kissimmee attraction Splendid China provides a completely different park experience, as does the mind-boggling Gatorland, with its alligators, crocs and gator shows (great value, too), and the one-off family centres like WonderWorks, the Orlando Science Center and Ripley's Believe It Or Not.

For more individual attractions, you have the unique aviation experience of Fantasy of Flight, and the Warbirds Air Museum, the hair-raising haunted house walk-through of Skull Kingdom plus a magnificent array of water fun parks.

The choice is yours, but it is an immense selection. Let's start here with One Giant Leap for Mankind.

Kennedy Space Center

The recent change to a fully ticketed entrance fee is a reflection of the massive amount of new development that has taken place at the home of

NASA's space programme. More than $120 million has been spent on revamping the Kennedy Space Center's Visitor Complex in the last few years and, while it was always a great visit in the past, now it is simply unmissable, in my opinion, for its hugely imaginative depiction of the past, present and future of space exploration.

There are five continually running shows or exhibitions, four static showcases, a kids' play area (and a new show designed specifically for them), an art gallery, the Astronaut Encounter, two splendid IMAX films and a full bus tour of the Space Center, which adds up to great value for the entrance fee.

You enter through the futuristic ticket plaza and can spend several hours wandering around the exhibits and presentations of the 70-acre complex itself.

Robot Scouts is a walk-through display-cum-show in the company of Starquester 2000, your robot host who will explain the history of NASA's unmanned space probes in surprising and often amusing style. Next door, the **Quest for Life** film – narrated by *Deep Space Nine* star Avery Brooks – provides another illuminating view in the Universe Theater. Head on out and see some of the hardware of space flight in the completely revamped **Rocket Garden,** which has a kids' water fountain and an Apollo space capsule gantry, to give you the feel of that last earthbound walk before the astronauts boarded the Saturn V rocket. Free guided tours are given twice a day. And don't forget to stop by the **Astronaut Memorial,** a stark, sombre but very moving tribute to the men and women who have died in advancing the space programme. **Shuttle Plaza** allows you to inspect a full-size replica space shuttle, while the **Launch Status Center** displays actual flight hardware, plus live mission briefings. Free walking tours are available several times a day.

Early Space Exploration is a clever and coherent walk-through trip into the recent past of the space programme, including the *Hall of Discovery*, the *Mercury Mission Control Room* – the original consoles from America's first manned space flights – and the *Hall of History*. The futuristic **Exploration in the New Millennium** exhibit provides more appeal for youngsters, with a fun educational element from the spaceship-like *Exploring Gallery*, the *Mars Rock* exhibit and a series of interactive panels. New in 2001 was the kid-friendly **Mad Mission To Mars 2025** show, a mix of educational messages and pure fun theatricals, with lots of special effects, audience participation and even its own hip-hop song, *The Newton Rap*. Children aged 8 up should have a laugh or two here.

Perhaps the most innovative feature, though, is the **Astronaut Encounter,** with personal briefings, Q&A sessions, video footage and anecdotes from various veterans of the Mercury, Gemini and Apollo programmes, plus several Space Shuttle astronauts. It is an amazingly insightful, inspirational and engrossing feature, and takes place up to three times a day at the Center Plaza. You can even take things a step further with the new **Dine With an Astronaut** opportunity (1pm, Mon–Sat only), whereby a small group gets to have lunch with the astronaut of the day. The featured astronaut will also give a special briefing adding extra insight

into their space missions. Various packages are available, starting at $29.95 for adults and $19.95 for children aged 3–11, and tickets may be purchased online (see below) or by phone at 321 449 4444.

Kids have their own playground, too, the **Children's Play Dome,** complete with a one-fifth scale space shuttle. Owners Delaware North Parks Services have lavished a fortune on upgrading the Center and, for my money, it's an essential experience for all but pre-school children. In many ways, it knocks the artificiality of Disney and Co into a cocked hat.

The air-conditioned **Coach Tour** (departures every 15 minutes), fully narrated throughout, makes two important stops in addition to driving around much of the working area of the Space Center, including the truly massive Vehicle Assembly Building. The first stop is the **LC39 Observation Gantry,** just one mile from shuttle launch pad 39A, a combination 4-storey observation deck and exhibition centre. The exhibits consist of a 10-minute film on the preparation of a shuttle for launch, models and videos of a launch countdown and touch-screen information on the shuttle programme.

Next is the awesome **Apollo/ Saturn V Center,** one of the area's truly great exhibits, where you can easily spend 90 minutes. It highlights the Apollo programme and first moon landing with two deeply impressive theatrical presentations on the risks and triumphs, with an actual 363-ft Saturn V rocket and a hands-on gallery that brings the past, present and future of space exploration into sharp focus. It is also quite a humbling experience. A third stop for the **International Space Station Center** had been discontinued with extra security considerations brought in after September 11. You should

7

ORLANDO'S OTHER ATTRACTIONS

A	Winter Park	S	Grand Cypress Equestrian Center
B	Aquatic Wonders Tours	T	Horse World Riding Stables
C	Boggy Creek Airboat Rides	U	Pirates Dinner Show
D	Port Canaveral	V	TD Waterhouse Center
E	Leu Gardens	W	Citrus Bowl Stadium
F	Warbird Air Museum	X	Osceola County Stadium
G	Green Meadows Petting Farm	Y	Central Florida Zoo
H	Sanford-Rivership Romance	Z	Sak Comedy Club
I	WonderWorks	A1	Sleuth's Mystery Dinner Shows
J	Trainland Inc	B1	Arabian Nights
K	Disney's Wilderness Preserve	C1	Forever Florida
L	Marriott's Orlando World Center	D1	Orlando Science Center
M	West Orange Trail Bikes	E1	Orange County History Center
N	Kissimmee Rodeo	F1	Lake Eola
O	Richard Petty Driving Experience	G1	Medieval Times
P	Black Hammock Fish Camp	H1	Hard Rock Vault
Q	Dave's Ski School	J1	Skull Kingdom
R	Dolly Parton's Dixie Stampede		

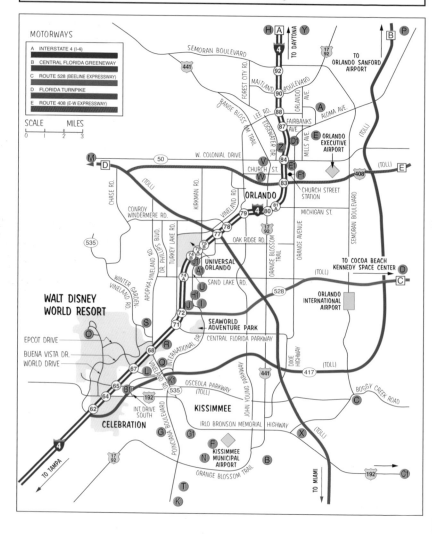

allow a good 2–3 hours to do the tour justice.

Additional tours are available at an extra $20 per person (adult or child). **Cape Canaveral: Then and Now** is a 2-hour-plus in-depth journey (security considerations permitting) into the early days of space exploration around the older part of the facility. Highlights include the Air Force Space Museum, Mercury launch sites and Memorial, original astronaut training facility and several active launch pads, all of which are otherwise off-limits. The 90-minute **NASA Up Close** takes visitors along the astronaut's launch day routine, with a look at both launch pads, the Vehicle Assembly Building and the gigantic crawler transports.

Equally impressive are the IMAX cinemas – 55-ft screens that give the impression of sitting on top of the action. The 37-minute film **The Dream Is Alive** puts you inside a space shuttle mission, while the new 3-D **Space Station** (narrated by Tom Cruise) is a breathtaking slice of science fact, living with the crew of the International Space Station as it comes together, and affording a heart-stopping look at the construction process. Both films are included in the admission price.

The Visitor Complex boasts an excellent **Space Shop,** four restaurants, including the full-service **Mila's,** and three snack counters. Even the Apollo/Saturn V Center has its own café where you can sit and marvel at it all.

Getting there: to get to the Kennedy Space Center, take the Beeline Expressway out of Orlando (Route 528, and it's a toll road, remember) for about 45 minutes, then bear left on the SR 407 (Don't follow the signs to Cape Canaveral or Cocoa Beach at this point) and turn right at the T-junction on to SR 405. The Space Center's Visitor Center is located 6 miles along SR 405 on the right-hand side. Opening

hours are 9am to dusk every day except Christmas Day, and it is busiest around lunchtime.

Admission to the complex is $25 for adults and $15 for children 3–11. Parking is free. It is open daily (but not on Shuttle launch days – call 321 449 4444 to check when those are) from 9am and the first tours and IMAX presentations start at 9.30am, while the final tour of the day is 2 hours before dark. For more details, log on to their website at www.kennedyspacecenter.com. Total attraction rating: AAAAA.

The greatest thrill of all, however, is an actual **shuttle launch,** of which there are six or seven a year. You can call the number above for information and Launch Transportation Tickets to a viewing area just 6 miles from the launch pad or buy them online via the Space Center's website above. Adult tickets cost $35.50 and $22.50 (including admission to the Visitor Complex), or $15 a head for the launch-viewing site only. However, in the event of a

Kennedy Space Center

launch cancellation, there are NO refunds, and the traffic in the area is usually humongous, taking anything up to 3 hours to get from Orlando to the Space Center. Alternatively, prime viewing sites are available outside the Space Center along Highway 1 in Titusville and Highway A1A through Cape Canaveral and Cocoa Beach. To be on hand for a shuttle launch is certainly an awe-inspiring experience.

Astronaut Hall of Fame

While the Kennedy Space Center tells you primarily about the machinery of putting men in space, the neighbouring Astronaut Hall of Fame (on SR 405, just before the main entrance to the Space Center) gives you the full low-down on the people involved. This museum to the space programmes houses some fascinating memorabilia, interactive exhibits and engaging explanations of the people behind the spacesuits. Prepare to be amazed at how incredibly small the cockpits of the early manned space flights were and amused by personal touches like Buzz Aldrin's High School report!

A chronologically coherent approach divides the Hall of Fame into six main sections. The **Entry Experience** introduces the visions of space flight, with an 8-minute video of the astronauts as modern explorers, and leads into **Race to the Moon,** the stories of the Mercury, Gemini and Apollo missions and their people. The **New Frontier** opens the way for Skylab and Shuttle missions, adjacent to the **Astronaut Hall of Fame,** the museum's heart and soul. **Space Explorers Today and Tomorrow** includes the audio-visual experience aboard the replica Shuttle to Tomorrow and a glimpse of the Space Camp for kids, before introducing the hands-on **Astronaut**

Adventure with its working models, G-force and flight simulators (a cabin that does six 360-degree rolls!), space-walk 'chairs', moon exploration, interactive computers and Mars Mission experience. Active minds will be more than rewarded. The First on the Moon exhibit also focuses on the selection of the Apollo 11 crew.

> BRIT TIP: Every Friday is Space Camp graduation day, so avoid the Hall of Fame then unless you want to be surrounded by dozens of highly enthusiastic 'space cadets' and their parents.

Admission is $13.95 for adults and $9.95 for kids aged 6–12 (5 and under free; 10% discount for seniors), with opening hours 9am–5pm (6pm in summer months), 7 days a week (except Christmas). The gift shop sells refreshments provided by the **Cosmic Café.** If you enjoyed the Kennedy Space Center, try to spend a couple of hours here. Total attraction rating: AAAA.

The residential **Space Camp** may be of interest to you if you have children of 9–12 who would like to train to be junior astronauts for 5 days. It's not cheap – $699/child – but it is a magnificent educational recreation for kids, and the camp is happy to take visitors from the UK. You have to book up about 2 months in advance, but then just bring your youngsters along on Sunday afternoon and pick them up again on Friday morning. They are arranged into groups and go through activities like flight and space-walk simulators, simulated space missions, studying rocket propulsion, space technology and other scientific experiments. For details, phone 407 267 3184 or visit www.AstronautHallofFame.com.

Cypress Gardens

Turning from the futuristic to the more natural, Cypress Gardens offers more than 200 acres of immaculate botanical gardens, spectacular flower festivals, world-famous water-ski shows and plenty of good ol' southern hospitality. It was the first 'theme park' in Florida, pre-dating *Walt Disney World Resort in Florida* by 35 years, and it has gradually expanded to remain a pleasant alternative to the usual water park experience. A new mini water park now provides a real child-friendly aspect for the first time.

It is about a 45-minute drive from Kissimmee, down I-4, turning off at Exit 55. Go south on Highway 27 for 20 miles and then right on to SR 540. Cypress Gardens is 6 miles along SR 540, on the left.

After the major tourist hustle of Orlando, the Gardens are an island of peace and tranquillity. Plan on spending the best part of a day here, too, as there is plenty to do. Start with a boat tour round the canals of the **Botanical Gardens** (NB: this attraction has had to close several times in recent years because water levels were too low to operate boats, due to drought), then stroll round the gardens themselves, taking note of the immense **banyan tree** (unlike Disney's Swiss Family Treehouse, this one is real!), the photogenic **Southern Belles** in their colourful period outfits and the beautiful **Gazebo,** which hosts more than 300 weddings a year.

Retracing your steps brings you to the spectacular **Water Ski Show,** the all-new 1950s-themed *Rockin' Around The Dock*, which features world-class skiers and breathtaking routines (odd fact: the ski show here is the world's longest-running single attraction, operating every day since 1942). There is also a water-ski adventure programme for $25 per person and a deluxe package with VIP backstage tour, T-shirt and souvenir photo for $50 (visit the Information Desk on your way in to book a place).

Continue on and have your picture taken in front of the **Mediterranean Waterfall,** then marvel at the delights of the centrepiece garden attraction: the **Spring Flower Festival** runs from March to May, the **Victorian Garden Party** (featuring clever topiary 'statues') all year long, the **Mum Festival** (featuring more than 2.5 million chrysanthemum blooms) in November and the **Poinsettia Festival/Festival of Trees** from the end of November to early January.

Next up are the **Plantation Gardens,** which offer the practical side of gardening with tips on how to grow herbs, vegetables, roses and other flowers. The **Wings of Wonder** exhibit is a huge butterfly house where more than 1,000 butterflies hatch from glass cabinets and flutter around in tropical splendour. Stop off for a *Gone with the Wind* experience at the beautifully restored **Magnolia Mansion**. The **Island in the Sky** will then lift you up 15 storeys on its circular revolving platform for a grandstand view of the park.

Model railway fans are also well catered for at the indoor, 20-train **Cypress Junction,** with replicas of various US landmarks on 1,100ft of track, while next door is **Carousel Cove,** a selection of games, rides and other activities to keep the youngsters amused for a while. New in 2001, just through Carousel Cove, is the **Wacky Water Park** (open from 10.30am–5pm daily; closed in winter), which offers kids – from toddlers to teens – the chance to really expend some energy on a series of pools, slides, flumes and splash areas. The main pool is geared primarily for under 8s, with a zero-depth entry and greatest depth of only 18in. It features an array of squirting animals, small slides and

Rockin' Around the Dock ski show

splash zones (including a tropical 'volcano'!), while the Flumarama section has six slides and one tube ride, from the rather tame (by *Disney's Blizzard Beach* standards) Coral Reef to the whizzier Typhoon Twister. Changing rooms and lockers are also available.

The huge **FloraDome** is a beautiful covered flower exhibit of thousands of blooms that changes several times a year, with the extra scenic elements of waterfalls, streams and a large-scale model railway.

In addition to the water-ski extravaganza, there are three other notable shows offering contrasting live entertainment at various times. The **Palace Theater** houses the spectacular Moscow on Ice show *Skate The States* (in great air-conditioned comfort), while **Nature's Arena** offers *Calling All Animals* – featuring parrots, a cotton-top tamarin, a 15ft-long albino python and two miniature horses – three times daily. New in 2002 was **Mystical Magic,** a show of mystery, surprise and fun (would you believe a mind-reading snake?!) by illusionists Fred and Kellie Becker.

The Southern Breeze paddle steamer

A mini zoo showcases the likes of wallabies, fallow deer and cotton-top tamarins in **Nature's Way** and **Nature's Boardwalk** (including the inevitable Gator Gulch), while the **Birdwalk Aviary** is a walk-through encounter with lorikeets and Australian parrots that eat out of your hand.

The pretty **Southern Breeze** paddle wheel riverboat provides historical excursions on Lake Eloise during the day for a small extra fee and themed dinner cruises in the evening and for Sunday brunch (separate ticket required – call 863 324 2111 to book, or call at the ticket booth during your visit).

The Gazebo at Cypress Gardens

There are 14 shops and gift stores to tempt you into buying yet more souvenirs, from the children-friendly **Butterfly Shop,** to **Sweet Creations** (home-made fudge and real citrus juice, marmalades and jellies). The **Village Fare** food court offers a good choice of eating, from freshly carved roast beef to pizza and salads, while the **Cypress BBQ** serves up barbecue-smoked chicken and ribs, and the **Crossroads Restaurant** is full-service dining in air-conditioned comfort. Again, there's no shortage of choice, quality is consistently high and value for money is good.

Cypress Gardens is open 9.30am–5pm, with extended hours during the festivals, including until 8pm for the spectacular **Spring Lights** (Feb 1–April 30) and 9pm for the **Garden**

Silver Springs glass-bottomed boat

of Lights Holiday Festival (Nov 21 to Jan 6), neither of which should be missed. The former features more than 4 million twinkling lights, a 110-ft Tree of Light and fireworks every Saturday evening, while the latter is themed to a Christmas story, with festive set-pieces and a positive explosion of glistening lights, and a 116ft-high Christmas tree which alone bears some 25,000 lights.

Admission is $34.95 for adults and $19.95 for 6–12s (under 6s free). Check out www.cypressgardens.com for the latest information. Parking is $5. AAAA.

Silver Springs

Continuing the theme of more natural attractions, we have Silver Springs, just under 2 hours' drive to the north of Orlando. This peaceful 350-acre nature park (don't worry, you won't have to walk round all of it) surrounds the headwaters of the crystal-clear Silver River. Glass-bottomed boats take you to watch the artesian springs (the largest in the world) that bubble up here, along with plenty of wildlife. Expect close encounters with alligators,

BRIT TIP: Silver Springs and Wild Waters are both busy at the weekend. You shouldn't encounter many queues here during the rest of the week.

turtles, raccoons and lots of waterfowl, while the park also contains a collection of more exotic animals, like bears, panthers, giraffes, camels and zebras that can be viewed from either land or water.

Four animal shows, an alligator and crocodile encounter, the world's largest bear exhibit, a petting zoo, a kids' adventure playground and a white alligator exhibit complete the attractions. To ruin a few more illusions of the film industry, this was the setting for the 1930s' and 1940s' Tarzan films starring Johnny Weissmuller. And, once you have absorbed the timeless tropical nature of the landscape, you will understand why they decided to save on the cost of shipping the film crew to Africa.

Silver Springs is located on SR 40 just through the town of Ocala, 72 miles to the north of Orlando. Take the Florida Turnpike north (it's a toll road, remember) until it turns into I-75 and, 28 miles further north, you turn off and head east on SR 40. Another 10 miles brings you to Silver Springs, just past the Wild Waters water park on your right.

The park's main attraction (dating back to 1878) is the **Glass-bottomed Boat Ride,** a 20-minute tour which goes down well with all the family and gives a first-class view of the seven different springs and a host of water life. Similarly, the **Lost River Voyage** is another 20-minute

Splendid China

boat trip down one of the unspoilt stretches of the Silver River, including a visit to the park's animal hospital where the local park ranger introduces you to all his current charges. The third boat trip, the **Jungle Cruise,** is a water safari, where animals from six continents, including giraffes, ostriches and antelope, are arranged in natural settings along the riverbanks.

As an alternative to messing about on the river, the **Jeep Safari** is a 15-minute ride in the back of an open trailer through a natural forest habitat, home to more animals from other corners of the world, such as tapirs, marmosets, antelope and vultures (plus a drive-through alligator pond!). Then there are the three **Ross Allen Island Animal Shows,** each one lasting 15 minutes and featuring an entertaining – and occasionally hair-raising – look at the worlds of reptiles, birds (including comical parrots, macaws and cockatoos) and creepy crawlies. The hair-raising part occurs only if you are the unlucky victim chosen to display a large tarantula, giant cockroach or scorpion. As you exit the animal shows take time to wander round **Big Gator Lagoon** and the **Crocodile Encounter** in a 1-acre cypress swamp habitat, viewed from a raised boardwalk. See the largest American crocodile in captivity, the 16-ft, 2,000-lb Sobek, as well as a collection of alligators, turtles and Galapagos tortoises. The **Florida Natives** attraction features a collection of snakes, turtles, spiders, otters and other denizens of the state. The **Botanical Gardens** then provide a peaceful haven to sit and watch the world go by for a while.

Other large-scale exhibits are the **World of Bears,** an educational presentation including conservation information in a 2-acre spread devoted to bears of all kinds (including the largest of its type in the world), from grizzly to spectacled and black bears, and the **Panther Prowl,** with a unique look at the endangered Florida panther and Western cougar. Both of these have educational presentations on their welfare several times daily.

Birds of Prey is a 30-minute show in the Silver River Showcase arena, highlighting the strengths, beauty and conservation issues of the park's collection of hawks, eagles, owls, falcons and vultures in a dramatic free-flight demonstration.

Children are not forgotten, either. **The Kids Ahoy!** playland, with its centrepiece riverboat featuring slides, rides, an air bounce, ball crawl, 3-D net maze, carousel, bumper boats and games, and **Doolittle's Petting Zoo,** with its deer and goats, are both big draws for the young ones.

The usual collection of shops and eateries are fairly ordinary here, in contrast to the slick appeal of Orlando's parks, although the **Deli** offers some pleasant sandwich alternatives for lunch and the **Springside Restaurant** is above average. In all, you would probably want to spend a good half day here, with the possibility of a few hours in the neighbouring 9-acre water park of **Wild Waters,** which offers slides like the Twin Twister, a pair of 60ft-high flumes, the free-fall Thunderbolt, the twin-tunnelled Tornado, the 220ft-long Silver Bullet and the helter-skelter Osceola's Revenge, as well as a 400-ft tube ride on the turbo-charged Hurricane, a huge wave pool, and various kid-sized fun in Cool Kids Cove and Caribbean Sprayground.

Admission fees are $32.99 for adults, $29.99 for seniors (55+) and $23.99 for children under 4ft tall (under 3s free). A joint ticket (Silver Springs and Wild Waters) is $36.99 and $27.99. Parking is $5. Open 10am–5pm, 7 days a week. Visit www.silversprings.com for more info or call 352 236 2121. AAAA.

Splendid China

New in 1994 and still expanding and modifying its various displays and exhibits, Splendid China is unique to central Florida and a completely different type of attraction. You won't find rides and other flights of fancy, but you will be taken on a fascinating journey through one of the biggest and most mysterious and breathtaking countries in the world.

This 76-acre park offers a range of intricate, miniaturised features like the Great Wall of China, the Forbidden City and the Stone Forest, some fascinating full-size exhibits, thrilling acrobats and martial arts experts and, naturally enough, some great food. There is a play area for young children but, realistically, the park will not hold their attention for long and in summer there is little escape from the relentless heat. But where it scores impressively is in its amazing eye for detail, its air of authenticity (genuine Chinese craftsmen were brought in to hand-build every miniature) and its peaceful atmosphere – quite an achievement in the tourist bustle of Orlando!

Splendid China is located at the western end of the main tourist drag of Highway 192, just 3 miles west of its junction with I-4, off the main road opposite the big Key W Kool Restaurant, on Splendid China Boulevard. The minimum time requirement is 3–4 hours, to take in all the different shows and attractions. Here's how its 10,000-mile journey through 5,000 years of history works. The four elements are essentially:

The exhibits: more than 60 painstakingly recreated scale models of China's greatest buildings, statues and landmarks. The **Great Wall** is one of the most striking, at half a mile long and up to $5\frac{1}{2}$ft high. It is constructed of more than 6 million tiny bricks, all faithfully put into place by hand. Other highlights include Beijing's **Imperial Palace and Forbidden City,** the 26-storey **Grand Buddha of Leshan** (reduced to a 'mere' 36ft tall), and the **Mausoleum of Genghis Khan.** The stairs by the side of the **Mausoleum of Dr Sun Yat Sen** afford a wonderful high-rise overview of the park, while the famous **Terracotta Warriors** exhibit offers a chance to get in the air-conditioned cool for a few minutes. Splendid China is three-quarters the size of the *Magic Kingdom Park,* so it demands a fair amount of leg work to appreciate all the exhibits.

The shows: There are four centres for the performing arts which showcase the talents of some top musicians, artists, acrobats and martial arts exponents. Inside the park, the **Temple of Light Theater** is the main centre, staging internationally acclaimed acrobatic exhibitions of around 30 minutes a time. On the opposite side of the park is the **Pagoda Gardens Show Area,** which features gold medal-winning Martial Artists from China's Shandong Province. In the heart of the park is the **Imperial Bells Theater,** with Chinese traditional music and instruments, including ancient bells and drums. The highlight, though, is the **Golden Peacock Theater** next to the park entrance. During the day, dance and folk costume shows are presented, and, in the evening, it features the 90-minute spectacular (not Mondays) *Mysterious Kingdom of the Orient,* which showcases the amazing talents of some 50 dancers, acrobats and martial artists in magnificent costumes.

You need to get your entry ticket validated if you leave the park early and want to return for this show, or you can pay the $16 (children 5–12 $10.95) for the show on its own, which includes a buffet-style meal in with the price.

7

The restaurants: the park sets great store by its food, whether it be in its sumptuous 5-star restaurant or its cafeteria-style buffet. The jewel in the crown is the elegant **Suzhou Pearl Restaurant** for full-service, gourmet cuisine, while more budget-priced is the **Seven Flavors,** a cafeteria-style diner offering American as well as Chinese dishes.

The shops: unlike the other theme parks, Splendid China's shopping opportunities are all located in the Chinatown front area of the park, which is open to the general public without park admission. The 10 gift shops are also one up on their counterparts by stocking a more upmarket and distinctive range of goods, from Bonsai trees to furniture, jewellery to T-shirts, silk and satin clothing to children's toys, and antique curios to contemporary artefacts. In many instances you can watch the Chinese craftsmen and women at work.

The mixture of Chinese and Floridian staff adds to the friendly atmosphere the park generates, but ultimately it is a difficult concept to describe so the best advice is to see it for yourself.

Admission is $26.99 for adults, seniors $23.99 and children (5–12) $16.99 (under 5s free). You can also take a guided tour for an extra $9/person. Opening hours are 9.30am–6pm, 7 days a week and parking is free. AAAA.

A Gatorland denizen

Gatorland

For another taste of the 'real' Florida, this is as authentic as it gets when it comes to the wildlife, and consequently it is popular with children of all ages. When the wildlife consists of several thousand menacing alligators and crocodiles in various natural habitats and four fascinating shows, you know you're in for a different experience. 'The Alligator Capital of the World' was founded in 1949 and is still family-owned, hence it possesses a home-spun charm and naturalism which few of its big-money competitors can match.

> **BRIT TIP:** If you have an evening flight home, Gatorland is handy to visit on your final day. Conveniently located, it is the ideal place to soak up half a day or so.

Start by taking the 15-minute **Gatorland Express** railway around the park to get an idea of its 110-acre expanse. This costs an extra $1 but is good for multiple rides, is fully narrated (usually in amusing style) and is especially good fun for kids. You also get a good look at the native Florida animal habitat, which features whitetail deer, wild turkey and quail. Wander through the natural Florida countryside beauty of the 2,000ft-long **Swamp Walk,** as well as the **Alligator Breeding Marsh Walkway,** with its 3-storey observation tower, and get a close-up view of these great reptiles, who seem to hang around the walkway in the hope someone might 'drop in' for lunch.

Breeding pens, baby alligator nurseries and rearing ponds are also situated throughout the park to provide an idea of the growth cycle of the Florida gator and enhance the overall feeling that it is the visitor behind bars here, not the animals. Many of the small-scale attractions have been designed with kids in mind and there is plenty to keep even the youngest amused, notably at **Lilly's Pad,** an imaginative water playground guaranteed to get them good and wet (swimming costumes definitely advisable). **Allie's Barnyard** is the petting zoo, while you can feed some friendly lorikeets at the **Very Merry Aviary.** Other animals on view include bats, iguanas, turtles, turkey vultures, tortoises, snakes, flamingos, emus, a Florida bear and deer.

However, the gators and crocs are the main attraction and it is the three shows which are the real draw (although you will never find yourself on the end of a queue here). The 800-seat **Wrestling Stadium** sets the scene for some real Cracker-style feats (a Cracker is the local term for a Florida cowboy) as Gatorland's resident 'wranglers' catch themselves a 7–8ft-long gator and proceed to point out the animal's various survival features, with the aid of some daredevil stunts that will have you questioning the cowboys' sanity.

The **Gator Jumparoo** is another eye-opening spectacle as some of the park's biggest creatures use their tails to 'jump' out of the water and be hand-fed tasty morsels, like whole chickens! **Jungle Crocs of the World** features some of the deadliest animals of Egypt, Australia and Cuba, with authentic lairs and brilliant presentation, while the show element has its scare-raising moments as the highly knowledgeable guides enter the pens to tell you all about the inhabitants. The revamped **Upclose Animal Encounters** is another entertaining and highly amusing showcase of various creatures, from the obvious snakes to less obvious scorpions and cockroaches. Brave children can provide some great photo opportunities here!

Obviously, face-to-face encounters with the park's living dinosaurs is not everyone's cup of tea, but it's an experience you're unlikely to repeat anywhere else. In addition, you can dine on smoked alligator ribs and deep-fried gator nuggets (as well as burgers and hot dogs) at **Pearl's Smokehouse,** with excellent kids' meals at $3.99. The park is also home to hundreds of nesting herons and egrets, providing a fascinating close-up of the nests from March to August. Gatorland is actually Central Florida's largest wading bird sanctuary and it adds an extraordinary aspect to this very user-friendly park.

Getting there: Gatorland is located on the South Orange Blossom Trail, 2 miles south of its junction with the Central Florida Greeneway and 3 miles north of Highway 192.

Admission: Gatorland also scores on its great value for money, with adult tickets at $17.93, children 3–12, $8.48, while there is also a $5 Walkabout Tour several times a day, offering more insight into the park's history and the behind-the-scenes areas, including an encounter with a baby gator. Hours are 9am–dusk and parking is free. www.gatorland.com for more info. AAAA.

Fantasy of Flight

A new venture worth noting here is Gatorland's Cypress Glades Adventure Tours, which provides more wildlife opportunities in St Cloud, some 25 miles to the south (see Chapter 8, Off The Beaten Track).

Fantasy of Flight

Another wonderful and fresh alternative on the Central Florida scene is this aviation museum attraction which is an absolute must, even for anyone not usually interested in the history of flight or the glamour of the Golden Age of flying. Just 25 minutes down I-4 towards Tampa (take Exit 44, Polk City, go north on SR 559 for half a mile, then turn left into the main entrance), Fantasy of Flight is a 5-part adventure featuring the world's largest private collection of vintage aircraft.

You start by entering the **History of Flight,** a series of expertly recreated 'immersion experiences' into memorable moments in aviation history. The entrance alone is eye-opening – you enter the fuselage of a DC-3 Dakota as if for a parachute drop, and step out into a moonlit night – and then visit set-pieces like a dogfight over the trenches in World War One and a bomber mission with a real Flying Fortress in World War Two. Audio-visual effects and film clips enhance the experience and give everything an awe-inspiring feeling of authenticity.

You exit into the **Vintage Aircraft** displays in two huge hangers, with the exhibits ranging from a replica Wright Flyer, to a Ford Tri-Motor, a Mk-XVI Spitfire and the world's only fully working Short Sunderland flying boat. From the museum's collection of 40 or so vintage planes, one is selected each day as the **Aircraft of the Day,** with a pilot holding a question-and-

answer session about that plane before performing an aerial demonstration over Fantasy of Flight. Two **Guided Tours** are given each day, one taking visitors into the Backlot and the other visiting the Restoration Shop, highlighting what it takes to restore and maintain these magnificent machines. Finally, **Fightertown** features eight realistic fighter simulators that take you through a World War Two aerial battle. You get a pre-flight briefing on how to handle your 'plane' (a Vought Corsair), and then climb in to the totally enclosed cockpit to do battle with the Japanese Air Force. It's difficult, absorbing, fun and totally addictive.

The whole experience is crafted in 1930s' art deco style, including a full-service diner (the excellent **Compass Rose**) and original gift shop. There is strong British appeal with the war depictions and the exhibits.

Admission is $24.95 for adults, $22.95 for seniors (60+) and $13.95 for kids 5–12 (under 5s free). It is open 9am–5pm and parking is free. Additionally, you can take a vintage **biplane ride** here with Waldo Wright's Flying service in an open-cockpit 1929 New Standard D-25 for $49/person (up to 4 passengers a time) or try the Fantasy of Flight 3-hour **balloon ride** experience for $160 (up to 3 passengers). Both operate seasonally and reservations are required.

Fantasy of Flight is the brainchild of American entrepreneur and aviation whiz Kermit Weeks and I have yet to encounter an attraction put together with more genuine affection. In fact, it is as much a work of art as a tourist attraction, and the masses have yet to discover it, too. For more info call 863 984 3500 or check them out on www.fantasyofflight.com. AAAA.

International Drive Area

The long tourist corridor of I-Drive continues to be a fast-developing source of hotels, restaurants, shopping and, more importantly, fun. It now has its own development council, advertising 'Orlando's Most Dynamic Destination', to emphasise its attractions. The I-Ride trolley brings it all together in transport terms and their website at www.InternationalDriveOrlando.com highlights all the possibilities. There is an Official Visitors Guide with an I-Ride map and valuable money-off coupons (which they can mail to the UK), and a freephone number – 1-866 2437 483 – to steer people in the right direction. Here's a look at the top attractions (see also chapters 9 and 11 – Orlando By Night and Shopping – to complete the picture):

Ripley's Believe It Or Not

You can't miss this particular attraction, next to The Mercado shopping village on I-Drive, as its extraordinary tilted appearance makes it seem as though it was designed by an architect with an aversion to the horizontal. However, once inside you soon get back on the level and, for an hour or two, you can wander through this museum dedicated to the weird and wonderful.

BRIT TIP: Ripley's, Hard Rock Vault and WonderWorks are all handy retreats to keep in mind for places to visit on the occasional rainy day.

Robert L Ripley was an eccentric and energetic explorer and collector who, for 40 years, travelled the world in his bid to assemble a collection of the greatest oddities known to man. The Orlando branch of this worldwide chain features 8,900sq ft of displays, including authentic artefacts, video presentations, illusions, interactive exhibits and music. The elaborate re-creation of an Egyptian tomb showcases a mummy and three rare mummified animals, while the Primitive Gallery contains artefacts from tribal societies around the world (some quite gruesome). Human and Animal Oddities, Big and Little galleries, Illusions and Dinosaurs all boast some recent up-dates and extra interactive elements.

The collection of miniatures includes the world's smallest violin and a single grain of rice hand-painted with a tropical sunset. Larger-scale exhibits include a portion of the Berlin Wall, a two-thirds scale 1907 Rolls Royce built entirely out of matchsticks and a version of the *Mona Lisa* textured completely from toast!

Admission is $14.95 for adults and $9.95 for 4–12s and it is open 9am–1am daily (last ticket sold at midnight). AAA.

Hard Rock Vault

Opening in December 2002, this is the interactive rock 'n roll museum from the worldwide and highly innovative restaurant chain. After the success of their Hard Rock Live venue (see page 227) at Universal's CityWalk and the Hard Rock Hotel, this promises to be another exercise in rock chic, with 17,000sq ft of dedicated space paying homage to the past and present of rock 'n roll in a Hall of Fame-type setting. There are both guided and self-guided tours through a 'living timeline', or chronological review, of music and its effect on society, era by era, from the 1950s on. The Vault also features some of the most prized pieces from the Hard Rock

Ripley's Believe It or Not!

collection from all over the world (more than 100 HR Cafes in more than 40 countries), as well as material which has never been seen before. The story is unfolded through video, artefacts, music and instruments, while the tour guides play a big part in bringing it all to life. There is a listening room, with a show of its own, a snack bar and a Hard Rock merchandise shop, and the creators estimate that rock devotees will want to spend from 2–4 hours here.

Admission is $14.99 for adults and $9.99 for children aged 5+ (under 5s free). For more info, visit www.hardrock.com. If you have youngsters keen to investigate a rock or pop career, the new **Hard Rock Academy** could be for them. This 5-day programme at Hard Rock Live for 12–17-year-olds in both vocal and stage performance offers

Skull Kingdom

tuition and advice in areas like talent agent counselling, audition skills and recording a CD and aims to make the classes both fun and practical. Orlando was the training ground for acts like Britney Spears, *NSYNC and O-Town, and the Academy can call on some top teaching talent, too. However, it's not a cheap course, with fees starting from $1,495. Call 407 445 7625 or visit the website for more details. AAAA (expected).

Skull Kingdom

The walk-through haunted house idea takes on a new dimension here. Not content with a house, this is a full-blown castle on I-Drive (opposite Wet 'n Wild) dedicated to frights, horrors and grisly goings-on at every turn. The setting and lavishness of the Kingdom of the

> **BRIT TIP:** Friday and Saturday evenings are peak periods for Skull Kingdom, with queues of up to 30 minutes.

Skull Lord marks it out as way above average, and the combination of elaborate light and sound effects, robotics and the scream-inducingly brilliant live actors (who are kept suitably creepy by full-time make-up artists) provides a hair-raising experience. The shock tactics are state of the art, with the best elements of horror films and haunted houses well maintained over the 2-storey spread of mazes, caverns and other demonic challenges (watch out for the monster spit!).

The Haunted Gift Shop and Ghoulish Arcade Games await you at the end of your 20–30-minute (depending on how much you 'enjoy' the experience!) Skull Kingdom immersion. It is open

6pm–11pm (Mon–Thur), noon–midnight (Fri–Sun), with extended hours in peak season, and admission $12.50/person (www.skullkingdom.com). Go with a few friends, or have a drink or three first! TTTTT (not recommended for under 12s).

> BRIT TIP: WonderWorks and Fun Spot are both open until midnight in high season, long after most of the theme parks are shut, meaning you can have a day at the park and then let the kids loose here for a while to really tire them out!

Fun Spot

Here is another choice for full-scale, family-sized fun, just off I-Drive on Del Verde Way (look for the 102ft-high big wheel past the junction with Kirkman Road). With four different and highly challenging go-kart tracks, bumper cars and boats, four quite daring fairground-type rides (check out the Spyder and Paratrooper), an impressive 2-storey video arcade (one of the largest in Florida) and food court, plus five Kid Spot rides for the little ones, the 4.7-acre park promises several hours of fun.

Admission and parking are free, but you must buy tickets for the rides, which are $3 each (or $22 for eight). Go-karts require 2 tickets, while the other rides are a ticket apiece. However, if you are planning on a visit of an hour or longer, their 'armband' tickets are better value. The Adult Armband (for ages 10+) includes all-day privileges on all Tracks and Rides for $29.95, while the Child Armband (2–9) allows all-day access to the 13 Family and Thrill Rides for only $14.95. It's

$5.25 for an all-day ticket to the Freeplay Arcade which contains 37 individual classic arcade games and a spread of more than 100 token-driven games (some of them state-of-the-art). It opens 10am–midnight (high season), or 2pm–11pm (Mon–Fri), 10am–midnight (Sat) and noon–11pm (Sun) in low season. Call 407 363 3867 or log on to www.fun-spot.com for more information. TTTT.

In a similar vein, **Magical Midway** on I-Drive (just north of Sand Lake Road) offers more go-karts, games and thrill rides (including 0–230ft in 3 seconds on the Space Shot Tower!). The two elevated kart tracks are both highly challenging, and then there are bumper cars, a giant slide, laser tag, bumper boats and a large arcade.

WonderWorks

I-Drive's most unmistakable landmark is the 'interactive entertainment centre' of **WonderWorks**, a 3-storey chamber of real family fun with a host of novel elements. Unmistakable? You bet – how many buildings do you know that are upside down? That's right, all of the 82ft-tall edifice is constructed from the roof up! The basic premise (working on the theory that every attraction has to

The upside-down WonderWorks

have a story behind it) is that WonderWorks is a secret research facility into unexplained phenomena that got uprooted by a tornado experiment and dumped in topsy-turvy fashion in the heart of this busy tourist district (yeah, right!). Well, you've got to give them full marks for imagination and, if the interior attractions aren't quite as entertaining as the exterior façade, there is still a lot here, especially for the 6–12 age group.

You enter through an 'inversion tunnel' that orientates you the same way round as the building (look out of the window to check!) and progress to chambers of entertaining and mildly educational hands-on experiences that demand several hours to explore fully. Without ever using the words 'science' or 'museum', WonderWorks steers you through five 'labs' of interactive activities, including the **Bermuda Triangle Corridor,** the **Mystery Lab** (experience earthquakes and hurricanes and see famous disasters on a bank of computer monitors), **Physical Challenge Lab** (virtual basketball, table tennis, hang-gliding and even horse racing, a baseball test, health and lifestyle quizzes and the wonderfully creepy Shocker Chair, a high-voltage simulation that gives you the feeling of 2,000 jolts rather than volts – it's weird!), **Illusions Lab** (with the Bridge of Fire static electricity generator, a computer ageing process and 'elastic surgery', hall of mirrors and bubble table), plus the **WonderWorks Emporium** gift shop, souvenirs and **Mazzarella's Pizzeria.** A Lazer Tag game centre on the top floor adds even more appeal for youngsters.

On no account miss the two virtual roller-coasters, a pair of amazing enclosed 'pods' which let you design and then ride your own coaster. If you have already been to *DisneyQuest,* this may seem tame, while it isn't as educational as the Orlando Science Center. But it offers a fun new dinner-show option, **The Outta Control Magic Show** (see Chapter 9, Orlando By Night), with a good value combination ticket.

Admission fees are $16.95 for adults, $12.95 for seniors (55+) and children 4–11; $4.95 for the Lazer Tag; $17.95 and $14.95 for the Magic Show on its own; $31.95 and $25.95 for the WonderWorks/dinner-show combo; $19.95 and $15.95 for WonderWorks/Lazer Tag; and $32.95 and $26.95 for all three elements. Open 9am–midnight daily. Visit www.wonderworksonline.com for more info. AAA/TTT.

Trainland Inc

The large-scale steam engine around the outside of the building (just south of the huge Race Rock restaurant) marks this out as a must for all train and model railway enthusiasts. New in 2001 and still developing, Trainland features a 4,000sq-ft G-gauge layout inside, beautifully crafted and with three main, highly elaborate sections – the Pennsylvania Backwoods, the Town, and the Industrial Area. The mountains, bridges, streets and buildings, coal mines, lakes, rivers and waterfalls have all been painstakingly hand-built from scratch, and some 8–14 trains are constantly on the go, with the longest track completing a mazy, 960-ft circuit of the whole premises. A scavenger hunt will keep children amused while they wander round and birthday parties can also be held here (call 407 363 9002 for details). The gift shop stocks a huge range of model trains, tracks and accessories and has a Thomas the Tank Engine play area for the young 'uns. The purpose-built outdoor locomotive Lady Liberty (with two open-sided – and wheelchair accessible – passenger cars) on the 2-ft narrow-gauge line is likely to be a magnet for children of the right age.

The quarter-mile route around the museum lasts just 5 minutes, but a ticket here is valid all day, which means youngsters can ride as often as they like.

Admission: the museum itself costs $6.95 for adults, $5.95 seniors and $4.95 children, while the combination pass (museum and outdoor rides) is $8.95, $7.95 and $6.95. For the train ride alone, the fee is $3 for adults and seniors and $2 for children. Opening hours are 10am–6pm (noon–6pm, Sun), with extended opening at peak periods. For more information call 407 363 9002, or visit www.trainland.net. AAA.

Downtown Orlando

The last couple of years have seen a significant move towards regenerating the city centre – the 'downtown' area – with new offices, apartments, shops and restaurants. This has also brought several significant developments in tourist attractions, too.

And, because this is Orlando, there is no such thing as a simple museum or science centre. Everything must be all-singing, all-dancing just to compete. Hence, the **Orlando Science Center** is more than a mere museum and far more fun than the average science centre. Here, you get a series of hands-on experiences and habitats that entertain as well as inform, and school-age children in particular will get a lot from it.

The Science Center has nine main components, plus an inviting café, a night sky observatory and an IMAX cinema. **Natureworks** is an immersion-style exhibit creating a number of typical Florida habitats (with several shows like the *Circle of Life Game* and a series of hands-on field stations). **Science City** introduces fun ways to understand

and use physical science and maths (including some mind-bending puzzles and challenges, notably in the Power Station), while the **Cosmic Tourist** offers a trip around our solar system with an amusing travel theme. **Bodyzone** provides some fascinating insights into the human body, with an interactive element called Measure Me which explores your size, strength, flexibility, agility and sensory abilities. A Healthy Lifestyles exhibit shows how bad habits like smoking affect a healthy body. Next door, **TechWorks** is a 4-part adventure into light, imaginary landscapes, showbiz science and a micro-world of microscopic investigation.

For those a bit too young for the educational element, **KidsTown** has plenty of junior-sized fun and games for under 8s. You'll be amazed at how much they learn in the course of having fun. **DinoDigs: Mysteries Unearthed** was a gift from the Walt Disney Company of their former Dinosaur Jubilee exhibit in the DinoLand USA area of *Disney's Animal Kingdom*. It has been recreated in the OSC as a palaeontological excavation site, complete with eight full dinosaur skeleton replicas and a number of genuine fossils. **Wired Science** was new in 2002, a series of networked multimedia information kiosks introduced by wacky characters, it illustrates basic scientific principles and supports other exhibits around the Center. The **Darden Adventure Theater** features science-themed musical comedy shows and demos,

BRIT TIP: The CineDome film and laser show can operate until midnight on Friday and Saturday for a show independent of the Science Center.

7

like PreHisto Rock (fun for all would-be palaeontologists) and the audience participation Science Spectrum.

In addition, the Center has two separate programmes in the **Dr Phillips CineDome,** a 310-seat cinema that practically surrounds its audience with large-format films, digital planetarium shows (a virtual tour of the universe, anyone?) and laser shows. It also boasts a 28,000-watt digital sound system that makes the experience unforgettable. The Science Center is on Princeton Street in downtown Orlando, just off Exit 85 of I-4 (as you go east on Princeton, the Center will be on your left but the multi-storey car park is on the right), and is open 9am–5pm Tue–Thur, 9am–9pm Fri and Sat, and noon–5pm Sun (closed Mon, except school holidays).

Admission is $9.50 for adults, $8.50 for seniors (55+) and $6.75 for 3–11s; or $12.50, $11.50 and $9.25 with one CineDome show (film or planetarium) and $14.50, $13.50 and $11.25 with two shows; the CineDome only is $6, $5.50 and

$4.50 for one film. Parking is $3.50. It is closed on Thanksgiving Day in November, Christmas Eve and Christmas Day. Visit www.osc.org for more info. AAAA.

Orange County History Center

This relatively recent addition offers an imaginative journey into central Florida history, from the wildlife and Native Americans to today's tourist issues and the space programme. Again, the accent is on the interactive, with hands-on exhibits and audio-visual presentations, and it is very much a journey through time, starting outside in renovated Heritage Square, complete with cypress trees and fountains. The History Center itself is in the former 1927 Orange County Courthouse, with the foyer converted into a dome featuring more than 150 icons unique to central Florida (see how many you can identify before and after your tour).

> BRIT TIP: Combine a visit to the History Center with lunch at the wonderfully eclectic Globe restaurant on the corner of the square.

The 4-storey adventure starts at the top with the **Orientation Theater's** 14-minute multimedia presentation as you sit in rocking chairs on the 'front porch'. Then you visit the Natural Environment and First Peoples exhibits (12,000 years ago), before First Contact brings in the European element. Jump into the 1800s and you visit a Seminole settlement, a Pioneer Cracker home (the first true 'cowboys'), hear tales of the old cattle-ranching days and learn about the citrus industry.

Bodyzone at Orlando Science Center

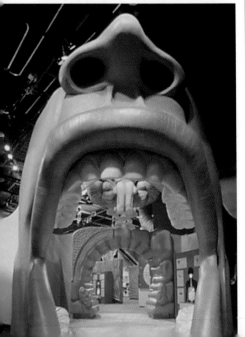

The early 20th century brings the story of Transportation, Tin Can Tourists, Aviation and the great land boom, Selling Central Florida. Then witness how the region dramatically altered with the development of the Space programme and the arrival of a certain Walt Disney in The Day We Changed. From there, you move on to the beautifully restored Courtroom B for some more real-life Orlando history. Finally, you hit the present in the Community exhibit, a spotlight on famous places, people and activities in the area, and a chance to view the dome from the top, testing all your new-found knowledge of the icons. You will also find various periodical travelling exhibits here (the story of World War Two in Florida is due in summer 2003), as well as the **Historium** gift shop.

Admission is $7 for adults, $3.50 for 3–12s and $6.50 for seniors (60+), and it is open 10am–5pm (Mon–Sat) and noon–5pm (Sun). The History Center can be found off Central Boulevard and Magnolia Avenue downtown (Exit 82C off I-4, left on to Magnolia, right on to Central Boulevard). Best place to park is the Orlando Public Library multi-storey car park on Central Boulevard (History Center admission includes 2 hours free parking there if you show your ticket). For more information, call 407 836 8500 or visit www.thehistorycenter.org. AAA.

Other downtown developments include the free **Lymmo** bus service which connects the central stretch along Magnolia Avenue, from South Street to the TD Waterhouse Center (formerly the Orlando Arena for sports and concerts) on Amelia Street, the **Downtown Arts District** and **Arts Market** (on Wall Street, off Orange Avenue, second Saturday every month, 11am–9pm Oct–April), seasonal concerts and firework shows, plus new shops and restaurants around **Lake Eola**.

The **Cultural Corridor** links the Downtown Arts District (which includes the Bob Carr Performing Arts Center and the Centroplex), with the Loch Haven area (where you can find the Orlando Museum of Art, Mennello Museum of American Folk Art, The Orlando Philharmonic Orchestra and the Orlando-UCF Shakespeare Festival), via the Dr Phillips Performing Arts Center, which is home of the Orlando Opera and Orlando Ballet.

The Saturday **Farmers' Market** (7am–1pm) has become a real downtown focal point (under the I-4 flyover at Church Street), with vendors now including local artisans, such as glass and dressmakers, as well as wonderful fresh produce. The **Thornton Park** area is currently the most happening part of Orlando, with the new Thornton Park Central (at the junction of Summerlin Avenue and Central Boulevard, just south-east of Lake Eola) offering a mix of unique small boutiques and trendy restaurants, with the monthly Third Thursday street party (5–10pm) attracting sizeable crowds. Visit their website www.downtownorlando.com for the latest info (see also Chapter 9, Orlando By Night).

The Holy Land Experience

Not so much a conventional attraction but right in the heart of the tourist mainstream is this 15-acre 'living Biblical museum', which sets out to recreate in great detail the city of Jerusalem and its religious significance from 1450BC to AD66 and provide an explanation and celebration of the Christian faith.

The staff are all in period costume, the architecture and landscaping are impressive and the background music in both the indoor and outdoor areas is all original and suitably atmospheric. From the **Jerusalem Street Market** entrance to the **Qumran Dead Sea Caves, Calvary's Garden Tomb** and on to the highly impressive **Temple of the Great King** (destroyed by the Romans in AD70), everything is portrayed in literal Biblical terms. The **Theater of Life** shows a 25-minute film of Bible landmarks, from Adam and Eve to the Crucifixion, while the **Wilderness Tabernacle** is a 25-minute theatrical portrayal of Old Testament worship, featuring the Holy Ark with lasers and pyrotechnics. A huge replica Jerusalem Model – which took more than a year to build – is explained in great detail several times a day in the form of a guided tour. Live performances include the *Garden Tomb Music & Drama* celebrating the Resurrection and an original musical drama *Today's The Day*, which plays out in the Plaza of Nations. There is even a Middle Eastern-style café where one of the menu items is a Goliath Burger. Recently opened is the **Scriptorium** centre for Biblical antiquities, another themed environment showcasing various rare artefacts. It is a thoroughly unusual 'attraction' (although they don't call it that), and sits rather awkwardly among the main tourist offerings, but it may well pique the interest of some.

The Holy Land Experience can be found immediately off Exit 78 of I-4, on the junction of Conroy and Vineland Roads (just north of Universal Orlando). It is open 10am–6pm (Mon–Fri), 9am–6pm (Sat) and noon–6pm (Sun).

Admission is $22 for adults and $17 for children 4–12. Parking is free. Call 407 367 2065 for more information or check them out on www.theholylandexperience.com. AA.

The Water Parks

If anyone has been down the slides and flumes at the local leisure centre, they will have an inkling of what Orlando's four big water parks are all about. Predictably, Disney has the two most elaborate ones, but the Universal-owned Wet 'n Wild and Water Mania are equally adept at providing hours of fun in a variety of styles that owe much to the flair of the theme park creators.

> BRIT TIP: While water parks are a great way of cooling down, it is easy to pick up a 5-star case of sunburn. So don't forget the high-factor, waterproof suntan lotion.

All four require at least half a day of splashing, sliding and riding to get full value from their rather high prices but, if you prefer to get your kicks in watery rather than land-borne fashion, these are definitely for you. Lockers are provided for valuables and you can hire towels.

Disney's Typhoon Lagoon Water Park

Until *Disney's Blizzard Beach* water park opened in 1995, *Disney's Typhoon Lagoon* was the biggest and finest example of Florida's water parks. In high season, it is also the busiest, so be prepared to run into more queues. Situated on Buena Vista Drive, just half a mile from the *Downtown Disney* area, the park's 56 acres are spread out around the 2½-acre lagoon fringed with palm trees and white-sand beaches. If it wasn't for the high-season crowds, you could easily convince yourself you had been washed up on some tropical island paradise. *Disney's*

Typhoon Lagoon also goes in for some of the most extravagant landscaping and introduces some unique and clever details. The walk up Mount Mayday, for instance, provides a terrific overview of the park as well as adding scenic touches like rope bridges and tropical flowers. Sun loungers, chairs, picnic tables and even a few hammocks are provided to add to the comfort and convenience of restful areas like Getaway Glen. However, you need to arrive early to bag a decent spot with some shade.

> BRIT TIP: As the busiest of the water parks, *Disney's Typhoon Lagoon* can hit capacity quite early in the day in the summer. Call 407 824 4321 in advance to check on the crowds.

The park is overlooked by the 90-ft Mount Mayday, on top of which is perched the luckless *Miss Tilly*, a shrimp boat that legend has it landed here during the typhoon that gave the park its name. Watch for the water fountains that shoot from *Miss Tilly's* funnel at regular intervals, accompanied by the ship's hooter, which signal another round of 6ft-high waves in the **Surf Pool** (you can hire inner-tubes to bob around on or just try body-surfing). Circling the lagoon is **Castaway Creek,** a 3ft-deep, lazy flowing river that offers the chance to float happily along on rubber tyres.
The series of slides and rides are all clustered around Mount Mayday and vary from the breathtaking three body slides of **Humunga Kowabunga,** which drop you 214ft at up to 30mph down some of the steepest inclines in waterdom (make sure your swimming costume is SECURELY fastened!), to **Ketchakiddee Creek,** which offers

a selection of slides and fun pools for all youngsters under 4ft tall. In between, you have the three **Storm Slides,** more body slides which twist and turn through caves, tunnels and waterfalls, **Mayday Falls,** a 460-ft inner-tube ride down a series of banked drops, **Keel Haul Falls,** an alternative tube ride that takes slightly longer, and **Gangplank Falls,** a group or family ride whose tubes take up to 4 people down 300ft of mock rapids. The hugely imaginative (but chilly) **Shark Reef** is an upturned wreck and coral reef, which you can snorkel around among 4,000 tropical fish and a number of real, but quite harmless, nurse sharks. Like all the areas, this one is carefully supervised, and those who aren't quite brave enough to dive in can still get a close-up view of the fish through the underwater port holes of the sunken ship (the Reef is closed during the coldest of the winter months).
There are height and health restrictions on Humunga Kowabunga (it's not suitable for anyone with a bad back or neck, or for pregnant women), while the queues for this slide, plus the Storm Slides and Shark Reef, can touch an arduous hour at times, which can take a lot of the fun out of it. Getting out of the sun can also be slightly problematic as the provision of shaded areas is not overwhelming, but a quick plunge into Castaway Creek will usually sort out any overheating problems.
For snacks and meals, **Lowtide Lou's** and **Let's Go Slurpin'** both offer snacks and drinks while **Typhoon Tilly's** and **Leaning Palms** serve a mixture of burgers, sandwiches, salads and ice cream. It is essential to avoid main mealtimes here if you want to eat in relative comfort. You can, however, bring your own picnic (unlike the main theme parks) which you can eat in special scenic areas (but no alcohol

7

or glass containers are allowed). You CAN'T bring your own snorkels, inner-tubes or rafts, but snorkels are provided at Shark Reef and you need to hire inner-tubes (if required) only for the lagoon. If you have forgotten a vital item like a sunhat or bucket and spade for the kids, or even your swimsuit, they are all available (along with gifts and souvenirs) at **Singapore Sal's.**

BRIT TIP: Ladies, please remember, down some of the whizziest slides it is advisable to wear a one-piece swimsuit rather than a bikini. Your modesty could be at stake here!

To avoid the worst of the summer crowds (when the park's 7,200 capacity is often reached), Monday morning is about the best time to visit (steer clear of weekends at all costs), while, on other days, arrive either 30 minutes before opening or in mid afternoon, when many decide to dodge the daily rainstorm. Early evening is also extremely pleasant as the park lights up.

Disney's Typhoon Lagoon

Disney's Blizzard Beach

Admission is $29.95 for adults and $24 for kids 3–9 (under 3s free), or it is free as one of the options with the Park Hopper PLUS Tickets. Parking is free. It opens from 9am to dusk every day. TTTT/AAAAA.

Disney's Blizzard Beach Water Park

Ever imagined a skiing resort in the middle of Florida? You haven't? Well, Disney has, and this is the wonderful result. *Disney's Blizzard Beach* water park puts the rest in the shade for size as well as extravagant settings, with the whole park arranged as if it were in the Rocky Mountains rather than the sub-tropics. That means snow-effect scenery, Christmas trees and water slides cunningly converted to look like skiing pistes and toboggan runs. It delivers a real feast for water lovers and Disney admirers in

BRIT TIP: You can save money on your day at the two Disney water parks by buying refillable drinks mugs – about $10.95 each – when you arrive and using them all day.

general, and the basic premise of snow-surfin' USA is an unarguable 5-star knockout.

Feature items are **Mount Gushmore,** a 90-ft mountain down which all the main slides run (including the world's tallest free-fall speed slide, the terrifying 120-ft **Summit Plummet,** which rockets you down a 'ski jump' at up to 60mph!), **Tike's Peak,** a kiddie-sized version of the park's slides and

a mock snow-beach, and **Ski-Patrol Training Camp,** a series of slides and challenges for pre-teens. **Melt-Away Bay** is a 1-acre pool fed by 'melting snow' waterfalls (actually blissfully warm), and **Cross Country Creek** is a lazy-flowing half-mile river around the whole park which also floats guests through a chilly 'ice cave' (watch out for the mini-waterfalls of ice-cold water!).

A ski chair-lift operates to the top of Mount Gushmore, providing a magnificent view of the whole park and surrounding areas. Don't miss the outstanding rides – Teamboat Springs, a wild, family inner-tube adventure, Runoff Rapids, a 1-, 2- or 3-person tube plunge, and the Snow Stormers, a daring head-first 'toboggan' run. Toboggan Racers gives you the chance to speed down the 'slopes' against seven other head-

7

Disney's Blizzard Beach

© Disney

first daredevils. All four go to new heights of water park imagination and provide good-sized thrills without overdoing the scare factor.

The **Downhill Double Dipper** is two side-by-side slides which send you down 230ft-long tubes in a race that is timed on a big clock at the bottom, and which gives you a real jolt halfway down! For those not quite up to Summit Plummet lunacy, the wonderfully named **Slush Gusher** is a slightly less terrifying speed slide. There is also a 'village' area including the **Beach Haus** shop and **Lottawatta Lodge** fast-food restaurant, offering diners a grandstand view of Mount Gushmore and Melt-Away Bay beach. Snacks are also available at **Avalunch** (ouch!), the **Warming Hut** and **Polar Pub & Frostbite Freddie's Frozen Refreshments**. Predictably, the crowds are suitably massive, so avoid the weekends and from mid morning onwards on Wednesdays to Fridays.

Admission: located just north of *Disney's All-Star Resorts* off Buena Vista Drive, *Disney's Blizzard Beach* costs $29.95 per adult and $24 per child (3–9); again it is one of the free optional extras with Hopper PLUS Tickets, with opening times from 9am to early evening. TTTTT/AAAAA.

Adjacent to *Disney's Blizzard Beach* is the amazing **Winter Summerland Miniature Golf Courses** (where Santa's elves hang out!), with two wonderfully elaborate courses that make for a great diversion with children. Watch

> BRIT TIP: The Children's Playground at Wet 'n Wild was built especially for those under 4ft in height – right down to the only junior wave pool in the world.

out for a riot of visual gags and puns, as well as some tricky mini-golf.

Disney's oldest water park, **River Country,** was closed throughout 2002 and it seems it is not likely to re-open in its old form.

Wet 'n Wild

If Disney scores highest marks for scenic content, Wet 'n Wild, the world's first water park back in 1977, goes full-tilt for thrills and spills of the highest quality. And this place will really test the material of your swimsuit to the limit!

Wet 'n Wild is repeatedly one of the best-attended water parks in the country, and its location in the heart of I-Drive makes it a major draw. Consequently, you will once again encounter some serious crowds here, although the 12 slides and rides, **Lazy River** attraction, an elaborate kids' park (with mini versions of many of the slides), **Surf Lagoon** and restaurant and picnic areas all manage to absorb a lot of punters before the queues develop. Amazingly, waits of more than half an hour at peak times are rare. Its popularity with locals means it is busiest at weekends, with July the month that attracts most crowds.

You are almost spoilt for choice of main rides, from the highly popular group inner-tube rides of the **Surge** and **Bubba Tub,** through the more demanding rides of **Raging Rapids** to the high-thrill factor of the 2-person **Black Hole** (like the *Magic Kingdom's* Space Mountain, but in water!), **Blue Niagara** (also enclosed, but this one's a body slide) and **Mach 5,** to the ultimate terror of **Der Stuka** and the **Bomb Bay.** The latter duo are definitely not for the faint-hearted. Basically, they are two 76ft-high body slides with a drop as near vertical as makes no difference. Der Stuka is the straightforward slide version, while the Bomb Bay adds the extra terror of being allowed to free-fall on to the top of the slide. And they call it fun! Suffice it to say, your author has not put himself at risk on these particular contraptions, and has absolutely no intention of doing so! For some reason, only 15–25% of the park's visitors pluck up the courage to try it. Can't think why. Height restrictions of 4ft are in force on the Bomb Bay, Der Stuka and Blue Niagara, while older kids get their own chance for thrills on the

> BRIT TIP: For all the water parks, it can be advisable to bring a pair of deck shoes or sandals that can be worn in water.

huge, inflatable **Bubble Up,** which bounces them into 3ft of water.

The thrilling toboggan-like **Fuji Flyer** takes 4 passengers in 8ft-long, in-line tubes which whoosh down more than 450ft of banked curves and speed-enhancing straights, and the bungee-like **Hydra Fighter** is a 2-person swing equipped with a fire-type hose that sends the contraption into mad gyrations as you increase the water pressure! New in 2001 was **The Storm,** a pair of identical circular slides which are billed as 'body coasters'! The enclosed tubes – complete with storm sound and light effects – send the rider plunging into a circular bowl, around which they spin at high speed before landing in the splash pool below. Huge fun.

For those under 4ft tall, the recently renovated **Kids Park** area has a full range of junior-sized slides, plus a new sandcastle structure with two semi-circular water slides and a giant bucket that fills and tips up at regular intervals. Uniquely, the children can use speciality tubes, beach chairs and tables designed specifically for their height.

The neighbouring lake is also part of the fun (although not in winter when its temperature drops below that of merely chilly), adding the opportunities to try the cable-operated **Knee Ski** and (for a nominal fee) ride the **Wild One** (large inner-tubes tied behind a speedboat). Alternatively, take a breather in the slow-flowing **Lazy River** or abandon the water altogether for one of several shaded picnic areas, which are quickly snapped up.

The energetic can play beach volleyball and ride the **Robo Surfer** at selected times, a watery version of the mechanical bucking bronco. Lockers, showers, tube and towel rentals are all available but, if you bring your own floating equipment, you must have it checked by one of the lifeguards.

For food, **Bubba's Bar-B-Q** serves chicken, ribs, fries and drinks, the **Surf Grill** features burgers, hot dogs, chicken and sandwiches and another seven snack bars offer similar fast-food fare, including a pizza bar and a kiddies' counter (peanut butter sandwiches, hot dogs and chips). Picnics can also be brought in to the park, provided you don't include alcohol or glass containers.

Wet 'n Wild is half a mile north of I-Drive's junction with Sand Lake Road at the intersection with Universal Boulevard and is open year-round (with heated pools in the cooler months) from 9am in peak periods (10am at other times) until variously 5, 6, 7, or 9pm.

Admission is $30.95 for adults, $24.95 for 3–9s and free for under 3s, alternatively, it is included with the Orlando FlexTicket. Tube rentals are $4 ($2 deposit), towels $2 and lockers $5 ($2 deposit), or $9 for all three ($4 deposit). Parking is $5. Check out www.wetnwild.com. TTTTT/AAA.

Water Mania

If Wet 'n Wild attracts the serious thrill seekers, Kissimmee's version, Water Mania, is more family-orientated and laid back, with the crowds highest at weekends when the locals flock in. That's not to say this park doesn't have its share of scary slides (or Wet 'n Wild doesn't cater for families), it's just their emphasis is slightly different and those looking to avoid the crowds often end up here. Where this 36-acre park scores a minor victory over its rivals is in the provision of 3 acres of wooded picnic area where you can bring your own picnic (although no glass items).

Eight different slides, including a patented non-stop surfing challenge called **Wipe-Out**, the usual **Cruisin' Creek**, a 720,000-gallon **Wave Pool** (waves every 15 minutes, up to 4ft high) and three separate kids' areas provide the main attractions – plenty to keep you

BRIT TIP: Kids are again extremely well catered for, and Water Mania can even host birthday parties in Mr Kool's Party Land. Call 407 396 2626 for details.

occupied for at least half a day. Top of the list for those daring enough to throw themselves down things like Der Stuka is the **Screamer**, an aptly named 72ft free-fall speed slide, and the **Abyss**, 380ft of enclosed-tube darkness. The **Anaconda** and **Banana Peel** both feature family-sized inner-tubes down long, twisting slides, while the **Double Berzerker** offers two different ways to be whooshed along and spat out into a foaming pool.

However, the outstanding feature, for both trying and watching, is the **Wipe-Out**, one of only two such attractions in the world. The challenge is to grab a body board

Wet 'n Wild – the Fuji Flyer

The Rain Forest at Water Mania

with sand beach and paddling area, added shade and refreshment hut.

In addition to the cooling picnic areas, there are several snack bars, a mini-golf course, volleyball and basketball courts and a large shop.

Water Mania is located on Highway 192, just a mile east of the I-4 intersection and is open 10am–5pm from early March to the end of September, and Wed–Sat only in October (hours are subject to change).

Admission is $19.95 for adults and $16.95 for children (3–9) and parking is $5. Call 407 396 2626 for more details or check out their website www.watermania-florida.com. TTTT/AAA.

Okay, that sums up the main large-scale attractions, but many people are now looking for the 'something different' factor, so let's explore some alternatives to the mass-market experience…

7

and try to ride the continuous wave, risking going over the edge into another pool if you stray too wide, or being sent flying backwards if you lose your balance. A real blast!

When it comes to pint-sized fun for the children, Water Mania is one of the best. The **Rain Forest** is designed for the 2–10s, with a 5,000sq-ft pool ranging from 3in to 2ft deep and featuring a selection of mini-slides, fountains and water guns, all arranged around a wonderful large-scale pirate ship, with more chances to climb, jump and generally swashbuckle. Other innovative recent additions are the **Rain Train,** a near life-size locomotive that sprays water out of its stack in the centre of a shallow pool, with other interactive play features and more slides; and **Tot's Town** for the toddlers (and their parents who want to relax a little), which is a partly fenced playground

Cruisin' Creek at Water Mania

Off the Beaten Track
(or, When you're All Theme-Parked Out)

After several days in the midst of the hectic tourist whirl of mainstream Orlando, you may be in need of a rest from the non-stop theme park activities. Or you may be a repeat visitor looking for a different experience. If either is the case, this chapter is for you.

Hopefully, you will already have noted the relatively tranquil offerings of Cypress Gardens and Silver Springs in the previous chapter but, to get away from it all more completely and to enhance your view of the area further, the following are guaranteed to take you well off the beaten tourist track. This chapter should really be subtitled 'A Taste of the Real Florida', as it introduces the areas of Winter Park, Seminole County, nature boat rides, eco-tours and journeys by airboat, balloon, ship, train and plane.

Winter Park

Foremost among the 'secret' hideaways is this elegant northern suburb of Orlando, little more than 20 minutes' drive from the hurly-burly of the likes of I-Drive and yet a million miles from the relentless commercialism. It offers several renowned museums and art galleries, fabulous shopping, numerous restaurants, several pleasant walking tours, a delightful 50-minute boat ride around the lakes and, above all, a chance to slow down.

The central area is **Park Avenue**, a classy street of fine shops, boutiques, two museums and a wonderfully shaded park. At one end of the avenue is Rollins College, a small but highly respected arts education centre which houses the **Cornell Fine Arts Museum**, with the oldest collection of paintings, sculpture and decorative arts in Florida (open 10am–5pm Tue–Fri, 1pm–5pm Sat–Sun, closed Mon and main holidays, admission free) and the **Annie Russell Theater** www.rollins.edu.

The **Morse Museum of American Art** is a must for admirers of American art pottery, American and European glass, furniture and other decorative arts of the late 19th and early 20th centuries, as it includes one of the world's foremost collections of works by Louis Comfort Tiffany. The dazzling Chapel restoration from the 1893 Chicago World Expo is now on display in its original form for the first time since the late 19th century and is worth the entrance fee alone. The museum is open 9.30am–4pm Tues–Sat and 1–4pm Sun, admission $3 for adults, children under 12 free (www.morsemuseum.org). The **Albin Polasek Museum** and **Sculpture Gardens** are also worth a look for culture buffs and for the serene setting devoted to this Czech-American artist. Open 10am–4pm Wed–Sun, admission is free and it is a superb setting for weddings.

The **Scenic Boat Tour** is located at the east end of Morse Avenue and offers a charming, narrated 12-mile tour of the 'Venice of America' (weather permitting – the drought of early 2001 severely restricted the route) around the lakes and canals for a fascinating glimpse of some of the most beautiful houses, boat houses and lakeside gardens (properties in the area start at $800,000 and several top $4 million!). Tours run 10am–4pm daily and cost $8 for adults and $4 for children 2–11, and it is one of the most relaxing hours you will spend in Orlando. Visit their website at www.scenicboattours.com.

Alternatively, a trip with **Home Town Bicycle Tours** gives a gentle but unique overview of this picturesque neighbourhood, including several parks and Rollins College, with full guide narration ($50/hour for groups up to 10; i.e. $5/person/hour, plus $20 bike hire; call 407 332 8703 or e-mail homehownbicycletours@hotmail.com). You can also take the **Park Avenue Walking Tour,** with useful free maps provided by the Chamber of Commerce on New York Avenue.

The shops of Park Avenue are a cut or two above anything you will encounter elsewhere and, while you may find the prices equally distinctive, just browsing is an enjoyable experience with the charm of the area highlighted by the friendliness of everyone hereabouts. For shops that are both unique and fun, look out for **Panache** (jewellery), **Park Avenue Gallery** (art), **Kendyl's Kloset** (children's clothes and toys) and **The Doggie Door** (for pets). Brand new are **Winter Park Teddy Bear Co** (make and stuff your own soft toys), **Olive this Relish that** (a wonderful gourmet food store with Mediterranean specialities) and **Peter Brook Chocolatier.** Regular pavement craft fairs and art festivals (especially the Spring Art Festival in March/April, which is a big part of the social scene) add splashes of colour to an already inviting scenario. In addition to the **Park Plaza Gardens,** which specialises in continental cuisine (see Chapter 10, Eating Out), you can sample French, Italian and Thai cuisines, among others. The new **Zak's on Park Avenue** has received rave reviews from the locals for its sparkling New Orleans-flavoured menu. Watch out, too, for Dress Up Thursdays, where the best-dressed diner in each of six restaurants receives a goody-bag full of great items from Park Avenue merchants. Street parking here usually allows 2 hours free, but the Sun Trust Building on the corner of Comstock and Park Avenue is a better bet.

The **Central Park** area alongside Park Avenue, notable for its fountains and flowers, is due to be expanded in the near future, which should enhance things still further. Check out www.wpfl.org and www.parkave-winterpark.com for more info.

Another high point of a visit to Winter Park is the **Kraft Azalea Gardens** on Alabama Drive (off Palmer Avenue at the north end of Park Avenue), 11 acres of shaded lakeside walkways, gardens and hundreds of magnificent azaleas. The main focal point, the mock Grecian temple, is a particularly beautiful setting for weddings. **Mead Botanical Gardens,** on Garden Drive (just off Highway 17/92) offers more trails through a sub-tropical forest, with native birds and plants from around the world. There is no admission charge for either.

To get to Winter Park, take Exit 87 from I-4, Fairbanks Avenue. Turn right on to Fairbanks and head east for 2 miles until it intersects with Park Avenue and turn left.

Midway between Winter Park and downtown Orlando is another botanical gem, **Leu Gardens,** a 50-acre retreat featuring formal gardens, peaceful walks and a boardwalk overlooking Lake Rowena. **The Leu House Museum** is open 10am–4pm (closed in July)

8

with tours every 30 minutes (last tour at 3.30pm). The gardens are open daily from 9am–5pm (9am–8pm in summer) and cost $4 for adults and $1 for under 13s (free entry from 9am–noon on Mon). You'll find them on the corner of Forest and Nebraska Avenues, via Mills Avenue and Princeton St from Exit 85 on I-4.

Getting off the beaten track

Aquatic Wonders boat tours

To go further into the real world of Florida nature and its wildlife, **Aquatic Wonders** operates a delightful break from the theme park business on Lake Tohopekaliga in Kissimmee (the bigger of the two lakes; NOT East Lake Toho). Operated by Captain Ray Robida and limited to a maximum of 6 people per trip, the choice of eight cruises offers a series of gentle adventures that are entertaining and educational as well as relaxing. Every cruise on the 30-ft covered pontoon boat is different depending on local conditions and Captain Ray's truly individual style, which is wonderfully laid back yet informative. His knowledge of the waterways and wildlife is outstanding and children with

enquiring minds will benefit.

The 3-hour **Aquatic Wonders cruise** studies the local lakes and rivers, water ecology and the fish, insects and other animals of the area ($35 for adults and children).

The **Eagle Watch Tour** is an ornithologist's delight as it goes out for 2 hours to look at the nesting bald eagles on the lake, rare ospreys and many other birds ($21 for adults, $14 for 3–12s). The rather romantic **Sunset Sounds** is another 2-hour trip aboard 'Eagle Ray' to enjoy the sights and sounds of dusk over the lake as the birds come home to roost ($18.95 and $12.95). **Starlight Wonders** is a 2-hour tour for a spot of star-gazing, gentle music and Native American stories surrounding the origins of the constellations ($25 and $16). **Rivers in Time** is a 2-hour journey back in time to the days of the river boat and the Seminole Indian War, a fascinating live history lesson with all the sights and sounds of the lake for good measure ($21 and $14).

BRIT TIP: Amazingly, the waterways feeding Lake Toho stretch all the way to Miami in the south. Captain Ray is a mine of fascinating geographical and historical information.

The **Gator Watch Tour** is a 2-hour night-time journey to view some of the locals hunting, nesting and just hanging out (and there are plenty of them out there! $25 and $16).

Family Fishing Adventures offers 4–5 hours of fishing fun with all bait and tackle (but not fishing licence) provided, especially for beginners ($200, takes up to 6). A new 2-hour tour of unspoilt **Makinson Island** is also available, providing an interpretive guided tour of this 132-acre nature preserve ($21 and $14).

Games and videos are provided for the kids in case their attention wanders! All tours supply non-alcoholic drinks and snacks (but you can take your own) and Captain Ray is fully licensed by the US Coast Guard, so you are guaranteed a high level of safety as well as entertainment. The *Eagle Ray* departs daily from 101 Lakeshore Boulevard in downtown Kissimmee (via Main Street and Broadway, turn left into Ruby and right at the end, Lakeshore Boulevard). Call 407 846 2814 for more details and to make reservations for these tours, which are proving increasingly popular, or visit www.florida-nature.com.

Makinson Island is worth highlighting here as it has quickly become a valuable place for boating, kayaking and hiking, after it was opened up to the public in spring 2002. It offers a series of marked hiking trails through a variety of pristine and secluded ecosystems, including cypress domes, citrus groves and beautiful pastures, with a picnic area set up under a covered pavilion. **Big Toho Marina** (on Lakeshore Boulevard) provides small fishing boat rentals here ($55 all day, $35 half-day), while **Richardson's Fish Camp** (1550 Scotty's Road) offers scheduled airboat rides to and from the island (call 407 846 6540 for rates). **WayFun Kayaks** operate from Richardson's, with 4–5 hour guided kayak and hiking trips (including snacks and refreshments at $49/person) or a 2-hour sunset trip around the island ($25/person). Visit www.wayfun-kayak.com for more information.

> BRIT TIP: Watch out for discount coupons in tourist literature offering up to $3 off airboat rides.

Airboat rides

The thrill of airboat rides can be experienced on many of Florida's lakes, rivers and marshes. An airboat is a totally different experience to any boat ride you will have had before, as it is more like flying at ground level. As much a thrill as a scenic adventure, it has the advantage of exploring areas otherwise inaccessible to boats.

> BRIT TIP: Best time for an airboat ride is first thing on a weekday morning when the wildlife is not hiding from the weekend boaters.

Airboats simply skim over and through the marshes, to give you an alternative, close-up and very personal view. Travelling at up to 50mph means it can be loud (hence you will be provided with headphones) and sunglasses are also a good idea to keep stray flies out of your eyes. It is NOT the trip for you if you are spooked by crickets, dragonflies and similar insects that occasionally land in the boat!

Several operations offer airboat rides in the area, from you-drive boats that do barely 5mph to much bigger ones, but for safety and quality my tip goes to **Boggy Creek Airboat Rides.** Their airboats can be found on Lake Toho at Southport Park (all the way down Poinciana

Airboat ride

Boulevard, off Highway 192 between Markers 10 and 11, and across into Southport Road – about a 30-minute drive) or on East Lake Toho (their main site). For the latter, you either take Exit 17 off the Central Florida Greeneway (417) and go south on Boggy Creek Road, then right into East Lake Fish Camp; better still, take Osceola Parkway all the way east until it hits Boggy Creek Road. Go left and then turn right at the Boggy Creek T-junction, then right into East Lake Fish Camp after 2 miles.

> BRIT TIP: Want to sample the Florida Everglades but don't fancy the 3-hour trip south? Boggy Creek Airboats are the perfect substitute, and at a fraction of the cost.

The **East Lake Fish Camp** is itself a little gem, offering a variety of boating and angling opportunities (call 407 348 2040 for details) as well as the wonderfully authentic rural Florida charm of the **restaurant and gift shop** (open 8am–9pm every day). If you are heading for a morning airboat ride, consider arriving early for a huge all-day breakfast at the fish camp first, while the more adventurous will want to try the local delicacies – catfish, frogs' legs and gator tail. For another great slice of local eating, try the Friday and Saturday night buffets. They are fabulous value at $9.95 and $12.95 each on an all-you-can-eat basis.

Boggy Creek's **half-hour ride** features three of the most modern 18-passenger airboats in Florida, skimming over the local wetlands for a close-up view of the majestic cypress trees and wildlife that can include eagles, ospreys, snakes and turtles, as well as gators.

You do not need to book in advance, just turn up and go (9am–5.30pm, daily), and rides cost $17.95 for adults and $12.95 for children 3–12 (don't forget the sunscreen as you can really burn out on the water). They also do a 1-hour **Night Tour** ($25, March–October only) for a completely different, and quite exhilarating, experience (gator eyes glow red in the dark!), but you do need to book at least 3 days in advance on 407 344 9550. Finally, they offer 45-minute **private tours** in their 6-passenger boat ($45/person) which provide an even more personal view of this amazing area. Check out www.bcairboats.com for more info.

Boggy Creek Parasail

A new operation in 2001 and complementary to the airboat rides, this is an opportunity to float over East Lake Toho for one of the most breathtaking views of the area. You float up with the greatest of ease from the back of their 16-passenger boat at heights of up to 400, 600 or 800ft (depending on the price you pay), descending again after about 15 relaxing minutes to land gently standing up – and completely dry. The sit-down harness they use requires no skill or effort on your part and makes it accessible to everyone (even me – see page 5!). The system is also deft enough to allow the operators to dip you in the water – upon request! Single flyers cost $45 (up to 400ft), $55 (600ft) and $65 (800ft), while double flyers are $75, $85 and $95. They also offer a romantic Sunset Cruise package for couples, with drinks and hors d'oeuvres at $180 per couple. Observers may ride free if there is space in the boat. Reservations are not usually required but it is often wise to check on 407 348 2700 (open 10am–5.30pm daily).

Cypress Glades Adventure Tours

Brand new and in conjunction with Gatorland, this is an adventurous series of offerings into the Florida countryside and waterways. Operated by Gatorland's enthusiastic head trainer Mike Hileman, there are six basic experiences, all of which can be customised to include other activities (such as airboat rides, kayaking or hiking). Based on beautiful Lake Cypress in St Cloud (25 miles south of Gatorland), the genuine feel of real Florida nature here is all encompassing. The local wildlife includes whitetail deer, Osceola turkeys, bald eagles and wild hogs, as well as the inevitable gators, and birdlife, such as ospreys, cranes, white pelicans, owls, Coopers hawks, cardinals, storks and ivies. The basic 40-minute **airboat ride** is $22.50 for adults and $12.50 for children, but you can then choose from their fully-guided **half-day airboat excursions,** including picnic lunch ($55 and $45); an **overnight campout** under the Florida stars, with a night-time airboat ride and dinner by the campfire (and toasted marshmallows! $77/tent, $93/cabin); a **night-time airboat ride** on its own ($38 and $28); a (seasonal) **night-time excursion** to a Florida east coast beach with a wildlife guide, looking to catch a glimpse of the loggerhead and green sea turtles as they lay their eggs ($44 and $35); the **gator egg collection** at Gatorland itself, a fairly labour-intensive tour for the true adventure seeker (12 and up only, $49); and the exclusive **Trainer for a Day** programme, also at Gatorland, with the opportunity to work behind the scenes at the park, finding out what it takes to handle such dangerous animals, behavioural training and a go at gator wrangling.

For more details, call 407 855 5496 or visit the Gatorland website.

To get to Lake Cypress (which has a Florida-style restaurant and fish camp), take Highway 192 west to St Cloud and head south for around 15 miles on Canoe Creek Road (County Road 523). Then turn right on an unmade road (Lake Cypress Road) for 2 miles into the fish camp.

Balloon trips

Florida is one of the most popular areas for ballooning and, if you are up early enough in the morning, you will often see several. The experience is a majestic one. If Orlando represents the holiday of a lifetime, then a balloon flight is the ride of a lifetime. The utterly smooth way in which you lift off into the early morning sky is breathtaking in itself, but the peace and quiet of the ride, not to mention the stunning views from 2,000ft above ground, are quite awesome. It is not a cheap experience, but it is equally appealing to all but the youngest children or those who have vertigo or a fear of heights. It is a highly personalised ride, taking up to 6 people. Some baskets take up to 9, but it's a squeeze!

> BRIT TIP: Dresses are not advisable for balloon trips and sensible shoes are essential.

Orange Blossom Balloons is the premier company in central Florida, with more than 17 years' experience and a wonderfully laid-back style that stems from their British-owned operation. You meet at the Days Inn Hotel Maingate West on Highway 192, half a mile past Splendid China, at 6am (the best winds for flying are always first thing in the morning)

8

WayFun Kayak expeditions

and then transfer to the take-off site, where you help the crew set up and inflate one of their three balloons. Owner-operator Richard Ornstein and his team are a real hoot, and you are soon up, up and away in awe-inspiring style, floating serenely up to 2,000ft or sinking down to skim the surface of one of the many lakes (disturbing the occasional gator or deer). After about an hour you come back to earth for a traditional champagne landing ceremony and return to Days Inn for a full breakfast and your special balloonist's certificate. The full experience lasts 3–4 hours and costs $175 per adult (inclusive of tax) and $95 for 10–15s (under 10s go free with their parents). Hotel pick-up is also available at $10 per person round-trip, or you can pay $20 to be part of the chase crew and just enjoy the champagne landing and breakfast. Call 407 239 7677 for reservations (they do get well-booked, even though they fly every day, weather permitting) or go to www.orangeblossomballoons.com.

Orange Blossom Balloons

Mount Dora Railway

New in 2002 was this wonderful and highly scenic opportunity to appreciate some of the central Florida countryside by train, all the way from Orlando to pretty Mount Dora in Lake County in the north-west. The 74-mile round-trip runs on Saturday and Sunday at 9am, returning at 5pm, and gives you plenty of time to explore the friendly little town of Mount Dora, which has a fine collection of antique and gift shops, boutiques, art galleries, cafes and parks. The train ride itself features a 1913 steam locomotive, completely overhauled in 2000, on a fairly gentle run from downtown Orlando (on Hughey Avenue) through orange groves and lake-filled countryside to the Mount Dora station on West Third Avenue.

Once in Mount Dora, you can take the 1-hour Cannonball service led by a vintage 1946 diesel loco to the town of Tavares at 11am, 12.40pm, 2.20pm and 4pm on Saturday and Sunday. Prices for the Mount Dora service are $27 for adults, $25 for seniors (55+) and $17 for children (4–12). The Tavares service costs $12, $11 and $8. To make reservations for this increasingly popular trip, call 352 735 4667 or www.mtdoratrain.com.

Everglades and the Bahamas

Day trips are increasingly common from Orlando to the Everglades, Miami, the Florida Keys and the Bahamas and, if you are prepared to put up with a long day out (up to 16 hours) you can see a lot of the state this way. However, it's a long journey for children for a half-hour airboat ride.

Real Florida Excursions and **International Divers** are two companies worth recommending.

Orlando & Mount Dora Railway

Real Florida has a variety of tours, from an Orlando Shop Til You Drop excursion to a Miami-Bahamas 2-day getaway. For the latter, you travel down to Miami (3½ hours) by coach, get to shop at the smart Bayside Marketplace or take the popular Miami waterways cruise, before the 22-minute flight to the Bahamas for an overnight stay. The following day can be spent on the beautiful beaches or at your hotel in Freeport, before a 5-hour cruise back to Fort Lauderdale with an excellent dinner buffet and then the (long) coach ride back to Orlando. This good-value package costs just $149 for adults and $99 for children 2–12 (plus another $76.30 in local taxes).

An overnight trip to **Miami** and the sizzling **South Beach** district, with its hot nightlife, is another attractive proposition. You get transport, a guided tour, good-quality accommodation and the best part of a day on the beach for $99 adults and $49 for 3–12s (plus $12/person tax). Another 2-day trip is the **Fort Lauderdale-Everglades** tour, which includes an overnight stay by the beaches of lovely Fort Lauderdale (plus a chance to shop at the world's biggest outlet mall, Sawgrass Mills) as well as a visit to the Everglades for an airboat ride, all for $99 for adults and $69 for children. Alternatively, their **Naples-Everglades Adventure** provides a taste of Florida in just a day (although much of the time is spent on the coach), with a 30-minute airboat ride through the Everglades, lunch in beautiful Naples and an afternoon cruise along the coast – $99 (adults) and $49 (3–12s), with an optional swamp buggy ride in the Everglades at $14 per adult (under 6s free). A new offering is their limo evening out to Universal's CityWalk, with dinner and a pass for the clubs. Called **Be A Star in a Great Big Car,** it involves a round-trip from your hotel to CityWalk in a stretch limo, and is proving highly popular at $69 for adults and $44 for 3–12s. A **Kennedy Space Center** day trip costs $56 and $46 (including admission,) and the **Shop 'til You Drop** (including buffet breakfast at Golden Corral and visits to World of Denim, Reebok Outlet Center, Belz Mall and West Oaks Mall) will set you back $29 and $19. Call Real Florida Excursions on 407 345 4996, ext. 3012 (or visit www.werusa.com).

International Divers offer several other contrasting and memorable tours, chief among which is their **Florida Adventure Tour,** a personal, all-day experience in the real Florida. It includes a breakfast buffet stop, a 2-hour boat

The author takes the front seat with Warbird Adventures

trip and snorkel on the picturesque Crystal River (where you often encounter the harmless manatees!), a relaxing lunch at King's Bay, 45-minute airboat tour on the Withlacochee River and a jeep safari through a wildlife refuge that includes tigers, lions, kangaroos and raccoons. It costs $94 for adults and $79 for children 3–9 (under 3s not permitted). Alternatively, their 2-day **Getaway to the Florida Keys** is an excellent proposition, visiting the Everglades en route, seeing an alligator wrestling and snake-handling show and taking an airboat ride before arriving at Key Largo for a beach barbecue. Part two of the adventure, after an overnight stay and breakfast at your beach resort, is the **dolphin encounter,** a 2-hour programme of instruction, observation and interaction with the Key's tame resident dolphins (including one-on-one swims, dorsal tows and foot pushes). With the dolphin encounter, the tour is $289 for adults and $279 for 7–9s, and $189 and $179 without (children must be at least 7 for the dolphin swim). Call International Divers on 407 352 5151 or visit www.swimdolphins.com.

Flying Tigers Warbird Restoration Museum

Vintage aeroplane and nostalgia buffs will want to make a note of this offbeat museum adjacent to Kissimmee Airport, which builds and restores World War Two fighters and bombers. Kids who enjoyed building Airfix kits will especially enjoy the 1-hour tour of the facilities, which basically represent a couple of large hangars with aircraft in various stages of restoration and repair. It is one of the most amazing programmes of its kind, with the exhibits ranging from a fully restored B-25 Mitchell bomber and a P-51 Mustang to scraps of fuselages and engines that will gradually be incorporated into the latest rebuilding project. It's a place where you see, smell and touch the history of the 1940s' newsreels, and the guides have a detailed knowledge of everything they show you.

You could be forgiven for thinking you have walked into a scrap yard, but the main hangars reveal the full scale of the operation, with the wholesale restoration of a B-17 Flying Fortress being their pride and joy. In fact, owner Tom Reilly insists: 'All those clean, tidy sterile museums you have seen in the past, well, this isn't one of them. We have oil on the floor we refer to as bomber blood and, if you are lucky, you might get some on you to take home as a souvenir.' Restoration projects include a Vought Corsair and a Lockheed Lightning, while a Lockheed Starfighter and MIG 21 are among about 13 planes on static display. Another 18 or so are flyable, including a Focke-Wolf 190 and a B-25 bomber. The site includes a charming gift shop that houses some more museum pieces, uniforms and memorabilia from World War Two. It is open 9am–5pm every day, and there's always some reconstruction work in progress. Charges are $9 for adults, $8 for 60+ and under 12s (under 8s free). This 'living museum' can be found off Highway 192, half a mile down Hoagland Boulevard on the left.

Anyone captivated by the sights, sounds and stories of this magnificent exhibit (also known as Bombertown) can also join in. **Warbird Restoration School** is an intensive 5-day course covering the whole rebuilding process, from sheet metal fabrication to welding and fuel systems. It culminates with a flight in a restored B-25J Mitchell bomber, but at a price of $995, it is definitely for enthusiasts only. Call 407 933 1942 for details or visit their website at www.warbirdmuseum.com.

Warbird Adventures

Once you have seen the displays, you should consider neighbouring Warbird Adventures. This is the best ride in town, bar none, guaranteed. Not only do you get to fly in one of their three 1945 T-6 Harvard fighter-trainers, but also, after a period of getting used to the front seat of this vintage 2-seater… you get to fly it! And you don't just handle the controls, your instructor will get you doing loops, barrel rolls and all manner of aerobatics. This is simply the most exhilarating ride I have ever done, enhanced by in-flight video and wingtip camera to record every moment. It is the only place where you can walk in off the street and, 20 minutes later, be flying a plane with no previous experience.

My instructor was the excellent Thom Richard and, despite my initial reluctance, he had me doing the full aerobatic business before long. Roller-coasters? They're for wimps! Mind you, this is not cheap – a 15-minute flight costs $150, while a 30-minute trip is $250 and an hour $450. Aerobatics (on 30- or 60-minute flights only) cost $30, while the PAL video is $40 and the stills $15 (or all three 'extras' for $70). Nevertheless, this is truly a memory to last a lifetime, and the thought of it still thrills me to bits. They also operate a 1966 Bell 47-G M*A*S*H helicopter for flights and instruction, call 407 870 7366 for details or visit www.warbirdadventures.com.

Green Meadows Petting Farm

From one extreme to another, here is guaranteed fun for kids of 2 up to about 11 and their parents (don't forget your cameras). It's the ultimate hands-on experience as, on your 2-hour guided tour, you (or rather, your children) can milk a cow, pet a pig, cuddle a chick or duckling, feed goats and sheep, meet a buffalo, chickens, peacocks and donkeys and learn what makes an animal farm tick. There are pony rides for the young ones and tractor-drawn hay rides for all, plus the Green Meadows Express steam train for a scenic ride through the farm and a play area of slides and swings. The shaded acres, free-roaming animals and peaceful aspect all contribute to another pleasant change of pace, especially as Green Meadows is barely 10 minutes from the tourist hurly-burly of Highway 192 (south on Poinciana Boulevard). It is open 9.30am–5.30pm daily (last admission at 4pm) and costs $17 per person ($13 for seniors, under 2s free), and you should allow 3–4 hours for your visit. Drinks, snacks and gifts are available, but it is also the ideal place to bring a picnic. Call 407 846 0770 or visit their website at www.greenmeadowsfarm.com.

Disney and cruising

8

Taking a cruise is fast becoming a regular option with your Orlando stay and, with the advent of *Disney Cruise Line* in 1998, you will now see a lot of publicity for these competitively priced 2-, 3-, 4- and 7-day sailings out of fast-developing Port Canaveral.

Although a newcomer to cruising, Disney has launched out with a couple of breathtaking ships, the 83,000-ton *Disney Magic* (1998) and *Disney Wonder* (1999), plus their own dedicated cruise terminal. Classic design plus the usual Disney imagineering have produced these two huge vessels incorporating special features for kids, teenagers AND couples without children. Both ships are a destination experience in their own right, each with four restaurants, a 1,040-seat theatre, cinema, nightclub complex, sports club and a full health spa, while they sail to the Bahamas, Caribbean and Disney's stunning private island. It is not a cheap option and the 3- and 4-night cruises can feel a little frenzied, but the 7-night Caribbean Cruises – either to St Maarten and St Thomas or Key West, Grand Cayman and Cozumel in Mexico – offer a genuinely relaxing style that is hard to beat anywhere in the world. They boast some novel touches with superb on-board entertainment, Disney character interaction and wonderful features like the adults-only champagne brunch. Many tour operators offer *Disney Cruise Line* packages but you can also book cruise-only at great rates with Dreams Unlimited Travel at www.dreamsunlimitedtravel.com.

The ships are identical in practical terms, and the week-long cruises allow you to enjoy fully the wide range of facilities. The impact of the four-restaurant set-up (where you dine in a different one each night, including the amazing *Animator's Palate* which comes to life all around you), the fabulous entertainment 'district', the vast array of kids' facilities (including Buzz Lightyear's Cyberspace Command Post) and the picturesque beaches of Disney's Castaway Cay island knock your socks off.

Other cruises out of Port Canaveral include the glitzy **Carnival Cruise Lines** (all-modern hardware, party atmosphere; call 1-888 2276 4825 in the US or 020 7940 4466 in the UK) with 3- and 4-day Bahamas voyages, and 7-day cruises to the Western Caribbean on one of their newest ships; **Royal Caribbean International** (more modern, glamorous ships, call 1-800 327 6700 in the US or 01932 834231 in the UK) with similar trips to Nassau and RCI's private island of Coco Cay; **Holland America Line** (more traditional cruise elegance, call 1-877 932 4259 in the US, 020 7940 4477 in the UK) offering 1-week cruises to the Eastern Caribbean and their private Bahamian island of Half Moon Cay; and, from May–October 2003, a unique 1-week cruise with **NCL**, one of the brightest and most quality-conscious brands, (call 1-800 327 7030 in the US or 08705 906060 in the UK), who will take their magnificent new *Norwegian Dawn* on a round-trip from Port Canaveral to Miami, the Bahamas and New York (yes, the Big Apple itself). For more advice, consult my book *Choosing A Cruise* or specialist UK travel agent, The Cruise Line Ltd, on 01273 835999.

For a smaller and more low-key approach, the **Rivership Romance** (daily out of downtown Sanford) is a great choice, especially for the lunch cruises on the wildlife-rich St John's River. The old-fashioned steamer can take up to 200 in comfort and adds a fine meal, live entertainment and a river commentary, as well as providing a relaxing alternative to the usual tourist scenario. Choose from the 3-hour lunch cruise (11am–2pm Wed, Sat and Sun) at $35 a head, the 4-hour cruise (11am–3pm Mon, Tue, Thur and Fri) at $45 or an evening dinner-dance voyage (7.30–11pm Fri and Sat) at $50. For reservations and info call 407 321 5091 (or visit www.rivershipromance.com). Their dock can be found off exit 101A of I-4, east into Sanford, then left on Palmetto Avenue.

Rivership Romance in Seminole County

Seminole County

Having arrived in the historic town of Sanford, the heart of Seminole County, it is worth pointing out the possible diversions of a day or two in this area that will get you well off

Spoonbill

the beaten track. The **Central Florida Zoological Park** is a private, non-profit-making organisation that puts a pleasant, natural accent on the zoo theme and is set in 109 wooded acres of unspoilt Florida countryside with boardwalks and trails around all the attractions. These include more than 100 species of animals, weekend feeding demonstrations, educational programmes, a picnic area, pony rides and a butterfly garden, plus the Zoofari Outpost gift shop. It's good value, too, at $7 for adults, $4 for seniors (60+) and $3 for kids 3–12, and the park (off Exit 104 of I-4) is open every day (except Thanksgiving Day and Christmas Day) 9am–5pm. For more info, visit www.centralfloridazoo.org.

St John's River Cruise, at Blue Spring State Park, features a 2-hour nature tour of this historic waterway, with interactive narration of the history, flora and fauna (which includes manatees in winter

months). This immensely personable, family-run tour costs $14 for adults, $12 for seniors (60+) and $8 for children (3–12) and leaves from Orange City marina several times a day (take Highway 17/92 north from Sanford to French Avenue and head west for 1 mile). Call 407 330 1612 to check times and book.

Bill's Airboat Adventures, on the St John's River east of Sanford, offers 90-minute tours in the company of conservationist and river historian Captain Bill Daniel for $30 ($15 for under 14s). Call 407 977 3214 to book. **Black Hammock Fish Camp and Restaurant** (off Exit 44 of the Central Florida Greeneway, take SR 434 east, turn left on Deleon St and left on to Black Hammock Road) is another peaceful backwater on Lake Jesup, where you can try fishing or Gator Ventures airboating – and don't miss their great restaurant for local specialities (call 407 365 1244). **Dana's Fishing & Scenic Tours** can take you out on to Seminole County's lakes and waterways for some brilliant bass fishing or guided scenic tours (by appointment only, call 407 645 5462 or visit www.fishingincentralflorida.com).

Of course, you can just head for one of the splendid **State Parks** in

8

Horse riding

this area and take your own tour of the well-marked trails. **Wekiva Springs State Park** offers hiking, canoeing and swimming, plus picnic areas and shelters, while **Little Big Econ** state forest has 5,048 acres of scenic woodlands and wetlands.

Sanford itself is a designated historic centre, full of brick-paved streets and antique shops. It is very much small-town America, having lost the growth battle with Orlando many years ago, but it makes a peaceful diversion with some lovely walks. It also offers the **Rose Cottage Tea Room,** one of the prettiest restaurants you will find in Florida, which serves a mouth-watering array of soups, sandwiches, salads and quiches, as well as fabulous fruit teas. This little treasure (open 11am–3pm Tue–Sat) can be found on Park Avenue, 13 blocks out of Sanford town centre (call 407 323 9448 for a reservation, which is usually necessary). If you fancy a day or two staying in the area (highly recommended), check out a quaint B & B accommodation such as The Higgins House (407 324 9238) or The Martin House (407 330 9013).

For more details of all the above, go to www.visitseminole.com or call in at one of their Visitor Centers, at Orlando Sanford Airport (in the Welcome Center as you exit the main building) and at 1230 Douglas Avenue in Longwood (one block west of Exit 94 of I-4; 407 665 2900).

Out on the Gulf Coast, just north of Homossasa Springs, the **Crystal River** offers another wildlife fiesta as it is home, seasonally, to the endangered manatee, and it is possible to go swimming with these wonderful creatures here. **Orlando Dive & Snorkel Tours** (call 407 239 3573 or visit www.diveorlando.com) offer organised excursions for $65, and it truly is a magical opportunity.

Eco-tourism

Genuine eco-tourism is still in its infancy, in general terms, in central Florida, but there are two major exceptions worth knowing about.

Forever Florida is, for my money, one of the most outstanding, non-theme park attractions. It is both a 4,700-acre wilderness preserve and a working ranch. As well as a close-up of Florida's flora and fauna and its conservation issues, you get a taste of the original cowboy life, Cracker style (Crackers were the 'real' cowboys, pre-dating their Western counterparts by 50 years), which is a fascinating slice of history. Eco-safaris, covered wagon tours, horse rides, bike trails, nature walks and, for the kids, pony rides and a free petting zoo, are the highlights, as well as the magnificent **Cypress Restaurant** and Visitor Center, which offers an essential 30-minute orientation programme into the conservancy's creation.

Beginning as a dream of gifted young biologist and ecologist Allen Broussard, Forever Florida was completed after his death (from complications of Hodgkin's disease) by his parents, Dr William and Margaret Broussard, who own the neighbouring Crescent J Ranch and continue to give their time and energy to building the wilderness as a non-profitmaking memorial to their son. The education element alone is awesome, and tours feature a strong conservation message in this tranquil, untouched corner of Florida. The **Cracker Coach Tour** (1½ hours at $18 for adults, $15 for under 13s, daily at 10am and 1pm, or 2½ hours at $28 and $18 at 3pm) – a kind of open-sided, large-wheeled buggy – is their stock-in-trade for a tranquil trundle around much of the woods, swamp and prairie that make up the ranch and conservancy. An education coordinator provides the low-down on the history and environmental issues of the ecosystems. You are likely to encounter alligators (at a safe distance), whitetail deer, armadillos and a host of bird life – including bald eagles – and leave with a good understanding of the real Florida. They also have a new 2-hour **Sunset Tour** on Saturday evenings at 6pm at $39.95 and $25.95 with dinner, or $28 and $18 without. **Guided horse rides** vary from $35–52 (1–3 hours; $24–31 for children), and **covered wagon tours** of the ranch are $28 and $18 (reservations required). **Trail bike** rentals are $8 an hour and **pony rides** $5 for the first ride, $3 for a second. There is even an **overnight trailride** or ranch experience for the ultimate Cracker appeal, but it is a touch expensive at $240/person (or $220 for 6–12 people, and $199 for groups of more than 12). The **City Slicker Roundup** runs three times a year, at $350 with an overnight stay, or $175 for a day ride. Regular tours run at 9am, 12.30pm and 3.30pm Fri–Sun but should be booked on 1-800 957 9794.

A new **BioPark** is in the offing, which aims to showcase only native Floridian animals, such as the panther and bear, and the original Cracker cattle (a distinctly 'ornery' beast, by all accounts). For more details, visit www.foreverflorida.com. The conservancy is a good 80-minute drive out of Orlando, some 40 miles east on Highway 192, through St Cloud as far as Holopaw, then 7½ miles south on Highway 441, but it is well worth the journey.

On an equally authentic scale is **Disney's Wilderness Preserve**, run by the Nature Conservancy in Poinciana, south of Kissimmee. This restoration of an 11,500-acre preserve is a work in progress and allows visitors in for various hiking trails, a 1-hour guided tour on Saturdays (at 9.30am) and 2-hour buggy tours on Sundays (1.30pm). Entry fee is $2 for adults and $1 for children, while the buggy tours are an additional $7 and $5. The preserve is located at the end of Pleasant Hill Road (follow Hoagland Boulevard south off Highway 192). Call 407 935 0002 for more information.

The **Kissimmee Convention and Visitors' Bureau** also publishes an excellent eco-guide, if you drop by on Highway 192.

Beach escapes

When it comes to beaches – another key component of a Florida holiday – you are again spoiled for choice. The sea, sand and surf of **Cocoa Beach** is only an hour's drive from Orlando (east on the Beeline Expressway – 528 – then south on Highway A1A) and offers some good shopping (including the unmissable **Ron Jon's Surf Shop**, a massive neon emporium of all things water related) in addition to the two main public beaches. As it's the Atlantic, the sea can be pretty chilly from November to March, but Cocoa Beach is rapidly developing into a major coastal resort, so the facilities are excellent.

Its more famous neighbour, just to the north, is **Daytona Beach**, which is still only an hour away if you take I-4 all the way east. This is the prime site of the Atlantic coast scene, with an array of good beaches (some of which you can even drive on – for a $5 toll, speed limit 10mph), boating and fishing trips, sightseeing (including the **Ponce de Leon Inlet Lighthouse**, a formidable 203 spiralling steps to the top of this magnificently preserved monument, but well worth it for the view (10am–5pm daily, $5 for adults, $1.50 for children) and surprisingly smart shopping at the redeveloped **Ocean Walk Village**, next door to the main beach, pier and boardwalk area, and the lively **Riverfront**

8

Marketplace along historic Beach Street (see below).

Newly opened is the **Marine Science Center** (just around the corner from the lighthouse), which showcases whale, mangrove, mosquito and sea turtle exhibits, along with turtle rehabilitation facilities and a 5,000-gallon artificial reef aquarium, as well as static and interactive educational displays. A boardwalk and nature trail system extends throughout the park, which naturally has a gift shop. It is open 10am–4pm Tue–Sat and noon–4pm Sun (closed Mon) and costs $1 for 5–12s and $3 for 13 and older (www.echotourism.com/msc/), under 5s free).

The **beaches** themselves are a lively affair around Spring Break (the big American pre-Easter college holiday) but fairly down to earth otherwise. Other highlights include the chance to cruise the intra-coastal waterway to see the local dolphins at play – check out **A tiny Cruise Line** (call 386 226 2343 or visit www.visitdaytona.com/tinycruise/) for details of their four cruises, which vary from $9.66–15.32 and include a lovely Sunset/City Lights tour from April to October.

The Riverfront Marketplace is the heart of downtown Daytona Beach, with a museum of local history, restaurants, nightclubs, coffee bars and a performing arts theatre, all in a quaint riverside setting. Dining out opportunities are many and inviting

Caladesi Island, one of the top five beaches in the US

and Lighthouse Landing among the best. The beaches themselves can be up to 500ft wide at low tide and are all open to the public year-round.

Lighthouse Point Park is especially worthy of note, a 52-acre stretch of nature trails, fishing, observation deck, swimming and picnicking (open 8am–9pm, $3.50 per vehicle). Check out the **Lighthouse Landing** here for lunch or dinner, a truly eclectic piece of Floridian restaurant life. For the latest on all Daytona Beach has to offer, call 020 7935 7756 in the UK or look up www.daytonabeach.com. Of course, one of the biggest attractions is the Daytona USA racetrack (see Motor Sport on page 222).

To the West you have the **Gulf Coast**, which is a good 90 minutes' drive down I-4 and through Tampa on I-275 south to **St Petersburg Beach** (105 miles) or **Clearwater Beach** (110 miles) or 2 hours-plus down I-4 and then I-75 to **Bradenton** (130 miles), **Sarasota** (140 miles) and **Venice** (160 miles), plus the beautiful islands of **Captiva Sanibel** (175 miles). The beaches are less 'hip', but more relaxed and refined, and the sea a touch warmer and much calmer, so it is better for families with small children. You will find it easier to get away from the crowds here, too. **Naples** is further south still on I-75 but is rated one of the most welcoming beach destinations in Florida.

Riverfront Marketplace, Daytona Beach

Florida's Beach

The huge stretch of beaches and 'cities' from St Pete Beach to Clearwater (collectively known as Florida's Beach) represent the heart of the Florida Beach experience, with a wonderful array of attractions as well as the 35 miles of lovely white sands and average 361 days of sunshine a year. **St Petersburg** itself, just across the Howard Frankland Bridge from Tampa, is a bright, attractive and happening city, with a range of developments, both recent and historical, which makes it a worthwhile visit. Take time here for the wonderful **Dali Museum** (open 9.30am–5.30pm Mon–Sat, 12 noon–5.30pm Sun; adults $10, under 11s free) and the new **Bay Walk** complex of shops, restaurants and 20-screen cinema. An additional assortment of surprising museums, pedestrian-friendly streets and the Pier all add up to a wealth of opportunity for the interested visitor, while fan-friendly **Tropicana Field** hosts the Tampa Bay Devil Rays baseball team – April to September – for another slice of pure Americana (tickets from just $5).

Out in the **Beaches,** from the 800-acre Fort De Soto Park in the south to stunning **Caladesi Island** in the north, there is a wonderful diversity of choice, too, with the likes of Treasure Island, Sand Key and St Pete Beach all receiving the Blue Wave Award for cleanliness and safety. **Fort De Soto Park** also offers free walking tours of its Spanish-American War era fort and wilderness areas, in addition to having one of the quietest and prettiest beaches. **John's Pass Village & Boardwalk** is an unusual shopping district full of art galleries and restaurants, while **Dolphin Landings** in St Pete Beach is another big draw for its dolphin watch cruises, Shell Island day trips and sunset sailings (the dolphin cruise is a real highlight for its guaranteed close-up animal encounters along the calm inland waterway; the 2-hour yacht voyage costs $25 for adults and $15 for children – call 727 367 4488 or visit www.dolphinlandings.com).

Along at Indian Shores, America's largest wild bird hospital, the **Suncoast Seabird Sanctuary,** is another must-see little hideaway, usually with more than 500 injured patients. **Clearwater Beach** boasts the Marine Aquarium and Pier 60, where the daily sunset celebration, complete with craft stalls and live music, is held. Reaching **Caladesi Island** brings you to one of the most picturesque beach spots in the world and another Blue Wave award-winner.

For those wishing to take it easy while they are here, rather than get back in the hire car, the **Suncoast Beach Trolley** is the perfect transport link both along the beaches and into St Petersburg ($1.50/ride or $3 for an all-day pass; call 727 530 9911 or visit www.psta.net). A new **hovercraft service** was due to start in summer 2002, offering trips from the Pier in downtown St Pete's to various Gulf beaches ($14 each way or $25 round-trip; call 727 578 4060 or look up www.hover-usa.com). **Duck Tours** offers 80-minute trips through the heart of downtown St Pete's and into Tampa Bay for a scenic view of the waterfront in a World War Two army amphibious vehicle ($18.50 for adults, $9.95 for children, call 727 432 3825 to book).

When it comes to accommodation, there is a suitably wide choice, too. A range of **Superior Small Lodgings** combine desirable beach-front locations with small-scale, personalised service (check out the Seahorse Cottages & Apartments on Treasure Island Beach as the perfect example – with weekly rates from $385 for a 1-bedroom cottage; call 727 367 2291 or go to www.beachdirectory.com). Of course, there are upmarket hotels, too, witness the superbly equipped **Tradewinds Beach Resorts** (a 1,100-room development of three resorts that combine their wide range of facilities; call 727 562 1221 or look up www.tradewindsresort.com) on St Pete Beach and the huge (and hugely impressive) **Sheraton Sand Key Resort** at Clearwater Beach, a 10-storey edifice with 10 acres of private beach and facilities ranging from floodlit tennis courts to a fitness centre, children's pool and playground (with supervised programmes in summer). Rates from $135–480, call 727 595 1611 or check out www.beachsand.com. The area also boasts more than 2,000 restaurants and they – and much, much more – can be looked up on www.floridasbeach.com.

Sport

In addition to virtually every form of entertainment known to man, central Florida is one of the world's biggest sporting playgrounds, with a huge range of opportunities either to watch or play your favourite sport.

BRIT TIP: Be warned, in summer months the locals all get the same urge to head for the beach at weekends, so unless you head out EARLY (i.e. before 9am) and come back late (i.e. after 8pm) you will encounter some serious traffic.

Golf

Without doubt, the number one activity is golf, with almost 150 courses within an hour's drive of Orlando. The weather, of course, makes it such a popular pastime, but some spectacular courses add to the attraction, and there are numerous holiday packages geared towards keen golfers of all abilities. With an 18-hole round, including cart hire and taxes, from as little as $40 on some courses (and they average around $75), it is an attractive proposition and quite different for those used to British courses. If you go in for 36-hole days, it is possible to save up to $30 by replaying the same course, while it is cheaper to play Monday–Thursday than Friday–Sunday.

Sculpted landscapes, manicured fairways and abundant use of spectacular water features and white-sand bunkers make for some memorable golfing. The winter months are the high season, hence the most expensive, but many courses are busy year-round. Be aware also that many courses pair up golfers with little thought for ability, handicap, etc. So, if two of you turn up, the chances are you will play with two complete strangers ('A little frustrating when you get paired with two middle-aged ladies from Switzerland who have only just taken up golf,' says reader John Cartlidge).

Virtually every course will offer a driving range to get you started, plus lockers, changing rooms and showers, while the use of golf carts is universal (and many include the amazing GPS positioning system which gives the yardage for every shot, plus the ability to order drinks or even lunch while you're on the course!). They all feature creature comforts like ice water stations and drinks carts that circulate the course (please don't forget to tip the trolley girls who drive them). A handful have swimming pools, while all can offer a decent bar and restaurant for that all-important 19th-hole session.

Your best starting point is to visit one of the five **Edwin Watts** golf shops around Orlando to pick up a free copy of the *Golfer's Guide* or the *Guide To Golf* for a handy introduction to most of the courses available (and even pick up a new set of clubs at the Watts National Clearance Center just south of Wet 'n Wild on I-Drive; call 407 352 2535 or visit www.edwinwatts.com). Alternatively, Tee-Times USA (1-888 465 3356) offers an excellent advice and reservation service. The **Visit Florida** organisation publishes an *Official Golf Guide* (call 850 488 8374 or www.flasports.com/fg.htm), as does Daytona Beach (1-800 881 7065, www.golfdaytonabeach.com).

For a unique and personable touch, you can't beat the all-in-one golf instruction service of **Professional Golf Guides of Orlando,** led by owner/operator and PGA member Phillip Jaffe, who is a mine of golfing lore and knowledge, as well as great company. They take up to 3 golfers at a time around some of the area's finest courses, and can supply transport and high-tech (graphite and titanium) clubs if required. The playing lesson is of the highest quality and includes full on-course instruction, course management strategies, full game analysis, game improvement suggestions, shot-making demos and a wrap-up lesson that will leave you with the knowledge and skills to take your game to the next level. It is an eye-opening experience to play alongside Phillip and his staff of PGA professionals (hey, he even managed to get me hitting the green from some way off, which is no mean feat!) and well worth it for the keen golfer who wishes to improve their game in one round. Call 407 894 0907 for rates or visit www.progolfguides.com.

> BRIT TIP: An early-morning tee-off in the summer can provide some of the most peaceful and scenic golf you will find.

Alternatively, the **Nick Faldo Golf Institute** on the lower portion of I-Drive (1-888 463 2536) is a great place to visit if you just want to hit a few golf balls.

Walt Disney World Resort in Florida has been quick to attract the golf fanatic, with five championship-quality courses, including the 7,000-yd **Palm**, rated as one of *Golf Digest's* top 25. Fees vary from $109–144 for *Walt Disney World Resort in Florida* guests and $114–149 for visitors, with half-price reductions after 3pm. Call 407 939 4653 for tee-times.

Another luxury experience is afforded by the nearby **Grand Cypress** on Vineland Road (407 239 1904, rates from $130–170 depending on season). It has three elegant 9-hole courses and a superb 18-hole links-style offering (all

designed by the legendary Jack Nicklaus), which presents a truly magnificent challenge.

MetroWest Country Club, on South Hiawassee Road to the north of Universal Studios (407 299 1099; $79–115), is a 7,051-yd masterpiece designed by Robert Trent Jones Snr and features elevated tees and greens, with pleasant rolling fairways and expansive bunkers.

The superb **Keene's Pointe** in Windermere to the north of *Walt Disney World Resort in Florida* is Nicklaus's newest and most exciting course, measuring 7,173yd if played off the pro Bear tees (there are always five tees for the various handicaps, ladies and seniors). Surrounded by lakes, it has a truly impeccable look, not to mention outstanding facilities, including a pool (407 876 1461; $65–115).

The **Legacy Club at Alaqua Lakes** is a masterpiece of conservation and tranquillity (it is part of the Audubon preservation and restoration scheme) as well as a tour de force of lush fairways and weird and wonderful greens (a signature feature of designer Tom Fazio). Winding through some spectacular forest in the suburb of Longwood in Seminole County, it is a serious challenge for serious golfers (407 444 9995; $54–64).

Also in Seminole, **Magnolia Plantation** is another wonderful contrast, a heavily wooded and peaceful haven that feels miles from the theme park world and yet is less

8

> BRIT TIP: Reader John Cartlidge, a keen Florida golfer, advises: 'Take your waterproofs with you. I was looking to buy some in Florida but could only find lightweight slipovers – no use in the UK.'

A Florida Beach sunset

than half an hour away up I-4. Woven among the lakes and ponds of the Wekiva River basin, Phillip Jaffe rates it a 'must play' course (407 833 0818; $55–85).

Falcon's Fire in Kissimmee is another standout course, featuring the 'ProShot' digital caddy system and water coolers on all golf carts. Plenty of water around the course assures a testing 18 holes, but it is wonderfully picturesque (407 239 5445; $75–150).

The **Orange Lake Country Club** is a huge vacation resort in Orlando (just 4 miles from Disney) with two 18-hole courses, a 9-hole course and a par-3, floodlit, 9 holes. The new Legends at Orange Lake course (designed by Arnold Palmer) is their top-of-the-range offering (407 239 1050; $70–90). **Kissimmee Oaks** features some majestic moss-draped oaks and local wildlife as well as 18 holes of memorable golf that wind around some pretty lakes, all just 3½ miles south of Highway 192 in Kissimmee in the Oaks Community off John Young Parkway (407 933 4055; $50–$80). Seminole County itself is another golf haven, with 18 public or semi-private courses, and offers golf-and-hotel packages from $65. Call 1-800 555 9589 for details or look up www.visitseminole.com.

Check when you book about each club's dress code, as there are a few differences from course to course.

Of course, this is only a small (if representative) sample and there are dozens of other choices.

Mini-golf

Not exactly a sport, but definitely for holiday fun, are the many quite extravagant opportunities for mini-golf around Orlando. They are a big hit with kids and good fun for all the family (if you have the legs left for it after a day at the theme park!). Several attractions and parks offer mini-golf as an extra, but for the best, try out the self-contained centres, of which there are six main ones.

Predictably, Disney has come up with some terrific ones of their own. **Disney's Fantasia Gardens Miniature Golf Courses,** next to the Swan Hotel just off Buena Vista Drive, is a 2-course challenge over 36 of the most varied holes of mini-golf you will find. Hippos dance, fountains leap and broomsticks march on the 18-hole crazy, golf-themed **Fantasia Gardens** – its style is taken from the Disney animated classic *Fantasia*, meaning lots of cartoon fun along the way as the park's Imagineers challenge you with a riot of visual gags as well as some diabolically difficult mini-golf. Watch out for *Toccata and Fugue in D Minor* where good shots are rewarded with musical tones, and *The Nutcracker Suite*, where obstacles include dancing mushrooms!

Fantasia Fairways is a cunning putting course, complete with fairways, rough, water hazards and bunkers to test even the best golfers. The 18 holes range in length from 40 to 75ft, and it can take more than an hour to play a full round. Each course costs $9.76 (adult) and $7.78 (child), and they are open 10am–11pm every day.

Disney's latest offering is the 36-hole **Winter-Summerland Miniature Golf Courses** at the entrance to *Disney's Blizzard Beach* water park. Divided into two 18-hole courses, these mini works of art feature a 'Summer' setting of surf and beach tests (watch out for squirting fish), and a 'Winter' variety of snow and ice-crafted holes, all with a welter of visual puns as befitting the vacation resort of Santa's elves (yes, that's the theme, and kids will love it – you can even see the skid marks where Santa landed his sleigh!). An adult round is $9.76 (3–9s $7.78), a double round is half price and it is open 10am–11pm.

Elsewhere, **Pirate's Cove** has a twin-course set-up at Lake Buena Vista (by the Crossroads shopping plaza) and I-Drive (just south of The Mercado), with mountain caves, waterfalls and rope bridges to test your skill and please the eye. **River Adventure Golf** (on Highway 192, almost opposite Medieval Times) offers a Mississippi River adventure with rolling rapids, waterfalls and an authentic water wheel. **Bonanza Miniature Golf and Gifts** (next door to the Magic Mining Co restaurant on west Highway 192) has an imaginative – and tricky – 36 holes with a gold mining theme. **Pirate's Island** (further along Highway 192 to the east) is another spectacular 36-hole spread, while arguably the most impressive of the lot is the **Congo River Golf and Exploration Co**, which has courses on Highway 192, I-Drive and Highway 436 in Altamonte Springs. They could almost be Disney-inspired, they are so artificially scenic. The Kissimmee location also has paddle boats to try, while I-Drive has the option of go-karts, and all three have games and video arcades. Charges are $6–8 per round, but look out for coupons which all have a couple of dollars off each one. They open 9am–10 or 11pm daily.

Million Dollar Mulligan is worthy of mention here, although it is neither mini-golf nor the real McCoy. Instead, Million Dollar Mulligan, just off Highway 192 on Florida Plaza Boulevard (next to Old Town – look for the giant golf ball), is a 9-hole, floodlit pitch-and-putt course that looks spectacular at night when its lake and fountains are illuminated. It costs $11.75 for adults and $7.50 for children and seniors and is open daily from 10am–midnight (407 396 8180).

Fishing

Fishing attracts a lot of specialist holiday-makers and is fast catching on as a highly enjoyable day out with us visitors as well. The abundance of lakes and rivers give plenty of choice, with bass the prime catch. A 7-day licence costs $17 (available from all tackle shops, fish camps, sports stores and Wal-Mart and K-Mart supermarkets), and there are dozens of boats for hire on the St John's River, Lake Toho in Kissimmee, Lake Kissimmee, and both coasts for some serious sea fishing. Expect to pay $160–195 for half a day and $200–295 for a full day bass fishing.

For the most complete angling service try **Cutting Loose Expeditions,** a highly experienced, personalised operator who can organise fresh or sea-water

Deep-sea fishing

expeditions and arrange hotel pick-up if necessary. All your bait and licence requirements are included. It is run by A Neville Cutting, one of America's leading fishing adventurers, who maintains high standards with his guides and other staff. Rates start at $200 for a half day's bass fishing (2 fishermen per boat with a licensed guide), and other trips, including offshore fishing for marlin, can be arranged with him. Call 407 629 4700, or write to Cutting Loose Expeditions, PO Box 447, Winter Park, Florida 32790-0447.

Alternatively, **AJ's Freelance Bass Guide Services** specialise in trophy bass fishing on Lake Toho in Kissimmee with professional guides (all US Coastguard-licensed captains). Day trips (9 hours from first light) are $275 for 1–2 people, a half day (4½ hrs) is $200 and it is $75 or $50 extra per person, plus your licence and bait (sodas and ice provided, but you need to bring your own snacks). Hotel pick-ups ($30) can also be arranged, call 407 348 8764 or visit their website at www.orlandobass.com. Seminole County has its share of fishing action, too. Check out **Spotted Tail** for a range of angling adventures with fly and light tackle, call 407 977 5207 or visit www.spottedtail.com.

Water sports

Florida is also mad keen on water sports of all persuasions. So, on any area of water bigger than your average pond, don't be surprised to find the locals water-skiing, jetskiing, knee-boarding, canoeing, paddling, wind-surfing, boating or otherwise indulging in watery pursuits. *Walt Disney World Resort in Florida* offers all manner of boats, from catamarans to canoes and pedaloes, and activities, from water-skiing to parasailing, on the main

Bay Lake, as well as the smaller **Seven Seas Lagoon Crescent Lake** and **Lake Buena Vista**. Parasailing (from *Disney's Contemporary Resort* – see page 55) costs $75 solo or $115 tandem, while boat rentals (from a range of resorts) vary from $8/hour (14-ft sailboats and catamarans) to $57/hour (21-ft pontoon boats). For reservations and information, call 407 939 7529.

Several operators serve the lakes around Orlando and Kissimmee, but some of them leave much to be desired safety-wise. **Dave's Ski School** on Lake Bryan at Lake Buena Vista (right next to the Holiday Inn Sunspree Resort on SR 535) gets our recommendation for their safety-conscious approach and their virtual guarantee to get beginners up and water-skiing. Their **Watersports Adventure** includes an hour's water-ski lessons and rides, a tube ride and a wave-runner ride ($55 adult, $48 child), and lasts up to 3 hours; an hour's water-ski school costs $40 and $36. You can also rent wave-runners at $35 for half an hour or try parasailing at $40/person. Many tour operators endorse this ski school and, for more details, call 407 239 6939 (or www.bvwatersports.com).

Horse riding

Orlando is home to one of the foremost equestrian centres in America – the **Grand Cypress Equestrian Center,** which is part of the 1,500-acre Grand Cypress Resort, and all its rides and facilities are open to non-residents. This stunningly equipped equine haven offers a dazzling array of opportunities for horse enthusiasts of all abilities.

A full range of clinics, lessons and other instructional programmes are available, from half-hour kids' sessions to all-summer academies, plus a variety of trail rides. Serious horse riders will note this was the first American equestrian centre to be approved by the British Horse Society, and it operates the BHS test programme. Inevitably, this 5-star facility does not come cheap but it is a worthwhile experience, especially for children. Private lessons are $55 per half hour or $100 per hour, while a week's package of 8 group 1-hour lessons is $280. Young Junior Lessons (15-minute supervised rides for under 12s) are $25, while the Western Trail Ride (an hour's excursion for novice riders) is $30 per person and the Advanced Trail Ride $100. The centre is open 8.30am–6pm Mon–Fri and 8.30am–5pm Sat and Sun, and it can be found by taking Exit 68 on I-4 on to Route 535 north, turning left after half a mile at the traffic lights and then following the road north for a mile (past the entrance to the Grand Cypress Hotel) until the equestrian centre is on your right (407 239 1938 or www.grandcypress.com/equestrian/).

On a smaller scale and none the less charming is the **Horse World Riding Stables** on Poinciana Boulevard, just 12 miles south of Highway 192. This gets you more out into the wilds and you can spend anything from an hour to a full day enjoying the rides and lessons on offer. The three main rides are the Nature Trail ($34), a walking-only tour of 45–50 minutes, for beginners aged 6 and up, through 750 acres of untouched Florida countryside, the Intermediate Trail (ages 10 and up) for nearly one hour ($39), and the Advanced Private Trail, a 75- to 90-minute trip for advanced riders with private guide ($49). There is also a picnic area with fishing pond, playing fields, pony rides for under 7s ($6) and farm animals to pet. Riding lessons are $25/hour with up to 4 in a group and $35/hour privately. The 3-hour Children's

Horse Camp (for 8 to 14-year-olds every Saturday at 9am) is $30 per child. There is no charge for just looking around, and the stables are open 9am–5pm daily. Call 407 847 4343 or www.horseworldstables.com.

Similarly out in the wilds (in the Rock Springs Run Wildlife Preserve in Seminole County, to be precise) are **Rock Springs Riding Stables,** another slice of native Florida, with rides varying from a 1-hour Turkey Trail to a full day's Wildlife Wander, all led by trained guides. The park's 6,000 acres guarantee plenty of wildlife, from otters and coyotes to the occasional wild boar and even bears, and the rides go out every day 9am–6pm, costing $25–100, with $10 pony rides for under 8s. To find Rock Springs, take I-4 to Exit 101C (Sanford–SR46) and go west 8 miles before turning left into the preserve. Take the dirt road first left and follow all the way to the horse barn, or call 407 314 1000 for more info.

Spectator events

When it comes to spectator events, Orlando is not quite so well furnished as other big American cities, but there is always something on offer for the discerning sports fan who would like to sample the local version of the big match. There are no top-flight American football or baseball teams, but there is an indoor version of gridiron, called Arena Football, plus a Minor League baseball team.

The main sport is **basketball** and the Orlando Magic of the National Basketball Association (NBA). The season runs from November to May (with exhibition games in October), and the only drawback is the 16,000-seat TD Waterhouse Center where they play (on Amelia Street, Exit 83B off I-4, turn left, then left again) is occasionally fully booked. Contact the Center's box office (407 649

8

3245) to see if there are any tickets left, although you will need to call in person to buy them (from $16 up in the gods to $60 courtside), or you can call TicketMaster on 407 839 3900 for credit card bookings.

The Orlando Predators, one of America's top **Arena Football** teams, are also popular at the same venue (from May to August, $10–30) and you would need to call several days in advance to avoid missing one of their lively home games that feature some great entertainment as well as their fast, hard-hitting version of indoor gridiron in the magnificent Center.

For the Real Thing in gridiron terms, the nearest teams in the **National Football League** are the Tampa Bay Buccaneers, 75 miles to the west, the Miami Dolphins, some ¾ hours' drive to the south, down the Florida Turnpike, or the Jacksonville Jaguars way up the east coast past Daytona, a 3-hour drive up I-4 and I-95. Again, TicketMaster can give you ticket prices ($25–50) and availability (Sept–Dec).

Disney's Wide World of Sports Complex™

The newest sports facility in the area is inevitably a Disney project to bring in some world-class events and competitors. *Disney's Wide World of Sports Complex*™ is a 200-acre, state-of-the-art complex, featuring more

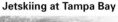
Jetskiing at Tampa Bay

The Tampa Bay Devil Rays in action

than 32 sports and is quite awesome to wander round even when no one is playing. The complex's main features are a 7,500-seater baseball stadium, a softball quadraplex, an 11-court tennis complex, beach volleyball and the **Official All Star Café**® with a massive array of sports memorabilia and even themed food. The baseball stadium is home for spring training of the mighty **Atlanta Braves**, and the crowds flock in for pre-season games in March. Once the season gets under way in April, *Disney's Wide World of Sport Complex*™ is home to the **Orlando Rays** (the minor league team of the Tampa Bay Devil Rays), who play 70 games a season, often with games on 6 or 7 evenings in succession, and Disney puts on an excellent stage, with plenty of hoopla, for every one. With tickets only $5–8 (and free parking), it is top-value entertainment as you check out America's future baseball stars in this family-orientated environment. Games and competitions are provided for kids between innings and the action is intense and exciting (I'll admit I'm a big baseball fan, but it is still a great slice of American life).

Other prime events include the Harlem Globetrotters basketball and international beach volleyball. The facilities alone should inspire world-class performances in any athlete. Standard admission is $8, but it is

The Richard Petty Driving Experience

one of your optional extras with a Park Hopper PLUS Ticket (although that does not cover special events), and *Disney's Wide World of Sports Complex*™ can be found off Osceola Parkway, on Victory Way. Call 407 939 4263 for events and prices.

The **Walt Disney World Marathon** is another major annual sporting event and, in 2003, it celebrates its 10th anniversary on January 12. Some 13,500 runners take part – including some of the world's leading athletes – but it also draws some huge crowds as the 26.2-mile route takes in all four theme parks. Be aware the parks face some serious disruption on the day, but, for anyone familiar with all the fun of the London Marathon, the Disney version also serves up a great spectacle. The annual **Half-Marathon** takes place on the same day. For more details visit www.disneyworldsports.com.

Rodeo

An all-American pursuit straight out of the Old West, the **Silver Spurs Rodeo** is staged twice a year at Osceola County Stadium. This is the biggest event of its kind in the south-east United States and is held the first week in October and the last week in February every year, but it sells out fast so you need to call at

least a month in advance for tickets on 407 677 6336. The event features classic bronco and bull riding and attracts top competitors from as far away as Canada.

On a slightly smaller scale but still worth seeing, the **Kissimmee Rodeo** is held every Friday at 8pm (except when the Silver Spurs is on) at the Kissimmee Sports Arena, on Hoagland Boulevard 2 miles south of Highway 192. Events include calf roping, steer wrestling and bull riding, and admission is $10 for adults and $5 for children 12 and under. Children especially seem to enjoy the live action, which can be surprisingly rugged (not to mention dangerous), and there is even a kids' contest – grab the ribbon from the calf's tail! The Catch Pen Saloon lounge is open 8pm–2am Friday and Saturday, and 6pm–2am Sunday, with line dancing 6–8pm and $1 drinks. Call 407 933 0020 for more details or look at www.ksarodeo.com.

Motor sport

8

For the guaranteed ultimate in high-speed thrills, *Walt Disney World Resort in Florida* has its own speedway oval where **Richard Petty Driving Experience** is based. Here you can experience one of their 650bhp stock cars as either driver or passenger at up to 145mph. The programmes have been devised by top NASCAR driver Richard Petty and offer the 3-lap **Ride-Along**

Daytona Speedway

Experience; a 3-hour **Rookie Experience** (with tuition and 8 laps of the speedway); the **Kings Experience** (tuition plus 18 laps in 2 sessions); and the **Experience of a Lifetime** (an intense 30-lap programme in three sessions).

The Ride-Along Experience will probably appeal to most – 3 laps of the 1.1-mile circuit with an experienced, race-proven driver lasting just 37 seconds a lap but an unbelievable blast all the way. Your initial take-off from the pit-lane takes you 0–60mph in a couple of seconds and you are straight into Turn One with your brain some distance behind. It is a bit like flying at ground level, it is hot and noisy and you must wear sensible clothes (you have to climb in through the window), but it is definitely the Real Thing in ride terms and a huge thrill.

You don't need to book for the Ride-Along Experience from mid February to the end of September and there is no admission fee, so you can come along just to watch. The three driving programmes all require reservations, while the track is occasionally closed for race testing from October to February. However, before you get carried away, wait for the prices: $89 for the Ride-Along Experience, $349 for the Rookie Experience, $699.99 for the Kings and $1,199.99 for the Lifetime Experience. For more details, or to book, call 407 939 0130 or visit www.1800bepetty.com.

Race fans will also want to check out **Daytona International Speedway** just up the road in Daytona (take I-4 east, then I-95 and Highway 92) for more big-league car and motorcycle thrills. It hosts more than a dozen race weekends a year, including stock cars, sports cars, motorcycles, go-karts and trucks, and highlights are the Daytona 500 (February 16, 2003), and Pepsi 400 (first Sunday in July). The big events attract more than 200,000 devotees and provide some of the most colourful sport anywhere in the world. Call 386 253 7223 or visit www.daytonainternationalspeedway.com).

Daytona USA, an interactive motor sport-themed attraction, is here as well, offering a series of hands-on exhibits, rides and films to give you a taste of all the high-speed action. Change tyres in a timed pit stop, design and video test a racing car, commentate on a race and experience the *Daytona 500* film. Other elements include Acceleration Alley (for an additional fee), with full-size NASCAR simulators combining motion, video and sound to capture the thrills of head-to-head racing at more than 200mph, and Daytona Dream Laps, another elaborate motion simulator to put riders inside the Daytona 500 itself. The history and great moments of Speedway are well detailed and there is a good gift shop. An optional extra is a half-hour, open-sided tram tour of the Speedway, stopping in Pit Road, to give you a real close-up of this amazing arena.

Race fan Alan Rogers, of Chester, rates the centre highly: 'Try the hands-on Pit Stop Live, the excellent *Daytona 500* movie and the 30-minute tour of the track. It's a real thrill.' Hours are 9am–7pm daily (not Christmas) and adult admission is $16, seniors (60+) $13 and children 6–12 $8 (under 6s free with a paying adult). The Combo ticket with the Speedway tour is $20, $14 and $17, while the tour on its own is $7 per person. Call 386 947 6800 or visit www.daytonausa.com. Finally, you can ride the **Richard Petty Driving Experience** here too, with the $99 fee for 3 laps of the world-famous, steeply banked 2½-mile tri-oval also including entrance to Daytona USA.

Okay, that's the full daytime scene, now let's check out all your night-

Orlando by Night
(or, Burning the Candle at Both Ends)

Hands up those who still have plenty of energy left! Right, this chapter is especially for you. If we can't wear you out at the theme parks and other attractions, we'll have to resort to a full-frontal assault on your sleep time – and take most of it away.

For, when it comes to night-time fun and frolics, Orlando again has a dazzling collection of possibilities, from its purpose-built entertainment complexes, through its range of evening dinner shows and on to a full array of bars and nightclubs. The choice is suitably widespread and almost always high in quality.

Unfortunately, the development that started the evening entertainment ball rolling has now closed down. **Church Street Station,** in the heart of the downtown area, shut in 2001 and there is, as yet, no firm news of what, if anything, will take its place.

Disney joined the big evening entertainment concept in 1987 with **Pleasure Island,** an imaginative range of clubs, discos and restaurants, and they continue to refine various elements all the time in order to keep it all fresh and appealing. **Disney's BoardWalk Resort** which opened in 1996, added more to their night-time amusement options.

International Drive (I-Drive) caught up with this process in 1997 when **Pointe*Orlando** opened. Although its prime focus is shopping and restaurants, it has a strong evening entertainment component with the big Muvico 21-screen cinema centre, its lively bars and two new nightclubs. Finally, Universal Orlando got with the beat in late 1998 with the opening of **CityWalk,** possibly the most elaborate and sophisticated centre of the lot. All these represent yet another slick opportunity to be dazzled and relieved of your cash in the name of holiday fun, but you should count on visiting at least one if your wallet can take the strain.

Downtown Disney

The large-scale development of what is now *Downtown Disney* (the old Village Marketplace and Pleasure Island) has evolved into a 3-part complex (*Downtown Disney* Marketplace, Pleasure Island and West Side) doubling the size of the old site and providing two key evening entertainment sources.

Downtown Disney Pleasure Island: this is the traditional nightclub zone which packs in the locals as well as the tourists and where every night is New Year's Eve. You must be 18 or over to enter (unless accompanied by a parent), while you must be at least 21 to enter two of the clubs (see below). Pleasure Island (which forms the centrepiece, or linking part, of *Downtown Disney*) consists of eight original club venues and just about every music type you can think of, plus several novel twists. The **Rock 'n Roll Beach Club** is a multi-level live music venue featuring 40 years of classic rock (and some outrageous

DJs) with a resident cover-version band. The **Pleasure Island Jazz Company** offers some excellent modern jazz and blues in a 1930s-style nightspot. Serious clubbers head for **Mannequins Dance Palace** (21and over only), a huge, popular disco, which features a revolving dance floor, mirrored walls and lasers, plus live entertainment from the Explosion Dancers. At the **Comedy Warehouse,** the Improv Co take centre stage for regular shows with guest 'volunteers'! For a touch of retro groovin', **8Trax** is a homage to 1970s' music, dance and styles (right down to the lava lamps). The unmissable **Adventurers' Club** is a personal favourite, a 2-storey live entertainment lounge, in 1920s' Gentleman's Club style, which comes to life all round you (watch the animal heads and masks!) and the stars of the shows in the different rooms mingle with the punters.

The **BET Soundstage Club**™ is a totally modern offering, with an interactive VJ/DJ and featuring the best of R&B, soul and hip-hop sounds (21 and over only). Finally, the newest venue **Motion** (formerly the Wildhorse Saloon) is a warehouse of a dance club, featuring Top 40 to Alternative music, animated DJs and a giant TV screen. Additionally, the outdoor **West End Stage,** which hosts Pleasure Island's resident band and occasional big-name acts, is the focus for the street party and fireworks at midnight, because every night is New Year's Eve, so get ready to party!

Downtown Disney looks superb at night

Cirque du Soleil® at Downtown Disney

As well as the clubs, Pleasure Island has a range of six shops, including **Reel Finds** for film memorabilia, **DTV,** an up-scale Disney fashion store and **Changing Attitudes,** offering some stylish men's and women's clothing. You can grab a snack at the **Missing Link Sausage Co** (hot dogs, burgers, sandwiches and fries) and stop for coffee, ice cream or frozen yoghurt at the splendid **D-Zertz.**

For a full-scale meal, the neighbouring **Portobello Yacht Club** offers excellent northern Italian cuisine in smart, lively surroundings. Of course, you can also visit the many eating outlets elsewhere around *Downtown Disney,* including **Planet Hollywood®** (the largest of this world-wide movie-themed chain, and the busiest restaurant of the lot), **Cap'n Jack's Restaurant** (for great chowder, crabcakes, shrimp or the Cap'n's 'fishbowl' margaritas), and **Fulton's Crab House** (for some of the best seafood in Orlando. Lunch is served from 11am–4pm and dinner from 5–11pm. As ever, to make a **Priority Seating** booking for a Disney restaurant, call 407 939 3463. *Pleasure Island* is free before 7pm when the entertainment kicks off, then the charge is $19.81, with strict age restrictions (taking your passport as ID is a good idea even if you are the 'wrong' side of 30). It stays open until 2am every night, and the admission fee is one of the options on

any Park Hopper PLUS Ticket.
Downtown Disney West Side is the newest element of the *Downtown Disney* expansion and incorporates the **AMC® Pleasure Island 24 Theaters Complex,** which has been increased to 24 screens, with more than 6,000 seats in state-of-the-art cinema surroundings.

Cirque du Soleil®

The most eye-catching part of West Side is home to the greatest show on earth (or at least, the greatest I've seen anywhere in the world), the **Cirque du Soleil®** production *La Nouba*™. Twice a day, 5 times a week, this purpose-built, 1,671-seater theatre stages the most stupendous combination of dance, circus, acrobatics, comedy and live music in a 90-minute show that includes more than 60 performers. Anyone familiar with the unique styling and outrageous costumes of the Cirque company will have an idea of what to expect, but even they will be left in awe by this multi-dimensional assault on the senses, featuring trampolines, trapezes, balancing acts and even mountain bikes, interspersed with innovative dance routines and spell-binding music, all with the most magnificent staging. Words alone do not do it justice – go and see it. Even at $67 a ticket ($39 for children 3–9), it is worth every cent, but you often have to book in advance, and reservations can be made up to 6 months beforehand on 407 939 7600. Performances are at 6 and 9pm Thur–Mon (no performances Tue and Wed), but try to arrive at least 30 minutes early for some excellent pre-show entertainment.

The other *Downtown Disney* elements are a fantastic mix of live music, fine dining, unique shopping and *DisneyQuest*, the ultimate in interactive game arcades.

The cavernous **House of Blues®**, a combination live music venue and restaurant in backwoods Mississippi style, is a must for anyone even vaguely interested in blues, rock 'n roll, R&B, gospel and jazz (call 407 934 2583 for info). Some top-name bands play here (check out www.hob.com for the event calendar), while their trademark **Gospel Brunch** on Sundays serves up some fabulous food with a full gospel show (10.30am and 1pm; $30 for adults, $15 for children 3-9). 'Praise the Lord and pass the biscuits', is their slogan, and it is a lot of fun. The 500-seat restaurant next door to the stunning main hall also offers some fine fare, including catfish, jambalaya and a host of other delicious Cajun dishes, and more live music is featured in the Blues Kitchen. The inevitable gift shop also stocks some quality merchandise.

Bongos Cuban Café™ (co-owned by Gloria and Emilio Estefan) brings the sights, sounds and tastes of Old Havana to another imaginative setting (check out the bongo-drum bar stools!), with red-hot Latin music and some of the best Cuban food in America. **The Wolfgang Puck® Café** offers a rich experience from the renowned Californian chef, with no less than four dining options: the café, gourmet food in a casual setting; Wolfgang Puck Express, the fast-food version; B's Bar for sushi, seafood, pizzas and micro-brew beers; and the Dining Room, an upscale restaurant (call 407 938 9653).

La Nouba™ **by Cirque du Soleil®**

© Disney

The shopping is also original and engaging, from the basic sweet shop **Candy Cauldron** that resembles a fairytale dungeon, through the one-off outlets like **Sosa Family Cigars, Celebrity Eyeworks** and the wonderfully stylish art, in both glass and ceramics, of **Hoypoloi Gallery**, to the more predictable souvenir stores and finally the truly mega **Virgin™ Megastore,** the largest music store in Florida, with 300 listening stations, a full-service café, hydraulic outdoor stage and a mean sound system!

The most unusual element opened in June 1998 and brought yet another novel idea to life. **DisneyQuest** is described variously as 'an immersive, interactive entertainment environment', the latest in arcade games, a series of state-of-the-art adventure rides or, as one Cast Member told me, 'a theme park in a box'. It houses 11 major adventures, like CyberSpace Mountain (design and ride your own roller-coaster), Invasion! An Alien Encounter (a fun VR rescue mission), Virtual Jungle Cruise (shooting the rapids, prehistoric style) and Aladdin's Magic Carpet (more virtual reality, riding in best cartoon fashion), a host of old-fashioned video games in the Replay Zone (do you remember Asteroids and Galaxian?), the latest sports games, a test of your imagination in Animation Academy and two futuristic cafés, one with computers and Internet tables, the other, Food Quest, straight out of a space-age comic book.

Two new elements in 2000 were Radio Disney SongMaker (a computer-generated professional audio system that creates a CD with you as the star!) and Pirates of the Caribbean: Battle for Buccaneer Gold (an amazing 3-D immersion into a swashbuckling adventure for pirate treasure). *DisneyQuest* is open 11.30am–midnight daily, but, if you want to avoid the queues (the building admits only 1,500), go during the day. A 1-day ticket costs $29 ($23 for 3–9s, although it is a bit too elaborate for most youngsters) and is an excellent way to keep teenagers amused.

Finally, the whole of *Downtown Disney* West Side is characterised at night by outstanding lighting and special effects and a vibrant, thrilling atmosphere that is almost intoxicating. Words alone do not do it justice – go and see it!

Disney's BoardWalk

Disney's other big evening entertainment offering is **Disney's BoardWalk Resort,** where the waterfront entertainment district contains several notable venues (not counting the excellent micro-brewery and restaurant of the Big River Grille and Brewing Works, the thrilling ESPN Club for sports fans and the 5-star Flying Fish Café). **Jellyrolls** is a variation on the duelling piano bar, with the lively pianists conjuring up a humorous and often raucous evening of audience participation songs ($6 cover charge; 21 and over only; 7pm–2am). The **Atlantic Dance** features more live music and a huge dance floor, all served up in a hot Latin style. The mix of salsa bands and DJ entertainment is hard to resist, and is especially popular on Friday and Saturday nights (when there is a $5 cover charge). It is strictly 21 and over each night (and it's closed Tue and Wed), so don't forget your ID to get in. *Disney's Boardwalk Resort* also features some amusing stalls and live entertainers, which add to the fabulous night-time atmosphere.

Universal's CityWalk

As part of the big Universal Orlando development – and in direct competition with *Downtown Disney –*

this 30-acre spread has just about everything in the entertainment world. The resort's hub is a busy, bustling expanse of shops, restaurants, snack bars, open-air events and nightclubs. It offers a huge variety of cuisine, from fast food to fine dining, an unusual mix of speciality shops and a truly eclectic nightclub mix, from reggae to Motown to salsa and high-energy disco. Unlike *Pleasure Island*, there is no entry fee, but you do pay a cover charge ($5–7) at the eight clubs. You can also buy a **CityWalk Party Pass** ($7.95) or Party Pass with Movie (one free film at the 20-screen Universal Cineplex; $11.95) for entry to all eight (except one-off concerts at Hard Rock Live), while the Orlando FlexTicket includes a Party Pass.

The area splits into three, with the main Plaza featuring shopping and restaurants. Among the most original (and entertaining) of the 13 shops here are **Endangered Species,** with merchandise designed to raise eco-awareness; **Quiet Flight,** a radical surf and beachwear store; the retro-American decor of **Fossil** for leather goods, watches and sunglasses; the wacky **Captain Crackers** for toys, moving animals and outrageous T-shirts; the inevitable **Universal Studios Store** for park merchandise; and **All Star Collectibles** for (American) sports fans.

When it comes to eating, you have the **NASCAR Café** (a must for motor-racing fans, 10am–late) with full-size stock cars and racing memorabilia, videos and interactive games while you dine on burgers, ribs, steaks and popcorn shrimp. **Pastamore** is a delightful al fresco Italian diner, with the choice of full-service dining (5pm–midnight) for pizza, pasta, grilled chicken and steaks or the **Pastamore Café** (8am–2am) for sandwiches, pastries and ice cream. **Emeril's** restaurant is at the 5-star end of the range, a sophisticated and vibrant journey into the cuisine of New Orleans master chef Emeril Lagasse. Fine wines and a cigar bar both add to Emeril's Creole-based gourmet creations, and if you don't try the Louisiana oyster stew here, you have missed a real treat (lunch 11.30am–2.30pm; dinner 5.30–10pm Sun–Thur, 5.30–11pm Fri and Sat). It also books up well in advance at weekends, so try weekdays to avoid missing out (or call 407 224 2424 to book). **Jimmy Buffet's Margaritaville** (11am–2am) is an island homage to Florida's laid-back musical hero, with 'Floribbean' cuisine (a mixture of Key West and Caribbean), live music and three bars, including the Volcano Bar which 'erupts' margarita mix (!) when the blender needs filling. There is a cover charge ($5) after 10pm when their live band hits the stage.

Across the CityWalk waterway is the **Lagoon Front** location of another huge dining experience, the 2-storey **NBA City** which is sure to thrill basketball fans with its Cage dining area, interactive Playground area and Club lounge where you can watch live and classic games (all 11am–2am). Right next door is the massive mock-Coliseum architecture of **Hard Rock Live,** a 2,500-seat concert venue with state-of-the-art staging and sound. Big-name bands and performers are on stage several times a week (and they do book British acts from time to time – Robbie Williams and Oasis have both played here) in this slightly retro rock 'n roll theatre; call 407 839 3900 for the latest information or check out www.hardrock.com. Of course, you can't miss dining at the **Hard Rock Café** here, the world's largest example of this international chain, with its collection of rock 'n roll memorabilia (including a 1959 pink Cadillac). It remains hugely popular, so try to get in early for lunch or dinner (11am–2am) to sample their classic diner fare (notably the Pig Sandwich). Collectors of Hard Rock souvenirs will also find prices a little more to their liking here than the UK in an excellent gift shop.

Finally, you come to the **Promenade** area, which offers a choice of nightclubs and some more fine dining (notably in the case of Latin Quarter). **Motown Café** (also with an entrance on Plaza level) is a homage to all the performers of the Motown record label, from the Four Tops and Jackson Five to modern artists, with a full-service restaurant, retro-style lounge and two revue stages featuring cover bands who emulate the likes of the Temptations and Supremes (11.30am–11pm Sun–Thu, 11–2am Fri and Sat; cover charge $5 from 9pm Sun–Thu, 10pm Fri and Sat). **Bob Marley – A Tribute to Freedom** is a clever re-creation of Marley's Jamaica home, turned into a courtyard live music venue, restaurant and bars. The bands are excellent, the atmosphere authentic and the place really comes alive at night (4pm–2am, 21 and over after 10pm; cover charge $5 after 8pm).

Next up is **Pat O'Brien's**, a faithful reproduction of the famous New Orleans bar and restaurant (4pm–1am), with its flaming fountains courtyard, main bar and special duelling piano bar (6pm–2am, cover charge $5 after 9pm, 21 and over, so remember your passport ID). Excellent Cajun food and world-famous Hurricane cocktails are the order of the day, but don't drink too many and expect to walk home! **CityJazz** is a real contrast, a hip, upmarket centre combining history, education and live music from a series of local and international musicians, with tapas-style food. Visually it is stunning, with good sound quality and, if you're keen on the live music (8pm–1am, Sun–Thur, 7pm–2am Fri and Sat, cover charge $5), you can easily spend all night here. For younger, club-minded visitors, **the groove** is the next generation in nightclub entertainment, a vivid, pounding, high-energy dance venue designed like a Victorian theatre but with the latest in club music, lighting and special effects (9pm–2am, cover charge $7 and 21 and over only).

Finally, completing the Promenade tour is the **Latin Quarter,** a truly sensational venue-cum-restaurant that serves up a genuine slice of Latin American style in its atmosphere, music, dance, decor and cuisine. Quite simply, the food is outstanding – a combination of beef, fresh fish and poultry with tangy fruit sauces, spicy salsas and mouth-watering marinades (don't miss their version of rack of lamb) – the ambience is mesmerising and the sounds are so wonderfully vibrant and alive, you can't help dancing, even in your seat. From Cuba to Chile, here is a great experience, with the live bands whipping up a samba and salsa storm. Drop in for dinner (5pm–2am) or just check out the music on Fri and Sat (cover charge $6 after 10pm).

Breathless yet? Well, there's still the **Universal Cineplex,** a 20-screen cinema complex with a 5,000 capacity and the latest in stadium seating, curved-screen visuals and high-tech sound systems. For all the venues, you park in the big Universal multi-storey car park, and there is no charge after 6pm. For the latest info, call 407 363 8000 or visit www.citywalkorlando.com.

Hard Rock Café

The Pointe*Orlando

This eye-catching development on I-Drive, almost opposite the Convention Center, is a mix of unique shops, cinemas, restaurants, the WonderWorks science centre (with its magic-themed dinner show), a new arcade-style entertainment centre and two new nightclubs. It is open all day but has plenty of evening appeal, too.

The big-name stores (open 10am–11pm) are all upscale and include some imaginative touches that make them stand out from the crowd. The collection of bars and restaurants strive to be different too. On the main ground level you have **Johnny Rockets,** a highly entertaining 1950s-style diner with an indulgent burger-and-milkshake menu (and waiters and waitresses who perform dance routines if the right song comes on the jukebox!). Nearby, **Monty's Conch Harbor** adds a touch of Key West cool for its seafood-orientated menu, while **Dan Marino's Town Tavern** is a particular personal favourite for its surprisingly elegant sports-themed dining (check out the football-shaped bar!), mix of lively and intimate areas and a well-balanced menu from this former American football star. Head upstairs to the second level and you find **Lulu's Bait Shack** leading the way for New Orleans-style cuisine and entertainment (it looks like an old shack blown in from Bourbon Street). Then there is **Adobe Gila's,** a fine Mexican *cantina* featuring more than 70 tequilas (!) and some south-of-the-border dining delicacies (try the Gila Wraps), and the 'soon to be relatively famous' wings, burgers and seafood of **Hooters** (with its equally famous 'Hooter Girl' waitresses). Lulu's and Adobe Gila's are especially popular with locals and are often packed at weekends, as they stay open until 2am, while they feature live outdoor music and DJs several days a week. On a Friday or Saturday, the atmosphere should be kicking from 6.30pm onwards, while weekdays it is more likely to be from 8.30pm.

The 21-screen **Muvico** cinema, with its wonderfully vast and themed (inevitably) entrance foyer, boasts state-of-the-art stadium seating and sound systems, and you can often see a newly released film here several months before it gets to the UK (watch out for some special film-and-meal deals here in future, especially for the Brits). Newest entertainment venue **XS Orlando** (motto: Too much is not enough!) offers 3 floors of fun and games where you can 'dine, dance and defend the world'. An upscale restaurant (try their excellent steaks or brick oven pizzas) occupies the ground floor, and you then ride the escalator up to the entertainment levels. Here, you will find more than 110 interactive games and attractions (including a virtual reality roller-coaster, rock-climbing challenge, several state-of-the-art shoot 'em up games, some arcade-style prize games and high-speed Internet access), fully stocked bars, live music with resident DJs and two roof terraces that enjoy views over

9

The Latin Quarter at CityWalk

I-Drive. XS Orlando is open noon–midnight Sun–Thur, and noon–2am Fri and Sat, and it is also an ideal venue for lunch (visit www.xsorlando.com for more info).

The Pointe also boasts two popular recent additions to the nightclub scene: **Matrix** (open 10pm–2am Thur–Sun), a high-tech, high-energy, high-volume club pulses to the techno beat for much of the time and has a kind of future-surreal decor that appeals to the younger (18–25) crowd. However only women are allowed in at 18, men have to be 21 except for college night on Thursdays when the age limit drops to 18 for everyone. The dance floor is huge and is ringed by two 10-ft video walls, sixteen 27-in TV screens and a multi-million dollar light show, while the lounge area features art deco loungers, chairs and loveseats. **Metropolis** (open 8pm–2am nightly) offers a more sophisticated atmosphere, with retro Top 40 music in a plush disco environment. It has seven Victorian billiards tables in the lounge area, various TV and video screens, and another large dance floor, and it tends to attract a slightly older crowd (25–35). It is only 21 and over here except for college night on Thursdays. At both clubs, the cover charge (after 10pm) varies per night (average is $10, free for ladies on Fridays). Stylish dress is required (no jeans or trainers). In 2002, every Monday was Teens Night for 14–17s. With a no-alcohol bar, it offers a great (and safe) environment to let your teenagers have some space of their own on holiday. For club info, call 407 370 3700 or visit www.metropolismatrix.com.

Pointe*Orlando is also in the process of developing another entertainment venue next door to XS Orlando, so visit their website at www.pointeorlandofl.com for details or call 407 248 2838.

Dinner shows

Another source of evening entertainment comes in the many and varied dinner shows which are a major Orlando phenomenon. From murder mysteries to magic shows, it's all wonderfully imaginative good fun, even if the food element is usually distinctly ordinary. As the name suggests, it's live entertainment coupled with dinner in a fantasy-type environment where even the waiters dress in costume and act out roles, accompanied by unlimited free wine, beer and soft drinks.

They always have a strong family appeal and you are usually seated at large tables where you can get to know other folks, too, but, at an average of $35–40 for adults, they are not cheap (especially when you add on the taxes and tips). Beware, too, the almost constant attempts to shake an extra few dollars out of you with photos, souvenirs, flags, etc.

Disney shows

Walt Disney World Resort in Florida's offerings here are often overlooked by visitors unless they are staying at one of the hotel resorts. For a night of South Seas entertainment, try the **Polynesian Luau Dinner Show** (at *Disney's Polynesian Resort*). It's a bit expensive at $39.50 for adults, and $20.50 for under 12s, but the entertainment is thrilling (fire jugglers, hula-drum dancers and clever musicians) although the food is nothing special. Beer, wine and soft drinks are all included. For reservations (usually necessary), call 407 939 3463, and shows are 5.15 and 8pm every Tue–Sat. The **Hoop-Dee-Doo Musical Revue** at *Disney's Fort Wilderness Resort & Campground* is an ever-popular nightly dinner show that carries on where the Diamond Horseshoe Saloon Revue in the *Magic Kingdom Park* leaves off, and has great food (all-you-can-eat ribs, fried chicken, corn on the cob, baked beans and strawberry shortcake). Especially loved by children, it features the amusing song and dance of the Pioneer Hall Players in a merry American hoedown-style show. Okay, it's corny and a tad embarrassing to find yourself singing along with the hammy action, but it is performed with great gusto, and you're on holiday, remember! The Revue plays nightly at 5pm, 7.15pm and 9.30pm at the Pioneer Hall, $39.50 for adults, $20.50 for under 12s. Reservations are ALWAYS necessary but can be made up to 2 years in advance on 407 939 3463.

An alternative is the nightly (and free!) **Electrical Water Pageant** which circles Bay Lake and the Seven Seas Lagoon, passing by each of the *Magic Kingdom Park* resorts in turn from 9pm. It lasts just 10 minutes (from around 9pm) so it is easy to miss, but it is almost a waterborne version of the park's SpectroMagic parade, with thousands of twinkling lights on a 1,000-ft floating cavalcade of boats and mock sea creatures. The usual schedule is 9pm at *Disney's Polynesian Resort*, 9.15pm at *Disney's Grand Floridian Resort and Spa* (and you get a grandstand view in Narcoosee's restaurant), 9.35pm on the shores of *Disney's Fort Wilderness Resort & Campground*, 9.45pm at *Disney's Wilderness Lodge* and 10.05 at *Disney's Contemporary Resort*. It can also be seen from the boat jetties outside the *Magic Kingdom Park* in high season.

Arabian Nights

This lovingly maintained, family-owned attraction is the largest-scale production and one of the most popular with locals as well as tourists. It's a real treat for horse lovers, but you don't need to be an equestrian expert to appreciate the

spectacular stunts, horsemanship and marvellous costumes as some 60 highly trained horses perform a 25-act show. Loosely based on the celebration of Princess Scheherezade's engagement to Prince Khalid, the show is staged in the huge indoor Moorish-themed arena at the centre of this 1,200-seater palace. The magnificent close-quarter drill of the Lipizzaner stallions, the daring riding and the thrilling chariot race all add up to a memorable show that kids, especially, adore. The recent addition of new characters (notably the comic Gaylord Maynard and his horse Chief Bear Paw), costumes and special effects, plus the incorporation of a bumbling genie, have given Arabian Nights a real boost and helped to keep their appeal fresh.

> BRIT TIP: Take a sweater or jacket with you as Arabian Nights is kept particularly cool for the benefit of the horses.

The food (green salad, oven-roasted prime rib with new potatoes, and a dessert, vegetarian lasagne on request) is above average, too. Arabian Nights, which is located just half a mile east of I-4 on Highway 192 (on the left, just to the side of the Parkway shopping plaza, or just past Water Mania if you are coming from the eastern end of 192), runs every evening at 7.30 or 8.30pm, with occasional matinees. It lasts almost 2 hours, and tickets ($44 for adults and $27 for kids 3–11) may be purchased at the box office between 10am and 6pm or by credit card if you phone 407 239 9223 (visit www.arabian-nights.com for a valuable money-off coupon). A new 'VIP' upgrade ($12 for adults, $10 for children) adds a stable tour, reserved priority seating (in the first three rows), a souvenir poster and a complimentary pre-show drink.

Pirates Dinner Adventure

This show (which has been revamped several times since it opened in 1997) features one of the most spectacular settings, with the Spanish galleon pirate ship centrepiece being 150ft long, 60ft wide, 70ft tall and 'anchored' in a 300,000-gallon lagoon. It also delivers good value with its pre-show elements, plentiful (if ordinary) food and drink, after-show Buccaneer Bash disco (until 10.30pm), plus the Pirate's Maritime Museum, which guests are free to wander around. The basic premise of the audience being 'hi-jacked' by the wicked 18th-century pirates is a clever one, even if the actual storyline is occasionally a touch hard to follow. Chaos and mayhem ensue, some of it inaudible thanks to poor acoustics, but there is swashbuckling galore, sword fights, acrobatics, trapeze artists and boat races, and the goodies (inevitably) triumph over evil Captain Sebastian and his crew. There are plenty of stunts and special effects (plus audience participation opportunities, which the kids will enjoy) and ticket prices are $43.95 for adults and $26.95 for 3–11s (look for discount coupons – see our offer on page 93). The show is located on Carrier Drive between I-Drive and Universal Boulevard, and runs daily from 6.30 or 7pm (plus a handful of 11.30am showings), with some pretty decent appetisers served until 7.45pm, when seating begins. A new Pirate Preferred seating upgrade provides front row priority and guaranteed cast interaction for a small extra cost. Call 407 248 0590 for reservations (or visit their website at www.orlandopirates.com).

Medieval Times

Eleventh-century Spain is the entertaining setting for this 2-hour extravaganza of medieval pageantry, sorcery and robust horseback jousts that culminate in furious hand-to-hand combat between six knights. It is worth arriving early to appreciate the clever mock castle design and the staff's costumes as you are ushered into the pre-show hall before being taken into the arena itself. The weapons used are all quite real and used with skill, and there are some neat touches with indoor pyrotechnics and other special effects. You need to be in full audience participation mode as you cheer on your knight and boo the others, but kids (not to mention a few adults) get a huge kick out of it and they'll also love eating without cutlery – don't worry, there are handles on the soup bowls! The elaborate staging takes your mind off the unexciting chicken dinner, but there is positively heaps of it and the serfs and wenches who serve you make it a fun experience. Prices, which include the Medieval Life exhibition, are $44 for adults and $28 for 3–11s (but check their website for discounts) and doors open 90 minutes prior to each show. Times vary according to the season, so call 1-800 229 8300 (or visit www.medievaltimes.com) for details.

The new Knights of the Realm show, with an all-new storyline and characters, opens here in January 2003. The castle is on Highway 192, 5 miles east of the junction with I-4. If you have 45 minutes to spare

Pirates Dinner Adventure

before the show, the Medieval Life exhibition makes an interesting diversion. This mock village re-enacts the life and times of 900 years ago, with artisans demonstrating pottery and tool-making, glass-blowing, spinning and weaving. It includes a Chamber of Horrors that might be a touch gruesome for small children.

Sleuth's Mystery Dinner Shows

This is a real live version of Cluedo acted out before your eyes in hilarious fashion while you enjoy a substantial meal (with a main course choice of honey-glazed Cornish hen, prime rib or lasagne) and unlimited beer, wine and sodas. You can choose between three theatres and eight different plot settings, including the new WKZY TV (a clever skit on trash television), that all add up to some elaborate murder mysteries. The action takes place all around you and members of the audience can take part in some cameo roles. The quick-witted cast keep things moving and you guessing during the 40-minute show, then during the main part of dinner you can think up some questions to interrogate them with (but be warned, the real murderer is allowed to lie!). If you solve the crime you win a prize, but that is pretty secondary to the overall enjoyment – and this is a show I do enjoy a lot. Prices are $40.95 for adults and $23.95 for children (3–11) and again show times vary, so call 407 363 1985 for details (or visit www.sleuths.com). Sleuth's Mystery Dinner Shows are located in Republic Square Plaza, on Universal Boulevard (half a mile north of its Sand Lake Road junction).

Purely for children is **Sleuth's Merry Mystery Dinner Adventure,** with a special kids'

Dolly Parton's Dixie Stampede

dinner, dessert and unlimited soft drinks. At $28 for adults and $16 for children (3–12), it is designed primarily for 6–12-year-olds (mainly on Saturday afternoons), and features one of two adventures, The Faire of the Shire and The Magical Journey of Juniper Junior.

WonderWorks: The Outta Control Magic Show

On a smaller scale but no less fun, this is a new offering at WonderWorks on I-Drive (on one corner of Pointe*Orlando). A novel mixture of improvised comedy and clever, close-up magic, the show is accompanied by all-you-can-eat pizza, beer, wine and coke. Set in the intimate Shazam Theater, it features live music, special lighting effects and some slick magic tricks from illusionist Tony Brent and sidekick Danny Devaney. The tricks are all fairly routine, but the show is served up in style and involves plenty of audience participation (which children love). Performed twice nightly at 6 and 8pm, it costs a reasonable $17.95 for adults and $14.95 for children and seniors. Or you could buy a Magic Combo ticket

9

for the show and unlimited use of WonderWorks afterwards (which stays open to midnight) for $31.95 and $25.95. For ticket information, call 407 351 8800 or visit www.wonderworksonline.com.

Masters of Magic

Brand new in summer 2001, this 90-minute Las Vegas-style magic review which, while it is not a dinner show as such, offers another major source of evening entertainment. The theme, A Magical Journey Through Time & Space, is designed to take guests through the different continents of the globe and the 272-seat theatre boasts a full surround-sound system, special effects and high-tech lighting to showcase the grand illusions prepared by Typhoon Lou (including one where he passes his body through a spinning industrial fan). His troupe of dancers/assistants add a fair bit of pizzazz to proceedings and, if the seating area (plain rows of tables and chairs) leaves something to be desired, the staging is excellent. Magician Typhoon Lou, a native American raised in Hawaii who has performed all over the world, has plenty of charm to go with his awe-inspiring illusions, the tour de force being making a Harley-Davidson motorbike disappear in mid air. Masters of Magic is performed at 6.30 and 9pm Wed–Mon (closed Tues), and is located next to the Bahama Breeze restaurant on I-Drive, just north of Pointe*Orlando. Prices are $29.95 for adults and $19.95 for children 4–12. Call the box office on 407 352 3456 or visit www.mastersofmagic.net.

The SoulFire Theatre & Dinner Experience

Opening in late summer 2002, this is a novel and ambitious venture into the comedy/audience participation style of dinner shows. Cutting-edge theatre company The SoulFire Traveling Medicine Show promises an evening of 'shenanigans, tomfoolery and general craziness' as you enter the United Brotherhood of Yaks Lodge and Reception Hall. The feature show is the *The Reunion of the Cursed Class of Herbert Hoover High* and, while American high school reunions may not mean a lot to us Brits, it should be an amusing exercise in both scripted and improv comedy. The basic idea is all the guests are characters in the big reunion and get to relive various memories and events from their high school days (you can play as big or minor a part in proceedings as you wish, and there is even an award for Best Outfit of the evening). Co-artistic director Rus Blackwell says: 'This is an Extreme dinner theatre experience – extreme meaning extremely original and extremely interactive, so much so that, as the night goes on, the line between audience and cast almost totally disappears.' They also promise the food will be above average, with the likes of tuna mousse, chevre chicken, pasta in wild mushroom cream sauce and chocolate cake, served with beer, wine or soft drinks.

The venue is a 200-seat theatre at the back of Lake Buena Vista Factory Stores on Apopka Vineland Road (SR 535), with shows at 7.30pm, plus a Sunday matinee. Call 407 465 1886 to book or visit www.soulfire.net. Tickets are $42 for adults and $28 for children (3–12).

Dolly Parton's Dixie Stampede

The biggest development in Orlando dinner shows for many a year is scheduled to open on May 23, 2003, when country & western queen Dolly Parton opens the fourth venue for her Dixieland extravaganza of music, comedy, horsemanship and ostrich races (!). The show features a high-energy competition (with lots of audience participation) between North and South, with various contests, speciality acts, song, dance and a huge Southern-style feast. Indeed, the food is a major part of the experience – which has been a big hit elsewhere in America – as you chow down on vegetable soup, whole rotisserie chicken, corn on the cob, home-made biscuit (that's savoury scones to us), barbecue pork loin, jacket potato and apple pastry. This is a no alcohol environment, though, hence your unlimited drinks are only Pepsi, tea and coffee. The quality of the entertainment should be high, however, and the $28 million development promises to provide a spectacular venue, with a 1,000-seat, 35,000-sq ft main arena to showcase the headlining abilities of their 32 horses and 30 riders. A separate Christmas show will be staged from November 1 to January 1, featuring a live Nativity scene and other seasonal festivities. The Dixie Stampede will operate once or twice a night, depending on the season, with a 30-minute pre-show in the (non-alcoholic) Dixie Belle Saloon. Tickets are $43.95 for adults and $28.95 for children (3–11). Call 407 238 4455 to book or visit www.dixiestampede.com.

And the rest...

Orlando is blessed with a huge variety of nightlife, from regular discos to elaborate live music clubs and no less then three 'duelling piano' bars. The majority are situated in the downtown area, i.e. away from the main tourist centres. The local paper *Orlando Sentinel* has a regular Friday section called *Calendar* which details the local

American radio

American radio stations come in a vast number of types and styles that conform to fairly narrow musical tastes. Here is a quick guide to finding the main ones in your car:

ADULT CONTEMPORARY
98.9 FM (WMMO)
99.3 FM (WLRQ)
105.1 FM (WOMX)
107.7 FM (WMGF)
POP
99.9 FM (WFKS)
106.7 FM (WXXL)
OLDIES
100.3 FM (WSHE)
790 AM (WLBE)
NEWS/TALK
90.7 FM (WMFE)
104.1 FM (WTKS)
SPORT
540 AM (WQTM)
CLASSICAL
90.7 FM (WMFE)
91.5 FM (WPRK)
JAZZ
89.9 FM (WUCF)
103.1 FM (WLOQ)
COUNTRY
92.3 FM (WWKA)
97.5 FM (WPCV)
98.1 FM (WGNE)
102.7 FM (WHKR)
ROCK
91.5 FM (WPRK)
93.1 FM (WKRO)
96.5 FM (WHTQ)
101.1 FM (WJRR)
105.9 FM (O-ROCK)

9

nightspots as well as individual events, and it is worth checking out the free *Orlando Weekly* (available in most supermarkets and tourist centres) for the latest happening scene. There is an amazing turnover rate of bars and discos, though, so don't be surprised if a nightclub you have visited before has suddenly undergone a complete change of name and personality. The basic distinctions tend to be **Live Music Clubs, Mainstream Nightclubs,** which also have the occasional live band, and **Bars** which specialise in evening entertainment.

Live music clubs

The following should give you a representative taste of the most popular venues (for those 21 and over only in most cases).

The rock 'n roll piano bar idea was pioneered here in Orlando, by the wonderfully named **Howl at the Moon Saloon** on West Church Street and is still going strong (6pm–2am Sun–Thur, and 5pm–2am Fri and Sat). Classic rock 'n roll, show tunes, current hits, the saloon's duelling pianists play them all, with full audience involvement and non-stop banter. There is no cover charge Sun–Tues, while Wed–Thur it is $4 after 7.30pm, on Fri it's $6 after 6pm and Sat is $6 after 5.30pm, and the live piano action begins at 8pm every night (it also gets distinctly rowdy and even bawdy later on, so remember your sense of humour).

Then, of course, you have **Jellyrolls** at *Disney's BoardWalk Resort* and **Pat O'Brien's** (the original New Orleans version) at Universal's CityWalk, which are both popular with locals and tourists alike.

CityWalk

Country music fans (and others in search of the 'in' crowd) will definitely need to check out **:08 Seconds,** a huge, multi-level entertainment centre. It earns its 'unique' tag by hosting live bull riding (!) and monster truck wars as well as having a huge dance hall with live bands, line dancing lessons, 12 bars (and bottled beer at $2, a real bargain), a pool hall, games room and classic country barbeque. The atmosphere is both authentic and infectious, right down to their well-priced gift shop. This is one of my favourite clubs in town. On West Livingston Street in the heart of downtown, it has bags of style, but call 407 839 4800 for the latest details (usually, ladies' night Wed – ladies get in free all night and drink free until 11pm – monster trucks Fri, and bull riding Sat). By the way, the :08 Seconds refers to the average time a bull-rider manages to stay on his bull!

Blues, rock and jazz are the staples of **The Social** (formerly Sapphire) at 54 North Orange Avenue, where resident DJs, a wide range of bands and special guest acts vary from week to week. Call for details on 407 246 1431. With San Francisco-inspired decor, this has the reputation for being one of the 'hippest' places to be seen in.

The **Volcano** on South Orange Avenue is another curious mix of styles that promises something for everyone, with local bands performing on their Wednesday Night Live slot, hip-hop sounds on Thursday, dance music Friday and Saturday and the Latin music scene on Sunday (Wed–Sun, 9pm–3am). Call 407 999 0033 for the latest info.

As a complete alternative from the music scene, **Sak Comedy Club** (on West Amelia Avenue in the Theatre Garage) is like a live version of the TV show *Whose Line Is It Anyway?* Fast-paced and funny (and with a 'no obscenity' rule for worried parents), the Sak performers do a mix of competitive improv comedy, with every show offering something different and the young performers living on their wits. On stage Tuesday to Saturday (with two different shows Thur–Sat, admission varies from $6–12). Their LabRats show (Tue and Wed) features Sak's 'students' and costs just $6. Call 407 648 0001 for reservations (advisable on Friday and Saturday) and find out why Sak's has been consistently voted the best live comedy in Florida.

Mainstream nightclubs

In addition to the mainstream DJ dance centres at *Downtown Disney's Pleasure Island* and Universal's CityWalk, **Tabu** (formerly the Zuma Beach Club on North Orange Avenue, just up from Church Street) appeals widely to the disco crowd with regular nightly line-ups, guest DJs and special events, usually of a fairly raucous nature! Call 407 648 8363 for the latest details, and admission varies from $7–12 (21 and over only). **Bar Orlando,** on South Orange Avenue, is another high-energy offering, with modern techno styles jostling with retro sounds from the 1980s and 1990s. **Cairo** has quickly become a haunt of the younger set on South Magnolia Avenue, with three rooms featuring dance music, reggae and out-and-out disco. House music also plays on Wednesday, and Friday is ladies night (no cover charge and free drink until 11.30pm for the ladies).

The **Independent** (formerly Barbarella) on Orange Avenue on the corner of Washington Street, offers alternative and new wave music 9pm–3am most nights. Again, it is more of a techno-dance sound, but features various retro-progressive, old wave and 'Bad Disco' nights. Friday is ladies' night, and the club has three contrasting levels, including an area with pool tables. Cover charge varies from $5–10, call 407 839 0457 for details. **The Club at Firestone** is also hard to categorise but scores well with the alternative/progressive crowd. It occasionally hosts rock and pop acts too big for Sapphire but otherwise ranges from mainstream disco to acid jazz lounge, with something different each night from Wednesday to Saturday (including gay nights on Wed). Two venues – the **Den** and the **Glass Chamber** – feature dance, house, jungle and hip-hop, with their Latin night, El Club Caliente, usually on Fridays. About half a mile north of Church Street on the corner of Orange Avenue and Concord Street, The Club is open 9pm–3am with cover charge ranging from $5–10. Call 407 872 0066 for nightly info (or visit www.theclub-online.com).

Bars

Bars of all types simply abound in Orlando but, again, several have a particular appeal to visitors, especially newcomers. Live entertainment, extrovert barmen, sports-themed bars and raw bars (offering seafood, often by the bucket!), the choice is, as ever, wide-ranging.

The area around Church Street is the core of this development (even since much of Church Street Station closed down), with a terrific range of restaurants and bars. Look out in particular for **Pebbles** and **Chillers** (they do an amazing range of daiquiris and frozen specialities). Upstairs to **Antigua** (which features DJ house music) is **Ybor's Martini**

Sunset over the Gulf of Mexico

Bar, an upscale cigar and cocktail emporium. Above Chillers is the highly recommended bar **Big Bellies,** which features its own micro-brewery and an impressive range of other beers (as well as an outrageous collection of wall art), and above that is the roof-top bar **Latitudes.**

Travel out past Church Street into Orange Avenue and you are into real locals' territory with the likes of **One-Eyed Jack's,** with its party pop atmosphere and live music sing-alongs, and its neighbouring connected bars the **Loaded Hog** and **Wall Street Cantina,** which are packed at weekends. Turn left on to West Central Boulevard and you find **Kate O'Brien's Irish Pub** for more lively bar entertainment (and a neat beer garden), the similarly Irish-themed **Scruffy Murphy's** is a block further north on Washington Street. Again, there is no cover charge and it has a real good-time atmosphere when it is busy (which is often). Heading south on Orange offers **Tanquerary's Bar and Grille** with live music on Friday and Saturday.

The eclectic duo of **Slingapore's** and **The Globe** (the latter an off-the-wall 24-hour diner) are also worth seeking out for a lively drink or three on Wall Street, just off Orange. The two are interconnected, which is mildly disconcerting, but boast a range of bars, a pool hall and live music, as well as The Globe's fun eating style.

Sports bars

Finally, with the multitude of sports bars that are another particularly American pastime, **Friday's Front Row Sports Grill** on I-Drive (just south of the Sand Lake Road junction) really sticks out as a major tourist trap which even the locals enjoy. Here you can catch ALL the action (and, yes, they do show soccer as well) on 84 TV screens, plus enjoy some 100 beers from around the world – and bar features such as $1 domestic 12oz drafts! – as well as try out their basketball nets, pool tables and shuffleboard, and rub shoulders with the local sports stars from time to time. The food is standard American diner fare and there is plenty to keep the kids amused, too (like crayons to colour in the paper tablecloths and a huge range of video games). The atmosphere varies according to the time of day and the sports event (pretty rowdy for Orlando Magic basketball games), so call 407 363 1414 for up-to-the-minute info. There is never a cover charge, reservations are not accepted and it is open 11am–2am Mon–Sat, 11am–midnight Sun.

Other choices for the sports bar experience include the massive **Players Sports Pub** on Curry Ford Road; 87 TV screens, with 12 big-screens, open 11am–2am every day (407 273 7363) and **Headlightz Sports Bar** on East Colonial Drive, which also offers live music (407 273 9600). A personal favourite is the **Orlando Ale House** on Kirkman Road, just opposite Universal Studios (407 248 0000). With more than 30 TVs, a raw bar and some great seafood, it also carries an above-average range of beers. *Walt Disney World Resort in Florida* can boast the excellent **ESPN Club** at *Disney's BoardWalk Resort*, a full-service restaurant with sports broadcast facilities, video games, more than 70 TV monitors, giant scoreboards and even a Little League menu for kids. No sports fan should miss it. Equally, **NBA City** at Universal's CityWalk, and the **Cricketers' Arms** in The Mercado should not be overlooked as great sports venues, especially for TV/video addicts.

Now, you will also want to know a lot more about where, when and how to tackle that other holiday essential – FOOD. So, read on…

Eating Out

*(or, Man, these portions
are HUGE!)*

Eating is a big deal in America.
Consequently, eating out is a
vital component in their
entertainment business. Whether
it be breakfast, lunch or dinner,
the experience needs to be well-
organised, filling and good value.
To say Americans take mealtimes
seriously would be the
understatement of the year.

It is sometimes hard to dispel the
notion that food is the be all and end
all of some Americans' holiday
experience, as the options for dining
are seemingly omni-present and
large scale. However, this is all good
news for us Joe Tourists.

Variety

The variety, quantity and quality of
restaurants, cafés, fast-food chains
and hot-dog stalls is in keeping with
the American tradition of eating as
much as possible, as often as possible.

At first glance, the full selection of
food is rather overwhelming.
Cruising along either I-Drive or
Highway 192 will quickly reveal a
dazzling array of eateries, the choice
of which can be quite bewildering.

As a general rule, food is plentiful,
relatively cheap, available 24 hours a
day and nearly always appetising and
filling. You will even encounter an
increasing number of fine-dining
possibilities, but the basic premise
remains you will get good value for
money and are unlikely to need
more than two full meals a day. Put
simply, portions tend to be large,
and of a heavily steak, chicken or
pizza-based variety, with service of

an efficient, friendly character. It is
actually hard to come by a BAD
meal. The one real exception (as
pointed out by several readers) is if
you like fresh veg. The US diet
often overlooks this staple, but if you
look up the vegetarian options lower
down or check out one of the outlets
of **Chamberlin's,** notably at the
Market Place on Dr Phillips
Boulevard and in the new Winter
Park Village shops, you will find a
healthy, balanced choice.

Exceptional deals

In keeping with the climate, most
restaurants tend towards the informal
(T-shirts and shorts are usually
acceptable) and cater readily for
families. This also leads to two
exceptional deals for budget-
conscious tourists, especially those
with a large tribe. Many hotels and
restaurants offer 'kids eat free' deals,
provided they eat with their parents.
The age restrictions can vary from
under 10s to under 14s, but it
obviously represents good value for
money and they are worth looking

BRIT TIP: As portions are
so large, you can save
money by sharing an
entrée, or main course,
between two. Your
waiter/waitress will be
happy to oblige (provided
you keep their tip up to the
full rate).

The fabulous Planet Hollywood®

for. The second item of interest is the 'all-you-can-eat' buffet, another common feature of many of the large chain restaurants. This means you can have a hearty meal for not too much and probably eat enough at, say, breakfast, to keep you going until dinner! A few establishments also offer 'early bird' specials, a dinner discount if you dine before 6pm.

Don't be afraid to ask for a doggy bag if you have leftovers (even if you haven't brought the dog!). It is common practice to take away the half of that pizza you couldn't finish, or those chicken legs or salad. The locals do it all the time and, again, it is highly wallet-friendly. Just ask for the leftovers 'to go'.

Don't hesitate to tell your waiter or waitress if something isn't right with your meal. Americans will readily complain if they feel aggrieved, so restaurants are keen to make sure everything is to your satisfaction.

And, please, don't forget to tip. The basic wage for waiters and waitresses is low, so they rely heavily on tips to supplement their income. Unless service really is shoddy, in which case you should mention it, the usual rate for tips is 10% of your bill at buffet-style restaurants and 15% at full-service restaurants. It is worth checking to see if service is added to your bill, although this is less common in the US.

With Orlando being the world's favourite holiday destination, and with the city springing up from such eclectic roots, you will encounter a monumental array of food types. Florida is renowned for its seafood, which comes at a much more reasonable price than in the Mediterranean. Crab, lobster, shrimp (what we call king prawns), clams and oysters can all be had without fear of breaking the bank, as well as several dozen varieties of fish, many of which you won't have come across before (by the way don't worry about eating 'dolphin', it's not a mammal related to Flipper but a totally different species called dolphin fish or mahi-mahi).

Cuban, Cajun/Creole and Mexican are other more local types of cooking which are well represented here, and there is plenty of Oriental fare from the Chinese and Indian to Japanese, Thai and Vietnamese.

The big shopping complexes and malls offer a good choice of eateries in their food courts, which are often particularly good value. Cracker (cowboy) cooking is original Floridian fare, and the more adventurous will want to try the local speciality – alligator meat. This can be stewed, barbecued, smoked, sautéed or braised. Fried gator tail 'nuggets' are an Orlando favourite. Of course, you can't leave Florida without trying the

Race Rock

great speciality Key Lime Pie, a truly decadent dessert. Look for the stall in *Pleasure Island* selling it at $1 a slice – true heaven!

How to order

Ordering your food can also be an adventure in itself. The choice for each item is often the cue for an inquisition of exam-type proportions from your waiter/waitress. You can never order just 'toast' – it has to be white, brown, wholegrain, rye, muffin or bagel; eggs and bacon come in a baffling variety of ways; an order for tea or coffee usually provokes the response 'Regular or decaf? Iced, lemon or English?' and salads have more dressings than the National Health Service. Whenever I've finished ordering, I'm tempted to ask 'Have I passed?' (NB: American bacon is always streaky and crisp-fried and sausages are chipolata-like.) Don't be afraid to ask to see a restaurant's menu if it isn't displayed. It is no big deal to Americans and the restaurant won't feel insulted if you decide to look elsewhere.

Vegetarian options

In a country where beef is culinary king, vegetarians often find themselves hard done by, and Orlando is little different to the general rule. However, there are a couple of bright spots, plus a handy hint when all seems lost.

Firstly, there are two speciality vegetarian restaurants in Orlando, The **Lower East Side** at 3401 LB McLeod Road (407 648 4830) and the Chinese **Garden Café** on West Colonial Drive downtown (407 999 9799), while the tapas-style **Café Tu-Tu Tango** on I-Drive serves a good variety veggie dishes.

Most of the upscale restaurants should be able to offer a vegetarian option and will be happy for you to ask in advance. *Walt Disney World Resort in Florida* is slightly more enlightened in that the **California Grill** (in *Disney's Contemporary Resort*), **Citricos** (*Disney's Grand Floridian Resort and Spa*) and **Spoodles** (*Disney's BoardWalk*) feature vegetarian dishes, while all the full-service restaurants (notably **Bongos Cuban Café**™ and **Wolfgang Puck's**® **Café** in *Downtown Disney*), plus some of the counter-service ones are usually keen to try to cater for non-menu requests. It is always worth asking.

Sweet Tomatoes is a salad buffet restaurant (distinctly vegetarian-friendly) with possibly the best meal deals in central Florida. On I-Drive (by its Kirkman Road junction), it offers an astonishing all-you-can-eat choice for just $6.69 at lunch ($7.49 at dinner, after 4pm) that includes a vast salad spread, a choice of soups, pizza, pasta, bread and pastries, plus fruit and frozen yoghurt. Drinks are $1.49 (with free refills) and kids meals are $1.49 for under 6s and

10

Hard Rock Café

$4.49 for 6–12s. Open from 11am–10pm, it should be sought out by all value- and health-conscious eaters. **Chamberlin's Market & Café** (with eight Orlando locations) is another more enlightened choice, with home-made soups, vegetarian chilli, sandwiches, salads and blissful fresh fruit smoothies (visit their website www.chamberlins.com).

An excellent section of the *Unofficial Walt Disney World Information Guide* also lists special dietary requests, including veggie, on www.wdwig.com/special.htm.

Drinking

The biggest complaint of Brits on holiday in the USA is of the beer. With the exception of a handful of English-style pubs (see pages 245–6), American beer is always lager, either bottled or on draught, and ice-cold. It goes down great when it's really hot, but, as a general rule, it is weaker and fizzier than we're used to.

BRIT TIP: If there are several of you, ordering a pitcher of beer will work out cheaper than buying it by the glass.

Of course, there are exceptions and they are worth seeking out (try Killian's Red, Michelob Amber Bock or Dos Equis for a fuller flavour), but if you are expecting a good, old-fashioned British pint, forget it. Spirits (always called 'liquor' by Americans) come in a typically huge variety, but beware ordering just 'whisky' as you'll get bourbon. Specify if you want Scotch or Irish whiskey and demand it 'straight up' if you don't want it with a mountain of ice! If you fancy a cocktail, there is a massive choice and most bars and restaurants have lengthy happy

hours where prices are very consumer-friendly (hic!). Good-quality Californian wines also work out better value than imported European ones. If you are sticking to soft drinks ('sodas') or coffee, most bars and restaurants give free refills. You can also run a tab in most bars and pay when you leave.

BRIT TIP: Tourist brochures often include money-off coupons for many restaurants so you can make useful savings. See our offer on page 93.

Another few words of warning. Florida licensing laws are stricter than ours and you need to be **21 or over** to enjoy an alcoholic drink in a bar or lounge. You will often be asked for proof of your age before you are served (or allowed into entertainment complexes like *Downtown Disney Pleasure Island*), and this means your passport or new driving licence with a photo. It's no good arguing or trying to reason with a reluctant barman. Licensing laws are strict and they can't afford to take chances. No photo ID, no beer! Anyone under 21 may not sit or stand near a bar either.

Right, that gives you the inside track on HOW to eat and drink like the locals, now you want to know WHERE to do it, so here's a handy guide to that veritable profusion of culinary variety. At the last count there were 3,600 restaurants in the metro Orlando area, with new ones being added and some biting the dust all the time and, while it would be a tall order to list every one, the following section covers the main tourist areas and chain groups, as well as providing an insight into some specialist, one-off establishments.

Fast food

If you are a **McDonald's** fan you are coming to the right place as there are no less than 59 outlets in the greater Orlando area, varying from small drive-in types to the mega, 24-hour-a-day establishment on Sand Lake Road (near the junction with I-Drive) that also has the biggest play area for kids of any McDonald's in the world and a number of differently themed eating areas. **Burger King** is also well represented, with 44 outlets, as is another familiar American franchise, **Wendy's,** which has 24 restaurants. If you're a burger freak and want to sample a variation on the theme, give **Checkers** (nine outlets) or **Hardees** (four) a try.

KFC has 18 restaurants around the area, but for something different on the chicken theme, try **Popeye's Famous Fried Chicken & Biscuits** (13). If it's pizza you're after, **Pizza Hut** has 46 restaurants and **Domino's** has 19 and both offer local delivery, even to your hotel room.

A particularly American form of takeaway is the 'sub', or torpedo-roll sandwich. This is what you will find at any one of the 48 local branches of **Subway,** or the 13 of **Sobik's** or seven of **Miami Subs.** They're a rather more healthy option than yet another burger, and offer some imaginative fillings. Two other variations on the fast-food theme are **Arby's** (with 13 outlets), which offers a particularly appetising roast beef sandwich and other beefy delicacies, and **Taco Bell** (17 outlets), which does for Mexican food what McDonald's does for the hamburger. If you've never had Mexican food before, this is probably not the place to start but, for anyone familiar with their tacos, nachos and tortillas, it's a quick and cheap spicy meal.

Most of these establishments will have a drive-through part, which will be fun to try at least once on your visit. Simply drive around the side of the building where indicated and you will find their take-away menu with a voice box to take your order. Please, don't wait for the food to be produced from the voice box! Carry on around the building and your food will be served from a side window where the cashier also takes your money. You will probably find your car has a slide-out tray from the central dashboard area that will take your coffee or soda cup.

Family restaurants

This section may, at first, seem similar to the American Diner type (on page 246), but there are two major differences. First, these are only restaurants. You usually won't find a bar here as with a diner. And second, they make a big effort for family groups in terms of kids' menus, activities (in many cases the kids' menu doubles up as a colouring and puzzle book) and budget-conscious prices. They also all serve breakfasts and you will find the best of the all-you-can-eat buffet deals here. Nearly all are chain groups in the same way as you find Little Chef and Happy Eaters all over Britain, but there are one or two worthy individuals, too.

The most popular are the **Ponderosa Steakhouse** restaurants and **Sizzler.** Whether it's breakfast, lunch or dinner, you will find great value and good, reliable food. In terms of style they are almost

10

BRIT TIP: A buffet breakfast at Ponderosa, Sizzler or any other similar establishment should keep you going until tea-time and is a good way to start a theme-park day.

indistinguishable: you order and pay for your meal as you enter and are then seated, before being unleashed on some of the biggest buffet and salad bars you will have seen. Ponderosa have the rather flashier style, but you'd be hard pushed to tell whose food was whose. Expect to pay about $4–5 for their breakfast buffets and $6–9 for lunch and dinner (there IS a difference in price depending on location, with the I-Drive area tending to be a dollar or two dearer than elsewhere). Standard fare includes chicken wings, meatballs, chilli, ribs, steaks and fresh seafood, while their immense salad bars in particular represent major value for money. Both are open from 7am until late evening and are handily located in all the main tourist spots.

A more homely touch can be found at the following selection, with equally good if not better value for money. For a hearty breakfast at any time of day, **International House of Pancakes** (otherwise known as IHOP) or the **Waffle House** will both appeal to you. You will struggle to spend more than $5 or $6 on a full meal, whether it be one of their huge breakfast platters or a hot sandwich with fries. Waffle Houses are also open 24 hours a day, while IHOPs open 6.30am–1.30am. Another traditional American 24-hour family restaurant is **Denny's Diner,** the nearest thing to our Little Chefs. Again, they make a traditional bacon and egg breakfast seem ordinary with their wide selection, and they do an excellent

Fulton's Crab House

range of hot, toasted sandwiches and imaginative dinner meals, like grilled catfish, as well as a Senior Selections menu, featuring smaller portions at reduced prices for the over 55s.

Similarly, **Perkins Family Restaurant** is open around the clock with a lookalike menu. For a really hearty breakfast try Perkins Eggs Benedict (two eggs and bacon on a toasted muffin with hash browns and fresh fruit), while their bread-bowl salads are equally satisfying. A new chain who impresses for its clean, fresh style is **Golden Corral,** who has already chalked up a number of reader recommendations, and offers a delicious Carver's Choice of hand-carved meats plus the usual buffet deals and a terrific dessert bar.

If you are travelling on the major highways of Florida, one of the 34 branches of **Cracker Barrel** may catch your attention, in which case you should definitely check out their delightful Old Country Store style, with mountainous breakfasts, well-balanced lunch and dinner menus, Kid's Stuff choices and a real old-fashioned charm that is a nice change from the usual tourist frenzy.

Two new alternatives worthy of note for any time but especially breakfast are the mushrooming chains of **Panera Bread** (wonderful pastries, salads and sandwiches) and **First Watch** (all manner of egg dishes, plus great coffee and pastries, and all served double-quick!).

One of the most popular one-off restaurants for wide family appeal is

Captain Nemo's on Highway 192 opposite Fort Liberty. It serves breakfast 8am–noon, lunch until 3pm and dinner until 11pm, and its seafood and steak menu means Mum and Dad can try oysters, lobster, salmon, swordfish or grouper while the kids are still able to get their burger fix. Prices are budget-orientated, with daily specials, and Happy Hour 3–7pm.

> BRIT TIP: Reader John Cartlidge says: 'While we agree with the recommendation for Sizzler and Ponderosa, one morning we found a huge line for their breakfast buffet, so we drove 200yd down the road to the Black Angus – and the biggest buffet we saw all the time we were there. And no queue!'

For a real fun family treat (and the biggest crossover into the diner-type restaurant), take the clan to one of the two **Jungle Jim's** in the Orlando area (at Crossroads of Lake Buena Vista, and West Church Street). From the parrots that welcome you to the restaurant, you know you are in for an unusual dining experience, and sure enough you will find an entertaining jungle setting, with the menu promising 'An epic dining adventure of lost legends, forbidden pleasures and ancient rituals'. There are 63 (!) choices of burger, including the World Famous Headhunter, a 1lb burger with ham, bacon and cheese and a full 1lb of fries – polish off the lot and your next one is free! The alternatives are ribs, steak or chicken, but it would be a shame not to try at least one of the 63 varieties. The kids' menu is suitably varied, and a huge cocktail

range is served by Dr S'Tiph Shotta Likker (ouch!). Open 11am–1.30am Sun–Thur, 11am–2am Fri–Sat.

Another one-off establishment worthy of high praise is **Everett's Old Tymes Eatery** at 2754 Orange Blossom Trail (just south of Osceola Parkway on the right heading south). This typical Florida family diner (open 6am–8pm Mon–Sat and 7am–2pm Sun) offers some of the best value fare in Kissimmee in best down-home style (all drinks are served in jam jars!). Portions are huge (the family breakfast, supposedly for six, includes a dozen scrambled eggs, 1lb of bacon, 1lb of sausage, fries and grits, biscuits and toast for just $18.99), while the daily breakfast special is $1.49. It's a bluff, no-nonsense kind of place, well used by the locals (and you'll often find the police here having breakfast), but don't be put off by appearances. Recommended by reader Liz Storey and her family, it more than passes the *Brit's Guide* test for a genuine, good value establishment that adds to your holiday experience.

Home from home

To complete this section it is appropriate to mention the handful of British pubs and diners which seek to attract the UK visitor. All offer a fairly predictable array of pub grub and a few imported British beers. You'll find the odd Brit or two working behind the bars, and you can happily take the kids into all of them,

10

Planet Hollywood® at Downtown Disney

providing they don't sit at the bar. First and foremost is the **Cricketers' Arms** in The Mercado on I-Drive. This has become a favourite haunt of British visitors due to the large selection of beers, appetising food, live evening entertainment and (soccer fans take note) live Premiership matches on their giant TV screen on a Saturday morning (from 10am – remember the time difference). It gets busy in the evenings, their live music is usually pretty good, and many of the staff are Chelsea fans, but we won't hold that against them! There is usually a cover charge for soccer matches.

Highway 192 in Kissimmee sports a number of fairly derivative pubs all keen to appeal to the home market. The best are **Harry Ramsbottom's** at Fort Liberty (between Markers 10 and 11), which also has its own fish 'n chippie, and the wonderfully kept **Stage Door,** 6 miles west of the junction with I-4 (and west of Marker 4, just past Lindfields Boulevard). This bar/restaurant gets full marks from the locals, too.

American diners

Not surprisingly, there are so many American-style restaurants, it would be a full-time job just to keep track of them all. Therefore, I will limit this particular survey to the main tourist areas, plus a couple off the beaten track that are well worth tracking down. The $ price listings are intended only as a rough guide for a 3-course meal:

$	=	$10–$15
$$	=	$15–$20
$$$	=	$20–$25
$$$$	=	$25–$30
$$$$$	=	$30 plus

Steak and Ale is a popular diner and can be found at five locations around Orlando (11.30am–10pm Mon–Thur, 11.30am–11pm Fri, noon–11.30pm Sat, noon–10pm

Sun; $$). They do some great steaks and ribs, plus tempting seafood and chicken dishes, with early bird specials of a 3-course set meal 4–7pm (4–6pm Nov–Mar), and two-for-one drink specials at the same time. The nationwide chain **Bennigan's** has four outlets in Orlando and is a particular personal favourite for their friendly, efficient service, smart decor and tempting menu, especially at lunchtime. They make the ordinary seem appetising and have a bar atmosphere straight out of the TV programme *Cheers!* Their Irish flavour really comes into its own on St Patrick's Day (March 17), and they have happy hour(s!) 2–7pm and 11pm–midnight. (11am–2am; $$)

Another enjoyable dining experience can be found at the two branches of **Darryl's** (one on I-Drive, the other at Fort Liberty on Highway 192). Their weird and wonderful decor is totally original; they also have a great bar area and a nicely varied menu with some interesting choices, like Cajun-fried shrimp. Thick, wood-fired steaks, delicious burgers and Southern-style dishes are their main fare, but they also offer tasty soups and quiches. (11am–1am; $$)

Hooters makes no bones about its style. 'Delightfully tacky yet unrefined' declares the menu proudly, and sure enough here is a relatively simple, lively establishment, especially popular with the younger crowd for its beach-party atmosphere – and the famous Hooter Girl waitresses (11am–midnight Mon–Thur, 11am–1am Fri–Sat, noon–11pm Sun; $). Their eight restaurants have a truly entertaining menu featuring great value seafood, salads, burgers and Hooters Nearly World Famous Chicken Wings in five strengths: mild, medium, hot, 3 Mile Island or Wild Wing. You have been warned!

By contrast, **Pebbles** (four

outlets) goes for the casual but sophisticated style, with a genuinely imaginative menu that will appeal to the amateur gourmet and won't cost a fortune (11am–midnight; $$$). You can eat burgers or roast duck, salad or steak and be sure of an individual touch with every meal. Their pastas are particularly appetising and they offer a kids' menu, too.

Uno Chicago Pizzeria is the place to go if Pizza Hut has become passé. Their three outlets offer great deep-dish pizzas with the addition of pastas, chicken dishes, steaks and salads. (11am–midnight; $$)

The **Olive Garden** restaurants (12 of them) are one of America's big success stories as they have brought Italian food into the budget, mass-market range (11am–10pm Sun–Thur, 11am–11pm Fri–Sat; $$). Their light, airy restaurants create a relaxing environment and, while they don't offer a huge choice, what they do they do well and in generous portions. Pastas are their speciality, but they also offer chicken, veal, steak and seafood and some great salads, and there are unlimited refills of salad, garlic breadsticks and non-alcoholic drinks that add to their good value. Their large, new property between Race Rock and Trainland on I-Drive is also a distinct cut above their other outlets for quality and style.

The two **Bahama Breeze** restaurants (one on I-Drive, the other on SR 535 at Lake Buena Vista, next to the Holiday Inn Sunspree) are a must for their striking Caribbean styling – and popularity (the I-Drive one features an hour's wait at peak periods!). As the Bahamas are not strictly in the Caribbean, their theming is a little suspect, but we'll forgive them as the food is well above average for a typical diner. Try West Indies Patties or Creole Baked Goat Cheese as a starter, while the main courses (primarily pastas, seafood, chicken,

beef or pizza) feature outstanding items like Black Pepper Seared Tuna or the Cuban beef stew Ropa Vieja, with every dish coming up immaculately fresh. The plantation-room styling, delightful outside wooden deck for a pre- or post-dinner drink, and live music most nights fully endorse their own slogan of: 'At Bahama Breeze there are no worries, just happy, friendly people and island hospitality!' (4pm–2am Mon–Sat, 4pm–midnight Sun; $$$)

Hard to categorise but well worth visiting is the **Cheesecake Factory** in Winter Park Village (and a new outlet in the Mall at Millenia). While they make a feature of their desserts, the rest of the menu is pretty impressive, too, not to mention the high-tech, cavernous setting. Mexican dishes jostle with pizza, pasta, seafood, burgers, steaks and salads, and they also offer a great brunch selection. (11am–11pm; $$$$)

Ribs

When it comes to steaks, ribs and barbecue food, Orlando has a magnificent array of restaurants that all proudly proclaim some kind of 'world famous' variety. In many instances they are right, and here's a good selection of the best on offer.

While in The Mercado, you may decide to try **Damon's,** which pronounces itself 'the place for ribs'. While they also do salads, chicken, seafood and burgers, their rib platters are simply humongous (11am–10pm; $$$). Try their onion loaf as a starter as it is rightly 'famous', while their lunch selections are particularly good value and, they promise, served within 15 minutes with their 'express' label. Damon's new restaurant in Old Town is one of their sports-themed Clubhouse variety, with interactive sports and trivia games to add to their appeal (and is owned by former American

10

football star Fred Marion of the New England Patriots).

Cattleman's Steak House (on Vineland Road, at the intersection of SR 535 and Highway 192, and on I-Drive south of The Mercado) goes for the cowboy approach once again, with a neat saloon bar, early bird specials 4–6pm and the Little Rustlers' Round-up menu for the kids. Steaks are again the order of the day, but you can also order chicken and seafood, and their Heavenly Duck is worth trying for something different. (4–11pm, saloon open until 2am; $$$)

The upmarket version of this type of establishment is **Wild Jack's** (on I-Drive, just north of Sand Lake Road) where you are greeted by the most magnificent wood-smoked barbecue aroma as you walk in the door. The huge, western-themed interior features a big, open-pit barbecue where you can watch your food being cooked (11.30am–11pm; $$$). Steaks, ribs, chicken and turkey represent your main choices and they are all served up with bags of panache and a big helping of Wild West style. Happy hour is 4–7pm, kids eat free with a full-paying adult and you can even buy yourself a Wild Jack's souvenir boot-shaped beer mug.

Another good choice which also pulls in a lot of complimentary

reader feedback is **Key W Kool's Open Pit Grill** on Highway 192 (just opposite Splendid China). Choice cuts of meat, mouth-watering steaks – check out the eye-popping 32-oz porterhouse! – prime rib, daily specials and a wonderfully succulent, inviting aroma add up to outstanding dining choice, and at good prices. (4–11pm; $$$)

I can also recommend any of the six restaurants of **Tony Roma's,** which rightly pronounce themselves 'famous for ribs'. The airy but relaxing decor and ambience, clever kids' menu (the Roma Rangers Round-up, full of puzzles and games), junior meals, and their melt-in-the-mouth ribs, try their Original Baby Backs, make a winning combination. You can still get chicken, burgers and steaks, but why ignore a dish when it's done this well? The Rib Sampler is a great platter, and there are chicken-rib and shrimp-rib combos. (11am–midnight Sun–Thur, 11am–1am Fri and Sat; $$)

Tex-Mex

What the Olive Garden does for Italian cuisine, **Chili's** (with 10 outlets) does for Mexican. Actually, it's an Americanised version of Mexican cooking that originated in Texas (hence Tex-Mex), with the emphasis more on steak and ribs and less on tortillas and hot spices (11am–1am Mon–Sat, 11am–11pm Sun; $$). Service is frighteningly efficient and, if you are looking for a quick meal, you'll be hard-pushed to find a quicker turnaround. The atmosphere is lively and bustling and they do a good kids' menu that is also a colouring/puzzle book. Similarly, the rather identikit **Chevy's** chain has eight restaurants in the area and offers a healthy slice of Mexicana, while still offering some reassuring American

Sunday brunch at the Renaissance Orlando Resort

selections. (4–11pm Mon-Thur,
4–midnight Fri, 11am–midnight Sat,
11am–11pm Sun; $$)

The most elaborate Mexican
offering is the cavernous **Don
Pablo's**, next to the Visitor Center
on I-Drive. Clever theming, lively
atmosphere (especially around the
Cantina bar!) and a classic, well-
explained menu add up to a real fun
experience. (11.30am–10pm Sun–
Thur, 11.30am–11pm Fri–Sat; $$)

Another one-off restaurant that
has a lot of Brit appeal is **Café Tu-
Tu Tango** on I-Drive, next to Vito's.
The accent is artist-colony Spanish
(whatever that means), with a really
original menu, live entertainment
and artwork all over the walls that
changes daily. Vegetarians will find
themselves well catered for here, and
you can try some particularly
succulent pizzas, seafood, salads and
paella. Mexican and Chinese dishes
also make an appearance, and there is
a thoughtful kids' menu (11.30am–
midnight; $$). The overall style is
based more on a tapas bar, so you
order a number of different dishes
rather than a starter and main course.
Ultimately, it is as much an artistic
experience as a meal, and the fun
atmosphere perfectly complements
the rich array of dishes.

Steakhouses

Serious steak-lovers will have to pay
a visit to **Ruth's Chris Steak House**
(with new restaurants in the Winter
Park Village and on West Sand Lake
Road) where prime beef in a mouth-

watering variety of choices is the
order of the day. It isn't cheap, but
you'll be hard-pushed to get a better
steak (5–11pm Mon–Sat, 5–10pm
Sun; $$$$$). 'Only the best',
proclaims their slogan. 'Come judge
for yourself, but come hungry'.

Similarly, the **Butcher Shop** (in
The Mercado on I-Drive) offers
steaks, steaks and more steaks.
Hugely impressive is the cold
counter, where you can select your
own piece of meat, and the hickory
charcoal grill where you can actually
cook your steak to the desired
degree with, of course, the help of a
chef to do it for you or offer advice.
(5–10pm Sun–Thur, 5–11pm
Fri–Sat; $$$$)

Charley's Steak Houses (of
which there are three, the biggest
being on I-Drive just north of The
Mercado) continue the theme of
excellent steaks, cooked over a
specially built pit woodfire. It's not
cheap (although their Orange
Blossom Trail location, 2 miles
north of the Florida Mall, is
noticeably cheaper than the other
two), but the decor and bar area are
splendidly furnished, and if you
don't fancy steak, which you can
watch being grilled on their large,
hardwood grill, you can have
seafood (5–11pm; $$$$$). Charley's
is frequently highly rated in
American steakhouse reviews.

Another imaginative choice is
Vito's Chop House in front of the
Castle Hotel on I-Drive. Their
choice beef cuts – check out the
Tuscan T-Bone – are aged 4–6 weeks

10

Morton's Steakhouse

and cooked over wood fires, while they also offer trademark pork chops, seafood and pasta, as well as an extensive wine list. (5–10.30pm Sun–Thur, 5–11pm Fri–Sat; $$$$)

For more steak-induced hedonism, **Morton's** of Chicago (on the Market Place on Dr Phillips Boulevard) is hard to beat. Its rather more upmarket (and sometimes pretty smoky) style is offset by a lively ambience that adds to the enjoyment of its trademark steaks, which you can watch being cooked on an open range. You are provided with a fully exhibited menu (they bring examples of the food to the table) and invited to enjoy some of the biggest, most succulent steaks it has been my pleasure to sample. The porterhouse is an inspired choice, as is one of the principal alternatives, Shrimp Alexander. Needless to say, this does not come cheap, especially as vegetables are extra, but it is a memorable experience. (5pm–midnight Mon–Sat, 5pm–11pm Sun; $$$$$)

Similarly, **Shula's Steak House** in the *Walt Disney World Dolphin Hotel* is both expansive (on your waistline) and expensive. The porterhouse and prime rib are outstanding, and this restaurant (the latest in a chain owned by famous former American football coach Don Shula) is extremely popular with locals. (5–11pm; $$$$$)

The **Outback Steakhouse** chain (in four Orlando locations) has an Australian slant with thick, juicy well-seasoned steaks, ribs and a small seafood selection. Appetizers include the 'Bloomin Onion', a large fried onion accompanied by their special dipping sauce. Queues build up in the evening, so try to arrive slightly before the usual dinner time or slightly after to avoid a wait (or visit the bar). They also feature a good kids' menu. (4–10.30pm Mon–Thur, 3.30–11pm Fri and Sat, 3.30–10.30pm Sun; $$$$)

Perhaps more fun is **Logan's Roadhouse** (with five central Florida outlets, notably on Highway 192 at its junction with I-Drive South) where the funky, rustic atmosphere is enlivened with masses of shelled peanuts, the shells of which liberally carpet the wooden floor by the end of the evening. Burgers, chicken, steaks and ribs are their stock in trade, while they also offer an Express lunch selection that is worth knowing about if you need to be quick (11am–10.30pm Sun–Thur, 11am–11.30pm Fri and Sat; $$$). **Black Angus** and **Western Steer** complete the line-up of steakhouses along more budget lines as they also serve breakfasts and aim for the family market. Black Angus (two outlets on Highway 192) offers an all-you-can-eat breakfast buffet as well as a typical range of steaks, and has a nightly karaoke session (7am–11.30pm; $$). Western Steer (on I-Drive, opposite Wet 'n Wild) has a breakfast buffet and dinner buffet. Steaks are the main fare, and with a large tribe to feed, it's great value. (7am–11.30pm; $$)

Seafood

You won't be surprised to learn that the choice of seafood eateries is equally large. **The Crab House** (locations on Goodings Plaza on I-Drive and Palm Parkway) should be self-explanatory. Garlic crabs, steamed crabs, snow crabs, Alaskan king crabs, etc. Yes, this is THE place for crab. You can always try their prime rib, pasta or other seafood, but it would be a shame to ignore the house speciality when it's this good. (11.30am–11pm Mon–Sat, noon–11pm Sun; $$$)

Red Lobster (10 restaurants) is from the same company that has made a success of the Olive Garden chain. This is seafood for the family market, with a varied menu, lively atmosphere and one of the best kids' menu/activity books. While lobster is the speciality, their steaks, chicken, salads and other seafood are equally appetising, and they do a great variety of combination platters. (11am–10pm Sun–Thur, 11am–11pm Fri–Sat; $$$)

Charlie's Lobster House (on I-Drive at The Mercado) has a similar menu, with nightly fresh fish specials and reservations recommended. The bar areas are immaculately furnished and service has that extra charm. (4–10pm Sun–Thur, 4–11pm Fri–Sat; $$$$)

Completing the chain restaurants here are the three outlets of the **Boston Lobster Feast,** with elaborate nautical decor and an unlimited lobster and seafood buffet (hence the 'Feast'). They have early bird specials from 4.30–6pm Mon–Fri, 2–4.30pm Sat–Sun which are excellent value, while their 40-item Lobster Feasts are guaranteed to stretch the stomach. (4.30–10pm Mon–Fri, 2–10pm Sat–Sun; $$$$)

Of the one-off restaurants, **Ocean Grill** (on I-Drive, just north of the Sand Lake Road junction) offers great seafood at moderate prices. Daily specials, including the early bird variety from 4–6pm, jostle with the likes of fried clams, south-western swordfish, fried catfish, shrimp Creole and seafood lasagne. Their fish and chips would put most British chippies to shame and, for the really hearty appetite, their surf 'n turf is superb (lobster or shrimp and steak), although at a hearty price. (4–11pm; $$$)

The **Atlantic Bay Seafood Grill** (on Highway 192, just east of I-4) surprisingly offers a breakfast buffet on top of its well-priced seafood dishes, early bird specials (4.30–6.30pm) and steaks, ribs and pasta. It's not gourmet but it is hearty and good value, especially their all-you-can-eat seafood bar. (4–11pm; $$)

Inside the new Omni Rosen hotel on I-Drive is the **Everglades Restaurant,** an upmarket seafood and steak choice which again combines unusual decor (an environmental look at the Everglades, complete with manatee, swamp scenery, tropical music and a 12-ft aquarium) with fine cuisine. Daily seafood specials jostle with wild boar, venison and buffalo steak, while the Gator Chowder is a must-try starter. There is a relaxing adjacent bar area in this cavernous hotel, and diners at the Everglades also enjoy complimentary valet parking. (5.30–11pm daily; $$$$)

Along at Pointe*Orlando is **Monty's Conch Harbor,** where Key West is the relaxed, casual theme and the specialities include conch chowder, clams, oysters, stone crabs and Cajun-spiced tuna. Their fresh fried seafood baskets are also a real treat and Key Lime Pie is a must for dessert. (11.30am–11pm; $$$$)

My vote for the most memorable seafood dining experience in town is a split decision, however. **Fulton's Crab House** in *Downtown Disney's* Marketplace is a wonderful choice. This mock riverboat has six differently themed dining rooms (albeit with the same menu), plus the Stone Crab Lounge which features a complete raw bar (and always seems to be busy). Nautical props, photos and lithographs fill the interior, giving it a wonderfully eclectic, period atmosphere, but the real attraction is the food – some of the freshest and most tempting fish, crab and lobster dishes in Florida. The Alaskan king crab is a rare treat, as is tuna filet mignon, but there are fresh specials every day (the air shipping bills for which are posted in the main hall), as well as a children's menu. Fulton's features an extensive wine list, micro-brewed beers and its own specialities, but the dining rooms often have a queue as early as 6pm, so it is advisable to book (407

10

Inside Race Rock

394 2628). The Stone Crab Lounge serves lunch and dinner 11.30am–midnight, while the restaurant is open for dinner. (5–11pm; $$$$)

The **Flying Fish,** at *Disney's Boardwalk Resort,* is, if anything, even better at what it does. The menu is not overburdened with choice, but what they do they do with great panache and wonderful presentation. Their 'Peeky Toe' Crab Cake starter is melt-in-the-mouth territory, while the Oak-Grilled Wahoo and Coriander Rubbed Yellowfin Tuna are both outstanding. They also offer steak and pork, plus a vegetarian option, but it's really the seafood you want to try here (4–11pm Mon–Sat, 4–10pm Sun).

Novel dining

There are four other restaurants that could be categorised as diners but are really delightful, one-off restaurants in their own right. All four provide a genuinely exciting dining experience in novel settings that will linger long in the memory, and without costing a fortune.

Planet Hollywood®, the largest restaurant in the recently troubled worldwide chain of this glitzy, showbiz-style venture, is next door to *Downtown Disney Pleasure Island* and is a pure fun entertainment venue. The food is fairly predictable diner fare, although everything is served up with pizzazz, but the cavernous interior lends itself to a party atmosphere, complete with numerous film clips and a stunning array of movie memorabilia. Some memorable house cocktails, too, but visit either mid-morning or mid-afternoon to avoid the serious queues. (11am–2am; $$$)

B-line Diner, inside the Peabody Hotel on I-Drive, pays an amazing art deco homage to the traditional 1950s-style diner, faithful in every detail, including the outfits of the staff. You sit at a magnificent long counter or in one of several booths, with a good view of the chefs at work and with a rolling menu that changes four times a day (which isn't bad when it is open around the clock). The food is way above usual diner standard, but the prices aren't, so you can munch away on catfish in a papaya-tartare sauce or pork chops with apple-sage chutney, as well as the traditional favourites of burgers, steaks and ribs, happy in the knowledge you won't break the bank. Their desserts are displayed in a huge glass counter and I defy you to ignore them. (open 24 hours; $$)

The two versions of **Rainforest Café,** an eco-aware, jungle-themed restaurant chain, are adjacent to *Disney's Animal Kingdom Theme Park* and in the heart of *Downtown Disney* Marketplace, one with a huge waterfall exterior and the other topped by an active, smoking volcano, and they have to be seen to be believed. You don't dine, you go on a 'safari adventure' in a rainforest setting amid audio-animatronic animals (including elephants and gorillas), thunderstorms, tropical birds, waterfalls, aquariums and some of the cleverest lighting effects I have seen. It is an amazing experience, especially for children, and the food is well above average.

Try the Rasta Pasta or Mo' Bones ribs, but the menu alone will take a while to negotiate. Unless you arrive before midday, you'll have to wait for a table, but that's no hardship given their locations. Beware the huge gift shop! (11am–11pm; $$$)

> BRIT TIP: Reader Penny Parker says: 'We tried Jungle Jim's at the Crossroads plaza at your recommendation and loved it but we also found a Chinese there tucked behind the IHOP, called Dragon Court – great food, great service and a fantastic price!'

Another unmistakable landmark on I-Drive is the super-charged, super-large restaurant of **Race Rock,** packed with rare motor-racing memorabilia and eye-catching machines of all kinds. This does for motor sport what the Hard Rock does for music, and how! Two giant car transporters line the entrance, which also boasts a giant-wheeled buggy, two dragsters and a hydroplane speedboat, welcoming you in to the circular, 20,000-sq ft restaurant itself. Giant TV screens and a host of regular TVs, video games, virtual-reality racing machines and loud, loud music and chequered flag tables complete the atmosphere, while the central bar sports an upside-down racing car circulating as the world's biggest ceiling fan! The food is traditional diner fare given a few tweaks like Start Your Engines (the starter selections), Circle Tracks (pizza), Stock and Modified (burgers and sandwiches), Pole Position Pastas and The Main Event (ribs, chops, chicken and salmon). I rate the Road Runner chicken, marinated in lime juice, olive oil and garlic and char-

grilled. A Quarter Midget menu costs $4.99 for children 12 and under. (11.30am–midnight; $$)

Chinese

Chinese food is well established in America and well represented in Orlando, although many outlets are pretty uninspired, not to mention downright insipid.

Ming Court on I-Drive, just south of King Henry's Feast, is the Rolls Royce of local Chinese restaurants. With the magnificent setting and live entertainment you can easily convince yourself you have been transported to China itself. The menu is extensive and many dishes can be had as a side order rather than a full main course to give you the chance to try more. (11am–2.30pm and 4.30pm–midnight; $$$)

Bill Wong's Famous Super Buffet (yes, they really do call it that) on I-Drive offers a cross between Chinese and diner-type fare. Their all-you-can-eat buffet features jumbo shrimp (and they mean Jumbo!), as well as crabs, prime rib, fresh fruit and salad. (11am–10pm; $$)

A rather classier version of this style is the **China Garden Buffet** at The Mercado. The elegant surroundings are the perfect complement to the extraordinary buffet choice, with more than 50 items – from spring rolls to chilled crab claws – on offer at any one time. There is also a full à la carte selection, but the buffet price of $15.95 for adults and $6.95 for 3–10s ($8.59 and $4.95 at lunch) make this one of the best deals going. (10am–11pm; $$)

Similarly, the **Sizzling Wok,** on Sand Lake Road, just across from the Florida Mall, offers an opportunity to get stuck into a massive Chinese buffet at a very reasonable price.

10

(11am–10pm Sun–Thur,
11am–10.30pm Fri–Sat; $$)

The **China Café** on I-Drive (at
the corner of Kirkman Road) is also
above average, with a lunch buffet
from 11am–3pm and a well
presented array of dishes (Crispy
Duck is outstanding). Daily specials
also feature. (11am–11pm; $$)

Japanese

The more adventurous (and those
already familiar with their cuisine)
will want to try one of the fine
Japanese restaurants with which
Orlando is blessed. **Shogun
Steakhouse,** on I-Drive under the
Rodeway Inn, is ideal for those who
can't quite go the whole hog and get
stuck into sushi (raw fish). If you
decide to 'chicken' out, you can still
order a no-nonsense steak or
chicken, but their full Japanese
menu is well explained and vividly
demonstrated by their chefs in front
of you at long, bench-like tables.
(6–10pm Mon–Thur, 6–10.30pm
Fri–Sun; $$)

Kobe brings a touch of Americana
to its dining content. With four
locations around the area, Kobe goes
for the mass market but still achieves
individual style with the chef
preparing your food at your table in
a style that is as much showmanship
as culinary expertise. (11.30am–
11pm; $$)

Ran-Getsu, on I-Drive opposite
The Mercado, does for Japanese
cuisine what the Ming Court does
for Chinese – it's stylish, authentic
and as much an experience as a meal,
and still reasonably priced. The
setting is simple and efficient, and
you can choose to sit at conventional
tables or the long, S-shaped sushi
bar. (5pm–midnight; $$$)

Benihana completes a formidable
quartet of outlets, situated in the
Hilton Hotel at Lake Buena Vista.
Again, it's a memorable experience,

with everything cooked in front of
you by their expert chefs, and their
steaks are among the most tender
you will ever taste. (5–10.30pm; $$$)

Indian

If you have come all this way and
still fancy a curry, believe it or not
you will be able to get one as good as
any you have enjoyed back home.
There are already more than a dozen
Indian restaurants around the
Orlando area and they all maintain
a pretty fair standard, from the
upmarket **Far Pavilion**, at the
intersection of I-Drive and Kirkman
Road, to the budget-price **New
Punjab** at the upper end of I-Drive
and on West Vine Street,
Kissimmee, with its excellent lunch
and dinner specials. For a medium-
range restaurant, **Passage to India**
(also on I-Drive) gets the locals' top
vote and is a cut above the average,
with unusual and exotic chicken
dishes and vegetarian Sabzi Dal
Bahar. It is a particular personal
favourite for its attentive service and
relaxed atmosphere, and you'll
probably find yourself dining with a
few fellow Brits. (11.30am–
midnight; $$$)

Thai and more

For other types of Oriental cooking,
the **Siam Orchid** (on Universal
Boulevard, round the corner from
Wet 'n Wild) offers exceptional Thai
food in a picturesque setting
overlooking Sandy Lake (5–11pm;
$$). **Little Saigon** (on East Colonial
Drive) will introduce you to
Vietnamese cuisine and a whole new
array of soups, barbecue dishes, fried
rice variations and other interesting
treats that take up where Chinese
food leaves off. (10am–9pm; $)

Possibly the best amalgam of all
the Asian cuisine styles is offered by
Haifeng, inside the Renaissance

Orlando Resort near SeaWorld. Here, in a suitably elegant setting, the fusion of Japanese and Chinese offerings is superb, with the service matching the high quality of the food. Their speciality tea is also a cut above. (5–11pm, Tue–Sun only; $$$$)

Cuban

Cuban food is a Floridian speciality and you will find some of the best examples at **Rolando's** (on Semoran Boulevard, in the suburb of Casselberry, head east from I-4 Exit 92). Try the red snapper or pork chunks and find out why the *Orlando Sentinel* rates this the best Cuban food north of Havana. (11am–9pm Tue–Thur, 11am–10pm Fri–Sat, 1–8pm Sun; $)

However, the new **Samba Room** on West Sand Lake Road is the 5-star experience hereabouts, an elegant lakefront restaurant full of Latin verve and ambience. The menu exhibits a wonderfully exotic touch, with the likes of mango-barbecued ribs, cachaca-smoked boneless chicken and sugar cane beef tenderloin (with chipotle mashed potatoes and mushroom sofrito), and their range of cocktails is suitably Cuban-laced (with lots of rum and martini). Definitely worthy of investigation, but also extremely popular, so reservations are advised. (407 266 0550; 11am–midnight Mon–Sat; noon–10pm Sun; $$$$$)

Italian

No survey of Orlando's restaurants would be complete without mention of its fine tradition of Italian cooking. **Pacino's** on Highway 192, opposite Old Town, goes for the family market and scores a big hit with value, a friendly atmosphere and Sicilian style, with clever animated puppet operettas, a fountain that occasionally spouts flame and a relaxing open-air feel that is enhanced by the clever use of the differently arranged seating areas. (4pm–midnight; $$$)

Bergamo's, in The Mercado, is actually German-owned but nonetheless authentic for all that. Don't be surprised if your waiter suddenly bursts into song – it's all part of the unique charm of this extremely tempting and highly entertaining restaurant. (5–10pm Sun–Thur, 5–11pm Fri–Sat; $$$$)

Italianni's (on I-Drive just south of its Sand Lake Road junction) won't hurt your wallet quite so much and does a great pizza among a typical selection of Italian fare. Don't miss their home-made cheesecake. (11am–11pm; $$$)

The 5-star version of Italian cuisine here belongs to two contrasting restaurants, **Christini's** on Dr Phillips Boulevard, and Michaelangelo on Kirkman Road. Strolling musicians, elegant surroundings and a 40-year history of award-winning cuisine characterise Christini's, where their home-made pasta and filet mignon are as good as anything you will find in Italy. (5–11pm; $$$$$)

Michaelangelo, just north of Universal Studios in Turkey Lake Village, promotes a candlelit atmosphere with live music in the cocktail lounge, formal, dinner-jacketed staff and a northern Italian cuisine that features delicious veal, snapper and pasta delicacies. Their pasta, bread and desserts are all home-made and it is all presented in an old-world style that is a million miles away from the tourist hurly-burly of the theme parks. (6–11pm, 6pm–2am in the bar; $$$$$)

10

German

A recent and highly worthwhile discovery is **Gain's German Restaurant** on the South Orange

Palm Restaurant

Blossom Trail (just past Oakridge Road going north), both for food and an excellent selection of bottled and draught beers. The friendly welcome, authentic Bavarian decor and tempting menu come as a real surprise in the heart of tourist Orlando, but owners Hans and Kessy Gain have lavished much care and attention on building up their trade here. A tasty ragout is an ideal appetiser, while there are sausage specialities (naturally), wiener schnitzel (of course), and rotisserie chicken and pan-fried rainbow trout (for something different). Apple strudel and Black Forest cake are the ideal desserts, while the Diebels amber ale is a fine choice for beer connoisseurs. Call 407 438 8997 for reservations. (11.30am–2.30pm and 4.30–10pm Tue–Thur, 4.30–11pm Fri and Sat, 4.30–10pm Sun; $$–$$$)

Splashing out

Finally, if you fancy really splashing out, here are some notable suggestions where both the food and ambience are way above average (albeit with the price tag to match). This fine dining aspect has become a real growth area in Orlando's culinary panorama, and long may it continue! Its popularity also requires that you book well in advance.

The **Park Plaza Gardens** is part of the Park Plaza Hotel on Park Avenue, Winter Park, and this beautiful courtyard restaurant gives you the feel of outdoor dining with the air-conditioned comfort of being indoors. Attentive service is coupled with an elegant, versatile menu that offers the choice of a relatively inexpensive lunch or a 3-course adventure featuring *escargots*, pasta with salmon, medallions of beef or one of several tempting fish dishes. Cuisine is distinctly 'nouvelle' rather than American, but nonetheless satisfying for all that. Its setting becomes even more intimate and charming in the evening with lights scattered among the foliage. Enjoy happy hour in the lounge (5–7pm, with complimentary buffet Thur and Fri), while their popular 3-course Sunday brunch features unlimited champagne and live jazz. (407 645 2475; 11.30am–3pm Mon–Sat and 11am–3pm for Sunday brunch, 6–10pm Mon–Thur, 6–11pm Fri–Sat, 6–9pm Sun; $$$$$)

Another highlight of the Renaissance Orlando Resort is the **Atlantis** seafood signature restaurant. This wonderfully elegant and quite intimate corner of an equally smart hotel not only offers fine dining in the normal course of events, but also a scintillating range of daily fresh Floridian seafood specials that just demand to be sampled. A fine wine list complements the full à la carte dinner menu. (5–10.30pm; $$$$$)

For another meal with a difference check out the **Renaissance's Sunday Brunch,** which is something of an Orlando tradition. Not so much a buffet as a 100-item banquet, it costs $30.95 for adults, $15.95 for children 4–12. Try this and brunch will never be the same again. (407 351 5555; 10.30am– 2.30pm)

A recent arrival in The Mercado and a pleasant addition to the upscale style in this largely mass-market location is **DiVino's,** a rural-themed Italian restaurant with the full essence of Tuscany. Relatively simple pastas jostle with wood-grilled swordfish, braised chicken and the trademark Osso Buco (roast veal shank), plus some excellent daily specials (seafood especially). It is not a cheap exercise (main courses run from $20–30) but the deep flavours, allied with excellent service, create a memorable meal. Reservations are advisable as it gets pretty busy most evenings around 8pm, on 407 345 0883. (5–11pm daily; $$$$$)

The opening of Universal's Hard Rock Hotel brought with it the **Palm Restaurant,** the latest in an upscale nationwide chain which has a big film-star and celebrity following. Founded in New York in 1926, it is famous for prime-aged steaks and jumbo lobsters, all served in spacious, elegant surroundings and with personable, knowledgeable service. The house speciality Jumbo Nova Scotia Lobster is truly spectacular. Of course, their steaks are a bit special, too (check out the Double Steak, a 36-oz New York strip for 2 at $60), while crab, swordfish and salmon, pork, veal and pasta are also on the menu. All this decadence is, however, reflected in the prices, and the vegetable dishes are extra, but the lunch menu shows a more modest touch while maintaining the quality. (407 503 7256; 11am–11pm Mon–Sat; noon–10pm Sun; $$$$$)

Sticking with the hotel theme, **Jiko** in *Disney's Animal Kingdom Lodge* is possibly their most imaginative and impressive culinary offering to date. Maintaining the hotel's African theming with its decor and lighting, Jiko ('The Cooking Place') features twin wood-burning ovens, a masterful menu and an exclusive selection of South African wines sure to please any connoisseur. The menu reflects influences from India and Asia as well as Africa and offers dishes like Banana-leaf Steamed Sea Bass, Whole Roast Papaya Stuffed with Spicy Minced Beef and Oven-baked Garlic Chicken Tagine with Grapefruit, Olives and Herbs. The personal level of service and ethnic ambience underline the adventure of any meal here and make it a real highlight of this amazing hotel. (407 939 3463; 5–11pm; $$$$$)

Old Hickory Steakhouse is another hotel-based offering in the new Gaylord Palms on I-Drive South. Its elaborate Everglades theming gives it an extra dimension, but the steak needs few gimmicks as the house speciality certified Black Angus beef is aged for 21–35 days and cooked to perfection. Side dishes are extra, hence it is an expensive option, but the attentive service and alternatives like oven-roasted swordfish and Maine lobster provide a memorable experience. Watch out, too, for their signature artisanal cheese course, imported by trendy New York chef Terrance Brennan. If you are fortunate enough to be staying at this amazing hotel, Old Hickory should definitely be on your to-do list. Otherwise, it is a great reason in itself to pay the Gaylord Palms a visit. (5–10.30pm Mon–Fri, 5–11pm Sat, 5–10pm Sun; $$$$$)

Now on to another of my favourite topics. The other main way in which Orlando will seek to separate you from your hard-earned money is shopping…

Jiko at Disney's Animal Kingdom Lodge

© Disney

10

11 Shopping
(or, How to Send Your Credit Card into Meltdown)

As well as being a theme park wonderland, the vast area that constitutes metropolitan Orlando is a shopper's paradise, with a dazzling array of specialist outlets, malls, flea markets and discount retailers. It is also a vigorous growth market, with new centres springing up seemingly all the time, from the smartest of malls to the cheapest of gift shop plazas – and you can hardly go a few yards in the main tourist areas without a shop insisting it has the best tourist bargains of one sort or another.

You will be bombarded by shopping opportunities every way you turn, and the only hard part is avoiding the temptation to fill an extra suitcase or two with the sort of goods that would cost twice as much back home. As a general rule, you can expect to pay in dollars what you would pay in pounds for items like clothes, books and CDs, and there are real bargains to be had in jeans, trainers, shoes, sports equipment, T-shirts and cosmetics.

But beware! Your duty-free allowance in the catch-all duty category of 'gifts' is still only £145 per person, and it is perfectly possible to exceed that sum by some distance. Paying the duty and VAT is still often cheaper than buying the same items at home, however, so it is worth splashing out, but remember to keep all your receipts and go back through the red 'goods to declare' channel on your return. You will pay duty (which varies depending on the item) on the total purchase price (i.e. inclusive of Florida sales tax) once you have exceeded your £145 allowance, plus VAT at 17.5%. Unfortunately, you cannot pool your allowances to cover one item that exceeds a single allowance. Hence, if you buy a camera, say, that costs £200, you have to pay the duty on the full £200, taking the total to £213.20, and then the VAT on that figure. However, if you have a number of items that add up to £145, and then another which exceeds that, you pay the duty and VAT only on the excess (and the customs officers will usually give you the benefit of the lowest rate on what you pay for). Duty rates are updated regularly and can be as little as 2.7% (golf clubs) or 15% (mountain bikes). If you have any queries, consult a Customs and Excise office before you leave (or visit www.hmce.gov.uk).

BRIT TIP: If you are tempted to use 'doctored' receipts to show a lesser value – don't, it is illegal. Your goods will be confiscated and there are heavy fines. Also, you can't escape the duty by saying the items have been used (in the case of golf clubs, for example) or that they are gifts for someone else.

Your ordinary duty-free allowances from America include 200 cigarettes and 1 litre of spirits or 2 litres of sparkling wine and 2 litres of still wine. Alligator products, which constitute an endangered species, require a special import licence, and you should consult the Department of the Environment first.

Be aware, also, of the hidden 'extras' of shopping costs. Unlike our VAT, the local version in Orlando, the Florida State sales tax, is NOT added to the displayed purchase price, so you should add 6 or 7% (depending on which county you are in) to arrive at the 'real' price. This frequently catches visitors out. The sales tax is added to everything that you buy in Orlando, from theme park tickets to a beer at the hotel you are staying in and all meals (but not groceries).

Here is a rundown of the main shopping attractions and the sort of fun and bargains to be had, divided into four categories. First, the purpose-built shopping complexes, specifically out to catch the visitor's eye; second, Orlando's speciality flea markets and discount outlets; third, the large shopping malls; and finally a few shops for the bargain-hunter. The best examples of the first category are all in the main tourist areas, starting, of course, with Disney.

Downtown Disney

The heart of *Walt Disney World* Resort in Florida in many ways is their *Downtown Disney* development. And the **Downtown Disney Marketplace** is typical Disney, a beautiful location, imaginative building and landscaping and a host of one-off elements that make shopping here a pleasure. Don't miss the awesome **World of Disney** store, the largest of its kind in the world, the **Lego Imagination Center** (an interactive playground

and shop), **Discover Garden Shop** for unique gifts and gardening accessories with an environmental awareness theme, the amazing **Art of Disney** and **Team Mickey's Athletic Club.** New in August 2002 was **Once Upon A Toy,** a gigantic toy emporium complete with a host of classic games, many with a novel Disney theme, for kids to try out. Dancing fountains and squirt pools (where kids tend to get seriously wet), the lakeside setting and boating opportunities all add to the appeal here. Restaurants include the superbly themed **Rainforest Café** and a **McDonald's,** plus the excellent **Cap'n Jack's Oyster Bar.**

Then you can stroll over to **Downtown Disney West Side** and see a film or visit the world's largest **Virgin Megastore.** The **Hoypoloi Gallery** is one of my favourites for a wonderfully eclectic range of artwork, from metal to glass. In all, there are 32 shops to browse, and the whole complex is open 9.30am–11pm every day. It is off Exit 67 on I-4 and is well signposted (avoid Exit 68 because of the congestion here).

I-Drive

This core tourist area has two cleverly built developments which offer some unique shopping attractions, starting with **The Mercado,** the original speciality complex, in the heart of the I-Drive corridor just south of Sand Lake Road. Although it is starting to look a bit tired compared to some of the newer developments, this Mediterranean-style 'village' includes 28 speciality shops, six high-quality restaurants (Italian duo **Bergamo's** and **Divino's, Charlie's Lobster House,** the **China Garden Buffet, Damon's** and the **Butcher Shop),** the **Cricketers' Arms** pub, evening entertainment (in the

11

ORLANDO'S SHOPPING CENTRES

A Downtown Disney Marketplace
B The Mercado
C The Pointe*Orlando
D Old Town
E Festival Bay
F Belz Factory Outlet World
G Quality Outlet Center
H Belz Designer Outlet Center
I Kissimmee Manufacturers' Outlet Mall
J Lake Buena Vista Factory Stores
K Orlando Premium Outlets
L Flea World
M Osceola Flea And Farmers' Market

N Florida Mall
O Colonial Plaza Mall
P Altamonte Mall
Q Seminole Towne Center
R Osceola Square Mall
S Orlando Fashion Square Mall
T Mall At Millenia
U Park Avenue
V Winter Park Village
W Kissimmee Historic District
X Goodings International Plaza

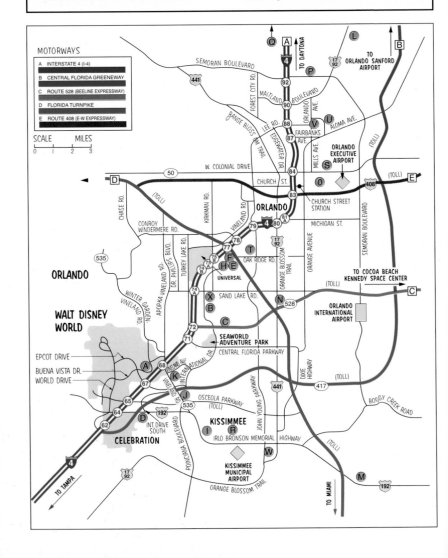

courtyard) and an impressive food court (especially for the budget-conscious – check out the All American Grill for great breakfasts). The Mercado is open 10am–10pm daily (from 8am in the food court and to 11pm at the restaurants), and will amuse you and your wallet for several hours. Shops like **Kandlestix, Andean Manna, Swings 'n Things, American Cola Company** and the new **Joseph's Place** (fishing apparel and accessories) are all good for a variety of unusual gifts, while hand-carts and artists also enliven the scene. **Internet City** offers the chance to check your e-mail and surf the Net, and there is a dedicated Mercado shuttle bus service to and from 15 I-Drive resorts throughout the day. A new live entertainment and dancing club, the **Vanguard,** is due to open in early 2003, too. Visit www.themercado.com for more info.

The second shopping complex to stand out on I-Drive is the 17-acre **Pointe*Orlando** (see Orlando by Night, Chapter 9), which is as much an evening adventure as mere shopping. The 60-plus stores here are all more upmarket than usual tourist fare, and you can indulge your passion for fashion at places like **Gap** and **Gap Kids, Banana Republic, Armani Exchange, Image Leather, Tommy Hilfiger, Abercrombie & Fitch** and the **Everything But Water** swimwear store, or stock up on gifts and souvenirs at **Disney Worldport, Bath & Body Works, Yankee Candle** (highly recommended), **Glow** and **Sunglass Hut.**

If nothing else, you should let the kids loose in the huge interactive toy shop **FAO Schwarz,** go to the state-of-the-art, 21-screen **Muvico** cinema complex, and finish up with a meal at lively **Johnny Rockets** American diner, where the staff all join in with various jukebox favourites (or one of the other six

fine restaurants). Visit www.pointeorlandofl.com for more details.

Kissimmee's version of the purpose-built tourist shopping centre is **Old Town,** an antique-style offering in the heart of Highway 192, with a tourist-friendly mix of shops, restaurants, bars and fairground attractions, all set out along brick-built streets. The shops – some 75 of them – range from standard souvenirs, novel T-shirt outlets and Disney merchandise to sportswear, motorbike fashions and other collectables (check out the **General Store** for a step back in time, too, or the **Old Town Portrait Gallery** for more period style). The **International Space Station** is new, with a host of NASA-inspired gifts and games, as is the fascinating **Petrified Rock Forest.** In addition, you will find 12 restaurants or snack bars, the 5-storey **Haunted Grimm House** ($7 for adults, $5 for children), and a host of rides, including the 60ft-tall Century Wheel, the Windstorm roller-coaster, go-karts, a **Kids' Town** area of junior rides and the all-new 365-ft **Slingshot** mega-ride (0–100mph in 2 stunning seconds!). Tickets are sold separately for most rides, but you can get an all-day pass for $25. Allow up to 4 hours here and try at all costs to take in the weekly **Saturday Nite Cruise** at 8.30pm, a drive-past of 300-plus vintage and collector cars (the biggest in America) which has become a real trademark here and

11

Park Avenue, Winter Park

celebrates its 13th anniversary on June 7, 2003. A **Friday Nite Cruise** features cars built from 1973–85, plus live music and prizes, and will reach its fifth anniversary on June 13, 2003. The second Thursday of each month is also **Motorcycle Mania** evening from 6pm. Parking is free and Old Town is open 10am–11pm daily (rides open from 4pm Mon–Fri, from noon Sat–Sun). **Damon's Clubhouse** restaurant is the stand-out dining choice, with great ribs, burgers and salads (and the chance to play various Trivia games and watch every kind of sport on their big screens) but the **Blue Max Tavern** is a fun alternative. **Del Boy's English Restaurant** offers repeats of *Only Fools And Horses*, as well as typical fare like shepherd's pie, a Sunday roast, and a fried breakfast with proper black pudding. Classic American diner **A&W** was due to open later in the summer in 2002. The whole of Old Town really comes alive in the evening, too.

Festival Bay, a 25-acre spread of shops, restaurants and entertainment with a **Cinemark** 20-screen cinema complex, at the top of I-Drive, is due to open its dramatic second phase in April 2003. This has been on-going since late 1999, with a delayed Phase I consisting of only the cinemas, the amazing **Bass Pro Shops Outdoor World** store and **Vans Skate Park.** However, all the signs have been that the project will be completed as planned, with major outlets of **Ron Jon's Surf Shop, Hilo Hattie** (Hawaiian-themed sportswear), **Kahunaville** (a tropically themed dining and entertainment venue), **Sheplers** (classic Western wear) and **FYE** – For Your Entertainment (a huge music, video and games store) – plus a host of fashion and designer label shops like **Victoria's Secret, Bath & Body Works, Ann Taylor Loft** and **Charlotte Russe.** Adding to the mix will be more themed restaurants and entertainment venues

such as the **Factory Fun House**, which will offer an indoor roller-coaster, a log flume, a games room and other interactive family rides. The recently opened Vans features a 50,000-sq ft skate park catering to all ages and skill levels, with an indoor wooden street course and an outdoor concrete street course. Festival Bay is another development of Belz Enterprises, and you can find out more about them on www.belz.com/factory/index.html.

Discount outlets

Belz Factory Outlet World is easily the biggest of this category of shops, the 'factory' or discount outlet, and is a big draw for British shoppers on I-Drive. It is a combination of mall and outlet centre spread over a huge area at the top of I-Drive at its junction with West Oak Ridge Road. It consists of more than 170 shops arranged in two indoor malls (both with lively food courts and one with a vintage carousel to amuse the kids), plus four separate annexes that all require a separate journey by car (unless you want to wear out a lot of shoe leather!). Avoid Belz at weekends, if you want to beat the crowds as the locals also do a lot of shopping here. The aim is to sell name brands at factory-direct prices and, while you may have to wade through a fair amount of stuff you wouldn't want if they were giving it away, you will find shoes, clothes, books, jewellery, electronics, sporting goods, crockery and more at bargain rates. Check out the Nike superstore

BRIT TIP: For the best value genuine Disney merchandise, try the Character Warehouse in Belz Mall 2 and Character Premiere in Mall 1.

(Annex 1), Calvin Klein outlet (Annex 2), Reebok footwear (Annex 4), the Van Heusen factory store (Malls 1 & 2), Oshkosh B'gosh kidswear, the Levis/Docker store, adidas and Guess Jeans (all Mall 2). Belz Factory Outlet World is open 10am–9pm Mon–Sat and 10am–6pm Sun.

Quality Outlet Center further down I-Drive offers much of the same, although not in the same quantity, but Disney Gifts for heavily discounted Disney merchandise is worth a look (9.30am– 9pm Mon–Sat, 11am–6pm Sun).

For a classier version, the **Belz Designer Outlet Center,** just south of Belz on I-Drive has a more upmarket range of 45 shops, including DKNY, Bose, Fossil, Fila, Liz Claiborne Shoes and Polo Ralph Lauren (10am–9pm Mon–Sat, 11am–6pm Sun).

Kissimmee's version of the discount outlet is the **Kissimmee Manufacturers' Outlet Mall** on Old Vineland Road (just off the central drag of Highway 192, between Markers 13 and 14). Again featuring brands like Nike, Levis and Van Heusen, plus Publishers Outlet for a wide range of discounted books, it is open 10am–9pm Mon–Sat, 11am–5pm Sun.

The newly expanded **Lake Buena Vista Factory Stores** offer another range of big-name products at discount prices, from Fossil, Sony, Reebok and Calvin Klein to a budget-priced Disney Character Corner, OshKosh B'Gosh Superstore and (the better-priced) Carter's Childrenswear, plus a lively food court and a kids' playground. A 1999 expansion added Gap and Liz Claiborne stores and, in 2002, shops for Old Navy, Perfume Outlet, SAS Shoes, Welcome Home, Rack Room Shoes and Danskin. And it all has the bonus of being one of the closest outlet centres to Disney's attractions. The new SoulFire Dinner & Theater Experience and the Travel

City Direct welcome centre are also here. The Factory Stores can be found on SR 535 (2 miles south off Exit 68 on I-4) and are open 9.30am–9.30pm Mon–Sat, 10am–6pm Sun. They also have a daily shuttle service that picks up at various hotels and timeshare units in a 10-mile radius (call 407 238 9301 for info or visit www.lbvfs.com).

Possibly the best of the lot, though, are the **Orlando Premium Outlets,** which were an instant hit with UK shopping devotees when they opened in 2000. Offering a fresh look and style, and with a legion of big-name designers (from Burberry and Ralph Lauren to Hugo Boss, Versace and Ermenegildo Zegna) they can be found on Vineland Avenue between I-Drive and I-4 (just south of SeaWorld; Exit 68 on I-4). In all, they offer 110 stores of well-known brand names (like Timberland, adidas, Reebok, Banana Republic, Nike and Calvin Klein) over four Mediterranean-themed areas (Plaza de las Flores, Plaza del Sol, Plaza de las Fuentes and Plaza de las Luces), with easy parking and the convenience of being at the southern end of the I-Ride Trolley (Main Line). New in 2002 were a Salvatore Ferragamo store and the upscale luggage and accessories of El Portal. Watch out also for big Disney bargains at the Character Premiere store and Universal items at Universal Studios Outlet Store. Even the food court is above average here, with a choice of six eateries (including Japanese, Chinese, Subway and Villa Pizza), plus a Starbucks, the mouth-watering Rocky Mountain Chocolate Factory and the A&W Diner. Opening hours are 10am–10pm (Mon–Sat) and 10am–9pm (Sun). Call 407 238 7787 or see www.premiumoutlets.com. Highly recommended (especially if you can get hold of their Discount Voucher booklet).

11

Flea markets

Flea World is America's largest covered market, with 1,700 stalls spread out over 104 acres, including three massive, themed buildings, plus a 7-acre amusement park, **Fun World,** to keep the kids amused for a good hour or two (rides cost about $2 each). It is open Fri, Sat and Sun only 9am–6pm and can be found a 20-minute drive away on Highway 17-92 (best picked up from Exit 90 on I-4) between Orlando and Sanford (to the north). The stalls include all manner of market goods (nearly all new or slight seconds), from fresh produce to antiques and jewellery (leather lingerie, anyone?) and a whole range of arts and crafts (try Rag Shoppe USA for some real bargains in materials and lace), while there is a full-scale food court and a 300-seat pizza and burger eatery, the **Carousel Restaurant,** plus free entertainment on the Fun World Pavilion stage. Call 407 330 1792 for more details.

On a slightly smaller scale is the **Osceola Flea and Farmers' Market** at the eastern end of the tourist area of Highway 192 in Kissimmee (Fri–Sun, 8am–5pm), offering food, clothing, household and kitchen supplies, electronics, sporting goods, collectables and handicrafts (call 407 846 2811 for more details). Similarly the **192 Flea Market,** on the central Vine Street stretch of Highway 192, has some 400 booths, plus a food court, in four bright-blue buildings under big oak trees, selling everything from

BRIT TIP: Need a good book? Make a beeline for Barnes & Noble by the Florida Mall or opposite the Colonial Plaza for a magnificent array of titles (especially travel) and a wonderful coffee shop.

Nintendo games to Florida souvenirs (open 7 days a week, call 407 396 4555).

Malls

The area's big indoor malls tend to run a touch more expensive than the outlets already mentioned, but they do have a huge range of pretty stylish shops. The outstanding **Florida Mall** features 264 shops, with seven large department stores and an excellent food court offering a choice of 17 outlets, plus the lively bar-restaurant **Ruby Tuesday**, the excellent **California Café Bar & Grill** and the chic little **Pebbles** in Saks Fifth Avenue. It is located on the South Orange Blossom Trail, on the corner of Sand Lake Road, and is open 10am–9.30pm Mon–Sat, 11am–6pm Sun. Highlights of this spacious and quite stylish Mall are the up-market (but expensive) Saks Fifth Avenue, Burdine's (Florida's oldest – and biggest – department store) and JC Penney. New in October 2002 were Nordstrom and Lord & Taylor, adding to the upscale line-up, along with Yankee Candle and Build-A-Bear. You can also benefit here from a discount coupon packet (from Guest Services) and the regular sales at many stores, which can make the Florida Mall as competitive price-wise as the discount outlets. Additional services include free wheelchair use, pushchair rental and video arcade (for the kids) in the food court.

The Mercado

There are even spa and beauty treatments available in the Lancôme Institut de Beaute in Dillard's, the JC Penney styling salon and day spa, and the Elizabeth Arden salon at Saks Fifth Avenue. It is also worth knowing you can visit the smart Adam's Mark hotel here for their Le Jardin restaurant and bar. For more info, visit www.shopsimon.com.

The huge 2-storey **Altamonte Mall,** on Altamonte Avenue in the suburb of Altamonte Springs (take exit 92 on I-4 and head east for half a mile on Route 436 and it is on the left), is also above average and slightly off the beaten tourist track. It is one of the largest in Florida, featuring 175 speciality shops, four major department stores – Burdines, Dillard's, JC Penney and Sears –15 outlets in the food court, plus four more restaurants, including Ruby Tuesday and the Orlando Ale House, and an elegant design with marble floors that makes shopping a pleasure. A major refurbishment is due to be completed in early 2003, adding an 18-screen cinema, a remodelled food court and a children's soft-play area. You can also get away from the usual tourist frenzy here to do some serious shopping from 10am–9pm Mon–Sat and from 11am–6pm Sun (weekdays are best, though), and they offer a VIP savings book for foreign visitors (go to the Customer Service Center). Visit www.altamontemall.com for more details.

One of the most extensive mall developments is **Seminole Towne Center** just off I-4 to the north of Orlando on the outskirts of Sanford. This vast complex (opened in 1997) offers another 2-storey wonderland of 100 designer shops and boutiques and five department stores (like Burdines and JC Penney) as well as craft stalls, a wide-ranging food court and six full-service restaurants (including Orlando Ale House, Olive Garden and Red Lobster).

Turn right off Exit 101C on I-4 and you are there, and it makes a handy place to while away your last few hours if you have an afternoon flight from the nearby Orlando Sanford Airport. The Towne Center is open 10am–9pm Mon–Sat, and noon–6pm Sun.

The spacious **Osceola Square Mall** (where Highway 192 mysteriously becomes Vine Street along its central stretch) is the only enclosed mall in Kissimmee, with 54 shops and a 12-screen cinema complex (open 10am–9pm Mon–Sat, noon–6pm Sun), including the local outlet of the retail store Ross, which deals in end-of-line items from big-names like Calvin Klein, Gap and Tommy Hilfiger. If you are prepared for a good rummage through their packed racks, you can collect some real bargains. 'Ross should be on every Brit's shopping list,' advises reader Mrs B Mair of Stockport.

Orlando Fashion Square Mall, just out of the city centre, has undergone a major redevelopment and now offers a 165-shop spread, four restaurants, a 14-counter food court and an eight-screen cinema complex. Four department stores – JC Penney, Dillard's, Sears and Burdines – anchor a typically broad range of outlets, including Gap, Everything But Water, Bath & Body Works, Zales and The Disney Store. Open from 10am–9pm Mon–Sat and noon–6pm Sun, Orlando Fashion Square Mall is on East Colonial Drive (Route 50), take Exit 83B

11

Charlotte Russe at the Florida Mall

off I-4 and head east 3 miles to Maguire Boulevard.

The big mall news, though, is the opening of the most upscale development to date, the **Mall at Millenia,** just off I-4 to the north of Universal Orlando (Exit 78). Opened in October 2002, it features the most upmarket, dramatic and technologically advanced shopping complex in Florida, with New York's most famous department stores, Bloomingdale's, Neiman Marcus and Macy's, leading the way among a select number of other top-name boutiques such as Tiffany and Louis Vuitton. And, having looked round it several months before its completion, I can confidently predict it will be a modern marvel of the retail world. The main entrance (of six) features a 60-ft glass rotunda with a water garden theme, there are marble and terrazzo floors, a 12-café food court (with orangery garden theming) and a bevy of restaurants. The grand architecture is also focused on five separate courts along a flattened, serpentine 'S' shape, which is topped with a flowing, arched glass roof like some gigantic conservatory. On two levels (three in Macy's and Bloomingdale's) and with eight 'Juliet' balconies connecting the two sides, the mall consists of a colossal amount of glass, plus a stunning central Grand Court, featuring a dozen 20-ft columns capped by curved plasma screens showing various images to support the theme of Man, Time and the Environment. And, while around 20% of the 150 outlets will be upscale and exclusive (Cartier, Chanel, Lacoste, etc, plus the ultimate luxury of Neiman Marcus, for brands like Gucci and Prada), the other 80% will offer more mainstream outlets like Gap, Banana Republic and Victoria's Secret. The six restaurants are also designed to be an attraction in themselves as they include The Cheesecake

Factory, gourmet seafood offering McCormick & Schmick, PF Chang's China Bistro and Brio Tuscan Grille. All in all, it should take the shopping experience to a new level in Florida (check out www.mallatmillenia.com for more details).

Traditional shopping

The attractions and possibilities of Winter Park's **Park Avenue** have already been detailed in Chapter 8, but the area also has the new **Winter Park Village,** a small, upscale, open-plan development of boutique shops, larger speciality stores like Borders Books, and some fine restaurants. The Village replaced the old Winter Park Mall and is on North Orlando Avenue (Exit 87 on I-4, head east on Fairbanks Avenue and then north on Highway 17/92, North Orange Avenue, for 2 miles, and it is on the right; website at www.shopwinterparkvillage.com). It has proved immensely popular with the locals and offers a nice change from the usual malls and plazas – as well as some excellent dining. Check out **PF Chang's Chinese Bistro** (their spicy Szechuan chicken is delicious), **Brio Tuscan Grille** (fine Italian fare) and the amazing (not to mention cavernous) new **Cheesecake Factory**.

More traditional shopping can also be found in the revamped **Historical District of Kissimmee** on Broadway, two blocks south of Highway 192 on Route 17/92, along Main Street and Broadway. These are a number of restored turn-of-the-century buildings featuring craft and gift shops, a children's boutique, country store and seven restaurants (including **Azteca's** for fine Mexican fare), plus antiques, western and sports wear. Every Thursday, the Downtown Farmers' Market displays its wares here, too. The Historical District shops are open 10am–5pm (10am–3pm on Sat).

Computer addicts may want to check out the **netkaffee** for the chance to send and receive e-mail (9am–9pm), www.kissimmeecra.com for more information.

> BRIT TIP: You can take advantage of free e-mail services at main public libraries (says reader Ann Tootell of Leicester).

Another recent development (and off the beaten tourist path) is the shops and restaurants of Disney's town of **Celebration,** a unique collection of speciality stores, an ice cream and candy shop, restaurants, cinemas, lakeside dining and a Saturday Farmers' Market, plus boat and bike rentals and the superb Celebration Hotel. Follow the signs to downtown Celebration along Celebration Avenue, just off Highway 192, a quarter of a mile east of its junction with I-4. The shops are open 10am–9pm Mon–Sat, noon–6pm Sun. This is a re-creation of the 'ideal' 1950s-style town, complete with white picket fences, while there are some lovely walks around the main lake.

Supermarkets

Apart from the big chemist chain stores, **Eckerd** and **Walgreens,** there are a few more typical large-group stores. The main supermarkets you will find are **Publix** and **Goodings,** which are comparable with Asda, Safeway or (in the case of Goodings) Marks and Spencer (and don't forget to visit Goodings on I-Drive, next to The Mercado, to pick up your *Brit's Guide* copy of the valuable *Entertainment* discount coupon book for $35 – see page 93). **Albertson's supermarket** on Dr Phillips Boulevard, is another well-priced choice.

For clothes, DIY, home furnishings, souvenirs, toys, electrical goods and other household items as well as groceries, the big discount stores are **K-Mart, Wal-Mart** (owners of Asda – see page 34 – and open 24 hours for serious shopaholics!) or **Target** (like a big version of Tesco's, but without the food). If there is anything you've forgotten, the chances are you can get it at one of the seven **Wal-Mart Supercenters** (notably on Highway 192 next to Medieval Times, another at the junction of Sand Lake Road and John Young Parkway, on Kirkman Road north of Universal, and a new one towards the east end of Osceola Parkway in the Buenaventura Lakes area).

For photographic supplies and film processing, try one of the many branches of **Eckerd Express Photo** (although they are dearer in the main tourist areas).

Specialist shops

Finally, a few worth making a note of for specific items are the various outlets of **World of Denim** (no explanation necessary), **The Sports Authority** and **Sports Dominator,** the former on Sand Lake Road and the latter north of Sand Lake Road, on I-Drive, which both offer all manner of sporting goods and apparel, while serious sportsmen and women will also want to visit the magnificent range of the five **Edwin Watts Golf** shops, including their national clearance centre on I-Drive, or any of the five **Special Tee Golf & Tennis** shops. On golf clubs in particular you can pick up some great deals and save a lot on the same equipment back home. Last but by no means least, **Greg's Western Weal** (on Highway 192 opposite Medieval Times) offers the chance to get yourself fully kitted out in the latest cowboy gear.

So now it is time to think about the journey home…

11

12 Going Home

(or, Where Did The Last Two Weeks Go?)

And so, dog-tired, financially crippled but (hopefully) blissfully happy and with enough memories to last a lifetime, it is time to deal with that bane of all holidays – the journey home.

If you have come through the last week or two relatively unscathed in terms of the calamities that can befall the uninformed or the plain unlucky, there are still one or two more little pitfalls that could possibly catch you out.

The car

First and foremost is the hire car. It has to be returned to Alamo, or whoever, and that can take a little time if you had to use an off-airport car depot. It is usually a lot easier and quicker to return the car and complete any outstanding paperwork (rare) than to get mobile in the first place, but it is wise to allow half an hour, just in case. The process tends to be even slicker with the firms who operate directly from the two airports.

Once negotiated, you are now back where you started in terms of your Orlando adventure, and probably with some time to kill, so here is a detailed guide to the two main airports.

Orlando International Airport

Orlando International is 46 miles from Cocoa Beach and 54 from Daytona Beach on the east coast, 84 miles from Tampa and 110 from Clearwater and St Petersburg to the west, 25 from *Walt Disney World* and 10 from Universal Studios; so always allow plenty of time for the journey. In these days of enhanced security (of which Orlando International is at the forefront), you also need to allow plenty of time for check-in – 2 hours for a domestic flight, 3 for an international one.

This modern airport is the 24th largest in the world, one of the fastest-growing and one of the most widely acclaimed for its overall passenger satisfaction values (regularly No 1 in America). It topped 30 million passengers in 2000 for the first time (some 80,000 a day on average), putting it level with Gatwick and Hong Kong, and with half the traffic of Heathrow (which has four terminals to Orlando's one). It can, therefore, get busy at peak times, but its 854-acre terminal complex usually handles the crowds with ease, and this is one of the most comfortable airports you will find. It boasts a great range of facilities, and its wide, airy concourses feel more like an elegant hotel than an airport (not too surprising when one end of the terminal is taken up by the airport-run Hyatt Hotel).

Ramps, restrooms, wide lifts and large open areas ensure easy access for wheelchairs, and there are special features like TDD and amplified telephones, wheelchair-height drinking fountains, Braille lift controls and companion-care restrooms to assist travellers with disabilities.

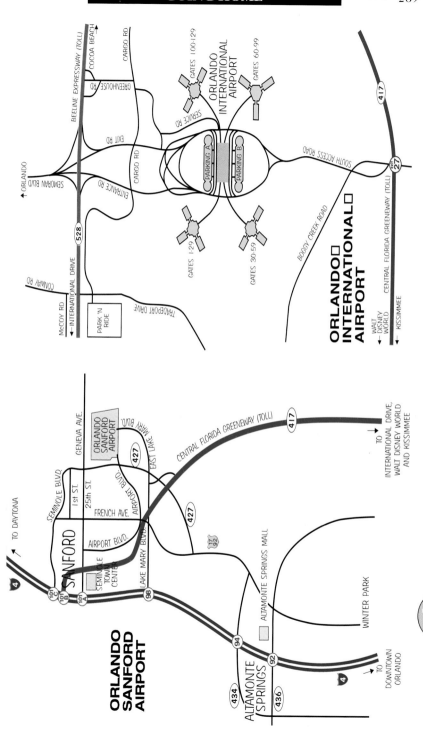

ORLANDO INTERNATIONAL AIRPORT

ORLANDO SANFORD AIRPORT

12

You will also find plenty to do here and, should you have more than a couple of hours to spare, it is worth leaving your hand luggage at the Baggage Checkroom and taking the 15-minute taxi ride to the Florida Mall, or checking in early, keeping the car and going to somewhere like Gatorland (about 20 minutes' drive away).

In keeping with the Orlando area, the International Airport is always engaged in staying a step ahead, and a major renovation through 2002/03 is due to add a host of new elements, including a major food court (with a feature McDonald's outlet) in the centre of the terminal and more shops. A fourth (and ultra-smart) satellite arm to the main terminal was opened in 2000, and a multi-billion dollar project to add a second terminal, a fourth runway, a new taxiway and control tower is under way, the latter phase due for completion in 2003.

Landside

As with all international airports, you have a division between **LANDSIDE** (for all visitors to the airport) and **AIRSIDE** (beyond which you need to have a ticket). Orlando's **LANDSIDE** is divided into three levels: **One** is the greatly enhanced area for ground transportation, tour operator desks, parking, buses and the car rental agencies; **Two** is for Baggage Claim (which you negotiated on the way in) and for any private vehicles meeting passengers; **Three** is where you should enter the airport on your return journey as it holds all the check-in desks, plus shops, restaurants, lockers, bank and information desks. Level Three is effectively sub-divided into four sections: **Landside 'A'** is the check-in section for **Gates 1–29** and **100–129**. Here you will find

American Airlines, ATA (American TransAir), Continental, Southwest, JetBlue and AirTran. Landside 'B' is home to the check-in desks for **Gates 30–99** and other main airlines, including Northwest, United, USAirways, BA, Delta and Virgin.

Once you have checked in, you can choose to explore the **East** and **West** sections of the main concourse, which occupies the centre of Level Three. The West end houses the **Great Hall**, with some more shopping and eating areas. Inevitably, Disney & Co make one last attempt to part you from what's left of your money, so you will find some more impressive gift shops for *Walt Disney World*, SeaWorld and Universal (and there is no airport mark-up either). Other outlets include Bunch-A-Books, Sunglass International, the Golf Gallery, two newsagents and a food court (including Burger King, Pizza Hut and Nathan's Famous Hot Dogs – although this will move after the big refurbishment). Up the escalators in the centre of the hall is a restaurant of the lively Chili's chain, a Tex-Mex diner and bar (this is also likely to change at some stage in 2003).

The **East** end of Level Three tends to be quieter and more picturesque as it is dominated by the 8-storey Hyatt Hotel atrium, featuring palm trees and a large fountain, and there are fewer shops. Universal and SeaWorld both have secondary (and different!) shops, while the Paradies Shop is a newsagent and gift store. Disney will also have a big feature shop here, too. For food and drink, there is a **Starbuck's** coffee shop and up the escalator is the entrance to the **Hyatt Airport Hotel** if you fancy seeing out your visit in style. **McCoy's Bar and Grill** (up and turn right) is a suitably smart bar-restaurant and has the bonus of a grandstand view of the airport runways (good for kids). The surroundings are immensely stylish and a long way removed from the average airport lounge.

If you want to go really upmarket, take the hotel lift to the ninth floor and **Hemisphere Restaurant**. Not only do you have an even more impressive view of the runways, its northern Italian cuisine is some of the best fare in the city. It's slightly on the pricey side, but the service and food are 5-star.

The central access corridors between the East and West ends will see the majority of the redevelopment work and new features. You will also find a bank, post office and a hair salon, as well as some stylish shopping with the likes of Body Shop, Perfumania, Electronics Boutique, Discovery Channel and a video arcade and playroom for the youngsters (some of which are also likely to be redeveloped).

If you still have time to kill, you can visit **Gates 100–129** (domestic flights) to examine some of the airport's magnificent art collection or view the large aquarium by the SeaWorld shop at the East end.

Airside

Once it is time to move on to your departure gate, you have to be aware of the four satellite arms that make up the airport's **AIRSIDE** (and the extra time required to clear security these days. They have installed Advanced Technology Checkpoint screening here, and you can encounter some long queues).

These are divided into **Gates 1–29** and **30–59** at the West end of the terminal, and **60–99** and **100–129** (American domestic flights only) at the **East** end. ALL the departure gates are here, plus duty-free shops, more restaurants and lockers.

The airport's four satellites are each connected to the main building by a shuttle service (as exists between the North and South terminals at Gatwick), so you need to be alert when it comes to finding your departure gate. There are no tannoy announcements for flights, so it's wise to check your departure gate and time when you check in. However, there are large monitors in the terminal which display all the necessary departure info. As a general rule, British Airways and Virgin use Gates 60–99, as do Delta. NorthWest, United and USAir usually use Gates 30–59, while ATA depart from Gates 1–29, along with American and Continental. Airlines using the new Gates 100–129 include low-cost carriers Southwest, JetBlue and AirTran.

In most airports, once you have moved Airside it is not possible to return to the Landside area again. However, that is not the case here, and, if you find the crowds milling around your departure gate too much to bear, you can always return to one of the terminal hostelries, for a bit of peace and quiet **(but bear in mind you will need to go through the security checkpoints again)**.

However, you should find the Airside areas just as clean and efficient as the main terminal, with the added bonus of three duty-free shops just in case your credit card hasn't already gone into meltdown.

As you pass through the ticket and baggage check at the West end of the terminal, you will find the **Alpha Retail Duty Free** immediately on your right. This is the biggest of their three shops and is open only to departing international passengers, so you will need your boarding card. Unlike other duty-free shops, you don't walk out with your purchases. Instead, they are delivered to the departure gate for you to collect them as you board the plane. This is because international flights are mixed in with domestic ones and, of

12

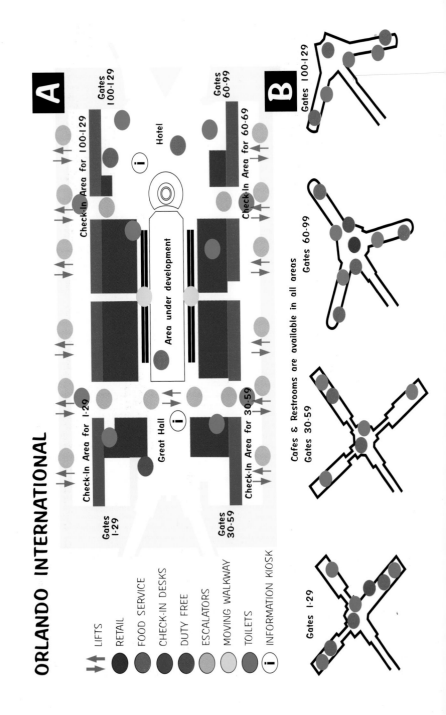

ORLANDO INTERNATIONAL

A

Gates 100-129

Check-In Area for 100-129

Hotel

Gates 60-99

Check-In Area for 60-69

Area under development

Check-In Area for 1-29

Great Hall

Check-In Area for 30-59

Gates 1-29

Gates 30-59

LIFTS
RETAIL
FOOD SERVICE
CHECK-IN DESKS
DUTY FREE
ESCALATORS
MOVING WALKWAY
TOILETS
(i) INFORMATION KIOSK

B

Gates 100-129

Cafes & Restrooms are available in all areas
Gates 60-99

Gates 30-59

Gates 1-29

ORLANDO SANFORD INTERNATIONAL AIRPORT

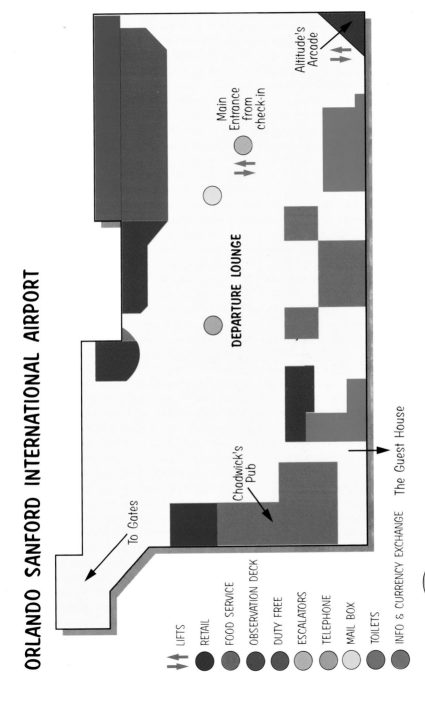

DEPARTURE LOUNGE

To Gates

Chadwick's Pub

Main Entrance from check-in

Altitude's Arcade

The Guest House

LIFTS
RETAIL
FOOD SERVICE
OBSERVATION DECK
DUTY FREE
ESCALATORS
TELEPHONE
MAIL BOX
TOILETS
INFO & CURRENCY EXCHANGE

12

course, duty-free shopping does not apply to internal flights.

At **Gates 1–29**, you will find another duty-free shop, plus a newsagents (the Keys Group News and Gifts), two **Café Azalea** lounge bars, a kids' play area and a mini food court, featuring **Burger King**, **Cinnabon** and **TCBY** (which stands for The Country's Best Yoghurt). **Gates 30–59** do not have a duty-free shop, so remember to bag your duty-frees back at the Airside ticket check. However, you will still find a **Café Azalea** lounge bar, **Don Pepe's Cuban Café**, a food court (with **Miami Subs**, **Villa Pizza** and **Freshens Yogurt**) and a WH Smith's.

Travelling from **Gates 60–99** gives you another duty-free shop, Disney's Flight Fantastic stores, a Stellar Partners newsagents and food court containing **Burger King**, **Nathan's Famous Hot Dogs**, and a lounge bar for that final beverage. As a bonus for parents with young children, there is a sea-themed play area here.

Gates 100–129 offer two outlets of the **Johnny Rivers Smokehouse Express**, a food court with **The Coco Oasis Bar & Lounge**, **McDonald's** and **Sbarro Pizza**, and two more shops.

For more details on Orlando International Airport, visit www.fcn.state.fl.us/goaa, which also features 'live' departure and arrival information.

Orlando Sanford Airport

Returning to what is now the main Orlando gateway for British charter flights should be a relatively simple experience, providing you retrace your route on the Central Florida Greeneway and come off at Exit 49. You go across one set of lights, turn right at the second set on to Lake Mary Boulevard and follow it all the way back to the airport. Signs have been posted on all the main routes to make the return journey straightforward, and the efficiency of the Alamo and Dollar car-rental return adds to this simplicity.

By way of a little more explanation, Orlando Sanford was created as a full international airport only in 1996, as an initiative between the airport authorities and several of the main British tour operators. And so My Travel (Airtours), Britannia, Monarch and Air 2000 all now go for the cheaper and simpler (in operating terms) option of Orlando Sanford. With its small, uncomplicated design (straight off the plane into Immigration, one baggage carousel and then a walk across the road to the Dollar or Alamo offices) it can get you mobile much quicker. Of course, you are further to the north to start with, so your journey time is 35–40 minutes longer and you have to pay an extra $4–5 in tolls, but, providing you follow the simple directions to the main tourist areas, you can save as much as an hour in overall time.

And, while this charter gateway lacks many of the extra amenities and creature comforts of Orlando International, it boasts an extremely spacious check-in area and works hard to make the departure as painless as the arrival process, especially with their new Guest House facility.

The problem of congestion in the departure lounge and a bottleneck at the gate access has been alleviated by the opening, in March 2001, of a second terminal, which provides overflow capacity. And its facilities are perfectly adequate for a comfortable stay, with **Chadwick's Pub** serving a decent range of food as well as British beers, a snack bar, cafeteria and ice cream shop, **Altitudes Arcade** (neatly located in one corner), a well-stocked duty-free shop, a Ron Jon gift store, Universal shop and a new Harley-Davidson inspired American Road store. There is also a large outdoor smoking deck (smoking is severely restricted inside).

The big addition here, though, is that of the **Guest House**, a premium lounge available to all passengers for a modest additional fee. The Guest House is located in a separate annexe from the main departure lounge, and is an oasis of comfort and quiet. The check-in area is more reminiscent of an upscale hotel, and it has all the facilities to match. There is a lovely little conservatory-style café, where you can take advantage of the unlimited tea, coffee, soft drinks and snacks (plus two alcoholic beverages per person), or opt for something extra from their exclusive lunch menu. It also provides a home theatre set-up, with widescreen TV and surround-sound, for recent release films, and a relaxing reading lounge, with newspapers and magazines. You can check your e-mail or surf the net while the kids enjoy the youth entertainment centre, with eight Sony Playstation 2 consoles. And, for the young 'uns, there is a separate playroom with various soft toys and games. It is billed as an airport lounge with the comforts of home and, to my mind,

it is well worth the $20 extra ($10 for children) to while away your last few hours here. You can see a full slide show of the Guest House on www.orlandosanfordairport.com.

Whether you are travelling from Orlando International or Orlando Sanford, you can expect your return flight to be somewhat shorter than the journey out thanks to the Atlantic jetstreams that provide handy tail-winds to high-level flights. Differences of more than an hour in the return journey times are not uncommon.

Finally, you will land back at Heathrow, Manchester, Glasgow, etc, rather more jet-lagged than on the trip out. This is because the time difference is more noticeable on eastward flights, and it may take a good day or two to get your body clock back on to local time. It is even more important not to indulge in alcoholic beverages on the flight if you are driving when you get home.

And, much as it may seem like a good idea, the best way to beat Florida jet-lag is NOT to go straight out to the travel agency and book another holiday to Orlando!

But, believe me, the lure of this theme park wonderland is almost impossible to resist once sampled – you WILL return!

Your chance to give something back

After hopefully having the holiday of a lifetime, you might like to know about a charity helping children with terminal illnesses to have a memorable time here, too. **Give Kids The World** is a unique, amazing organisation in Kissimmee which provides a week's fantasy holiday for terminally ill children who wish to visit the central Florida attractions. GKTW works with other wish-granting foundations around the world and basically provides all the local facilities for the child – and their family – to find some joy in their lives. It is set up as a village resort and includes all meals, accommodation, transport, attractions, tickets, use of video camera and many other thoughtful touches in a magical setting. It is a truly wonderful charity, one I am happy to support myself, and I hope you will help, too. You can make a donation through the charity's website – www.gktw.org – or send it to: Give Kids The World, 210 South Bass Road, Kissimmee, Florida 34746, USA. Thank you.

12

13 Your Holiday Planner

You can design your own holiday schedule on pages 278–79
with the aid of the theme park Busy Day Guide on page 280.

Example: with 5-day Park Hopper Plus Pass

DAY	ATTRACTION		NOTES
SUN	DAY		
	EVE		
MON	DAY		
	EVE		
TUE	DAY		
	EVE		
WED	DAY		
	EVE		
THUR	DAY	Arrive 2.40pm local time Orlando Sanford Airport	*NB: 55 mins to drive to hotel*
	EVE	Check out local shops and restaurants	
FRI	DAY	Welcome meeting/UNIVERSAL STUDIOS	
	EVE		
SAT	DAY	DISNEY'S ANIMAL KINGDOM THEME PARK	*(8am start)*
	EVE	Medieval Times Dinner Show	
SUN	DAY	THE MAGIC KINGDOM PARK	*(Open until 10pm today)*
	EVE		
MON	DAY	SEAWORLD	
	EVE		
TUE	DAY	BUSCH GARDENS	
	EVE		
WED	DAY	KENNEDY SPACE CENTER	
	EVE	Skull Kingdom/WonderWorks/Pointe*Orlando	

Disney's 5-Day Park Hopper Plus Pass gives 5 days at the main theme parks, plus TWO of Blizzard Beach, Typhoon Lagoon, Pleasure Island and Disney's Wide World of Sports™; there may be a separate charge for big events at Wide World of Sports.

DAY		ATTRACTION	NOTES
THUR	DAY	DISNEY-MGM STUDIOS	
	EVE		
FRI	DAY	ISLANDS OF ADVENTURE	
	EVE	Universal Orlando's CityWalk	*(until late!)*
SAT	DAY	Winter Park Lakes/shopping/museums	
	EVE		
SUN	DAY	EPCOT	*(open until 9pm)*
	EVE		
MON	DAY	Fantasy of Flight and Splendid China	
	EVE	Pleasure Island	
TUE	DAY	Aquatic Wonders Tours/Warbird Air Museum	
	EVE	Arabian Nights	
WED	DAY	Blizzard Beach/EPCOT	*(Arrive late this time)*
	EVE		
THUR	DAY	Gatorland/Back to airport	
	EVE		*Flight 6pm; return car at 3.30pm*
FRI	DAY	Return Gatwick 7am	
	EVE		
SAT	DAY		
	EVE		
SUN	DAY		
	EVE		

13

Blank form: your holiday!

DAY	ATTRACTION	NOTES
SUN	DAY EVE	
MON	DAY EVE	
TUE	DAY EVE	
WED	DAY EVE	
THUR	DAY EVE	
FRI	DAY EVE	
SAT	DAY EVE	
SUN	DAY EVE	
MON	DAY EVE	
TUE	DAY EVE	
WED	DAY EVE	

DAY	ATTRACTION		NOTES
THUR	DAY		
	EVE		
FRI	DAY		
	EVE		
SAT	DAY		
	EVE		
SUN	DAY		
	EVE		
MON	DAY		
	EVE		
TUE	DAY		
	EVE		
WED	DAY		
	EVE		
THUR	DAY		
	EVE		
FRI	DAY		
	EVE		
SAT	DAY		
	EVE		
SUN	DAY		
	EVE		

13

Busy Day Guide

Day	Busiest	Average	Lightest
Mon	Magic Kingdom	Disney-MGM Studios	Epcot Universal Studios Islands of Adventure Busch Gardens Kennedy Space Center SeaWorld Water Parks
Tues	Epcot Disney's Animal Kingdom Universal Studios	Magic Kingdom	Disney-MGM Studios Busch Gardens Islands of Adventure Kennedy Space Center SeaWorld Water Parks
Wed	Disney-MGM Studios Disney's Animal Kingdom	Islands of Adventure SeaWorld Water Parks	Magic Kingdom Busch Gardens Epcot Kennedy Space Center Universal Studios
Thurs	Magic Kingdom Universal Studios	Busch Gardens Epcot Disney's Animal Kingdom SeaWorld Water Parks	Disney-MGM Studios Islands of Adventure Kennedy Space Center
Fri	Epcot SeaWorld Water Parks	Disney-MGM-Studios Islands of Adventure Busch Gardens Kennedy Space Center	Magic Kingdom Disney's Animal Kingdom Universal Studios
Sat	Busch Gardens Magic Kingdom Islands of Adventure Kennedy Space Center SeaWorld Universal Studios Water Parks	Disney-MGM Studios	Disney's Animal Kingdom Epcot
Sun	Disney-MGM Studios Islands of Adventure Kennedy Space Center SeaWorld Universal Studios Water Parks	Disney's Animal Kingdom Busch Gardens	Epcot Magic Kingdom

The author wishes to acknowledge the help of the following in the production of this book:

The Orlando Tourism Bureau in London, The Orlando/Orange County Convention & Visitors' Bureau, Visit Florida, The Kissimmee/St Cloud Convention & Visitors' Bureau, Walt Disney Attractions Inc., Universal Orlando, The Greater Orlando Aviation Authority, Orlando-Sanford International Airport, The Busch Entertainment Corporation, The Orange County Sheriff's Office, Seminole County Convention & Visitors' Bureau, Central Florida Visitors & Convention Bureau, Visit USA Association, St Petersburg/Clearwater Area Convention & Visitors' Bureau, Daytona Beach Area Convention & Visitors' Bureau, Winter Park Chamber of Commerce, Alamo Rent A Car, Grand Theme Hotels Group, HM Customs and Excise Office, Airwave Communication.

In person, Oonagh McCullagh (Orlando Tourism Bureau) and Zoe Ward (Icas PR), Suzy Brown, Louisa French, Jason Lasecki (Walt Disney), Danielle Courtenay, Rick Gregory (Orlando CVB), Larry White, Geo Morales (Kissimmee CVB), Wit Tuttell (St Petersburg/Clearwater CVB), Susan McLain (Daytona Beach CVB), Michael McLane, Camille Dudley (Universal), Kate Burgess (Visit Florida), Carolyn Fennell (Orlando Aviation Authority), Craig Dorris (Orange County Sheriff's Office), Mike Moran (Airwave), Susan Flower (SeaWorld), Honoria Nadeau (Busch Gardens), Anthea Yabsley, Sarah Bolam (Synergy PR), Jack Wert (Seminole County CVB), Laura Richeson (Bennett & Company), Mary Kenny (Grand Theme Hotels), Heather Strickland (Kennedy Space Center), Al Riley (Splendid China), Steve Specht (Silver Springs), Michael Caires, Greg Dull (Orlando-Sandord Airport), Suzanne McGovern (Yesawich, Pepperdine & Brown), Joyce Couch (Travel City Direct), Allan Oakley (Alexander & Associates), Nigel Worrall (Florida Leisure), Bob Mandell (Greater Homes), Wrenda Goodwyn, Zina Talsma (International Drive/I-Ride), Sonya Snyder (Quill Communications), Todd Hansen (Ripley's), Loretta Shaffer (Old Town), Chris Tomasso (Hard Rock Café), Keith Salwoski (Gaylord Palms Resort), Melissa Gotlin (Orange County History Center), Jeff Stanford (Orlando Science Center), Donna Turner (Medieval Times), Michele Plant (Disney's Wide World of Sports), Phillip Jaffe (Pro Golf Guides of Orlando), Lisa Klemme (Pointe*Orlando), KT Budde Jones (Warbird Museum), Thom Richard (Warbird Adventures, Mella Jacobs (Forever Florida), Brian Wettstein (Winter Park Chamber of Commerce), Margie Long (Boggy Creek Airboats) and Naomi Lewis (Virgin Holidays), plus my research team Michele Carpenter, Marcia Harris, Michele Plant, Susan Haass, and travel writer Karen Marchbank. Special thanks to my youngest assistants Carly and Holly Feltham. Thank you all.

Very special thanks to Pete Werner and all at the DIS – you know who you are!

Got a red-hot Brit Tip to pass on? The latest info on how to beat the queues or the best new restaurant in town? We want to hear from YOU to keep improving the guide each year. Drop us a line at: Brit's Guide (Orlando), W. Foulsham & Co. Ltd, The Publishing House, Bennetts Close, Cippenham, Slough, Berkshire SL1 5AP. Or e-mail: simon.veness@spitfireuk.net

Reader tips from: Shirley Ahmed and family, Roy Carlisle, Geoff Avis, Gary Baldwin, The Tyler family, Hilary Stones, Penny Parker, Sally Jordan, Nicola Roberts, Andrew Bamford, Carole Agar, The Storey famiy, Ray Hoyle and Tim Smith (via e-mail); Mrs W Smith, Weston-super-Mare, the Feltham family, Sidcup, Kent.